14605011

TRANSBOUNDARY CONSERVATION

A NEW VISION FOR PROTECTED AREAS

SERIES PRODUCER
CEMEX BOOKS ON NATURE
PATRICIO ROBLES GIL

RUSSELL A. MITTERMEIER • CYRIL F. KORMOS • CRISTINA G. MITTERMEIER
PATRICIO ROBLES GIL • TREVOR SANDWITH • CHARLES BESANÇON

PREFACE BY
VALLI MOOSA

FOREWORD BY
PETER A. SELIGMANN

CEMEX

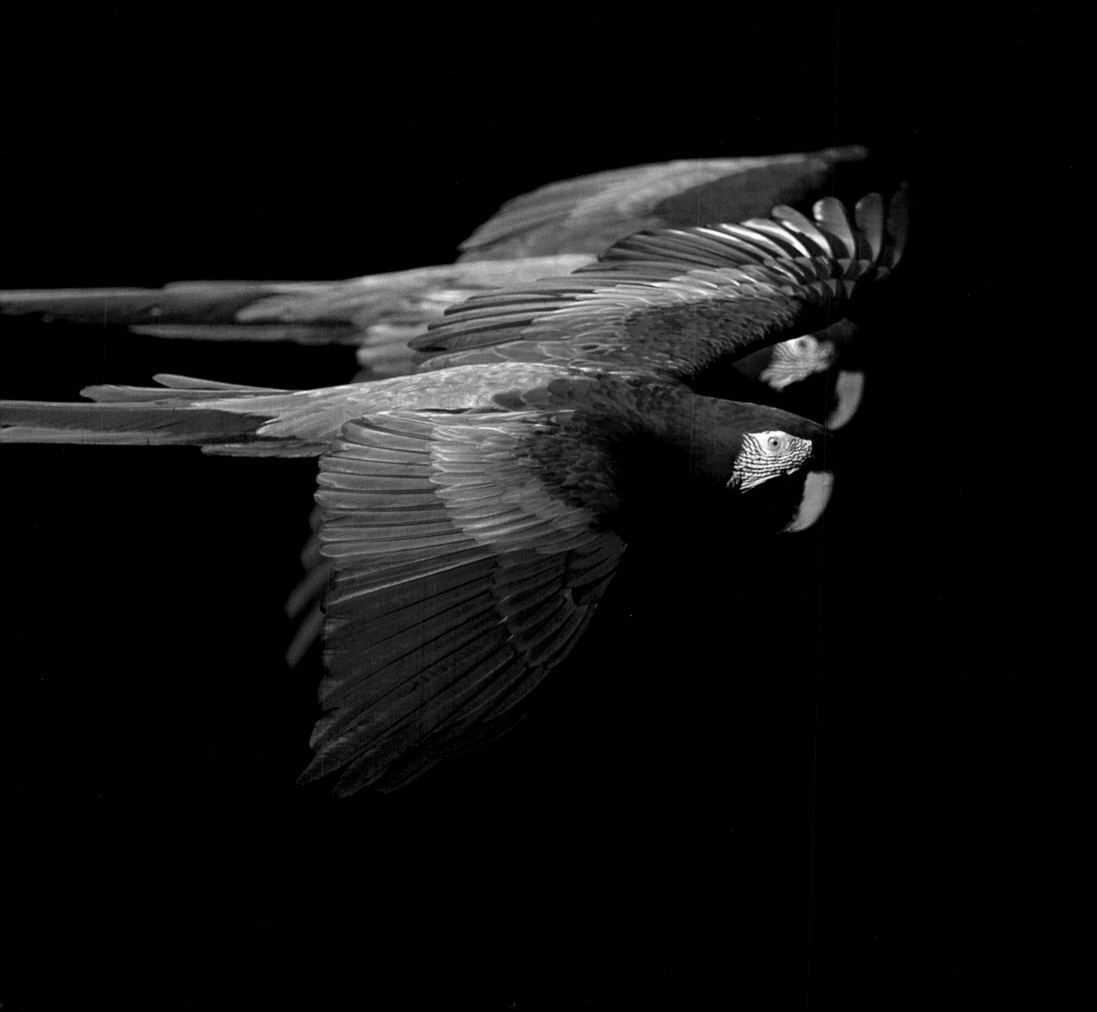

Territorial conflicts, migration, ethnic and religious wars, confrontations to gain access to natural resources and their control —these are a few of the sensitive scars man has left and leaves behind in his fight against man for the establishment of boundaries. Yet the natural world and its species do not recognize political borders and today give us the opportunity to promote collaboration within a boundary-less society.

The integration of two or more countries must not only involve financial criteria that favor trade. Real and dynamic integration entails considering the economic aspect while also allowing for environmental and socio-cultural aspects. Here lies the importance of creating sister parks, international parks, or peace parks, as the transboundary conservation areas are termed.

The first of its kind, Waterton-Glacier International Peace Park, between the Canadian and the U.S. border, was declared over 70 years ago. These conservation initiatives, however, have continued throughout seven decades and today involve encompass close to 200 transboundary parks world-wide, comprising almost 820 pro-tected natural areas in 112 countries.

The transboundary conservation initiatives emphasize the need to protect nature, landscapes, and biodiver-sity. Nonetheless, they also go beyond the environmental aspect to include national security, clashes over bor-der limits, the creation of alliances between or among nations, and more productive and just societies. From this perspective, nature becomes the crux of the analysis, and its care and protection, the alternatives for develop-ment policies.

This is why CEMEX is proud to present this book about this relevant and topical issue: The conservation of protected natural areas beyond political borders, where bioregions are defined by natural limits, where respect and the adequate use of resources, the guarantee of law enforcement, as well as political culture and adopted development models must be part of regional agreements that will lead to the care and protection of nature.

It should be mentioned that this book is a double source of pride for CEMEX because we now add, to our decade-long editorial efforts, our active participation over the past five years in the conservation and restoration of the natural province of El Carmen, Coahuila. In collaboration with private agencies, institutions, and gov-ernments, CEMEX has been working on the development of a 4-to-5 million-ha biological corridor, comprised of protected areas in Coahuila and Chihuahua, Mexico, and in Texas, U.S. The biological and ecological importance of this region has been highlighted by Conservation International, having identified it as one of its Top Global Priorities, one of the 34 Global Biodiversity Hotspots, one of five wilderness areas with the largest biodiversity and, finally, one of the three most exemplary transboundary natural areas in the world.

We thank Agrupación Sierra Madre for 13 years of joint editorial efforts, Conservation International for the co-edition of six books —making them of great value for scientists and for those in charge of decision-making on environmental issues at an international level—, and The WILD Foundation and The World Conservation Union for their collaboration and commitment to this book.

We also thank all those who fight day to day for the permanence of life, certain that the unity of natural areas will be part of our shared future.

CEMEX

As President of IUCN, I am delighted to see this publication on transboundary protected areas. At a time in human history when international cooperation is more important than ever, it is particularly pleasing to see that the conservation community is also contributing to improved international understanding. Today's international boundaries have been created through historical processes, many of which involved conflict. These borders often are in remote areas where government control may be weak, and where military installations are often located as a means of controlling transboundary problems. The newspapers are filled with reports of the security challenges of many international boundaries. But a very welcome source of reducing tension, and even building international cooperation, is now becoming an increasingly important element of national security. Transboundary protected areas now form close to 200 complexes involving over 800 individual protected areas. When protected areas are found on both sides of an international boundary, cooperation replaces the potential for conflict, lines of communication are opened, tourism becomes a force for peace, and problems are converted into opportunities.

This book provides a comprehensive introduction to the new international support for transboundary protected areas, identifying the major institutions involved, providing some excellent case studies of how cooperation has been built, and inspiring us to greater efforts to ensure that the rich biodiversity that is often shared between countries becomes a focus for cooperation. IUCN has long been a leader in the field of protected areas, and we have promoted transboundary cooperation for several decades. This book is an important milestone, but real success will come only when the principles and practices that are advocated in this publication become much more widespread, and the potential of protected areas for promoting peace is fully realized on the ground. This is certainly not going to take place overnight, but every step we take toward improved international cooperation in conservation is another step toward international peace and prosperity.

VALLI MOOSA
President
IUCN-The World Conservation Union

Conservationists have long recognized that successfully protecting the planet's biodiversity will require extensive cooperation between neighboring countries. Indeed, a look at global conservation priorities as identified by Conservation International highlights the need for regional cooperation very clearly. Of the 34 Global Biodiversity Hotspots and five High Biodiversity Wilderness Areas that Conservation International has recognized as the top global priorities, only a small percentage is entirely contained within the national borders of a single country. Most span at least two or three countries. Devising regional conservation strategies is therefore a matter of necessity rather than convenience.

Nonetheless, to date, most biodiversity conservation efforts have been implemented mainly at the national level. Of course, many countries have pledged to do their share in protecting regional resources through international agreements and treaties, and many international organizations have played major roles in conservation efforts around the world. But in terms of implementation, there have been relatively few projects managed jointly between countries.

In recent years, however, this has begun to change. Countries are increasingly establishing transboundary conservation areas, i.e., parks and protected areas adjacent to protected areas in neighboring countries. Just as importantly, countries are working together to develop shared management plans for these transboundary protected areas, despite the fact that they are separated by a national border. In some cases, border controls are even being relaxed so that park rangers can travel freely between countries while remaining within the park boundaries. As this book indicates, this trend is gathering momentum, and transboundary conservation areas are being established on an unprecedented new scale. We are now entering into a new era of transboundary conservation, and we are opening the door to an exciting array of possibilities for international cooperation —for biodiversity protection and beyond.

From the biodiversity perspective, transboundary conservation areas have many benefits. First and foremost, they allow for a much more effective, more organic conservation strategy, ensuring that protection does not stop at a national border when the ecosystem itself extends well beyond political boundaries. They also create the potential for more efficient management; for example, by allowing protected areas agencies to share scarce resources and by helping them to avoid duplication of certain tasks.

Transboundary conservation areas can also have a number of vitally important non-biodiversity benefits. They can help resolve long-standing and contentious territorial disputes between countries by providing an attractive way to reach a settlement. They can also help countries reconcile after periods of conflict. If designed properly, transboundary conservation areas can also have far-reaching social implications, making it possible for local communities and indigenous groups to once again have a voice in the management of their traditional lands. In some cases, transboundary protected areas are allowing communities that have for decades been separated by an arbitrarily drawn national border to be reunited. Also of great importance, transboundary conservation areas, often quite large in size, can play a key role in the maintenance of critical ecosystem services like watershed protection. In other words, we are finding that transboundary conservation areas can have the same transformative effect on an international scale that protected areas have at a national level —helping to create a more functional, coherent landscape, and using the ecological integrity of an area to generate social, political, and economic progress.

Much remains to be done —both in terms of increasing the number of transboundary parks and improving prospects for joint management of these parks so that the benefits cited above can be fully realized. But the potential gains we stand to make from transboundary conservation are tremendous. This book offers an overview of the many benefits that transboundary conservation can generate, and of the spectacular places that will be better protected as a result of transboundary conservation efforts.

Last, but not least, we would like to thank our principal partner organizations in the development of this book: CEMEX, Agrupación Sierra Madre, The WILD Foundation, and the Transboundary Protected Areas Task Force of the Commission on Protected Areas of The World Conservation Union, as well as the many other collaborating institutions that have worked with us on this important publication.

PETER A. SELIGMANN
Chairman and CEO
Conservation International

Transboundary conservation is a great opportunity to establish cooperation bridges between governments and societies. This book focuses on protected natural areas straddling both sides of the political division between or among two or more countries, highlighting the efforts made to join them. Protecting and ensuring the permanence and integrity of these areas will be one of the means to solve past and future social, political, and environmental conflicts among nations.

Many of these are legendary areas whose names are deeply ingrained in the history of each country. There are currently 112 nations sharing one or several protected areas with neighboring countries. This book centers on 28 transboundary conservation areas with the purpose of assembling a representative sample of each continent and the most important ecosystems.

The efforts that governments, organizations, and individuals have undertaken are explained in the description of each area, making these pages a priceless medium to transmit knowledge and experiences which, in many cases, represent the evolution of conservation models in an ever-changing world. Ensuring the preservation of these areas is one of the main challenges we face today.

In Agrupación Sierra Madre and Unidos para la Conservación we have worked for the conservation of three transboundary areas: The Maya Tropical Forest, one of the largest and most important blocks of tropical forest in the Western Hemisphere; the great Sonoran Desert, which Mexico shares with the U.S., and, on the same border, between the states of Coahuila and Texas, an archipelago of mountain islands in the middle of the Chihuahuan Desert, where several private and governmental conservation agencies —both at a state and federal level— protect the great corridor between Mexico and the U.S. The diversity and contrast these three areas display is as great as their challenges and threats.

We have faced many of the most usual problems in transboundary areas: Damage to the ecosystem because of the coming and going of vehicles patrolling the area, looking for illegal aliens or drug-dealers, together with the instability and the mobilization that lead to armed conflicts. These phenomena are related not only to the loss of biodiversity but also to the occasional fragmentation of the soil, additionally isolating the few still-remaining wilderness areas.

Unifying a whole region and making it secure requires major efforts and concrete actions. By purchasing land for conservation, negotiating and establishing agreements with their owners through ecological servitude, and providing funds to sustain conservation actions it is possible to influence new policies and laws to strengthen these activities.

This is why we consider the publication of this book to be so valuable. We are grateful to CEMEX for its commitment and the confidence it placed on Agrupación Sierra Madre for the management of this project; to Conservation International for its leadership in conservation; and to The WILD Foundation and The World Conservation Union for its support and foresight. Only through unity shall we be strong and successful.

Seventy years ago, a group of Americans and Mexicans had a dream: Uniting both countries through an internationally protected area in what today are Big Bend National Park, in southeast Texas, and the flora and fauna protection areas Maderas del Carmen and Cañón de Santa Elena in Coahuila and Chihuahua, respectively. Six decades went by before that dream was officially fulfilled. At the same time, another history developed naturally. In 1944, when Big Bend was designated as a national park, there were no more black bears due to the persecution they had been subjected to —only a few of them were able to take refuge in the mountains on the Mexican side, to the south of the park. Thanks to the conservation efforts of several Mexican ranchers, however, the bear population grew and expanded, crossing the Rio Grande into Texan territory. This has been one of most important achievements for Big Bend National Park ever since it was created. The efforts of the ranchers and the connectivity of natural areas, as biological corridors, allowed the success of this great event.

Although this book stresses the importance of protected natural areas, it also emphasizes that of the biological corridors adjoining them. An example of this is the black bear, proving that there are no borders in the natural world and that animals have no nationalities.

PATRICIO ROBLES GIL
President
Agrupación Sierra Madre
and Unidos para la Conservación

TRANSBOUNDARY CONSERVATION
A NEW VISION FOR PROTECTED AREAS

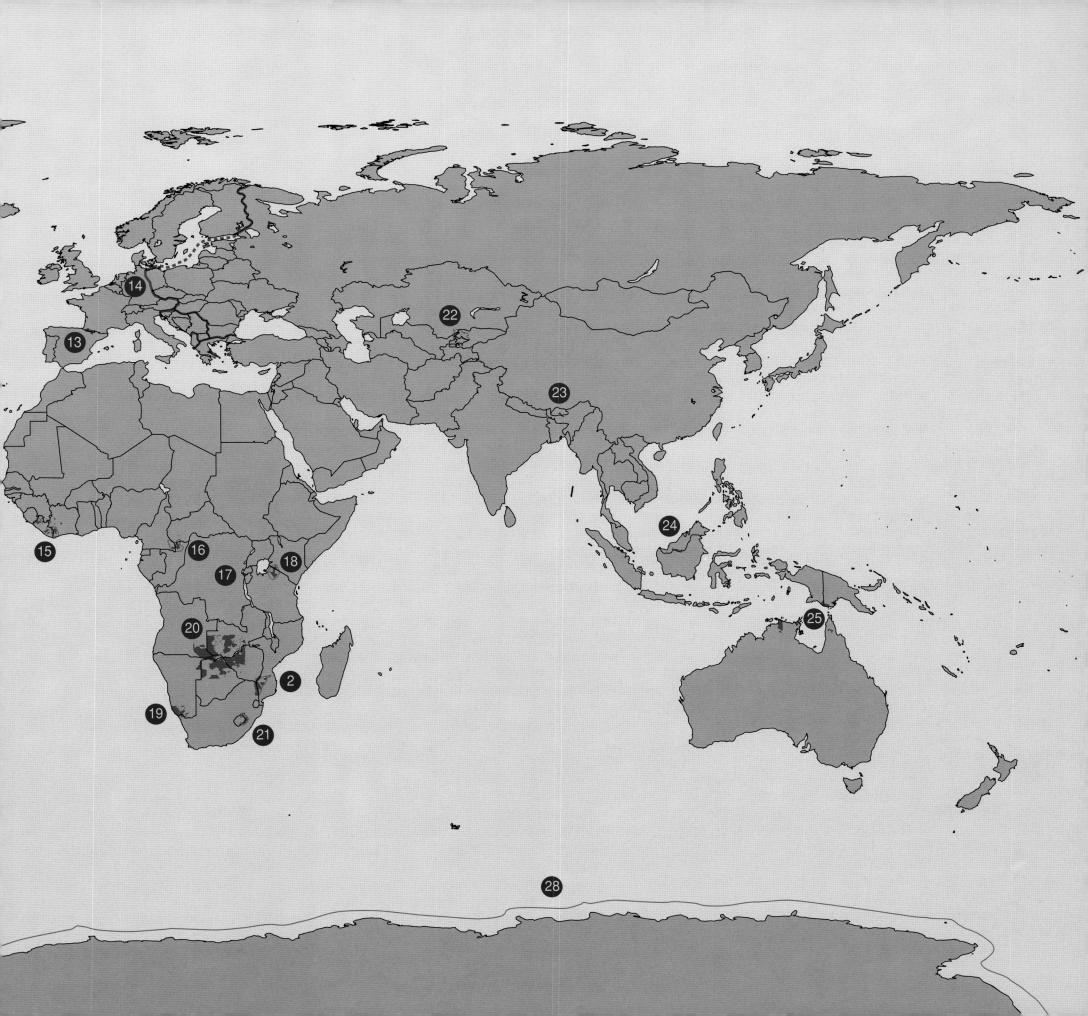

AN INTRODUCTION TO TRANSBOUNDARY CONSERVATION

Transboundary conservation is not a new phenomenon. The first transboundary protected area, the Waterton-Glacier International Peace Park between Canada and the U.S., was established in 1932, although the idea of transboundary conservation had been in discussion since the early 1920s. If not new, however, it is certainly a concept whose time has come. Although the number of transboundary conservation areas (TBCAs) around the world did not expand significantly for several decades after the first few were created, their numbers have increased dramatically in the last 30 years.

In 1988, 59 places were identified in which two or more protected areas (including all the World Conservation Union [IUCN] protected area categories) adjoined across international boundaries; by 1997, this number had more than doubled to 136 complexes of internationally adjoining protected areas, including 488 individual protected areas (Zbicz and Green 1997). In 2001, the number of complexes had increased to 169 with 666 individual protected areas, of which 31 involved three countries and one had four countries (Zbicz 2001). This most recent analysis in 2005 indicates a total of 188 complexes involving 818 protected areas in 112 countries. Although this latest increase is due in part to inclusion of smaller sites that were not included in earlier versions, the growth is still real and the trend unmistakable. It is clear that the number of transboundary protected area complexes continues to grow, and that there are many sites in the planning stages.

This growth in numbers belies the complexity of purpose, scope, and socioeconomic context for transboundary conservation, and the resulting difficulty in establishing transboundary institutional arrangements. For example, with respect to cooperative management of sites, research in 1997 revealed that, although some cooperation existed in 82% of the pairs of adjoining protected areas around the world, most of this cooperation was minimal, with less than 20% of the pairs engaged in substantive cooperative management (Zbicz 1999b). Furthermore, there are many transboundary conservation projects where the constituent areas on either side of the border do not currently meet the IUCN criteria for designation as protected areas, but where conservation objectives and land management arrangements would nonetheless qualify them as transboundary conservation initiatives. We therefore refer to this wider all-encompassing group as transboundary conservation areas (TBCAs) rather than the more restrictive term, transboundary protected area (TBPA).

The most up-to-date list of internationally adjoining protected areas and transboundary conservation initiatives is included as Appendix. This list will form the basis to identify the global network of TBCA sites and professionals. In many cases, the column indicating the names of these complexes is blank because many of these are so new, or their inclusion as transboundary complexes so recent, that they do not yet have formal names.

TBCAs represent a new conservation paradigm with enormous potential. Although the development of such areas presents many challenges, we believe that they are not a passing fad, but a very progressive approach that will continue to bring about more effective biodiversity conservation, improved relations between countries, involvement and re-integration of divided communities, and a range of other socioeconomic benefits to many regions around the world. In particular, transboundary conservation has been highlighted in regional socioeconomic initiatives (e.g., the European Union and Southern African Development Community) as a mechanism for integration of regional conservation and development goals. In a broader forest management context, the Yaoundé Declaration issued in Yaoundé, Cameroon at a Ministerial Conference on Africa Forest Law Enforcement and Governance in 2003, highlighted the central importance of transboundary conservation and management of forest resources in several places. As with any new development, there is cause to celebrate innovative progress. But there is also a need to examine critically and to reflect on the contribution that these initiatives can make in the achievement of global conservation and development objectives, as well as in the participation and livelihoods of communities who live in and around these areas.

This book highlights 28 TBCAs. Our selection includes TBCAs from every continent, though with an emphasis on high-biodiversity tropical regions. The first three chapters focus on three major transboundary protected areas of particular importance. The first is the Waterton-Glacier International Peace Park, the first peace park ever established. The second looks at the Great Limpopo Transfrontier Park, one of the largest transboundary projects in the world, one with deep political significance, and one that has the capacity to transform local economies. And the third is the El Carmen-Big Bend complex because it involves not just government-level activities, but also the role of private sector actors in such endeavors and is rapidly becoming a model for public-private partnerships.

We have also chosen one area not always discussed in the context of transboundary conservation, namely Antarctica. Antarctica does, however, fall under IUCN's definition of a transboundary protected area, which includes areas beyond national jurisdiction. This concept is important because of the potential for new protected areas and TBCAs in neutral zones or demilitarized zones, such as those between Jordan and Israel or the demilitarized zone between the two Koreas, and because of the potential for setting aside TBCAs on the high seas. In light of the latter, we also include several examples of marine TBCAs. Though it is a well-accepted mechanism in a terrestrial context, the potential for marine TBCAs s remains very underutilized.

Finally, although the term "transboundary" is generally understood to include borders within countries (i.e., between states or provinces), as well as between countries, we have chosen to focus exclusively on TBCAs that straddle international boundaries, because the social and political benefits are most significant in the international context.

On the opposite page, Reynolds Mountain amid layers of fog over Reynolds Creek Falls, with flowering beargrass (Xerophyllum tenax) in the foreground. Glacier National Park, Montana.
© Jack Dykinga

Above, southern white rhino (Ceratotherium simum simum) in South Africa, now the most abundant of the world's five rhino species.
© Patricio Robles Gil/Sierra Madre

Successful biodiversity conservation requires an effective network of protected areas. Although protected areas often have massive financial shortfalls for their management (e.g., Bruner et al. 2001), they remain the most effective mechanism to prevent species extinctions and to ensure the persistence of global biodiversity over the long term. For example, one of the greatest conservation success stories of the past century —saving the southern white rhino (*Ceratotherium simum*) from the brink of extinction, from around 50 individuals to some 12 000 animals today— was only made possible by the strategic creation of protected areas (coupled with intensive management) in their remaining habitats (Emslie and Brooks 1999). Indeed, the value of protected areas in shielding areas from anthropogenic disturbances and in particular habitat loss —the number one threat to global biodiversity (Baillie et al. 2004)— has been clearly demonstrated (e.g., van Schaik et al. 1997; Bruner et al. 2001; Sánchez-Azofeifa et al. 2003).

Studies have shown that species abundance is higher in protected areas than in surrounding landscapes (Sinclair et al. 2002), and protected areas are often the last remaining places where native species communities persist (as was the case in many of the studies cited above). The most extreme evidence of this is seen in those species whose entire global population is confined to protected areas, such as the pygmy hog (*Sus salvanius*, CR), which now only occurs in India's Manas National Park, or the Walia ibex (*Capra walie*, CR), which is found just in and immediately around the Simien Mountains National Park and World Heritage Site in Ethiopia. Large protected areas, in particular, can confer benefits to populations of wide-ranging species, such as the African wild dog (*Lycaon pictus*, EN), that would otherwise come into conflict with humans outside of these protected areas (Woodroffe and Ginsberg 1998), though they may provide insufficient protection to some migratory species across their entire migratory routes, such as the wildebeest (*Connochaetes taurinus*) in the Serengeti (e.g., Thirgood et al. 2004).

This is not to suggest that protected areas are a global panacea. Without adequate management plans, protected areas are as vulnerable to habitat loss as any other parcel of land. In Indonesia, for example, extensive logging has taken place within a number of protected areas, such as Bukit Barisan Selatan National Park, where forest loss between 1985 and 1999 averaged around 2% per year (Kinnaird et al. 2003), and Gunung Palung National Park, where deforestation between 1999 and 2002 was nearly 10% per annum (Curran et al. 2004). Furthermore, some threats, particularly invasive species and disease, cannot be mitigated through protected areas alone. For example, the golden toad (*Bufo periglenes*) ultimately went extinct in the Monteverde Cloud Forest Preserve in the Cordillera de Tilaran, near Monteverde, despite the fact that the species occurred within a protected area with a pristine habitat.

Nonetheless, for most species, and certainly for those whose habitat loss and degradation is the most pervasive threat, habitat preservation remains the primary conservation response, and a strong protected area network continues to be the most effective (though not always sufficient) means of conserving biodiversity. It is against this background that this book aims to investigate the history and value of transboundary protected areas, by showcasing their importance in contributing to a strengthening of the global protected area network for the benefit of worldwide biodiversity conservation.

On the opposite page, the imposing gemsbok (Oryx gazella) is a true desert dweller and an important flagship species for several of Southern Africa's transboundary conservation areas.
© Patricio Robles Gil/Sierra Madre

HISTORY OF TRANSBOUNDARY CONSERVATION AREAS

In 1895, Canada established its fourth national park: Kootenay Lakes Forest Park in southern Alberta. This park, adjacent to the border with Montana in the U.S., was renamed Waterton Lakes National Park in 1911, and expanded over the years from its original 14 000 ha to 52 500 ha. Glacier National Park, U.S.'s tenth national park, covering an area of approximately 410 000 ha, was established fifteen years later in 1910. In 1932, as a result of an initiative by Rotary Clubs in Alberta and Montana, the parks were officially designated as the Waterton-Glacier International Peace Park, and in 1995 were added to the World Heritage List as a single site. The park officially commemorates the long-standing peace and friendship between the two countries, as well as the cooperative management of shared natural resources. Waterton-Glacier International Peace Park (Chapter 1, p. 71), therefore, enjoys the status of being the first transboundary protected area with cooperative management, and also the first peace park; i.e., a transboundary protected area established explicitly to further the peace between two countries or to celebrate long-standing peaceful relations.

Nonetheless, the concepts of transboundary protected areas and peace parks predate Waterton-Glacier and, in fact, the first TBPA plan originated in Europe rather than in North America. In 1925, the Krakow Treaty between Poland and what was then Czechoslovakia called for peace parks in the Tatras Mountains to help resolve a contentious border dispute. These did not come into existence until after World War II when six parks were established: High Tatras National Park in Czechoslovakia in 1949 (now in Slovakia) and Tatrzanski National Park in Poland in 1955; Karkonoski National Park in Poland in 1959 and Krkonose in Czechoslovakia (now in the Czech Republic) in 1963; and Pieninski National Park in Poland in 1955 and Pienini National Park in Czechoslovakia in 1967 (now in Slovakia).

In Africa, Portuguese ecologist Gomes de Souza first articulated the idea of transboundary conservation in 1938. De Souza proposed that Mozambique's colonial administration should undertake negotiations with neighboring states regarding a transboundary park. Although this proposal was reiterated by a number of biologists over the years, it was not until 1992, when peace returned to Mozambique, that plans for a TBPA between South Africa and Mozambique could be revived. Africa's first formally declared transboundary protected

area was implemented when the Kgalagadi Transfrontier Park between South Africa and Botswana (incorporating Kalahari Gemsbok National Park in the former and Gemsbok National Park in the latter) was officially launched in May 2000 by South Africa's President Thabo Mbeki and Botswana's President Festus Mogae.

The concept of transboundary conservation was formally introduced in Central America in 1974 at the First Central American Meeting on the Management of Natural and Cultural Resources, which stated that border areas with natural and cultural characteristics of interest to both countries, and which might benefit from an integrated protection strategy, should be jointly managed. Central American transboundary protected areas were launched in the 1970s. The first actual TBPA was established between Colombia and Panama. Los Katios National Park in Colombia was expanded by 20 000 ha in 1979, bringing its northern extent to the border with Panama, and Panama in turn created Darien National Park in 1980, completing the link. The impetus for this park was the onset of foot-and-mouth disease in Panama and the need to prevent its spread southward into South America. The driving force was thus neither joint biodiversity management nor a desire to improve relations between the two countries, but rather a policy device to deal with the livestock disease problem —nonetheless nature conservation was advanced in the process.

The first transboundary protected area in Central America explicitly established to manage natural resources jointly and to promote peaceful relations was La Amistad (Chapter 8, p. 159) between Costa Rica and Panama. The presidents of both countries issued a joint declaration on the need for the park in 1979, followed by an implementation agreement in 1982. The first TBPA in South America was the iconic Iguaçu/Iguazú complex (Chapter 12, p. 191), straddling Brazil and Argentina, near the Paraguayan border to the west. Both protected areas are National Parks and World Heritage Sites. The government of Argentina initially reserved the area for Iguazú National Park in 1909, though the park itself was not established until 1934. Iguazú received World Heritage Site status in 1984. Iguaçu National Park in Brazil was established by decree in 1939, and then extended by subsequent decrees in 1944 and 1981. Iguaçu was listed as a World Heritage Site in 1986.

Asia has the distinction of having established the world's first marine TBPA, with the development in 1996 of the Turtle Islands Heritage Protected Areas in the Sulu Sea between Malaysia and the Philippines. With this, the significance of the Turtle Islands as a traditional nesting area of green (*Chelonia mydas*, EN) and hawksbill (*Eretmochelys imbricata*, CR) sea turtles was recognized, as was the fact that bilateral efforts are necessary to ensure the survival of marine turtles in the region. The areas include six islands designated by the Philippines (Boaan, Langaan, Great Bakkungaan, Lihiman, Taganak, and Baguan) and three designated by Malaysia (Palau Selingaan, Palau Gulisaan, and Palau Bakkungaan Kechil).

TERMINOLOGY

Although transboundary protected areas and peace parks have existed for some time, attempts to sharpen definitions in this field are quite recent. Until the last few years there has been little standardization in the terminology of transboundary conservation, leading to an array of terms used somewhat interchangeably, often with confusing results. *Transboundary protected areas, transfrontier conservation areas, transboundary natural resource management areas, parks for peace*, and *peace parks* are a few of the terms that have been used widely. Fortunately, a number of organizations have made a concerted effort to define terminology more precisely, and a consensus seems to be emerging.

Transboundary Protected Areas and Parks for Peace

The IUCN has led the way in convening experts on the subject of transboundary conservation through a number of workshops dating back to 1988. Workshops held in Bormio, Italy in 1997 and Gland, Switzerland in 2000 led to a landmark 2001 IUCN publication entitled *Transboundary Protected Areas for Peace and Co-operation* (Sandwith et al. 2001). In 2003, IUCN and the International Tropical Timber Organization (ITTO) partnered to organize a workshop in Thailand entitled "International Workshop on Increasing the Effectiveness of Transboundary Conservation in Tropical Forests." In May 2004, IUCN, ITTO, and InWent (the German Capacity Building Organization) sponsored a transboundary workshop at the Bonifacio Transboundary Marine and Terrestrial Protected Area on the island of La Maddalena in Sardinia, Italy, and discussed legal and institutional issues and governance in the transboundary context, the results of which will be published through IUCN in 2005.

Based on the many years of study and debate on transboundary conservation, IUCN put forth two terms to define areas that are both protected areas and that straddle international boundaries. The first, *Transboundary Protected Area* (TBPA), is defined as:

An area of land and/or sea that straddles one or more boundaries between states, sub-national units such as provinces and regions, autonomous areas and/or areas beyond the limits of national sovereignty or jurisdiction, whose constituent parts are especially dedicated to the protection and maintenance of biological diversity, and of natural and associated cultural resources, and managed cooperatively through legal or other effective means.

This definition has a number of dimensions. One key aspect is its insistence on some degree of cooperation between the protected areas on either side of the boundary. Although the threshold for such cooperation is not high, and at a minimum level only requires communication between the protected areas, those parks with no cooperation at all are not deemed TBPAs. The expectation is that

On the opposite page, a rainforest landscape on the Panamanian side of La Amistad, one of Central America's most important and oldest transboundary conservation areas.
© Art Wolfe

On pp. 32-33, Iguazú Falls from the Argentinian side. These falls are shared by Brazil and Argentina, with each side providing completely different views of this truly magnificent spectacle.
© Günter Ziesler

most areas will develop increasing degrees of cooperation over time, moving beyond communication to consultation, collaboration, coordinated planning, and ultimately fully integrated cooperative management, at least on specific issues of common concern. Most of the chapters in this book cover areas that have at least some level of cooperation, although a few are at such an early stage that collaboration is not yet a realistic objective.

Another important element is its inclusion of sub-national jurisdictions within the term "transboundary," a useful approach when so many countries have suffered tragic civil conflicts and where international borders have emerged or disappeared over time. This inclusion also recognizes that there can be many sub-national boundaries within the TBPA complexes, creating linkages in the landscape in any of the participating countries. Furthermore, this definition is also forward thinking in that it recognizes that it is also important to include areas "beyond the limits of national sovereignty or jurisdiction" under the TBPA umbrella. There is of course international precedence for protecting areas beyond the limits of national sovereignty in the Antarctic Treaty System (Chapter 28, p. 333), and in the demilitarized zone between Israel and Jordan. And there might well be potential for additional areas in the future —in other demilitarized zones (DMZs), including in particular that between South Korea and North Korea, or possibly on the high seas. This issue is discussed at greater length below.

The second term proposed by IUCN was *Parks for Peace*, which was defined as:

> ...transboundary protected areas that are formally dedicated to the protection and maintenance of biological diversity, and of natural and associated cultural resources, and to the promotion of peace and cooperation.

Despite the apparent focus on transboundary protected areas, the Parks for Peace concept has been applied differently in other circumstances. For example, IUCN notes that the United Nations University for Peace in Costa Rica uses the term "Peace Park" to indicate any protected area where there is a history of conflict, regardless of the transboundary nature of the protected area. This distinction is particularly useful for countries that have limited terrestrial borders (e.g., Indonesia). It also prevents the term from being used in an area that is not transboundary because there is no crossing of an international or domestic boundary, but which has nonetheless suffered due to serious conflict.

Transboundary Conservation Area/ Transfrontier Conservation Area

At the time of the 2001 IUCN publication, IUCN's World Commission on Protected Areas (WCPA) Task Force on Transboundary Protected Areas recognized that the definition of a TBPA given above applied only to a subset of the broader array of transboundary conservation areas and initiatives that might or might not lead ultimately to the establishment of TBPAs. During the preparations for the Fifth IUCN/WCPA World Parks Congress in 2003, and building on work conducted by the Biodiversity Support Programme (BSP was a consortium of the World Wildlife Fund, The Nature Conservancy, and the World Resources Institute funded by the U.S. Agency for International Development) in Sub-Saharan Africa, it became clear that the scope of transboundary conservation had to include the broader concepts of conservation initiatives beyond adjoining protected areas, including transboundary natural resource management initiatives. This view gathered momentum at the ITTO/IUCN conference in Thailand in 2003, which called for a revised typology of transboundary conservation initiatives.

Mohamed Bakarr, the keynote speaker at the ITTO/IUCN conference, suggested that it might be worthwhile to formally adopt the term "Transboundary Conservation Area" (TBCA) to avoid restricting "conservation initiatives to just those areas where protected areas are adjoining across international borders." The rationale was that "TBCAs should apply even to areas where protected areas could be miles away from international borders, and yet fall within a landscape that makes sense for integrating biodiversity conservation efforts across those borders." As part of its current program, the IUCN/WCPA Task Force on Transboundary Conservation is developing an all-embracing global learning network of transboundary conservation sites and practitioners to provide guidance across the whole spectrum of types. The recommendation in favor of TBCAs resonated strongly with materials presented jointly by IUCN and ITTO.

One example cited in the materials was the Central Asia Transboundary Biodiversity Project between the Kyrgyz Republic, Kazakhstan, and Uzbekistan, which consists of four currently "discontiguous protected areas in a three-country transborder region." This case was cited as an example of "a cluster of protected areas and the intervening land" linked by a common bioregional management plan. The materials also suggested that a TBCA could include a cluster of protected areas with cooperative management, though without joint management of the intervening land. Several parks in Africa's Great Lakes region, including Kibiria National Park in Burundi, Virunga National Park in the Democratic Republic of Congo, and Volcanoes National Park in Rwanda are examples of this type of TBCA (Chapter 17, p. 239). These parks were not linked by joint management of intervening lands, but their biodiversity and management challenges were so sufficiently similar that information-sharing on a regular basis proved to be helpful.

The ITTO/IUCN meeting resulted in proposals for a typology of transboundary conservation initiatives, which were further debated at the meeting held in La Maddalena, Sardinia, and which will be incorporated into a new IUCN publication. In essence, the typology includes four types which are proposed as an organizing framework

for transboundary conservation and development initiatives. The four main types are:

1] *Transboundary Protected Areas (TBPAs)*

Protected areas that adjoin across an international boundary, and that involve cooperative management, have provided the most easily defined of transboundary conservation initiatives. These conform to the IUCN definition of a TBPA cited above.

2] *Transboundary Conservation (and Development) Areas (TBCAs)*

There are numerous examples of transboundary conservation initiatives where protected areas may be, but are not necessarily, a feature of the regional landscape, but where conservation and sustainable development goals have been asserted within a framework of cooperative management.

3] *Parks for Peace*

Some transboundary conservation initiatives have the explicit objective of securing or maintaining peace during and after armed conflict, or of commemorating past warfare. These conform to the IUCN definition of Parks for Peace cited above.

4] *Transboundary Migratory Corridors*

This type includes situations in which the habitat needs of species require the persistence of areas in several countries, e.g., all elements of a migratory route.

In addition to these main types, there are two other official designations of transboundary conservation initiatives, which can be superimposed on any combination of the above four types, namely:

1] *Transboundary World Heritage Site*, where protected areas on either side of an international boundary fall collectively into the designation of the area as a World Heritage Site. These initiatives are likely to be a small sub-set of Transboundary Protected Areas.

2] *Transboundary Biosphere Reserve*, where areas on either side of an international boundary fall within a biosphere reserve designated under UNESCO's Man and the Biosphere Programme. Transboundary conservation areas (as defined above) conform most closely to the concept of a biosphere reserve, provided they meet UNESCO's designation criteria (see UNESCO guidelines on transboundary biosphere reserves).

Apart from IUCN and many international organizations fostering transboundary conservation programs at the global level, the only organization specifically established solely to promote transboundary conservation programs is the Peace Parks Foundation (PPF), which operates in the Southern African Development Community (SADC) area. PPF was founded in 1997 when WWF-South Africa determined that a separate organization was necessary to give adequate time and attention to transboundary initiatives in the SADC region. Acting as a facilitator rather than implementer, PPF involves itself in many

activities, including advocacy, fund-raising, negotiating with governments, conservation planning, and management support.

PPF adopted the term Transfrontier Conservation Area (TFCA), rather than TBCA, to describe its activities in the region, though the terms are interchangeable, and both are widely used. PPF describes a TFCA as "a cross-border, (usually international) park." In a departure from the most recent IUCN terminology discussed above, PPF also uses the term "Peace Park" interchangeably with TFCA, the rationale being that transboundary conservation leads to new economic potential through ecotourism and that economic growth in the region will promote peaceful relations. Establishing this linkage makes particular sense in Southern Africa where ecotourism is a major industry because of the high concentration of world-renowned protected areas. Equating TFCAs with Peace Parks is also a natural linkage given the decades-long history of conflict in the region.

SADC has also adopted the term TFCA, which it defines within its Protocol on Wildlife Conservation and Law Enforcement signed by 13 heads of state in August 1999, as follows: *Transfrontier Conservation Area* "means the area or the component of a large ecological region that straddles the boundaries of two or more countries, encompassing one or more protected areas, as well as multiple resources use areas."

This definition captures some of the key elements that current transboundary conservation practitioners would like the TBCA concept to represent, namely: *a*] a large ecological region (or regional ecosystem approach); *b*] that straddles an international boundary (with all the attendant benefits of transboundary cooperation and collaboration); *c*] encompassing one or more protected areas (including a core, high status protected area where conservation of biodiversity is the primary focus, with other component areas that may have a slightly lower emphasis on biodiversity); and *d*] multiple resource use areas, capturing the modern reality that people and wildlife need to live together or at least alongside each other in complementary ways.

The TBCA/TFCA approach provides a useful broadening of the TBPA concept outlined in IUCN's 2001 publication to a corridor vision that encompasses a wider array of conservation mechanisms, centered around core protected zones. The TBCA/TFCA terminology is therefore an important complement to IUCN's definitions.

Transboundary Natural Resource Management

A third term that has been used in the transboundary context is "Transboundary Natural Resource Management," or TBNRM. In 1999, the Biodiversity Support Program (BSP) published an important document on this topic, entitled "Study on the Development of Transboundary Natural Resource Management Areas in Southern Africa" (Griffin et al. 1999). This study suggested the need for TBNRM terminology on the grounds that the definitions of TFCA and TBCA were overly restrictive and failed to take into account certain key dimensions. Specifically, it cited the need to include multiple use zones within the TFCA concept, and the need for greater attention to the role of communities in managing natural resources.

Given that this publication was released before IUCN's 2001 document, the TBNRM terminology was put forth as an alternative to a now somewhat outdated World Bank definition proposed in 1996. That definition stated that TFCAs were "relatively large areas that straddle frontiers (boundaries) between two or more countries and cover large-scale natural systems encompassing one or more protected areas." BSP raised a number of valid concerns with respect to the World Bank's definition, many of which were later addressed in IUCN's 2001 definitions. Nonetheless, the TBNRM concept as described in BSP's study expresses some fundamental differences with TBCAs that require attention.

The central concern expressed in BSP's publication is that TBPAs or TFCAs are excessively protected areas focused at the expense of local communities. Thus, BSP's publication contends that "[f]rom a community perspective, TBNRM describes the situation more accurately than the notion of TBCAs, which emphasize conservation ahead of sustainable use. Tension between conservation and development objectives and TBCA/TFCA development should not be an excuse for a retreat into the old fortress of 'command and control' conservation." The study then notes that in Africa in the twentieth century, many communities lost land-rights, and a range of other property rights, including rights to wildlife, and that new land-use policies often separated wild animals from the ecological and economic systems of which they were an inherent part.

In our view, these approaches are not mutually exclusive. It is important to establish and manage TBPAs and TBCAs within a context of legitimate TBNRM, where the rights and obligations of communities and authorities alike are recognized and negotiated through appropriate forms of governance. BSP quite accurately cites the plight of many African communities that were dispossessed by the establishment of new protected areas, as well as the critical need to avoid the "command and control" protected-area models of the past.

However, new models embraced by the World Parks Congress, the Programme of Work on Protected Areas of the Convention on Biological Diversity, and IUCN's Third World Conservation Congress in 2004 demonstrate that it is possible to move beyond the traditional "command and control" approach to involve communities in the establishment and management of protected areas, and to include community-conserved areas as components of a regional landscape approach to conservation. The work of government agencies, NGOs, and communities around the world, from the Terai Arc in Nepal and India to the Cóndor region shared by Peru and Ecuador, shows that it is possible to combine community-based natural resource management and multiple use zones into larger frameworks including core protected areas.

Nor do we think it is advisable to de-emphasize protected areas in favor of a more general sustainable use approach. The premise used to justify a TBNRM/Sustainable Use approach in the BSP publication

—that there is an inherent tension between conservation and development objectives— is in our view too sweeping a generalization. We believe that retaining protected areas at the core of a TBCA strategy is necessary to generate the full range of biological, social, and economic benefits that a conservation corridor can provide. Moreover, the sustainable development concept can itself be amorphous, making it unclear precisely what the management objectives are in a given landscape. Lessons learned from integrated conservation and development projects suggest that, under certain conditions, they can be quite effective in relieving pressure on a protected area in the short term, but that in the long term they cannot substitute for policy changes, community involvement, and appropriate government response.

Despite these differences, TBNRM seems to describe a process that is not far removed from TFCA planning as it is currently understood. Although TFCAs focus more explicitly on biodiversity conservation, whereas TBNRM focuses more on the process of managing transboundary resources (e.g., fisheries, migratory wildlife, or shared water bodies), in practice there is very often an overlap in objectives. For example, a protected area that safeguards a watershed will help sustain transboundary water supplies, while a TBNRM project that manages migratory wildlife can help ensure viable populations within a protected area and throughout a corridor. Furthermore, although TBNRM focuses on the process of decision-making at the community level, whereas protected area management almost always includes regional government and national authorities, protected area management requires extensive local consultation, while an effective TFCA requires TBNRM-type management for biodiversity conservation to succeed in the intervening lands between protected areas.

Terminology in this Book

The current use of terms is non-binding, and any country is free to use its own terminology —for example, by choosing to designate a park within its borders as a "Peace Park" to commemorate lives lost in a civil conflict. IUCN emphasizes that its definitions are not internationally sanctioned designations established via treaty, such as World Heritage or Ramsar designations. Furthermore, although IUCN provides detailed best-practice guidelines for TBPAs (discussed below), it also stops short of establishing even an informal certification process for TBPAs.

On the other hand, IUCN provides the only consistent leadership in this field and is in the process of developing more refined and general definitions, as well as guidance for transboundary conservation initiatives, including the broader scope of TBCAs. For the sake of consistency and clarity, we have adopted the IUCN terminology in this book using Transboundary Conservation Area (TBCA) as the broad all-encompassing term, and Transboundary Protected Area (TBPA) as the more restrictive term for those areas that meet both protected area and cooperation criteria.

Furthermore, and although IUCN has not established a formal certification process, there is some momentum in that direction, in part because IUCN's guidelines are quite detailed, providing a core from which a certification process could be derived, and in part because the EUROPARC Federation has established a process for certifying good management practices in TBPAs, giving the idea of a certification process greater credibility. In our view, an IUCN certification, or perhaps even a certification granted by a United Nations body in cooperation with IUCN under an international treaty, would be a positive development. Although the World Heritage and Ramsar Conventions have no enforcement capacity, and limited funding to grant as incentives, they provide official international status that can raise the profile of protected areas, attracting visitors, attention from the public and decision makers, and donor funding.

ORGANIZATIONS INVOLVED IN TRANSBOUNDARY CONSERVATION

The World Conservation Union (IUCN)

The role of IUCN in promoting effective approaches to transboundary conservation has already been discussed above. Its principal effort has been through its volunteer networks of professional protected area managers, coordinated by the WCPA Task Force on Transboundary Conservation, but also involving the Commission on Environmental Law (CEL) and the Commission on Economic, Environmental and Social Policy (CEESP). Its ambitious program, contained within the Durban Action Plan emanating from the World Parks Congress 2003, and subsequently endorsed by the Third World Conservation Congress, is to establish and maintain a global learning network, supported by regional coordination hubs and catalyzing implementation priorities worldwide.

The Programme of Work on Protected Areas, adopted by the Seventh Conference of the Parties to the Convention on Biological Diversity in February, 2004, requires the Parties, with specific reference to the supportive role of IUCN, to, *inter alia*:

1] Apply the ecosystem approach by extending protected areas beyond national boundaries, including *transboundary protected areas* and protected areas in marine areas beyond the limits of national jurisdiction;

2] Establish, where appropriate, *new transboundary protected areas* with adjacent Parties and countries, and strengthen effective collaborative management of existing TBPAs;

3] Compile and *disseminate information* on regional networks of protected areas and *transboundary protected areas*, and to provide an enabling *policy environment for transboundary protected areas*;

4] Develop and adopt minimum standards and best practices for national and *regional protected area systems*; and evaluate and improve the effectiveness of protected areas management by establishing frameworks for monitoring, evaluating, and reporting protected areas management effectiveness at sites, national and regional systems, and *transboundary protected area* levels.

In addition to IUCN, a number of organizations, including donors, funding agencies, and conservation organizations have promoted and supported the establishment of transboundary conservation areas worldwide. Significant funding has been allocated to these initiatives by, among others, the Global Environment Facility (GEF) and its implementing agencies. This section provides additional information on some of the organizations mentioned above, as well as information on several other institutions that have played an important role in transboundary conservation, either by encouraging further study or by providing funding.

Peace Parks Foundation

The Peace Parks Foundation's (PPF) pioneering role is discussed at greater length above in the Terminology section. PPF remains a leader in transboundary conservation, though it continues to maintain its focus on areas adjoining South Africa. With the exception of serving in an advisory capacity to organizations working on formal conservation status for the DMZ between South Korea and North Korea, PPF has not expanded its expertise to other parts of the world.

Conservation International

Conservation International (CI) focuses its efforts on three global priority regions: terrestrial biodiversity hotspots (Mittermeier et al. 2004), high-biodiversity wilderness areas (Mittermeier et al. 2002, 2003), and key marine regions. The 34 biodiversity hotspots (Mittermeier et al. 2004) are regions that harbor a large number of species found nowhere else, and at the same time have lost a significant amount of their original vegetation due to human activities. To qualify as a hotspot, a region must hold at least 1 500 endemic plant species (0.5% of the global total) and must have lost at least 70% of its original native habitat. What remains of these 34 hotspots covers only 2.3% of Earth's land surface, yet contains at least 50% of all vascular plants, 42% of all vertebrates (mammals, birds, reptiles, amphibians, and freshwater fish), and more than three-quarters of all species listed by IUCN as "Critically Endangered" or "Endangered."

The five high-biodiversity wilderness areas (Mittermeier et al. 2002, 2003) are vast regions of undisturbed land, with at least 70% original vegetation still intact and very low human populations. These areas are important as major storehouses of biodiversity, and are critical for watershed protection, carbon sequestration, pollination, disaster prevention, and other ecosystem services. The five high biodiversity wilderness areas recognized by CI are Amazonia, the Congo Forests of Central Africa, the island of New Guinea, the Miombo-Mopane Woodlands and Savannahs of Southern Africa, and the North American Deserts straddling the border between Mexico and the U.S.

CI has a broad-based approach to conservation that involves scientific research, capacity building, collaboration between governments and national institutions, and community-based efforts focused on the role of biodiversity conservation in poverty alleviation. The organization's range of activities in transboundary areas reflects this, from fund-raising for de-mining conservation areas in Angola, to research on elephant populations in the Kavango Zambezi TFCA region, to development of sustainable livelihoods on the border between Costa Rica and Panama in La Amistad (Chapter 8, p. 159).

Perhaps more so than in any other region in which it works, CI has organized itself around transboundary corridors in much of Central and South America. CI has restructured itself to work through regional nodes called Centers of Biodiversity Conservation (CBC) that are focused on regional corridors rather than focused exclusively on individual countries. Although CI continues to work at a national level, especially insofar as certain conservation priorities are not part of transboundary corridors, CI's restructuring into CBCs has enabled the organization to concentrate on several major transboundary corridor initiatives, such as the Maya Tropical Forest shared by Mexico, Guatemala, and Belize (Chapter 7, p. 147); La Amistad on the Costa Rica-Panama border (Chapter 8, p. 159); the Vilcabamba-Amboró Corridor between Bolivia and Peru (Chapter 9, p. 167); and the Chocó-Manabi corridor between Colombia and Ecuador. In addition, CI has engaged in two highly innovative marine projects —the Eastern Tropical Pacific Seascape in the waters of Ecuador, Colombia, Panama, and Costa Rica (Chapter 27, p. 321), and the Mesoamerican Reef System, involving Mexico, Belize, Guatemala, and Honduras (Chapter 26, p. 313).

In South Africa, CI has also established a branch office dedicated to facilitating the establishment of TBCAs throughout southern Africa. The CI Southern African TFCA Unit has a small staff and works through fund-raising and partnerships with governments and NGOs to implement a variety of activities. The current focal areas for support and facilitation are the Kavango-Zambezi TFCA and the western Orange River region straddling Namibia and South Africa, although it also assists in two other areas (Chapters 20 and 19, pp. 265 and 257 respectively).

World Wildlife Fund (WWF)

One of the most comprehensive efforts to address landscape-level conservation priorities has been WWF's identification of ecoregions based on a variety of biogeographical characteristics (Olsen et al. 2001). WWF's ecoregional classification was designed to assist conservation action, and within the 867 ecoregions identified, global priorities for ecoregion conservation were highlighted in 237 areas, known as the Global 200 Ecoregions, many of which straddle international boundaries. For example, in Africa, 85% of the 119 terrestrial ecoregions occur in more than one country, mostly with direct connectivity across borders (Oglethorpe et al. 2004).

In addition to promoting conservation action in many transboundary sites through regional and country-driven programs, WWF has invested in approximately 60 ecoregions in the first phase of its global ecoregion conservation program. Planning and management teams have been systematically working with governments and other partners to develop ecoregion visions, identify priority landscapes within ecoregions, and apply conservation planning tools and developing strategies that address key threats and opportunities. The approach focuses on conservation in broad landscapes where there are often several different forms of land use besides protected areas. Even when applied within countries, these are challenging multi-institutional models for conservation, necessitating horizontal and vertical integration of sectoral policies, plans and programs, as well as activities in various tiers of government.

The complexity is increased in many ways by the introduction of a transboundary element, but transboundary collaboration is often essential to increase conservation effectiveness, and WWF has developed several high profile transboundary projects. One is the Tri-National de la Sangha Project (Chapter 16, p. 231). Another is the Tri-National Dja-Odzala-Minkebe or TRIDOM Project, which links the Minkebe National Park in Gabon, Odzala National Park in the Republic of Congo, and the Dja Faunal Reserve in Cameroon —three critically important protected areas in the Congo Basin. TRIDOM covers 147 000 km^2 of forest, approximately 7.5% of all of Central Africa's forest area, comprises 35 000 km^2 of protected areas, including one World Heritage Site, and has received over $10 million in funding from the GEF. The GEF grant will address threat mitigation to the TRIDOM area and provide funds to develop the long-term financing and management mechanisms necessary to protect the area.

African Wildlife Foundation

The African Wildlife Foundation (AWF) recently launched a new Heartlands Program, designed to protect those large and cohesive conservation landscapes in Africa that can sustain healthy populations of wild species and ensure natural processes for future generations. These landscapes are also areas in which tourism or other natural resource-based activities can contribute significantly to local livelihoods. Most of the AWF's "Heartlands" are transboundary areas, and include TBCAs or have TBCAs planned. Perhaps the most high-profile of the TBCAs is the Virunga Heartland, which is discussed in greater detail in the "Political Benefits" section below and in Chapter 17, p. 239.

EUROPARC Federation

The Federation of Nature and National Parks of Europe, or EUROPARC Federation, was founded in 1973 to form a network of professionals working in European protected areas. An independent, non-governmental organization based in Germany, EUROPARC is in some respects similar to IUCN, though with a more limited mission in that they focus on protected areas. Like IUCN, EUROPARC brings together a membership that includes governments, non-governmental organizations, academic institutions and individuals, and their network links the organizations responsible for managing over 400 protected areas. At the World Parks Congress in 2003, EUROPARC launched an initiative entitled "Transboundary Parks Following Nature's Design," which consists of a program for certifying transboundary parks that meet EUROPARC's management criteria (discussed further below).

InWent

An organization that has partnered with the IUCN/WCPA Task Force on Transboundary Conservation and has acted as a convenor on transboundary conservation issues in the Southern Africa region is Germany's InWent (Internationale Weiterbildung und Entwicklung Gemeinnützige GmbH, or Capacity Building International, Germany). InWent is the product of a merger between the Carl Duisberg Gesellschaft e.V. (CDG) in Cologne, Germany, a non-profit organization dedicated to international advanced training and human resource development, and the Foundation for International Development (DSE), a foundation acting on behalf of the Federal German Government, also focused on training and policy dialogues. InWent held a series of regional workshops on transboundary conservation in Southern and Eastern Africa in 2002 and 2003, and these helped capture the rapidly growing body of experience on TBCA development and management in the region.

The International Tropical Timber Organization (ITTO)

ITTO's Yokohama Action Plan, in force for 2002-2006, provides a mandate to ITTO to include biodiversity concerns and especially transboundary protection of tropical forests among its goals, and is pursuing a two-pronged action program to implement this mandate. The first component is to reduce biodiversity loss by improving management in timber-producing tropical forests, and the second involves technical assistance and funding to establish and manage protected areas. As a result, ITTO is supporting the establishment and management of 10 million ha of transboundary conservation areas, including the Lanjak-Entimau/Betung Kerihun Transboundary Conservation Area between Sarawak (Malaysia) and Indonesia (Chapter 24, p. 299), and the Cordillera del Cóndor Transboundary

Conservation Area between Ecuador and Peru (see below). ITTO has also worked with IUCN to develop case studies from lessons learned, and continues to assist at the international level in the development of transboundary conservation policies.

The World Bank

In 2000, the World Bank published a working paper entitled "Transboundary Reserves: World Bank Implementation of the Ecosystem Approach." The paper adopted the CBD's Malawi Principles (see below), described World Bank-funded projects underway implementing this approach generally, and summarized lessons learned from World Bank TBCA projects around the world. These projects include the World Bank's contribution to management of shared freshwater resources (such as in the African Rift Valley Lakes), initiatives to improve transborder cooperation on the management of large marine ecosystems, and financing for trust funds that provide reliable funding for the management of transboundary wildlife resources.

BENEFITS OF TRANSBOUNDARY PROTECTED AREAS

How can we explain the tremendous increase in the number of transboundary protected areas in the last few decades? And why has this phenomenon generated such tremendous enthusiasm in the conservation community? The answer is that the transboundary element can act as a multiplier, greatly amplifying the benefits protected areas already provide. Transboundary conservation area initiatives allow conservationists to operate at a larger scale, moving across political boundaries to protect a transboundary ecosystem in its entirety, rather than stopping at political borders that rarely correspond to natural systems. By the same token, a TBCA can create unique social opportunities; for example, by reuniting communities divided by borders or allowing mobile peoples to move across their traditional territories more easily.

TBCAs also add an enticing political dimension to conservation, which is the capacity to reduce tensions or even to help resolve conflicts between countries, in particular those stemming from boundary disputes. This peace-making dimension enlarges the range of benefits parks provide in a significant way. It also provides powerful evidence for one of the central tenets of conservation —that protected areas are not only necessary to secure the planet's ecological integrity but, more broadly, that they are an essential component of any healthy, peaceful, and productive society. The following sections review in more detail the many benefits TBCAs can provide, besides their obvious biological benefits inherent in any well-managed protected area.

On pp. 42-43, the late afternoon sun on the rim of the Cerro Colorado Volcano in El Pinacate and Gran Desierto de Altar Biosphere Reserve of Mexico.
© Jack Dykinga

Political Benefits

The attraction of TBCAs and Parks for Peace stems in large part from their regional political benefits. TBCAs can help reduce tensions between countries that have strained relations, they can help resolve border disputes, or they can be used after a political settlement has been reached, as a goodwill gesture to rebuild peaceful cooperation. And of course, as in the case of the first Park for Peace, they can celebrate historically good relations and a shared commitment for the joint management of natural resources. In this section, we focus on the role of TBCAs in the resolution of international border disputes, and in bringing peace and reconciliation to regions that have experienced violent conflict. For an additional example, please see Chapter 20, p. 265, on the Kaza TFCA, highlighting the role of that TFCA in bringing reconciliation and economic renewal to Southern Angola, and in building new ties between Angola and its neighbors.

Resolving Boundary Dispute: The Cordillera del Cóndor

To the extent that Parks for Peace can play an important role in the settlement of disputes and are an effective vehicle for reducing tensions, their geopolitical significance is potentially far-reaching, especially given the substantial number of unresolved border disputes around the world. The Carpathian mountain parks between Poland and Czechoslovakia established between 1949 and 1967 and cited above, provide one example of the use of TBPAs to secure a settlement of a boundary dispute and to begin the process of reconciliation. A more contemporary example is the Cordillera del Cóndor Transboundary Protected Area between Peru and Ecuador, established as part of a boundary dispute resolution between the two countries. According to peace agreements between Peru and Ecuador, signed on October 26, 1998, both countries recognized Areas of Ecological Protection on both sides of the border. Later, in 1999, Peru created an additional protected area, the Santiago-Comaina Reserve, which will eventually lead to the creation of the Cordillera del Cóndor National Park (Carlos Ponce, pers. comm.).

The dispute had its origins in a conflict over several Spanish royal decrees during the eighteenth and nineteenth centuries, relating to the administration of certain lightly populated areas in the western Amazonia. As a result of these decrees, several areas were shifted back and forth between two Spanish colonial administrations, the Viceroyalty of Peru and the Viceroyalty of Nueva Granada. The shifts in the administration of these provinces made it unclear to which subsequently independent country they belonged. If they were part of Nueva Granada, they would seem to be Ecuadorian. If under the administration of the Viceroyalty of Peru, it would seem to be Peruvian territory. The issue was geopolitically important given the considerable size (32 500 ha) of the region at issue, as well as the fact that it constitutes a key access corridor to the Amazon River.

Despite numerous attempts to mediate a settlement over the next century, efforts to resolve ownership of these provinces, and to define the border, failed, and hostilities between the two countries broke out in 1941. After a ceasefire was signed in 1942, and a boundary agreed to, the U.S., Brazil, Chile, and Argentina brokered the Protocol of Rio de Janeiro in 1942 to solidify the cease-fire agreement.

Unfortunately, efforts to demarcate the border under the Protocol were frustrated. As has so often been the case, the border was established using a general description of geographic features in a landscape that was not yet well mapped or explored. In this instance, the Protocol established the border based on a watershed formed by the Zamora and Santiago Rivers, along the Cordillera del Cóndor. The discovery of a third river, the Cenepa, in 1947, made implementation of the Protocol's terms more difficult in this region. Although the area in dispute only entailed a 75 km stretch of the border, Ecuador viewed this development as an opportunity to extract itself from an unfavorable settlement, and ultimately withdrew from the Protocol in 1960.

Hostilities again flared up in 1981, and continued sporadically until 1995, despite the appearance of détente when President Fujimori of Peru visited Ecuador in 1991. The old conflict ignited in 1995, leading to a 19-day shooting war. Official reports, after a cease-fire was established, indicated that 50 Peruvians had been killed, with about 30 dead on the Ecuadorian side. Significant mobilization in both countries suggested that there was a very real risk of further military escalation. In contrast to previous engagements, Ecuador is credited with having prevailed in this conflict. As a result, and as a matter of national honor, Ecuador was extremely reluctant to submit to a demarcation process that would likely favor Peru's stronger historical claim to the region and that would result in the loss of territory, including several military outposts. Particularly sensitive and of great emotional importance to Ecuador was the potential loss of a military base at Tiwintza, which its soldiers had strongly defended in the 1995 conflict. When an expert commission ruled that the Rio Protocol was enforceable, despite the existence of the Cenepa River, which in their view did not materially affect the Protocol's intent, it seemed that negotiations had reached an impasse.

The impasse was resolved in 1998 through a package of measures, including grants of commercial access to Ecuador in Peru's Amazon region, and certain property (though not sovereign) rights within Peru. A major element of the settlement was the proposal of several transboundary protected areas. Although the parks were small, the proposal was that they be jointly managed, free of any sign of national demarcation. These protected areas would also include the sites of the Ecuadorian military bases that were awarded to Peru, and a monument to the fallen soldiers to both countries and to newfound peace to be built in the park.

These proposals were supported by a series of surveys in the region to establish the biological importance of the area. The surveys found that the region had extremely high levels of biodiversity and high levels of endemism, and provided an important habitat for a number of threatened species, several of which had very limited distributions. Establishing the global importance of the region was therefore a useful building block in the drive towards a final settlement (Conservation International 2002).

Immediately after parks were established on either side of the border, several foundations and multilateral organizations (ITTO, The John D. and Catherine T. MacArthur Foundation, and the United Nations Foundation) were invited to help define a broader conservation strategy for the area, including protected areas in the region not adjacent to the newly created ecological protection zones on both sides of the border. The presence of these international organizations helped to establish a sense of neutrality and mutual confidence, and led to the creation of the TBPA.

Of course, conservation was only one aspect of the settlement. More important was that neither country wanted the conflict to escalate, and the recognition that even low-level conflicts had a very high human and economic cost. The fact that Ecuador had prevailed in the 1995 engagement perhaps also created a window of opportunity for the country to accept a solution from a position of strength. So a key to the settlement was the commitment to a $3 billion development plan for the region, which was launched in 2000 and is scheduled to end in 2009.

The park's deep symbolic importance provided a critical element in the resolution of the dispute. International support for nature conservation in the formerly disputed area will play a continuing role in building peaceful cooperation between the two countries and generating economic benefits for the region.

Reconciliation: The Iron Curtain-The Greenbelt Initiative and Beringia

Another example of the usefulness of TBCAs in bringing reconciliation and renewed communication and cooperation to a region that has suffered from political strife and conflict can be found in Eastern Europe. Conference proceedings from IUCN's 1997 Parks for Peace conference in South Africa noted that TBPAs were flourishing between Warsaw Pact countries. Indeed, of the 50 existing and 26 proposed TBPAs in Europe, 22 or about 29% were found on borders separating Warsaw Pact countries from each other, or from Western Europe.

This phenomenon can be explained in a number of ways. As a result of the tight control of border areas during the Cold War, wildlife in these border areas was able to regenerate. Thus, as in the case of the DMZ between the Koreas, biodiversity benefited from the political conflict, making these extensive areas logical locations for protected areas. A second explanation has to do with the fact that despite the Cold War, conservationists made efforts to work across borders wherever possible. In some cases, such as between Austria and Hungary or between the former Czechoslovakia and Germany, there was already a history of goodwill and cooperation on the ground. Finally, the fall of the Iron Curtain created great enthusiasm for international cooperation and exchange, and, combined with the impetus provided by the European Union, the EUROPARC Federation, and a variety of NGO initiatives, led to a rapid growth in the number of transboundary initiatives.

The European Greenbelt Initiative (Chapter 14, p. 209), which is being coordinated by IUCN and the German Federal Agency for Nature Conservation (BfN), is an attempt to manage and consolidate the network of protected areas along the former Iron Curtain. This initiative has three components: 1] the Fennoskandian Greenbelt between Norway, Finland, and the Russian Federation; 2] the Central European Greenbelt, running through Germany, between the Czech Republic, Austria and Hungary, to the Adriatic Sea; and 3] the Balkan Greenbelt, running along the separation between the Balkan countries, to the Black Sea.

The term "Beringia" comes from the eighteenth century Danish explorer Vitus Bering, who explored the North Pacific for the Russian Czar, and after whom the Bering Strait was named. In the late 1920s and early 1930s, the word "Beringia" came into use as a geographic descriptor for a large area between the Kolyma River in the Russian Far East and the Mackenzie River in the Northwest Territories of Canada. Because the Bering Straits have at various times been above sea level, linking the Russian Far East and Alaska by land, Beringia is still characterized by many biological and cultural linkages.

In 1986, at a time when U.S. and Soviet relations were beginning to improve, and shortly before the fall of the Berlin Wall, a working group was established to address a number of environmental issues, including "Conservation and Management of Natural and Cultural Heritage." The idea for a Beringian Heritage International Park emerged from these discussions, and, in 1989, the concept began to be introduced at the local level in native villages in northwestern Alaska and the Chukotka Peninsula in Russia. At a summit in 1990, Presidents Bush and Gorbachev announced they would be creating an international park spanning the Bering Strait, emphasizing the need for cooperation in the study and management of the respective parks.

Unfortunately, implementation of the agreement stalled. In the U.S. the reason seemed to be a lack of local support for the project, ostensibly because local consultations were not sufficient. As a result, the U.S. and Russia have engaged in a Shared Beringia Heritage Program since 1991 to develop stronger transboundary ties in the region, and to build stronger support for the project. Since 1991, this Program has been supplemented by the now annual Beringia Days Conference, which provides a mechanism to review the activities of the Shared Beringia Heritage Program. The Beringian Heritage International Park therefore remains very much alive, though legislation from both governments will be necessary to make this park a reality.

Maintaining Channels of Communication during Conflict:
The Virunga-Bwindi Region

The forests at the border of Rwanda, Uganda, and the Democratic Republic of Congo (D.R.C.) are the last habitat of the mountain gorilla (*Gorilla beringei beringei*). With only about 385 mountain gorillas left, this is one of the most threatened species on the planet. Their remaining habitat is almost wholly contained in four national parks: Bwindi Impenetrable National Park (which may in fact have a distinct subspecies), Mgahinga Gorilla National Park in Uganda, Volcanoes National Park in Rwanda, and Virungas National Park in the D.R.C. This region is under intense population pressure and suffers from extreme poverty and recurring ethnic and military conflict. The most shocking of these episodes occurred in Rwanda in 1994 when nearly a million people, mostly ethnic Tutsis, lost their lives in less than three months in a chilling genocide.

For over a decade, a consortium of international NGOs has been working alongside protected area authorities to help conserve mountain gorillas and their habitat. The International Gorilla Conservation Programme (IGCP), formed in 1991, is managed by three partners: the AWF, Fauna and Flora International (FFI), and the WWF. The partnership also includes protected area authorities from the three countries in which IGCP works: the Office Rwandais de Tourisme et des Parcs Nationaux, the Uganda Wildlife Authority (UWA), and the Institut Congolais pour la Conservation de la Nature (ICCN).

Through more than 10 years of war in the Great Lakes region, IGCP's staff worked with everyone who could influence the survival of the mountain gorillas and their habitat. The park authorities, government and military authorities, and local people all impact what happens in the parks, and conservation objectives can only be attained if they work together. Development, humanitarian, and relief organizations also affect the natural resources, the people, and the forests. IGCP meets regularly with military officers, government and administrative authorities, and representatives of local communities to explain how the national parks of the Virunga Mountains are vital to the people of the region. Intact forest in the Virungas helps prevent erosion and helps to ensure dependable water supplies and much-needed tourist income, as well as providing a habitat for biodiversity. The military commanders operating in the region have worked closely with IGCP and the parks to help ensure the protection and conservation of mountain gorillas.

Although mountain gorillas remain under tremendous pressure, the efforts of the IGCP have enabled a small increase in their population in recent years. This incredible success is a reflection of the deep commitment of the parties involved and also of the high stakes of the endeavor. Failure to protect this flagship charismatic

On the opposite page, a common piping guan (Aburria pipile) *sitting on a tree above a clay lick in the lowland rainforest of Peru's Bahuaja-Sonene National Park, part of the Vilcacamba-Amboró transboundary corridor.*
© André Bärtschi

species would mean certain extinction and a loss of approximately $3 million per year in tourist revenues —a considerable sum in one of the poorest regions in Africa. But this success is also testament to the regional transboundary approach that IGCP has adopted.

Fundamental to IGCP's transboundary approach is regional collaboration —i.e., cooperation between the adjacent countries in the region for the purpose of protecting and enhancing this Afromontane ecosystem. This is achieved through hosting periodic meetings of the wardens of the gorilla parks, periodic meetings of the wider community of NGOs and government authorities that are active in the region, and joint patrols and capacity building for park rangers and other protected area staff. IGCP's transboundary approach has led to a rich web of cross-border relationships between government and non-government entities that have persisted during times of conflict. These relationships build resilience into a social and political system strained to breaking point by war and poverty, and provide a valuable network for humanitarian and relief organizations working in a region so often subjected to chaotic violence.

Facilitating Progressive Engagement in Areas of Prolonged Conflict

There remain many areas worldwide where diplomatic initiatives have failed, but where shared conservation objectives may over time provide the impetus to settle long-standing disputes. In these cases, continuing talks regarding the potential for establishing TBCAs often create neutral common ground and an inspiring objective that parties can embrace without losing face. In particular, highly visible events, such as international conferences, can provide an excellent platform for neighbors to work towards dispute resolution, using transboundary conservation as a basis for negotiation. In this section we highlight two high-profile examples where transboundary proposals may yet bear fruit. They are the Siachen Glacier-Saltoro Ridge Area in Kashmir, between India and Pakistan, and the DMZ between South Korea and North Korea.

The Siachen Glacier
The Siachen Glacier is the longest glacier in the world, and the site of the highest battlefield in the world, with troops stationed at an altitude of 6 700 m. The territorial dispute arises from an imprecise definition of the Line of Control established between India and Pakistan subsequent to the 1971-1972 conflict between the two countries. As a result, both countries claim the Siachen Glacier and Saltoro Ridge, and troops have been facing off in this region for several decades. The conflict has of course taken a human toll, including casualties from the fighting itself and many more from the harsh environment. There has also been an environmental toll from human waste, which decomposes slowly at high altitudes, from chemical contamination, oil, and kerosene, all of which are draining into watersheds upon which millions of people depend.

There have been a number of proposals for turning the Siachen Glacier and Saltoro Ridge area into a transboundary Siachen Peace Park. In the last few years, there have been several climbs for peace, including a 2002 expedition in Switzerland sponsored by the International Institute for Peace through Tourism (IIPT), IUCN, and the International Mountaineering and Climbing Federation (UIAA), involving both Pakistani and Indian climbers. While the establishment of a Siachen Peace Park may not become a reality in the short term, a number of factors appear to work in favor of such a proposal. Two such important factors are increasing détente between the two countries in recent years and the fact that a Siachen Peace Park could serve as an initial overture towards lasting peace without requiring an immediate and permanent resolution to the underlying Kashmir conflict. The work of IUCN, the UIAA, and the IIPT in keeping the idea alive and promoting high profile events that encourage communication and cooperation between India and Pakistan are therefore vital, because this kind of preparatory groundwork is essential to move quickly should the opportunity for a Siachen Peace Park arise.

The South Korea-North Korea Demilitarized Zone (DMZ)
Perhaps the most high-profile standoff in the world, the conflict between North Korea and South Korea has shown some encouraging signs of a thaw in recent years, even though a resolution over what to do about the DMZ, let alone reunification, still seems far away. Nonetheless, it is difficult to imagine a better location for a Peace Park. The DMZ is an important monument to fallen soldiers from Korea, as well as the many other nations involved in the conflict. Largely untouched since 1953, the 4-km wide, 250-km long area of the DMZ is also an ecological time capsule where much of Korea's biodiversity remains intact. As such, it represents the heart of what remains wild on the peninsula. Threatened Asian species, many of which are gone from other parts of the Korean peninsula, persist in the DMZ, including the Asiatic black bear (VU), the Eurasian lynx, the goral sheep, the leopard, and possibly even the Amur tiger, though tiger reports remain unconfirmed. Indeed, in addition to discussing the possibility of establishing a DMZ Peace Park, there is also talk about designating the area a World Heritage Site.

Preparatory work for a potential peace park in the DMZ between North Korea and South Korea has been ongoing for some time on the South Korean side, including a conference in July 2004 hosted by the DMZ Forum, a U.S.-based NGO, and by the Gyeonggi Province and Gyeonggi Cultural Foundation. Korea's Ministry of Culture and Tourism, and Non-Hyup, Korea's agricultural industry association, funded the conference.

Progress on a DMZ peace park and World Heritage designation will require approval from both South Korea and North Korea, which makes it difficult to assess the likelihood of a breakthrough. As with India and Pakistan, however, dialogue between South Korea and North Korea seems to have improved. Another encouraging sign is the opening of the Mount Keumgang site in North Korea to tours from South Korea. Finally, as with the Siachen Glacier case, the engagement of NGOs and international organization ensures that discussions will continue. The fact that local and national government agencies from South Korea were not only involved, but hosted and sponsored the conference in Seoul in 2004, demonstrates that, at least from the South Korean side, the idea of establishing a World Heritage Site and Peace Park is alive and well.

Social Benefits

Border areas are often important from a biodiversity perspective because their remoteness from large urban centers works to ensure their intactness. Nonetheless, border areas are also places of great social complexity for several reasons. First, they are often home to unique cultures that have evolved in varying degrees of isolation. Second, colonial borders were frequently drawn without regard to cultural patterns and ethnicities, so that ethnic groups, and sometimes even families, found themselves separated by political boundaries. The latter is an especially big problem for traditionally mobile communities that follow wildlife migrations to hunt, or mirror wildlife migrations as they seek grazing areas for livestock, or both. Thirdly, border areas can be particularly volatile in regions prone to conflict and can suddenly become staging grounds for armies or rebel groups during times of armed conflict. They can also be flooded with refugees fleeing a war zone, and seeking a safe haven where they can access subsistence resources.

The unique character of border areas therefore creates special conditions in which a TBCA can either become a unique opportunity —a stabilizing force making it possible to restore the social and ecological integrity of the landscape— or a potentially complicating factor, creating new barriers for local communities. Which of these is the case depends in large part on the willingness of those designing the TBCA to understand and address the social intricacies of the region in which they are working.

To date, TBCA planning has not sufficiently integrated social considerations and, as a result, the provision of social benefits has not reached its full potential. This is unfortunate given that TBCAs could become very useful in helping to rectify problems caused by political boundaries established without regard to social and ecological boundaries. TBCAs can involve local communities in the management of an area that more closely resembles the area traditionally under their management and, with the proper agreements in place between governments, can allow communities to circulate more freely between countries, making it possible to reunite families divided by borders.

There is evidence that TBCAs facilitate cultural exchanges between ethnic groups separated by borders, even where the cultural dimension is not an explicitly articulated objective of the TBCA's design. For example, the proposed |Ai-|Ais-Richtersveld TFCA seems

On the opposite page, a giant otter (Pteronura brasiliensis) resting on a branch along the Rio Távara in Peru. This imposing aquatic predator is one of the most important flagship species of the Vilcabamba-Amboró region.
© André Bärtschi

49

to have encouraged exchanges between Nama people on both sides of the South Africa-Namibia border, and could be instrumental in bringing families on opposite sides of the border back together. The Andean region provides another example. Although social considerations were not key to the establishment of the El Cóndor TBCA, the management plan for that TBCA seeks to reestablish traditional linkages between the Awajún, Wampis, and Shuar indigenous groups, setting an important precedent for future TBCAs. Although there are many other examples where TBCAs, or plans for TBCAs, are indirectly bringing greater attention to the needs of local communities and indigenous groups, the fact remains that these benefits could be increased significantly if this aspect were included in planning efforts more systematically.

TBCAs can also provide an uplifting economic effect through tourism, to local communities, and to the country as a whole. Tourism is now the world's fastest growing industry. The World Tourism Organization (WTO) estimates that in 1999 over 663 million people spent time as tourists, spending more than $453 billion. The WTO expects over one billion travelers a year by 2010, and 1.6 billion by 2020. Moreover, the tourism industry is the world's largest employer, generating approximately 200 million jobs, or about 10% of the jobs around the world (World Tourism Organization 2004).

The nature-based tourism market represents roughly 7% of expenditures on tourism and 20% of all international travel. Furthermore, nature-based tourism is growing at a much faster rate than the general tourism sector —10 to 30% versus approximately 4%. In some areas, such as the South African Development Community (SADC) region, tourism is the biggest job creator and an essential source of foreign exchange. Based on current trends, over 1.2 million new jobs are expected to be created between 2002-2012 in the SADC countries, many of which will be based on visits to protected areas and wildlife viewing.

The economic potential of nature-based tourism is therefore enormous, and protected areas that have the added international cachet of being designated TBCAs are well placed to capitalize on this potential. This is particularly true if the protected area also benefits from other international designations —for example, as a UNESCO World Heritage Site. Nevertheless, there are also important caveats. Current levels of infrastructure in many developing countries are inadequate to meet growing tourist demand. In addition, there are serious risks associated with depending too much on a tourist economy, which discourages investment in the necessary infrastructure. Political shocks resulting from terrorist attacks or civil strife can have immediate and radical impacts on tourism, with disastrous effects on local economies. Tourism therefore requires careful planning and integration into national and regional development plans.

Another reality of the nature-tourism industry (and of tourism generally) is that many of the jobs created are unskilled and low-paying, and much of the profits tend not to remain in local communities, but rather are concentrated in cities or exported to developed countries. It is therefore essential to implement mechanisms to ensure that some of these profits remain in the local communities where the ecotourism actually takes place. In addition, tourism benefits can be unevenly distributed between countries sharing TBCAs if one of the countries has inferior infrastructure. All of these issues must be taken into consideration in planning for TBCAs.

Management Benefits

A third factor explaining the rise in TBCAs has to do with the many management advantages that accrue to countries with adjoining protected areas. These benefits are listed at greater length in IUCN's "Transboundary Protected Areas for Peace and Cooperation" mentioned above. They include the greater efficiency —both financial and in terms of human resources— of combining efforts on a range of management challenges, from invasive species and pest control, to wildfire prevention, to search and rescue operations. Coordinated management can also avoid expensive duplication of efforts —for example, research programs, *ex situ* banks or nurseries, training programs for park staff, and educational and interpretation materials for visitors. And, of course, coordination creates a more dynamic problem-solving environment, increasing the pool of expertise that can be applied to any given situation and generally raising morale for park staff.

In addition, cross-border coordination frequently raises the profile of the parks, giving them special status at the global level and facilitating designation as World Heritage Sites or other international designations, as well as creating opportunities for donors and assistance agencies. The higher profile created by the transboundary status of protected areas often gives government officials, from customs and immigrations officials to protected area staff, added incentive to address problems and threats, or simply to honor commitments to the protected areas in question. This may help improve a range of conditions that previously impacted management —for example, smuggling or other criminal activities in and around a protected area, or illegal immigration in the region.

The Whole is Greater than the Sum of the Parts

Given the massive loss of human life and social strife in a century that was more often than not characterized by rampant nationalism and armed conflict, it is not difficult to see why the idea of TBCAs, including TBPAs and Parks for Peace, gathered such momentum during the last few decades of the twentieth century. Conservation that transcends national borders, and, in so doing, generates benefits to wild nature, eases political tensions, reduces protected area management burdens, has an uplifting effect on local communities and indigenous groups, and creates economic opportunity, is an exciting prospect.

Some of this excitement must be tempered by the fact that while transboundary conservation projects can simplify certain aspects of protected area management, they can also add complexity. Requiring consensus from two governments, when previously approval from only one was sufficient, can slow decision-making. Where the two protected areas are of different classifications, managed by different administrative agencies —such as a national park on one side of the border and a wildlife refuge on the other— differing mandates can complicate attempts at cooperation. Differences in language across borders can also be a limiting factor, and disproportionate financial resources on one side of a border can also cause an imbalance in the distribution of benefits. And, as highlighted above, border areas are characterized by their own array of special challenges —from refugee crises, to smuggling, to militarization as result of political tensions, to outright conflict. Thus, at least in the short-term, transboundary protected areas may not simplify management appreciably.

However, the potential of TBCAs is nonetheless real, and it is this enormous potential that makes them interesting. TBCAs are not a fail-safe mechanism —not all TBCAs deliver on their promise or do so quickly, and not all TBCAs provide the full range of benefits described above. But TBCAs do create opportunities. Whether they evolve slowly over time as a result of informal contacts between protected areas or whether they benefit from diplomatic efforts at the highest levels, TBCAs are attractive because they establish cooperation and create new channels of communication that previously did not exist. By virtue of these mechanisms, and the peaceful cooperation that TBCAs encourage, action suddenly becomes possible not just on biodiversity conservation, but on a wide range of diverse but interrelated concerns, from natural resource management, to human rights, to cultural preservation, to economic development. It is the potential for this chain reaction in the landscape —this cascade of benefits that necessarily begins with a more effectively managed ecosystem— that makes TBCAs such an exciting prospect.

ESTABLISHING TBCAS-BEST PRACTICES AND SOCIAL GUIDELINES

The rapid increase in the number of TBCAs around the world has led to a substantial growth in the understanding of how to make transboundary conservation successful. Thanks to efforts of organizations like IUCN and its partners, this body of knowledge is being translated into lessons learned and guidelines and, in the case of the EUROPARC Federation, has even led to a certification process for good management practices of TBCAs. These principles, guidelines, and certification processes for transboundary protection are of great value from a practitioner's standpoint. They represent the cutting edge in knowledge and experience in the field and a useful synthesis of a much larger body of information, and facilitate the creation of new TBCAs as well as the more efficient management of existing ones.

The following sections first review principles, guidelines, and best practices for TBCA projects generally, and then focus in particular on one important aspect of TBCA projects, i.e., how to address linkages between social issues and transboundary conservation efforts. Of special concern are issues relating to migratory or mobile peoples, and the challenges of protected area management in times of conflict.

Best Practices

The Convention on Biological Diversity and the Ecosystem Approach: The Malawi Principles

The Second Conference of the Parties to the Convention on Biological Diversity (CBD) in 1995 adopted the "ecosystem approach" as the primary framework for actions taken under the CBD. The Fourth Conference of the Parties in Bratislava in 1998 then assigned the Subsidiary Body on Scientific, Technical, and Technological Advice to develop the ecosystem approach in more detail, resulting in the Malawi Principles on the ecosystem approach. The principles were endorsed by the Fifth Conference of the Parties in Nairobi in 2000 (Decision V/6).

Although not explicitly addressing TBCAs, and necessarily more general than a set of guidelines or certification criteria, the Malawi Principles nonetheless provide a useful starting point for developing a TBCA. The Malawi Principles encourage multi-sectoral conservation planning at a landscape scale, and emphasize the need for adaptive management strategies that take into account socioeconomic factors and changing ecosystems. The Malawi Principles therefore call for an approach in many ways similar to implementing a TBCA, but that will in some instances be even broader in scope.

The status of these Principles as the product of a scientific body convened by the secretariat of an international convention gives them greater weight, and although they are not binding, they nonetheless carry meaningful authority. They are also backed by decades of scientific study and growing efforts by countries to develop mechanisms to regulate shared natural resources, either via TBPAs or TBCAs, or via treaties governing pollution, shared water bodies, etc. As a reflection of this body of scientific knowledge, and of the growing custom of international management of shared natural resources, these Principles represent an important step forward.

IUCN: Good Practice Guidelines

IUCN's 2001 publication includes a series of nine Good Practice Guidelines for transboundary protected areas, addressing all aspects of designing, implementing and managing TBPAs. These guidelines

On the opposite page, a silverback mountain gorilla (Gorilla beringei beringei) in the Virunga Volcanoes; the flagship species for this tri-national transboundary area on the Rwanda-Uganda-Democratic Republic of Congo border.
© Anup Shah

On pp. 54-55, a devil ray (Mobula spp.), a smaller relative of the manta, from Cocos Island, Costa Rica, a key component of the Eastern Tropical Pacific Seascape.
© Sterling Zumbrunn

in many ways mirror IUCN's Cardiff Series of Protected Area Management Guidelines. They are advisory rather than prescriptive, and are intended as an evolving product, to be refined as new experiences and lessons learned come in from the field. The Good Practice Guidelines range from advice on building support for the project and designing the project to benefit local peoples, to the mechanics of developing cooperative management mechanisms across borders, obtaining long-term funding and dealing with political tensions and conflict. They provide a common-sense approach for building a solid transboundary protected area project, emphasizing the need for early and open dialogue with all parties concerned, as well as the need for developing projects incrementally, given their inherent complexity.

Supplementing the Guidelines is a scale for assessing levels of cooperation between internationally adjacent protected areas. The highest level of cooperation, Level 5 or "Full Cooperation," is described as closely integrated planning, where common goals and joint decision-making are implied and, in the case of a transboundary protected area involving a shared ecosystem, the joint plans approach the combined protected areas as a single unit. At this highest level, joint management may occur in addition to joint planning; though at a minimum a joint committee is in place for consultation on transboundary protected area issues.

Conversely, the minimum level of cooperation, Level 1, establishes the threshold for what constitutes a transboundary protected area according to IUCN's standards. Level 1 requires some two-way communication between the protected areas, including meetings or communications at least once a year, occasional information sharing, and occasional notification across borders of actions that may affect the other protected area.

While stopping just short of developing an institutionalized certification process, IUCN's Good Practice Guidelines and its cooperation scale nonetheless provide a very clear road map for what constitutes a well-designed and well-implemented transboundary protected area. These tools, combined with the Draft Code described below, provide a framework that might easily be developed into a certification process in the future.

EUROPARC Federation's Certification:
"Transboundary Parks-Following Nature's Design"

EUROPARC's certification process was established "to encourage best practice and facilitate daily cooperation between European protected areas borders." The certification is a voluntary process by which protected areas apply to EUROPARC for a manual of the certification standards and the evaluation processes. Protected area managers then assess their performance and, if ready for certification, submit the full set of application documents, indicating how they meet EUROPARC's standards. Upon receipt of the completed application,

EUROPARC appoints independent verifiers to review the application and conduct site visits. The independent verifiers' reports are then submitted to a EUROPARC Evaluation Committee, which takes the final decision regarding the award of a formal Certificate.

EUROPARC's standards are summarized through quality criteria applied to five fields of work. The criteria include the development of a common vision for the TBCA, official cooperation agreements and joint work plans, funding for continued cooperation, and regular staff cooperation, including sharing of information, joint field work, and joint decision making. These criteria are then applied to five areas: nature and landscape conservation, education and communication, recreation and sustainable tourism, research and monitoring, and mutual understanding and the promotion of peace. These standards were pilot-tested in three TBPAs: Alpi Marittime and Mercantour in Italy and France, Krkonose and Karkonosze on the Czech Republic-Poland border, and Neusiedler See and Fertö-Hanság on the border between Austria and Hungary. Fertö-Hanság was awarded EUROPARC's first certificate in 2003, just prior to the official launching of the Certification Program at the World Parks Congress.

EUROPARC's approach assesses existing cooperation in a TBPA, and therefore differs significantly from IUCN's bird's-eye view of the entire process of establishing a TBPA, managing it effectively, and trouble-shooting, particularly in times of conflict. It is also a program designed for and implemented strictly in Europe, rather than the global view adopted by IUCN. Taken together, however, EUROPARC's certification and IUCN's guidelines provide critical information on the mechanics of TBCA implementation and management, and EUROPARC's work in particular is an important step forward as it represents the first application of a mechanism for monitoring and assessing TBCAs.

Social Guidelines

It is now widely accepted that consulting with local communities and indigenous peoples is an essential step in establishing any protected area. Creating a participatory management structure that provides these groups with a meaningful opportunity to provide continuing input into protected area management is also increasingly a standard measure. Numerous IUCN publications (including the 2001 publication as well as IUCN's Guidelines on Indigenous and Traditional Peoples and Protected Areas and the Cardiff Guidelines) address the issue of local involvement in management and establish guidelines on participatory design and implementation of protected areas. In the case of TBCAs, however, two social issues in particular deserve special mention.

The first is the question of how to take into account mobile peoples who have traditionally lived in or made use of an area to be included in a TBCA. The second is the potential for TBCAs to act as demilitarized areas. Though not exclusive to TBCAs, these questions

are especially relevant because of the additional leverage transboundary protected areas can generate. Some of the benefits TBCAs can provide for mobile peoples were highlighted in the section on social benefits above. In part because of these successes, and in part because discrimination against mobile peoples continues around the world, this issue has received renewed attention in recent years.

International Labor Organization Convention 169

The first document to address the linkage between conservation and mobile peoples, at least in general terms, is the International Labor Organization (ILO) Convention 169 concerning Indigenous and Tribal Peoples in Independent Countries. The ILO adopted the Convention in 1989, which entered into force in 1991. Convention 169's preamble states that the Convention is necessary for two reasons. First because ILO's Convention 107 concerning Indigenous and Tribal Populations adopted in 1957 was in need of revision —the preamble refers in particular to the outdated "assimilationist policies" in that document. And second because fundamental human rights continue to be denied to tribal and indigenous peoples, contributing to the need for an updated ILO Convention.

Convention 169 therefore provides a clear and strong call for governments to ensure that indigenous and tribal peoples "enjoy the full measure of human rights and fundamental freedoms without hindrance or discrimination" (Article 3) and "to undertake special measures as appropriate for safeguarding the persons, institutions, property, labor, cultures and environment of the peoples concerned" (Article 4). With respect to mobile peoples, Article 14 calls on governments to recognize traditional ownership of lands, and to give particular attention "to the situation of nomadic peoples and shifting cultivators in this respect." Article 14 is reinforced by Part V of the Convention, entitled Contacts and Cooperation Across Borders, which consists of a single Article 32, and states that:

> Governments shall take appropriate measures, including by means of international agreements, to facilitate contacts and cooperation between indigenous and tribal peoples across borders, including activities in the economic, social, cultural, spiritual and environmental fields.

The Dana Declaration

In 2002, a group of experts from a range of NGOs and multilateral organizations gathered at the Wadi Dana Nature Reserve in Jordan at a conference titled "Mobile Peoples and Conservation: Crossing the Disciplinary Divide." Referring to themselves as a "group of concerned professionals," participants in this gathering issued a declaration, entitled the Dana Declaration on Mobile Peoples and Conservation.

The Dana Declaration opens with the premise that the world faces an unprecedented global crisis both in terms of loss of biodiversity, as well as the loss of cultural and linguistic diversity, and that in many cases the forces leading to ecological and cultural erosion are the same. The Dana Declaration further notes that mobile peoples are particularly discriminated against, and that at the same time they make important contributions to ecosystem conservation and biodiversity protection. Given these facts, the Dana Declaration notes the urgent need for a "mutually reinforcing partnership between mobile peoples and those involved with conservation" and represents a commitment on the part of its signatories to develop such partnerships. The balance of the Dana Declaration consists of principles for achieving such a partnership, emphasizing the need to respect traditional knowledge, and to integrate traditional knowledge into mainstream science through adaptive management approaches that build on traditional cultural models and customary laws and through collaborative management structures.

Principle 1 states that "conservation approaches with potential impact on mobile peoples and their natural resources" must recognize the rights of mobile peoples and "should lead to effective empowerment" —in essence a restatement of IUCN Best Practices with respect to indigenous peoples and of ILO Convention 169. While it is a given that conservation projects must always respect and seek to enhance the rights of all peoples, it is important to note that conservation planning processes can in and of themselves be an important step in changing perceptions of mobile peoples, bringing attention to their plight, integrating them into management structures, and ultimately helping to secure the rights to which they are entitled. Thus, delaying a conservation planning process while waiting for official government action conferring certain rights could in some instances delay the process by which full rights are ultimately achieved.

The Dana Declaration served as a timely reminder of the urgent need to respect the rights of a group of peoples who continue to be marginalized around the world. Accordingly, one of its key functions seems to have been as a catalyst, designed to generate greater attention to the issue of mobile peoples at the World Parks Congress, and subsequently at the Seventh Conference of the Parties to the Convention on Biological Diversity (COP 7) in Malaysia, and IUCN's Third World Conservation Congress in Bangkok. In this respect, the Dana Declaration generated immediate results, leading to the creation of the World Alliance of Mobile Indigenous Peoples (WAMIP) at the World Parks Congress, and bringing this issue more prominently before the international conservation community. Launched at the World Parks Congress, WAMIP held its second meeting at the CBD's COP 7 and has begun the process of developing its membership, establishing strategic objectives and raising additional funds. WAMIP has established a 10-year horizon for its strategy, which includes working towards securing rights for mobile peoples, helping them to maintain and strengthen their cultural identities, facilitating their free movement, and influencing policy and legal instruments to support their mobile lifestyles.

Although merely a proposal put forth by IUCN, and not currently under the umbrella of any international agreement, the IUCN's Draft Code for Transboundary Protected Areas in Times of Peace and Armed Conflict ("Draft Code") nonetheless deserves special mention. First, it is important because it provides a particularly cogent and concise synthesis of the many beneficial roles transboundary protected areas can play —ecological, political, and economic. Furthermore, it seems to take this reasoning one step further, recognizing at least implicitly that TBPAs not only provide benefits, but that they are in fact a fundamental building block, in many cases vitally necessary for achieving social, economic, and political stability in a particular region.

The importance of the TBPA as a fundamental building block is reflected in the very broad scope of issues that the Draft Code encompasses, many of which are not directly related to biodiversity conservation or ecosystem management. Indeed, the Draft Code is presented as deriving from a growing international body of international law that addresses a range of environmental and humanitarian issues. These issues are currently governed by a long list of international instruments on: 1] conservation of biodiversity and ecosystem services, 2] human rights, and 3] prohibitions on environmentally damaging means of warfare and/or mandating protection of the natural or cultural environment against avoidable harm in areas of armed conflict.

Thus, the Draft Code's reach goes well beyond the traditional vision of what protected area management entails, particularly in its clauses relating to managing military activities in times of peace and in conflict situations. Although this is unfortunately out of necessity —brought on by repeated crises around the world, perhaps most visibly in West and Central Africa— the Draft Code goes quite far in addressing this issue.

For example, the Draft Code proposes that states develop, publish, and distribute guidelines on rules of engagement in or near TBPAs. It also encourages states to define offenses relating to damage caused to TBPAs during conflict and to actively prosecute violators. It also proposes that certain high-priority TBPAs, including World Heritage Sites or sites designated for protection under the 1954 Convention on the Protection of Cultural Property, could be designated as non-defended localities or demilitarized zones under the Geneva Convention.

The Draft Code not only argues that TBPAs should in essence be demilitarized zones that should neither become a military objective nor used to strategic advantage during war, it even more specifically proposes several general guidelines for rules of engagement in or near TBPAs. For example, the Draft Code states that in the event that a TBPA becomes a legitimate military target, and an opposing force determines that a military response impacting the TBPA is in order, that decision should be made "only by its highest level of operational level of command." In addition, that decision should only be made "on the basis of exercising the legitimate right of self-defence" and only if an attack "is the sole military feasible option." The Draft Code also states that the response should be proportionate to the military objectives involved, with a view to "minimizing direct and incidental damage to the TBPA," and that should it appear that damage to the TBPA might be "excessive or disproportionate," the attack should be canceled.

The Draft Code is not by any means the first document linking environmental health to socioeconomic stability and national or regional security. That nexus is well established and benefits from considerable study and analysis. What is more interesting is the Draft Code's insistence that one essential mechanism for achieving stability is the establishment of TBPAs. Placing protected areas at the center of a spectrum of environmental, social, political, cultural, and humanitarian concerns, and proposing explicit mechanisms to protect the integrity of transboundary areas so that they may fulfill their full range of functions, is a significant step forward.

MAINTAINING MOMENTUM: TRANSBOUNDARY GLOBAL NETWORKING AND CAPACITY BUILDING

Global Networking

The challenges of operating in the transboundary context are considerable due to the complexities of operating across international boundaries. Protected area management is already complex, but when differences in language and culture (both between and among countries and institutions) are added, as well as the fact that transboundary conservation inherently involves issues of diplomacy and international relations protocols, the result is one of the most challenging types of conservation in the world. Retaining existing knowledge and building on it in other areas of the world requires coordination among the many governments and other institutions working in this field.

IUCN has taken on the responsibility of maintaining a global network through its WCPA Task Force on Transboundary Conservation. This network, still in its infancy, consists of a website (www.tbpa.net) and a network of partners linked through e-mail list servers and other informal arrangements. The network acts as a focal point to bring together transboundary practitioners, donors, researchers, national and international NGOs that operate in the transboundary context, and the general public interested in these topics. The Task Force also contributes to and convenes specialist meetings to consider and develop best practices based on contemporary experience and research.

The grand vision of the global network is to build regional nodes around the world that can act as storehouses of knowledge about specific projects, organizations, and people. Existing organizations active in this field are best situated to take on this regional role. For example, the Peace Parks Foundation in Southern Africa and the EUROPARC Foundation currently serve in this role in their respective regions. This grand vision furthermore calls for IUCN to act as the global hub in this network by supporting the work of all the regional nodes and providing an overall global perspective.

A network is only as strong as the contributions from its constituent parts and, just as there are significant gaps in the existing global protected areas' network, the global transboundary network is also far from complete. Additional strong partners need to take an active role in the network and a greater funding base needs to be developed. IUCN is well situated to build this network and should continue to do so.

Monitoring and Evaluation

Developing a better ability to monitor the successes and failures of TBCAs around the world is as important as the formation of the regional and global networks described above. Many TBCAs are made up of protected areas that suffer from lack of capacity, making monitoring and evaluation of the individual protected areas, let alone the functioning of the complex as a whole, a difficult proposition. But monitoring and evaluation of TBCAs is also constrained by a variety of factors special to TBCAs that make monitoring and evaluation a complex undertaking.

One limiting factor with TBCA monitoring and evaluation, as with TBCA management generally, has to do with the added layer of complication created by the international dimension. Language barriers, the need to work with multiple land management agencies in different countries, the need to develop socioeconomic indicators for each country, and the need to work at a larger scale created by TBPA complexes with two or more protected areas all combine to make monitoring and evaluation more difficult.

A second challenge is the fact that many of the tools and guidelines for protected area management are site-specific and do not extend much beyond the boundaries of the protected area. This is a problem given that the impacts of TBCAs are often intended to reach far beyond the protected areas themselves, particularly when the TBCAs involve large complexes. In southern Africa, for example, many TBCA initiatives include several protected areas of different types, as well as intervening lands that have no formal protection, but whose management is an integral part of the TBCA.

Existing monitoring and evaluation tools also do not focus specifically on the transboundary elements of the protected area complex, failing to measure and monitor those value-added benefits created by the transboundary nature of the complex. They also do not focus sufficiently on assessing benefits beyond biodiversity conservation, such as socioeconomic, and peace and cooperation benefits. Since regional development and promoting peaceful relations are key functions of TBCAs, and given that TBCAs in theory should act to magnify benefits of conservation in a way that individual protected areas cannot, these are significant gaps to fill.

Monitoring and evaluation of TBCAs is generating greater attention and analysis. As capacity develops in individual projects, and as communication between projects improves as a result of better TBCA networks, more customized tools will develop to fill gaps that cannot be addressed by extrapolating from generic protected area guidelines. There are indications that this is already happening. For example, the IGCP's mountain gorilla project in the Virunga-Bwindi region is using Peace and Conflict Impact Assessments (PCIAs) developed for use by humanitarian and aid organizations, and adapting this tool to their project. In such a volatile region, the PCIA has a vital function —it gauges the social-political "temperature," hopefully to measure improvement, but also to assess whether the project is creating new stresses rather than making things better.

TRANSBOUNDARY CONSERVATION AND GLOBAL SPECIES CONSERVATION PRIORITIES

Given that *in situ* conservation of viable populations of species in natural ecosystems is recognized as a fundamental requirement for the maintenance of global biodiversity (for example, the Convention on Biological Diversity; CBD 1992), governments have invested considerably in the creation of over 100 000 protected areas in 227 countries or territories, occupying around 11.5% of the Earth's land surface area (Chape et al. 2003). This is no small accomplishment, surpassing the 10% target proposed a decade earlier at the Fourth World Parks Congress in Caracas, Venezuela (IUCN 1993). However, various regional studies over the last decade have revealed that the coverage of biodiversity in the existing protected areas' network is still inadequate (e.g., Scott et al. 2001), and that many existing protected areas are biased away from areas of high biodiversity value and threat (largely due to the historical ad hoc, opportunity-driven approach to establishing protected areas, e.g., Pressey, 1994).

A recent comprehensive study investigating the effectiveness of the current global protected areas' network (Rodrigues et al. 2004a) used global data sets on the distribution of protected areas and terrestrial vertebrates to highlight that the global protected area network is indeed far from complete, with some 21% of threatened amphibians, mammals, birds, and turtles analyzed not represented in any protected area. These results were even more compelling when considering only "Critically Endangered" species, with 43% being gap species. A companion study (Rodrigues et al. 2004b) identified those unprotected regions of the world with remarkably high

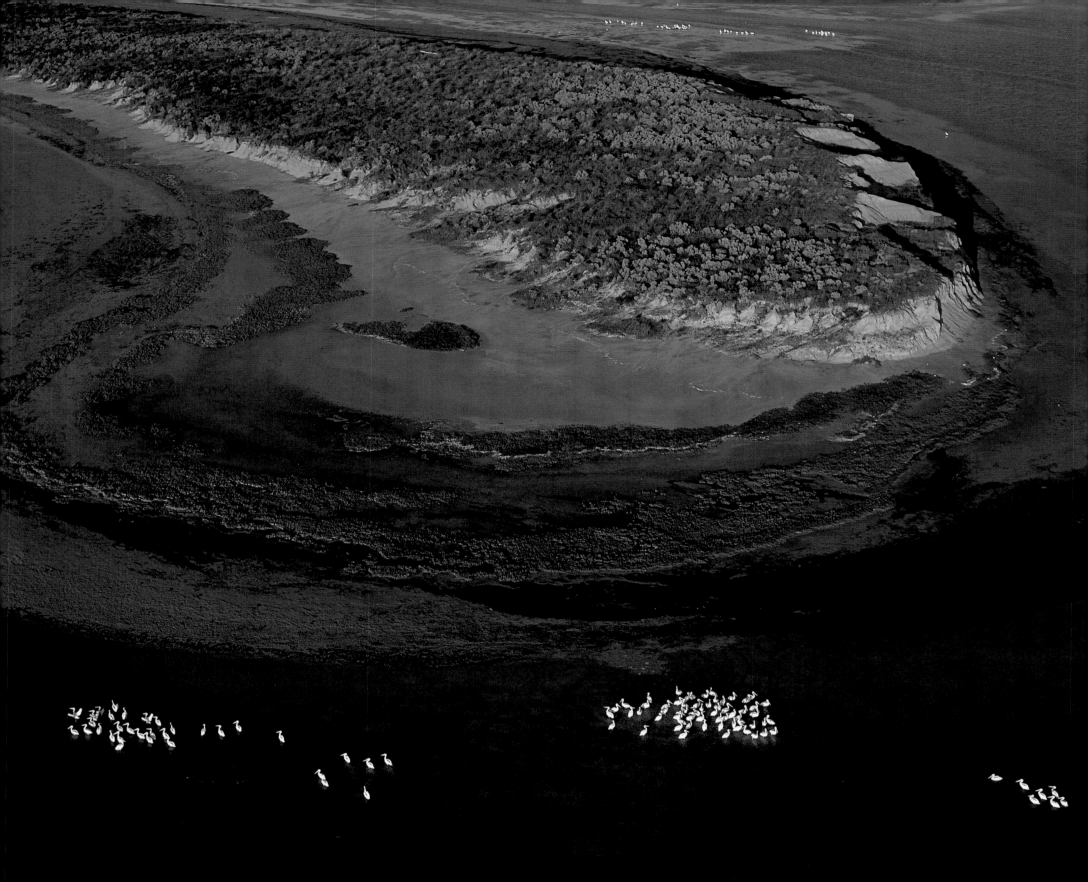

conservation value and that are simultaneously under serious threat. These regions lie overwhelmingly in tropical and subtropical moist forests, particularly on tropical mountains and islands, and represent urgent priorities for expansion of the protected areas' network.

Although these "gap" studies represent global analyses, they point to the many priorities for building up protected areas' networks in places such as Central America, the Tropical Andes, the Caribbean, the Albertine Rift, the Guinean Forests of West Africa, the Himalaya, and parts of Southeast Asia —regions well known for having exceptional endemism and a high level of threat (Myers et al. 2000; Mittermeier et al. 2004). Some of these regions also straddle international boundaries, indicating that they offer much potential as priorities for the establishment of effective transboundary conservation areas.

However, analyses such as these are at a coarse-scale; on their own, they are of limited use in directing conservation on the ground. This requires fine-scale assessments, conducted at the national or regional level to give sufficient resolution. An exciting concept relevant at this level of planning is that of "Key Biodiversity Areas," a criteria-based, data-driven approach to defining targets for site-scale conservation (Eken et al. 2004). The concept is built on that of "Important Bird Areas," which was developed and refined by BirdLife International over a period of some 25 years, in such a way that today more than 6 000 Important Bird Areas (IBAs) have been identified worldwide, holding in particular important concentrations of threatened, restricted-range, and congregatory species (BirdLife International 2004). Key Biodiversity Areas aim to incorporate detailed information on the biological requirements of such species (and across taxonomic groups), and on the adequacy of particular sites for the conservation of these species, in order to systematically identify a set of sites across the globe that will form the platform for strengthening and expanding the protected area network. It is likely that many Key Biodiversity Areas will involve sites straddling international borders (as is already the case with many contiguous IBAs).

As the identification and delineation of Key Biodiversity Areas proceed in many priority regions across the globe, one subset of these sites is already in an advanced stage and deserves immediate incorporation into protected areas' planning. These sites are only the tip of the iceberg of Key Biodiversity Areas —sites known to hold the last remaining populations of "Critically Endangered" or "Endangered" species. The examples of the pygmy hog and the Walia ibex, cited at the beginning of this introduction, are examples of such sites (albeit both already protected). These sites have been highlighted by the Alliance for Zero Extinction —a partnership of international, national, and regional non-governmental organizations, representing known places where species extinctions will occur unless immediate conservation action is taken. Of course, some of the threatened species at these sites will require action in the form of species-based approaches, such as captive breeding or control of invasive species,

but many, particularly those not protected, are in dire need of habitat protection (or strengthened protection).

Of the 595 sites identified by the Alliance for Zero Extinction, several represent immediate opportunities for transboundary conservation initiatives. The most urgent example concerns that of Mount Nimba, a 1 760-m peak that straddles the three West African nations of Guinea, Liberia, and Cote d'Ivoire (Chapter 15, p. 221). Designated as a World Heritage Site in 1981 (though excluding the Liberian portion), this site, part of which is currently conserved by three contiguous protected areas (Mount Nimba Strict Nature Reserve/Mounts Nimba/Nimba Mountains), is home to six highly threatened species found nowhere else on earth, including four amphibians (*Arthroleptis crusculum*, *Hyperolius nimbae*, *Nimbaphrynoides liberiensis*, and *Nimbaphrynoides occidentalis*) and two mammal species, in addition to a bat (*Hipposideros lamottei*) and an otter shrew (*Micropotamogale lamottei*). Mount Nimba is under particular threat from habitat destruction, iron-ore mining, poaching, and increasing human pressure.

Two other important examples in Africa are Mount Elgon National Park and Mount Elgon National Forest Reserve in Uganda and Kenya, the only known site for Du Toit's torrent frog (*Arthroleptides dutoiti*, CR) and for two species of "Endangered" otomyine rodents (*Otomys barbouri* and *O. jacksoni*), and the Chimanimani Mountains between Zimbabwe and Mozambique, the only known site for the cave squeaker (*Arthroleptis troglodytes*, CR), an amphibian species that has not been reliably recorded for 40 years and that is currently only partially protected by the Chimanimani National Park on the Zimbabwean side.

Other priority transboundary sites can be found in Latin America, including the Parque Nacional El Tamá between Colombia and Venezuela, the only known site for *Atelopus tamaense* (CR) and for the Táchira antpitta (*Grallaria chthonia*), a species not recorded since 1956; the Cerro El Pital between Honduras and El Salvador, a site protected only on the Honduran side of the border by the Cerro El Pital Biological Reserve and the only place in the world where the frog *Bolitoglossa synoria* (CR) occurs; and the Parque Nacional La Amistad (Chapter 8, p. 159), on the border between Costa Rica and Panama, which has the only known population of the salamander *Oedipina grandis* (CR).

Sites identified through data-driven methods, such as those discussed above, represent examples of priority places where effective and collaborative transboundary management can have positive and immediate benefits for the irreplaceable and globally threatened species they are known to hold. Of course, they are only the "tip of the iceberg;" many other transboundary priorities exist and will become obvious not only as the Alliance for Zero Extinction expands its remit to other taxa (i.e., beyond vertebrates and conifers), but also as the process of identifying Key Biodiversity Areas expands and progresses. Nonetheless, there is no cause for

On the opposite page, a flock of white pelicans (Pelecanus erythrorhynchus) *flying over the Laguna Madre on the Tamaulipas-Texas border.*
© Patricio Robles Gil/Sierra Madre

delay. The need for transboundary planning to incorporate these sites into existing schemas immediately, and to begin focusing on already identified Key Biodiversity Areas that straddle country borders, cannot be overemphasized.

CONCLUSION: NEXT STEPS IN TRANSBOUNDARY CONSERVATION

Viewed in its historical context, the wave of new TBCAs is not surprising. The half-century since World War II witnessed an enormous amount of new international bilateral, regional, and global environmental agreements, regulating everything from clean air to toxic chemicals, to trade in endangered species, to agreements on international watercourses. There has been a corresponding increase in attention to international environmental issues from all sectors of society, including bilateral and multilateral funding institutions, non-governmental organizations, private foundations, private corporations, the media, and the public. As a result, it is widely accepted that shared natural resources cannot be managed in isolation and that the health of the planet depends on cooperation on environmental issues. In this light, the dramatic increase in TBCAs is a logical development.

However, this then begs the question as to how transboundary conservation might continue its evolution. One answer is that the success of TBCAs will encourage a wider range of applications of the concept at a larger scale; for example, including protected areas that are far apart and not connected through a traditional corridor strategy per se, but are nonetheless critical for migrating fauna and therefore in need of cooperative management. The broadening of definitions beyond the subset of TBPAs to encompass all TBCAs or TFCAs, discussed above, as well as Parks for Peace and transboundary migratory corridors, suggests that there is room for new applications of the concept. Another possibility is that TBCAs will see a dramatic increase in the marine context, protecting critical seascapes around the world and in areas beyond national jurisdiction (Chapters 26 and 27, pp. 313 and 321 respectively).

Yet another possible development is that TBCAs will be increasingly used as mechanisms to resolve political disputes, especially boundary disputes. The potential for this application is broad, given that there are hundreds of border disputes around the world, many of which are in areas of very high biodiversity. In addition, the number of agreements regulating shared resources, such as international watercourses, or resources in the global commons, such as fisheries on the high seas, indicates that it is becoming more acceptable to governments to relinquish some national control over natural resources to ensure that their use is well regulated and peaceful.

More fundamental is the realization that transboundary conservation, perhaps more so than other forms of conservation and development, embraces the mainstreaming of biodiversity conservation into virtually every form of human endeavor. The rationale for transboundary conservation has traditionally been the conservation of biodiversity or other natural resources. Increasingly, conservation of biodiversity is emerging as one of the *added values* of transboundary initiatives that were established for a range of other purposes, including restitution of human rights in marginalized areas on country borders, reconciliation of divided communities, socioeconomic integration of adjacent countries, mutually beneficial economic development based on sustainable use of natural resources, restoration and maintenance of peaceful relations, fostering of cooperative national and institutional development, integration of sectoral policies and programs, harmonization of laws and policies, development of appropriate systems of international governance, capacity-building at systemic, institutional and individual levels, and innovative research in the sciences and other disciplines.

The easiest answer regarding the future of transboundary conservation is that, given the many proposed TBCAs in various stages of development, growth in TBCAs is likely to continue for the foreseeable future. TBCAs have reaffirmed the central importance of protected areas, not only as havens for biodiversity but also as wellsprings for healthy and productive societies. We hope that this book will serve to stimulate further interest in this exciting and important concept that is assuming an ever-greater role in the global conservation and development agenda.

RUSSELL A. MITTERMEIER
CYRIL F. KORMOS
CRISTINA G. MITTERMEIER
TREVOR SANDWITH
CHARLES BESANÇON
DOROTHY C. ZBICZ
PATRICIO ROBLES GIL
JOHN HANKS
LEO BRAACK

MICHAEL HOFFMANN
MOHAMED BAKARR
DAN MARTIN
VANCE MARTIN
RODERIC MAST
OLIVIER LANGRAND
GUSTAVO A.B. DA FONSECA
CLAUDE GASCON
THOMAS LACHER

On the opposite page, a group of African buffalo (Syncerus caffer) *in the Zambezi River at the Caprivi Strip, a vital wildlife corridor shared by five countries: Namibia, Botswana, Zimbabwe, Zambia, and Angola.*
© Patricio Robles Gil/Sierra Madre

THREE EXEMPLARY CASE STUDIES

THE WATERTON-GLACIER INTERNATIONAL PEACE PARK: THE FIRST OF ITS KIND

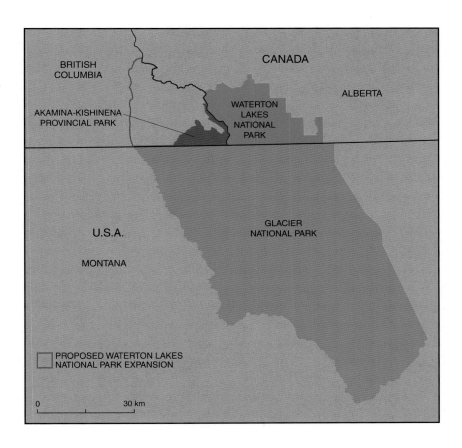

With few interruptions, a great mountain range runs the length of the Americas from Alaska to Tierra del Fuego. Called the "Backbone of the World" by the Blackfeet people, it forms the Continental Divide, separating the Atlantic and Pacific watersheds. Consisting of many ranges made up of every kind of rock, this massive linear uplift passes through the full spectrum of life zones native to the Americas from the Arctic to the tropics, from desert to rainforest. In the heart of the Rocky Mountains of North America, straddling the Canada-U.S. border, four life zones come together in one of the most biologically productive and ecologically intact parts of the continent. A significant part of this rich landscape is protected in Waterton-Glacier International Peace Park (the Park), the first of its kind in the world.

Long known for its scenic beauty and abundant wildlife, the Park's largely intact western slope has recently been confirmed as the most important area for the full range of native North American carnivores. Homeland to First Nations and part of the Old North Trail that runs from Yellowstone to the Yukon, the Park came under the protection of national governments at the turn of the twentieth century and is today the engine that drives the regional economy, despite the fact that its boundaries are incomplete and that it is at risk of becoming an ecological island. Fortunately, steps are underway to secure the future of this remarkable area.

The Waterton-Glacier landscape lies at the Northern Rocky Mountains, one of 37 wilderness regions of global importance that were recently identified by Conservation International and which collectively cover close to half the planet's terrestrial realm (Mittermeier et al. 2002). The Park falls squarely within the North Central Rockies Forests Ecoregion portion of this 245 000-km^2 area, which is dominated by coniferous forests and dramatic topographic relief that yields varied micro-climates and abundant biological diversity (Ricketts et al. 1999). The combined area of the transboundary Park is approximately 4 320 km^2. Surrounding it are land units that are subject to varying degrees of protection or exploitation from their respective governments. On the Canadian side of the border, British Columbia's Akamina-Kishinena Provincial Park and the Flathead and Bow-Crow Provincial Forests lie to the west and northwest, and Alberta's Blood Indian Reserve to the northeast. South of the 49th parallel in Montana, the Blackfeet Indian Reservation and Lewis and Clark National Forest abut Glacier National Park's eastern perimeter, while the Flathead National Forest and Great Bear, Scapegoat, and Bob Marshall Wilderness Areas lie to the immediate south and east. There are

also private lands around the parks that are important to the ecological function of the region, notably the Rocky Mountain/ Waterton Front to the east, the Elk Valley to the north, and the Swan Valley to the southwest.

The Waterton-Glacier International Peace Park is situated at the southern end of the area where the two great ice masses of the Wisconsin Ice Age met. When the Cordilleran and Laurentide ice sheets began to melt about 12 000 years ago they separated, allowing people from ice-free Beringia in the Yukon to travel along the mountain front down the Old North Trail. Various cultures occupied the region through the millennia. At the time of European contact, the Blackfeet (called Blackfoot in Canada) were the dominant indigenous people of the northern Great Plains, making their home from the foothills far out onto the prairie bounded by the North Saskatchewan and Yellowstone Rivers. Chief Mountain on the international border is a sacred site to their tribe, a place where thunder lived and vision quests were held. The Ktunaxa (anglicized to Kootenay in Canada or Kootenai in the U.S.) lived to the west in the Rocky Mountain Trench in places like the Tobacco Plains, which remain snow-free in winter, as well as elsewhere in the northern headwaters of the Columbia River system. Annually they crossed the Continental Divide to hunt buffalo on the Great Plains via the North, Middle, and South Kootenay passes that still bear their name. Both these indigenous peoples still inhabit the region, and the area of the Park remains central to their cultures.

Triple Divide Peak in Glacier National Park is a special place. A drop of water falling on its summit could travel through elaborate river systems to one of three great ocean basins —Hudson's Bay in central Canada, the Gulf of Mexico, or the Pacific Ocean at the Oregon Coast. On its east side, through a series of valleys that radiate like fingers from the Continental Divide, mountains of the Livingston and Lewis Ranges form the headwaters of the Milk, St. Mary, and Oldman Rivers. The low Milk River Ridge is a major dividing point. It separates rivers that flow south through the Missouri-Mississippi River system to the Gulf of Mexico from rivers that flow north through the Saskatchewan-Nelson River system that drains into Hudson's Bay. Along the western slopes the South, Middle, and North Forks of the Flathead River drain the entire area and converge at Flathead Lake, one of the largest lakes in all the Rocky Mountains. Ultimately, all westward waters flow to the Pacific through the Columbia River.

The wilderness value of this region did not escape North American conservationists in the decades leading up to the twentieth century, an exciting era for conservation that began in 1872 with the creation of the world's first national park at Yellowstone. Banff became Canada's first national park in 1885. Ten years later, what is now Waterton Lakes National Park was added to the country's list of protected areas and later named for British naturalist Sir Charles Waterton (Lothian 1976). The Waterton Lakes had been a favored camping area for native people. They were explored during the Palliser Expedition of 1857-1860 and later became the focus of preservation efforts by frontiersman John George "Kootenai" Brown and rancher F.W. Godsal, who helped to persuade government leaders to establish what was first known as Kootenay Lakes Forest Park (Lothain 1976; Rodney 1969). By 1900, additional national parks had been established in both Canada and the U.S. In the same period, the Migratory Birds Convention Act was adopted by the two countries and large mammals that had almost been hunted to extinction began to be brought back through the creation of special protected areas in both nations.

At the same time, however, proprietary rights to the Montana wilderness had been systematically wrested from Native Americans in response to reports from explorers of precious resources and scenic natural wonders (Buchholtz 1976). Notable for a different sensibility was George Bird Grinnell, a founder of the Boone and Crockett Club and editor of *Forest and Stream* magazine. Grinnell wrote extensively about the "Crown of the Continent" and of the local Blackfeet people and called for protection of the region's glaciers, lakes, and wildlife. Grinnell worked tirelessly for the establishment of a national park (Diettert 1992). When railroad tycoon James Hill, whose Great Northern Railroad tracks headed directly toward the high mountain glaciers and lakes, lent his weight to the effort, it helped ensure the establishment of Glacier National Park in 1910.

Twenty-two years later, due largely to the efforts of Rotary International chapters in Alberta and Montana, Waterton Lakes and Glacier were ceremoniously joined as the world's first international Peace Park, celebrating the longstanding friendship between Canada and the U.S. Next came the Park's nomination to the UNESCO Biosphere Reserve Program in the mid-1970s, in recognition of its ecological importance on a global scale. Designation as a World Heritage Site followed in 1995, testament to the region's incredible natural beauty, cultural value, and contribution to the survival of threatened wildlife. However, the evaluation that accompanied that designation noted there was an anomaly on the western boundary of Waterton that made the Park incomplete. In 2002, the government of Canada announced an interest in expanding the Park into a portion of British

Columbia's Flathead Valley to fill in the missing piece, provided the Province of British Columbia and the Ktunaxa First Nation agree. Such an expansion could effectively double the size of Waterton.

A mix of geophysical features contributes to exceptionally high levels of plant diversity and endemism in Waterton-Glacier International Peace Park, which are representative of the region's overall biological richness. The enormous Lewis Overthrust Fault brought deep basement rocks to the surface and thrust them into the sky above what today is prairie. As a result, grasslands plants from the Great Plains penetrate mountain valleys. A cool climate allows northern arctic and boreal plants to reach the southern limit of their distribution along the high mountains, yet the climate is so mild that alpine plants from the Southern Rockies also reach the northern limit of their distribution here. Low mountains to the west allow Pacific air masses to retain their moisture until they collide with the towering rock walls of the Continental Divide, where it is deposited in great quantities of rain and snow, allowing Pacific plants to reach the eastern limit of their distribution.

The result is a giant ecotone, with the greatest diversity of vascular plants in all of Canada. This astonishing variety can be experienced by an 80-km drive along the Going to the Sun Road in Glacier. From west to east it passes through dark wet cedar hemlock forests of giant trees to the open subalpine zone at Logan Pass where vast gardens of brilliant wildflowers spread out between clumps of dwarf krummholtz trees, through mid-elevation montane forests of pine and Douglas fir, and down onto open sunny grasslands. Enjoyed by most of the Park's million annual visitors, this biological tour de force can be seen in a day or absorb a lifetime of study.

A recent compendium of vascular plants found in Glacier National Park tallies 1 132 species —1 005 of them native and 127 introduced— representing the Cordilleran, Boreal, Arctic-Alpine, and Great Plains Floristic Provinces (Lesica 2002). It is believed that these numbers also include all the taxa occurring across the border in Waterton Lakes. This floral diversity is not only impressive regionally but on a global scale as well, matching or exceeding levels of plant species-richness in Botswana's Okavango Delta, East Africa's Serengeti Plains, and the lush temperate rainforests of America's Pacific Northwest. All of these areas are of far greater expanse, underscoring the special nature of the Waterton-Glacier plant communities.

Terrestrial vertebrate diversity within the Northern Rockies varies widely among the four taxonomic classes. The Waterton-Glacier International Peace Park lies along a major North American migratory flyway. As a result, 272 species of birds have been identified as inhabitants of the park complex, if only as transients. The golden eagle (*Aquila chrysaetos*) is common throughout the region, but the "Endangered" trumpeter swan (*Cygnus buccinator*) represents a rare sighting. Amphibians, as one would expect, are rather poorly represented in high altitude temperate ecosystems. Historical surveys have identified as many as a dozen species, but recent field investigations suggest that perhaps only as many as seven species of frogs, toads, and salamanders remain within the Park (Marnell 2004). Reptiles are even less represented with only two garter snakes and a pond turtle as local inhabitants.

Sixty-three species of mammals have been documented as residents within park boundaries (Shea 1995). Rodents are well represented with two dozen species, but it is the large hoofed mammals that are most conspicuous throughout the Park's elevations. Moose (*Alces alces*), elk (*Cervus elaphus*), white-tailed deer (*Odocoileus virginianus*), and mule deer (*O. hemionus*) represent the cervid family, while two bovids call these mountains home —the bighorn sheep (*Ovis canadensis*) and the mountain goat (*Oreamnos americanus*). The entire assemblage serves as a prey base for the region's meat-eating mammals.

The Waterton-Glacier area has special importance for carnivores. At least 19 species of meat eaters occur in the Park area and no carnivore native to this region of North America is missing. The highest density of grizzly bears (*Ursus arctos*) in the interior of North America resides on the western side of the Peace Park in the North Fork of the Flathead Valley. On the east slope, in Waterton's Blakiston Valley, it is not uncommon in the course of a twenty-minute drive on a summer afternoon to see half a dozen black bears (*U. americanus*) feeding on berry bushes. Both species are commonly seen on either side of the Continental Divide. In addition to the two species of bears there are cats: lynxes (*Lynx canadensis*), cougars (*Puma concolor*), and bobcats (*Lynx rufus*); dogs: wolves (*Canis lupus*), coyotes (*C. latrans*), and red foxes (*Vulpes vulpes*); and a host of mustelids including wolverines (*Gulo gulo*), fishers (*Martes pennanti*), pine martens (*M. americana*), badgers (*Taxidea taxus*), river otters (*Lutra canadensis*), minks (*Mustela vison*), long-tailed weasels (*M. frenata*), short-tailed weasels (*M. erminea*), least weasels (*M. nivalis*), and striped skunks (*Mephitis mephitis*). The Park is a great place to see a grizzly bear digging in a sunny alpine meadow for ground squirrels and glacier lily bulbs or perhaps to hear wolves and coyotes howling on a moonlit night.

On the opposite page, the wapiti or elk (Cervus canadensis) is a common, frequently-seen species in the Waterton-Glacier system.
© Patricio Robles Gil/Sierra Madre

Above, Lewis monkeyflowers (Mimulus lewisii) and heartleaf arnica (Arnica cordifolia) below Oberlin Falls, Glacier National Park.
© Jack Dykinga

On pp. 76-77, Wynn Mountain and Allen Mountain overlooking Lake Sherburne and meadows of lupine (Lupinus sp.) and fireweed (Epilobium angustifolium) in Glacier National Park.
© Florian Schulz/ visionsofthewild.com

The Park is part of the Crown of the Continent ecosystem, a subset of the broader Yellowstone to Yukon region, the last stronghold of many large mammals in western North America. Populations of grizzly bears in the lower 48 states of the U.S. are confined to habitat corridors from Yellowstone to the border and their survival is linked to what happens in Canada. One of the largest populations remaining is centered on the rich wilderness of the Park, the nearby Bob Marshall Wilderness complex, and the unprotected Flathead Valley in British Columbia.

The survival of this grizzly population, and that of most other large carnivores, depends on linkages in Canada between the Waterton-Glacier area and the gene pool further north in Banff and Jasper National Parks and west to the Purcell Range. The low-elevation break that connects these populations across the southern Canadian Rockies runs through Crowsnest Pass and Elk Valley. There a highway and railway pass through several towns and beneath large open-pit coal mines. Fortunately, significant efforts are being made by the Yellowstone to Yukon Conservation Initiative, The Nature Conservancy of Canada, and the forestry company Tembec, Inc. to secure close to 450 km² of forested private lands through which wildlife can move safely. This is the largest such private conservation project ever undertaken in Canada. Similar efforts are being made by The Nature Conservancy in Montana to secure large, low elevation tracts on private land owned by the Plum Creek Timber Company in Swan Valley, located southwest of the parks.

Private lands elsewhere are also critical to the long-term viability of resident grizzlies. The eastern front of the mountains is snow-free much of the year due to warm Chinook winds, and foothill grasslands there are the first to green up in the spring, attracting bears that have just emerged from a long winter's dormancy. On both sides of the international border, The Nature Conservancy has been particularly successful working with landowners to secure many thousands of hectares of these important spring grasslands. The Blackfeet of Montana have also started a land trust to keep their grasslands that border Glacier National Park from being fragmented by development.

Rising in British Columbia, the North Fork of the Flathead River flows entirely undammed through what the *New York Times* recently called "America's Wildest Valley." Canadians refer to it simply as the Flathead, a remote, uninhabited, and still unprotected region. Upon reaching the U.S., the North Fork is treated as a very special resource. Half of it is protected in Glacier National Park, where it has been designated a Wild and Scenic River, and water withdrawals along its course are strictly regulated. Studies have shown that the North Fork is unique because, unlike most mountain rivers, it flows for its entire length through a broad valley that is unconstrained by canyon walls (Stanford 2001). Waters that well up through the gravel river bed create a shifting mosaic of habitats across its floodplains that support rich cottonwood forests, high levels of species diversity, and ecological connectivity to its British Columbia headwaters. The river also benefits from large upstream lakes, like Lake MacDonald, that act as heat sinks and moderate water temperatures. A compilation of recent research efforts, in fact, concluded that a unique carnivore community resides in the transboundary Flathead region, unmatched in North America for its variety, completeness, and species density (Weaver 2001). Simply put, the North Fork of the Flathead is an ecological jewel of global significance.

There is, however, a conservation anomaly in this region. Obvious to anyone who looks at a map, the southern boundary of Waterton Lakes National Park corresponds very well with the northern boundary of Glacier National Park along the east side of the Continental Divide, yet there remains a large gap to the west of the watershed; the American portion of the valley is protected but the Canadian side is not. In his first superintendent's report for Waterton Lakes, Kootenai Brown (1911) noted this deficiency, stating that "It seems advisable to greatly enlarge this park. It might be well to have a preserve and breeding ground in conjunction with the U.S. Glacier Park." Over the years, various efforts have been made to remedy the situation. Most recently, in 2002, the government of Canada declared its interest in expanding Waterton Lakes National Park westward if there is agreement from the Ktunaxa First Nation and the Province of British Columbia. Neither has yet agreed, but determined efforts to augment Waterton Lakes National Park continue by the Canadian Parks and Wilderness Society, the East Kootenay Environmental Society, the Yellowstone to Yukon Conservation Initiative, and the National Parks and Conservation Association.

Waterton Lakes National Park was established in part at the urging of local rancher F.W. Goodsal and it has enjoyed the support of the vast majority of its ranching neighbors ever since. Their voluntary commitment to share with wildlife the grasslands they own adjacent to the Park and to prevent fragmentation through housing development in a formal Waterton vicinity protection zone has been longstanding. Their efforts were recognized in the 1970s through the establishment of a UNESCO biosphere zone. In the 1990s, however, a combination of deteriorating economic conditions for ranching, provincial weakening of

land use planning controls, and increasing land prices put their continued stewardship at risk. The Nature Conservancy of Canada worked cooperatively with the ranching community and, through a combination of conservation easements and buy-outs with leasebacks ranching families, they have been able to remain on the land and share it with wildlife. The result is permanent protection of an 11 000-ha buffer zone which preserves the ranching culture, as well as the visual and ecological integrity of the Waterton Front.

On the American side, people in the Great Falls area east of the Park supported the establishment of Glacier National Park, but many residents in Kalispell in the Flathead Valley on the west side bitterly opposed it due to the loss of access to timber and mining. Today, the park is acknowledged by their successors to be the economic engine of Montana's Flathead Valley. While the parks in both countries support a robust summer tourism industry, it is primarily the permanent residents they attract that drive the economy, particularly in Montana. As a result, the economy of the Flathead Valley is outperforming that of the rest of the state, and diversification beyond tourism within the regional business community bodes well for long-term stability and growth (Swanson 2003).

On the British Columbia side, the absence of a national park is reflected in the below-average economic performance of that region. In 2004, information regarding positive benefits to the economy of Montana's Flathead Valley, due to Glacier National Park, significantly affected a vote by municipal government leaders in the Regional District of East Kootenay. The result was approval of a feasibility study into expanding Waterton Park and into British Columbia's Flathead Valley.

The Waterton-Glacier region has benefited from philanthropy based outside the area. Non-governmental sources of capital have enabled much of the conservation efforts around the parks. Remarkable work done on the Waterton Front has been supported by the W. Garfield Weston Foundation and Barbara and John Poole. The Wilburforce, Paul Allen Forest Protection, and Woodcock Foundations have been critical to private land conservation efforts in the Elk Valley and Crowsnest Pass. The Henry P. Kendall Foundation and Wilburforce Foundations have been critical to the Park's expansion efforts, and there are many other benefactors as well.

Over the course of the last century-and-a-half, the western wilderness of North America has been transformed from a vast undeveloped region to a center of economic development amid pockets of wilderness. Each succeeding decade has brought with it new threats from growing markets to the region's environmental and cultural integrity. Trappers were the vanguard at the turn of the eighteenth century, taking a toll on fur-bearing animals but otherwise leaving little evidence of their presence. Prospectors arrived in the mid-1800s, staking claims and panning for gold. Hunters followed in search of large game, killing off the last of the bison herds by the early 1880s. Railroad tracks crossed the Continental Divide in the 1890s. At the turn of the twentieth century, underground coal mines proliferated in the Elk Valley and Crowsnest Pass area, becoming in the 1960s open pits that removed whole mountain tops. Natural gas was discovered in the mountains north of Waterton and developed in the last half of the twentieth century. Fortunately, some of the government authorities that carved up large chunks of the mountainous terrain into timber and coal reserves and the valleys into agricultural parcels also had the wisdom to establish national parks and wilderness areas that today serve millions of visitors every year. The lure of protected places also brings more and more businesses and permanent residents, affecting prospects for sustainable development.

The ongoing threats to the region have been documented in several reports. In 1980, a report by the U.S. National Park Service ranked Glacier National Park the fourth most endangered of more than 300 national parks surveyed, and several more recent studies echo similar concerns on both sides of the international border. In 2000, the Panel on the Ecological Integrity of Canada's National Parks determined that Waterton Lakes faced negative impacts both from external and internal sources, and a 2002 study prepared by the National Parks and Conservation Association warned of threats to the Park due to the "cumulative impacts from proposed highway expansion; conversion of working ranch and forest lands to recreation, commercial and residential developments, clear-cut logging; a growing number of sightseeing air tours; invasions of non-native species into parklands and waters; and potential extraction of coal, oil and gas resources." These threats translate into degraded wildlife habitats and restrictions on the movements of large, wide-ranging vertebrates, and the loss of native fish unable to compete with invasive species. In addition, this most recent report identifies potential long-term threats of global warming and atmospheric pollution, as well as the perennial shortage of financial resources needed to monitor ecological processes and to manage wildlife and visitors.

Human presence in the Rocky Mountains manifests itself in railways and the proliferation of roadways, which many wildlife

On the opposite page,
an alpine pool in Glacier
National Park, Montana.
© Carr Clifton/Minden Pictures

Above, a Canada goose
(Branta canadensis)
on Waterton Lake.
© Patricio Robles Gil/Sierra Madre

authorities regard as impediments and even potential barriers to the movements and reproductive success of large animals such as grizzlies, elks, and mountain goats. The proposed expansion of Highway 2 in the U.S. and Highway 3 in Canada are of major concern, as is the oft-discussed paving of the North Fork Road in Montana's Flathead Valley, due to the development pressures that would follow. In addition, the seasonal ranges and dinning sites of several species are being increasingly encroached by expanding residential, commercial, and resort developments, as well as off-road vehicle and snowmobile use.

Exotic game fish introduced by sportsmen into Flathead Lake have found their way into Glacier National Park where they have driven down numbers of native species, such as the cut-throat trout. At the same time, in Alberta, Canada, the hunting season on gray wolves spans nine months and there is no limit on how many can be trapped each year. As a result, wolf populations in the Park are at risk and this impacts prey populations as well.

Clear-cut logging and the extraction of natural gas are among the heaviest impacts to the once pristine landscape that surrounds the Park. Only a public outcry from both countries in 2004 prevented the construction of an open-pit coal mine in Canada's Flathead Valley. Open-pit mines create enormous surface disturbance and are known to have a negative impact on water quality and native fish populations. New plans for the extraction of coal-bed methane —natural gas trapped alongside coal deposits— create additional problems, based chiefly on the amount of contaminated water that the process generates and the land surface disturbance by roads and well sites. This is a particularly contentious issue in areas northwest of the Park in British Columbia. The effort to expand natural gas extraction is also a prominent concern along the Rocky Mountain Front both in Canada and the U.S., particularly in Alberta's Castle Wilderness to the north of the parks and on federal land in Montana south of the parks. These practices bring with them large road infrastructures that readily displace wildlife, especially large carnivores such as grizzlies, introduce exotic species, and reduce suitable habitat for ungulates. They can also threaten the integrity of sites sacred to indigenous people.

Perhaps the most insidious long-term threats to the Waterton-Glacier region stem from global warming. The potential for environmental change —especially for high-latitude, high-altitude landscapes— is great. According to the best available information, increasing atmospheric concentrations of greenhouse gases such as carbon dioxide, methane, and nitrous oxide, have already raised average global temperatures, which could increase by several more degrees over the course of the next few decades. Within the Park, the effects of such warming are already becoming apparent with a rapid reduction in glaciers, measured since the parks were established. There is a real concern that global warming could completely eliminate all of the region's glaciers (the ultimate irony for a national park that was named for them), shrink alpine zones, eliminate species for which park populations represent the southern limit of their distribution, affect water levels in rivers and lakes, reduce native fish populations, and perhaps cause the extinction of plant species endemic to the region. In recognition of such threats, park authorities have already established research programs to detect and monitor expected environmental changes due to global warming, the initial emphasis having been placed on rare alpine plants (Lesica and McCune 1992). Canada has ratified the Kyoto Protocol, pursuant to a global treaty to reduce the harmful effects of global warming, but the U.S., where some politicians and industries deny the problem, has not.

The future of the Waterton-Glacier International Peace Park will be considerably brightened if plans to expand the Park on the Canadian side proceed, bringing under protection some of the most important habitat for large carnivores in North America. Expansion into the Flathead Valley would also protect the headwaters of several streams that flow south into Glacier and protect the remarkably rich low-elevation Flathead riparian zone. But no park is viable as an island. Conservation here cannot succeed unless it is linked to broader efforts across the Yellowstone to Yukon region. Ensuring connections for wildlife from the Park north to the Canadian Rockies and west to the Purcell Mountain Range is essential to the long-term survival of all wide-ranging species in the southern part of the region. Such connections will also be important to the survival of the area's remarkable plant diversity as those species struggle to adapt to climate change. Fortunately, there is a committed constituency of people and two strong park services dedicated to the region's long-term well-being.

WILLIAM R. KONSTANT
HARVEY LOCKE
JACK HANNAH

The Waterton-Glacier area has large populations of black bear (Ursus americanus) *and grizzly* (Ursus horribilis). *Above,* © Patricio Robles Gil/ Sierra Madre; *opposite page,* © Florian Schulz/ visionsofthewild.com

THE GREAT LIMPOPO TRANSFRONTIER PARK: A BENCHMARK FOR INTERNATIONAL CONSERVATION

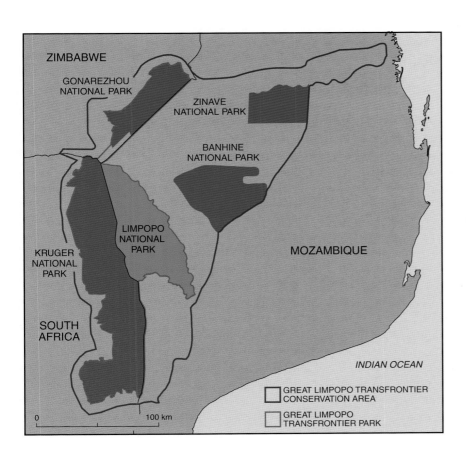

ZIMBABWE

GONAREZHOU
NATIONAL PARK

ZINAVE
NATIONAL PARK

BANHINE
NATIONAL PARK

LIMPOPO
NATIONAL
PARK

KRUGER
NATIONAL
PARK

MOZAMBIQUE

SOUTH
AFRICA

INDIAN OCEAN

☐ GREAT LIMPOPO TRANSFRONTIER
CONSERVATION AREA

☐ GREAT LIMPOPO
TRANSFRONTIER PARK

0   100 km

At close to 3 600 000 ha in extent, the Great Limpopo Transfrontier Park (GLTP) represents one of the crowning jewels of
conservation efforts in Africa. At its heart lies South Africa's
Kruger National Park (KNP), conserved for over a century and
making up more than 1 900 000 ha of the total area, and Mozambique's Limpopo National Park (LNP), at almost 1 100 000 ha,
while a sweep of land reaches northwards through the Sengwe
communal land of Zimbabwe to embrace the Gonarezhou National Park. Straddling this elongate area as a near-continuous
backbone are the rock-strewn Lubombo Mountains, while four
major river systems drain the region as they flow eastward
towards the Mozambican coast.

Broadly categorized as lowland flat savannah, a diverse mix
of landscape types contributes toward the mosaic of habitats that
supports a wealth of biotic diversity in the GLTP. Reaching in
from the east are broad tongues of deep sands with a dense cover
of exceptionally diverse sandveld vegetation communities. Vast
basalt plains lie west of the Lubombo Mountains, supporting
extensive grasslands, which in the KNP host large herds of
Burchell's zebra (*Equus burchelli*), blue wildebeest (*Connochaetes
taurinus*), buffalo (*Syncerus caffer*), and many other species.
Further south the open grassland changes to woodland dominated by knobthorn (*Acacia nigrescens*), marula (*Sclerocarya birrea*),
leadwood (*Combretum imberbe*) and interspersed stands of sick-
lebush (*Dichrostachys cinerea*), tamboti (*Spirostachys africana*),
and others. North of the Olifants River, the vegetation changes
dramatically to almost uniform stands of mopane (*Colophospermum mopane*), with occasional communities of baobab (*Adanso-
nia digitata*), tamboti, and various species of *Commiphora*. These
mopane plains are prime habitat for large numbers of buffalo
and elephant (*Loxodonta africana*). The western margin of the
GLTP is more undulating with granitic soils, giving rise to mixed
communities where red bushwillows (*Combretum apiculatum*)
tend to be most abundant. Craggy hills also adjoin the Luvuvhu
River and much of the western part of the LNP, and the valleys
of these hills host dense stands of Lubombo ironwood (*Andros-
tachys johnsonii*).

Rivers contribute to and sustain a large part of the biotic
diversity of the GLTP, and the banks contain rich alluvial soils
which in many cases are home to a lush riverine fringe of tall
trees comprising a mix of *Ficus sycamorus* figs, natal mahogany
(*Trichelia emetica*), jackalberry (*Diospyros mespiliformis*), sausage
trees (*Kigelia africana*), nyala trees (*Xanthocercis zambesiaca*), with

stands of fever trees (*Acacia xanthophloea*), palms (*Phoenix reclinata* and *Hyphaene natalensis*), and others.

The GLTP receives the bulk of its approximate 550 mm average annual rainfall during the summer months from November to March. Temperatures are mild in winter —rarely reaching freezing point— but daytime temperatures in summer typically exceed 30°C, and often reach well above 40°C. Malaria is endemic in much of the region, although effective control programs in the tourist areas keep the number of cases to a minimum.

There are considerable differences in development and facilities between each of the component areas that comprise the GLTP, reflecting the very different histories of the three partner countries. The KNP has the advantage of many decades of tourism development, offering some 4 700 beds in 40 tourist camps, linked by a network of 2 677 km (917 km tarred) of well-maintained roads. A staff of about 2 500 people is employed in KNP, representing a diverse mix of skills ranging from anti-poaching units to civil engineers, internationally acclaimed scientists to finance managers, and many others. In order to boost the annual income required to support not only the budgetary needs of KNP but also to cross-finance other national parks in South Africa, a sophisticated system of privatization and outsourcing initiatives has been embarked upon to run restaurants, shops, and other business activities deemed as "non-core functions" of national parks. Certain wilderness areas in Kruger are leased to concessionaires for 20-year cycles, in which low-volume high-income tourism is practiced for an upmarket visitor segment. Most facilities in KNP, however, are targeted at people in the middle-income range. Close to a million visitors pass through KNP annually. Although they are mostly South Africans, over 25% of them are from overseas, mainly Europe but also the U.S. Despite this picture of sophistication, advanced infrastructure, and high level of servicing, KNP has retained a balance of good quality amenities combined with a wilderness experience that continues to draw thousands of visitors who return year after year. Most of these people come for self-drive game-viewing, but there are many organized tour operators servicing the region. Once in KNP, a wide range of opportunities exist, such as wilderness trails spanning several days in remote settings, shorter morning or afternoon bush walks from almost all main camps, game drives with a park guide, and night-drives in open safari vehicles. New options continue to be identified and made available.

Across the borders into Mozambique and Zimbabwe, the picture is somewhat different. Infrastructure and tourism is minimal, at least for now. With the contractual commitment to administer the GLTP as a regional asset, investors are showing keen interest to develop tourism lodges and products. National governments have already started establishing an improved road network to enable access to the different areas, and a new border post at Giriondo has been created to supplement the existing border link at Pafuri between KNP and LNP. The Zimbabwean component of the GLTP still poses substantial challenges in terms of direct access and true integration with the other components of the GLTP, but all of this is currently in the planning stage.

In terms of the Memorandum of Understanding signed between the three countries in November 2000, and confirmed by the Establishment Treaty of December 2003, the Great Limpopo Transfrontier *Park* will be the core area of a much larger Great Limpopo Transfrontier *Conservation Area* (GLTFCA) to be developed in time. Most of the additional area lies within Mozambique, including the Banhine and Zinave National Parks, but substantial contributions, mainly in the form of private nature reserves and conservancies, will also come from South Africa and Zimbabwe. The eventual TFCA as envisaged will make up an area of very nearly 10 000 000 ha.

The GLTP represents an area of convergence of several ecological zones which includes tropical and subtropical elements. Varying topography, together with considerable differences in soil types and rainfall, all contribute to a rich mosaic of habitat types. The combination of physical and climatic factors allows a variety of some 2 000 species of plants to thrive in the area, clustered into distinct communities which form the basis for the extraordinary wealth of animal life present in the GLTP. The area contains 147 species of mammals, 505 species of birds, 116 reptiles, 49 fish, and 34 amphibians, the latter including the knocking sand frog (*Tomopterna krugerensis*) discovered in and known only from the GLTP.

One of the major success stories has been the restoration and nurturing to fully viable status of the populations of both black (*Diceros bicornis*) and white rhino (*Ceratotherium simum*). Previously hunted to extinction in the region, founder populations of both species of rhino were reintroduced in the 1960s from KwaZulu-Natal, and today the KNP hosts steadily growing populations, already numbering close to 500 black rhino and in excess of 6 000 white rhino. As fences continue to drop between the component parts of the GLTP, these animals will spread and recolonize traditional rangelands. The white rhino population is now the biggest in Africa, while the black rhino —having started from a much smaller founder population— will achieve that

On p. 84, the Olifants River is one of the major waterways running through the woodland savannahs of Kruger National Park.

Above, the Defassa waterbuck (Kobus ellipsiprymnus defassa) is a common species in the Greater Limpopo system.

*On the opposite page, the greater kudu (Tragelaphus strepsiceros) is one of Africa's most majestic antelope species and is well represented in the Greater Limpopo area.
All photos,*
© *Patricio Robles Gil/Sierra Madre*

status in time given its current rate of reproduction and the abundance of available habitat.

Buffalo number about 30 000 while the total number of elephants in KNP and Gonarezhou exceeds 16 000. These are expanding populations much in need of additional habitat, currently being provided by the extended area now offered, especially by the LNP. Rivers abound with hippos (*Hippopotamus amphibius*) and crocodiles (*Crocodylus niloticus*), the latter reaching some of the highest densities in any of the African rivers.

Predators are present in much of the GLTP, maintaining their intrinsic natural interaction with prey species in this extensive system. Lions (*Panthera leo*) abound, as do leopards (*P. pardus*), and spotted hyenas (*Crocuta crocuta*). Wild dogs (*Lycaon pictus*) number approximately 300 and cheetah (*Acinonyx jubatus*) slightly less. Smaller species, more secretive and less visible, are nevertheless common and include the black-backed jackal (*Canis mesomelas*), the side-striped jackal (*C. adustus*), the caracal (*Caracal caracal*), the serval (*Leptailurus serval*), the civet (*Civettictis civetta*), two species of genets (*Genetta genetta* and *G. tigrina*), and the African wild cat (*Felis silvestris lybica*).

Birdlife is particularly prolific in the GLTP, and there is constant background twittering and chirping everywhere to remind one of the exceptional diversity of avian fauna. Some of the more exceptional species include various species of storks, including the magnificent saddle-bill stork (*Ephippiorhynchus senegalensis*), black stork (*Ciconia nigra*), open-billed stork (*Anastomus lamelligerus*), woolly-necked stork (*Ciconia episcopus*), and marabou stork (*Leptoptilos crumeniferus*); an abundant array of raptors, including the majestic bateleur (*Terathopius ecaudatus*), steppe eagle (*Aquila nipalensis*), martial eagle (*Polemaetus bellicosus*), crowned eagle (*Stephanoaetus coronatus*), and long-crested eagle (*Lophaetus occipitalis*), as well as the striking secretary bird (*Sagittarius serpentarius*), Ground hornbill (*Bucorvis leadbeateri*), and Kori bustard (*Ardeotis kori*). But it is the sheer beauty and grace of so many other species which makes it such a pleasure to behold and constantly be surprised by the diversity of feathered life all around: multiple species of rollers, bee-eaters, kingfishers, orioles, exquisitely reflective sunbirds, and the master architects of all, the array of boldly colored weavers.

Rare and unusual species confined to the GLTP or with very limited distribution elsewhere include the knocking sand frog (*Tomopterna krugerensis*) and an as yet non-described new species of *Eptesicus* bat, both discovered in KNP. The GLTP is home to three species of the beautifully colored *Notobranchius* tropical killifish, which occur in seasonal pans and have drought-resistant eggs that survive in dry soil to ensure a next generation. Lungfish (*Protopterus annectens brieni*) are also present here in seasonal pans, surviving the annual dry season by encasing themselves in a protective cocoon of dried mud. Seven species of lizards, geckoes, and snakes have endemic or near endemic status. New species of insects are described from the GLTP almost on an annual basis, reflecting the volume of research that is done in the area, for the moment mainly within the KNP. The very rare king cheetah is also found here, a striking color variant of the more usual spotted variety.

Biodiversity, however, is not only about species-richness; it also embraces the particular mix of species into distinct communities and genetic sub-types, as well as the ecosystem processes that ensure their persistence. The extensive area of the GLTP and its largely pristine state allow for natural evolutionary ecosystem processes to proceed unhindered, a critical prerequisite for long-term resilience and viability of species and communities. Diseases such as anthrax are endemic and periodically sweep through the system and test the immune responses of wildlife populations, and regular droughts are sometimes severe enough to almost halve the populations of some animals, as in 1992 when buffalo declined to below 14 000, although they have now regained their former abundance and continue to increase. Dramatic floods are regular occurrences in wet climatic cycles which scour reedbeds and riverbanks and re-calibrate river-systems, depositing life-supporting layers of sediment. Fire, such a characteristic feature of African savannahs, burns through about one third of the area each year, clearing moribund growth and allowing fresh vegetation to emerge. The GLTP is a dynamic example of life systems naturally at work, a vibrant system, healthy and diverse in most of its components.

As the oldest National Park in Africa, having its foundations in the proclamation of the Sabi Game Reserve in 1898, KNP represents a very large area of original, untransformed habitat. It contains the full spectrum of wildlife known to have occurred in the region from earliest recorded history, almost all present in strong, viable populations. It is this ample reservoir of wildlife stock that will serve as primary source area for the 1 100 000 ha LNP, whose fauna was practically totally destroyed during two decades of civil war in Mozambique. Nevertheless, with the essential habitat in LNP still in surprisingly good condition, major translocation operations have already resulted in many animals being captured in KNP and moved to their new home in Mozambique, including 111 elephants, 51 buffalos, 12 white rhinos, 702 zebras, 594 blue wildebeests, 957 impalas, and a variety of other animals. In time, as the

*On the opposite page, one of Africa's largest remaining populations of elephant (*Loxodonta africana*) is to be found in the Greater Limpopo area.*

*Above, the crested guineafowl (*Guttera pucherani*) is one of two guineafowl species common in this region. Both photos, © Patricio Robles Gil/Sierra Madre*

89

The red-billed oxpecker (Buphagus erythrorhynchus) *spends most of its time searching for ticks and other parasites in the fur of the large African mammals, such as the giraffe* (Giraffa camelopardalis) *and the impala* (Apycerus melampus). *Both photos,*
© Patricio Robles Gil/Sierra Madre

Zimbabwean areas have also become more fully integrated, wildlife from KNP will also cross the Limpopo River more freely to repopulate the corridor area leading up to Gonarezhou, and reciprocally trickle south into the corridor from Gonarezhou.

The long history of conservation in a major part of the GLTP, including KNP since 1898 and Gonarezhou since 1934, has resulted in the development of strong skills in conservation management. Both Zimbabwe and South Africa have long records as leaders in many fields, especially in game capture techniques, veterinary disease management, general wildlife management skills, and a strong research base, all now being harnessed for the benefit of this three-nation linkage of protected areas. The KNP in particular has a long history of in-house research done either by the core group of scientists employed full-time by KNP, or the numerous collaborating scientists from all corners of the world who annually produce research papers and books on all aspects of wildlife, geology, fire, aquatic systems, climate, and many other topics. At any one time, there are some 200 ongoing projects registered within KNP, and it is without doubt the most intensively studied protected area in Africa. One of its greatest assets is a detailed series of long-term datasets on climate, annual vegetation monitoring, various environmental parameters, water quality and quantity, annual aerial census figures of herbivores, and several others.

Aside from these broader benefits of the GLTP, where localized skills and assets are brought to bear for conservation benefits throughout an extensive transboundary region, there are also some very specific species-level benefits. Elephants and the management of elephant populations has long been a controversial public issue, particularly in South Africa. Decades of relentless hunting for ivory had by the early 1900s reduced the elephant population in what is now KNP to almost zero. Since its proclamation, the very few remaining animals slowly increased, supplemented by refugee elephants escaping hunting pressure in Mozambique. By the early 1960s, the wildlife managers of KNP were concerned about the steep rate of increase in the elephant population, and there was a growing belief that such an unchecked population would soon have a negative impact on at least some other species and communities. This was, after all, a national park for the benefit and conservation of all species, not only elephants. And so, after workshops and head-scratching, a decision was reached in 1966 that the elephant population would henceforth be managed. The KNP was considered to have a "carrying capacity" of approximately 7 500 elephants, and that would be considered the optimum number managed for in this park.

An annual aerial survey of elephants would be the basis for determining whether or not to reduce numbers. At the same time, a decision was made to manage the rapidly escalating buffalo population through annual culling, with the occasional removal of hippo and some other species.

For almost three decades, this annual culling exercise was maintained, each year removing several hundred elephant and several thousand buffalo to maintain their numbers at approximately 7 500 and 28 000, respectively. But the practice was subject to cycles of condemnation and furor in the media, until eventually a strong lobbying effort forced South African National Parks (SANParks) to cease elephant culling in 1995. During a public meeting, SANParks conducted a total review of the KNP wildlife management plan. This was done with the participation of experts worldwide, who advocated a zoning system of high-elephant density and low-elephant density to achieve a mosaic of impacts which could be shifted as the level of impact became high. Nevertheless, the recommended policy still involved removal of substantial numbers of elephants in the low impact zones. With a limited market for live elephants to be relocated to other conservation areas, it meant that some culling would have to be done. In the face of public pressure, the politicians would have none of this, and the KNP elephant management policy remains at the mercy of political considerations. Extensive research on elephant contraception in KNP yielded valuable understanding, but no solution, as the technical aspects associated with using contraception as a means to manage almost 10 000 elephants are not financially or otherwise practical. On the order of 4 000 elephant cows would have to be immobilized and treated twice a year, something that is simply not feasible under field conditions. But the establishment of the GLTP has brought relief to wildlife managers concerned about mounting evidence of excessive elephant impact. Elephants will now, at least in some areas, be able to disperse into adjoining areas, relieving the pressure inside this park while at the same time re-colonizing areas such as the LNP. This will be a slow process over many years, but with long-term benefits for wildlife and also tourism.

Aside from the many lessons learned as part of the elephant management program —watched and assimilated by conservation agencies throughout the subcontinent— other powerful insights have also been gained regarding management of large mammal populations. Buffalo were also subjected to an annual cull to maintain their numbers at around 28 000, but the severe droughts of 1983 and 1992 in southern Africa showed that in

extensive systems such as those represented by KNP, buffalo populations can be left to be regulated by purely natural processes (including other contributory elements such as periodic epidemics of anthrax). Culling of buffalo was therefore discontinued in 1992.

The removal of fences and a commitment to complementary management on a regional basis is also good news for certain rare species with special habitat requirements. Certain species occur naturally as low-density populations, and roan antelope and tsessebe are examples of these. Present for many decades in numbers hovering around 200, both species experienced precipitous drops in the late 1980s. Subsequent studies suggest that a well-intended but misguided policy caused this decline. In an attempt to boost the numbers of these rare species, additional boreholes and watering points were established in their preferred focal areas of distribution, which tended to be arid and open mopane veld hosting relatively few other large mammals. The net effect of this additional water was to attract growing numbers of zebra into the region, followed by more lions, and over just a few years populations of both roan and tsessebe had dropped to below 50 individuals each. With closure of some of the key watering points a positive trend of growth has returned, but the real solution lies in the additional habitat provided by LNP, directly adjoining the prime area of distribution of roan and tsessebe in KNP.

The initial phase of development of the GLTP has shown that grossly disparate areas can nevertheless find common goals in conservation sufficiently worthwhile to each party so that true partnership and commitment is entered into. In this respect, the well-endowed, internationally renowned, well-stocked, and well-managed KNP is contrasted with the war-ravaged and wildlife-devastated LNP, starting with near zero staff or infrastructure. Furthermore, the three countries have had recent histories of bloody conflict and stark differences in economies and resources. The GLTP is regarded as an opportunity to overcome these differences and ensure that the respective experience in each country is brought to bear on the whole. This is surely an example not only to other African countries, but to nations around the world.

A detailed and integrated Joint Management Plan has been developed and accepted by all three countries as the basis for harmonized and complementary land-use planning, wildlife management, tourism management, and a range of factors having common impact. The GLTP has become an example where lessons can be learnt for the benefit of the many other TFCAs currently in the planning or implementation phase in Africa. Indeed, most of the processes and institutional structures followed during the formation of the GLTP have been adopted by other TFCAs in the region.

But the GLTP is not only about biodiversity and economic potential, there are other intangibles difficult to quantify, yet deeply needed and sought by many people. It is a sense of wilderness, remoteness, being able to stand at one point and scan the horizon from side to side and imagine convincingly that this is what it must have been like thousands of years ago. These places are precious and few, and they need to be preserved because they are irreplaceable. They represent a quality rather than a thing, and without ever really being fully conscious of it, it is this quality of wilderness that draws people to places like the GLTP. People come here partly because of the lions and elephants and other wildlife, but also to quietly savor the vast expanse, to absorb the simple pleasure of being in a place that is authentic, and as it should be, to rediscover perspective and harmony —a personal unspoken satisfaction that this place is good. We have many protected areas on our planet; by and large we have set aside and indeed exceeded the 10% target of IUCN, but what about the issue of scale and this matter of "wilderness"? It is here that large-scale protected area corridors, including transboundary conservation areas, truly come into their own, for they fulfill not only a need to conserve biodiversity and to enable ecosystem processes such as migration, disease, fire, and so on to proceed at evolutionary scale, but also a human need for space, remoteness, and experiencing nature in its unique authenticity.

The GLTP has come to represent the achievement of some of the very best of what is intended by the broader objectives of a transboundary conservation area (TBCA). Fundamentally, throughout the world, TBCAs strive to achieve three main objectives, that of improved regional biodiversity conservation, socioeconomic benefits, and to contribute towards a culture of peace and collaboration amongst participating nations or partners. With the Establishment Treaty just signed in December 2003, the GLTP has already made major strides in progressing towards those objectives.

For proper appreciation, the GLTP should be seen in the context of the regional wars and political tensions that existed in the region for most of the late twentieth century. Zimbabwe and Mozambique were engaged in bitter civil wars, covertly fueled by neighboring South Africa, anxious to destabilize and prevent hostile governments being entrenched along its borders. South

On the opposite page, the imposing Goliath heron (Ardea goliath) is the largest of the world's heron species.

Above, Kruger National Park is one of the few areas in Africa where one can still encounter huge old tuskers like the one shown in this photo. Both photos,
© Patricio Robles Gil/Sierra Madre

Africa itself was a pariah state due to its apartheid policies, with guerrilla fighters infiltrating through Mozambique and Zimbabwe, thereby further escalating the hostility between South Africa and its neighbors.

With a return to peace in Mozambique and Zimbabwe, and with a truly democratic government in South Africa in 1994, the need and opportunity for economic collaboration meant that somewhat suspicious neighbors now had to talk to each other about potential partnerships. Regional economic integration, and especially through developing ecotourism in border areas, offered an obvious opportunity not fraught with political trip wires. Biodiversity conservation and associated ecotourism therefore provided an ideal bridge for previously hostile nations to talk to each other in an amicable manner for their mutual benefit, forging just one of the avenues for neighboring countries to embark on a peace-building and reconstruction initiative.

Nonetheless, South Africa itself had serious challenges to face at the time of democratization in 1994. The 1 900 000 ha-KNP represented "unused" pristine land with an abundance of natural resources eagerly eyed by a high density of impoverished subsistence communities living along its western boundary, people trapped by unemployment rates of almost 40% at the time, and the land heavily overgrazed by cattle and low rainfall not conducive to high agricultural yields. KNP had its origins through the resettlement of many of its earlier inhabitants early in the twentieth century, and several land claims were lodged in terms of the Restitution of Land Rights Act of the new democratic government. One of the earliest successful claims was won by the Makuleke Community Property Association, which in 1998 was awarded ownership of the northern portion of KNP between the Limpopo and Luvuvhu Rivers. As an unpopulated area exceptionally rich in floodplain vegetation, birdlife, small mammals and insects, and highly scenic with magnificent riverine gorges and baobab landscape, the Makulekes entered into a contractual partnership with SANParks, whereby the Makuleke region would be jointly managed and administered as a contractual national park as part of KNP for the next 50 years. Here again a "transboundary" partnership has proven successful, for mutual benefit, with lodges now established to attract tourists and biodiversity well-managed and secure. Other land claims are still in progress for various other parts of KNP, but the Makuleke example is a powerful incentive for communities to engage in similar ventures that bring economic benefits to the people but also safeguard natural resources in the area.

Negotiating and developing a Concept Plan for what would eventually be the GLTP really commenced in 1996, resulting in close interaction through an international technical committee of mainly state conservation agencies of the three countries, guided by a tri-national Ministerial Committee, supported financially by the three governments, donor institutions (Krediet-Anstalt fur WiederAufbau KfW, USAID), and various NGOs such as IUCN, Peace Parks Foundation, African Wildlife Foundation, CAMPFIRE, and others. This process also resulted in the development of trusting partners, and sharing of skills and resources, based on common needs and objectives, finally resulting in the Memorandum of Understanding signed in November 2000 and the Establishment Treaty in December 2003. Many of the key processes developed during the formation of the GLTP, particularly the establishment of various specialized committees dealing with Security Issues, Joint Management Plans, Community Issues, Tourism, Financing, and so on, have now been adopted by other TBCAs in the region, which again reunites stakeholders from the different nations to work together, share experiences, and explore solutions as collaborating partners. These are the foundations of peace and collaboration that achieve true regional integration.

In terms of the Establishment Treaty, the GLTP is collaboratively managed by a Joint Management Board with equal representation from all three countries. This Establishment Treaty was discussed and approved at national government level in each of the three countries, with the Treaty eventually being signed by the three heads of state. The political commitment represented by the GLTP is therefore significant, a truly regional project with the highest-level political support, and therefore with a far higher degree of longer-term sustainability as a regional conservation endeavor.

The GLTP serves as a clear example of the financial potential that protected areas in Africa can achieve —without sacrificing any conservation principles or compromising biodiversity. As the core area of the GLTP, KNP annually attracts close to a million visitors to view and experience its wildlife splendor. These visitors bring in tens of millions of dollars in revenue each year, sufficient to cover over 80% of the budget for the entire network of national parks in South Africa. This makes it possibly the only park system in the world that is almost entirely self-supporting and worthy of closer inspection by other conservation agencies facing financial challenges. It is this tourism pool that will spread into the adjoining components of the TFCA, once infrastructure and tourism facilities are in place. So sure is

*Above, the lilac-breasted roller
(Coracias caudata),
though widespread
and common, is one of Africa's
most beautiful birds.*

*On the opposite page,
the white-faced duck
(Dendrocygna viduata)
lives in large flocks and is a
frequently-seen inhabitant
of the Greater Limpopo's
wetlands.
Both photos,*
© Patricio Robles Gil/Sierra Madre

the international community that the GLTP will be a success that the German Government has committed approximately 12 million euros for the development of the LNP, with the Peace Parks Foundation supporting implementation of this ambitious development program in Mozambique.

Despite the long history of conservation and state-of-the-art wildlife management in some of its component areas, the GLTP nevertheless has some serious challenges, almost all having their origins outside its boundaries, including a plethora of alien invasive plants and alien diseases such as bovine tuberculosis. The abstraction of water from feeder rivers through impoundments, irrigation farming, and water-thirsty plantations of alien trees in catchment areas, and pollution from fertilizers and mining, have affected water quality and modified river flow regimes affecting habitats for fish and other aquatic species. All of these aspects are subjects of intensive research and management actions to understand and mitigate their impact.

Much still remains to be done to achieve the objectives of full integration of the component areas making up the 3 600 000-ha Great Limpopo Transfrontier Park, let alone embarking on the far more ambitious vision of a 10 000 000-ha Great Limpopo Transfrontier Conservation Area. Although the GLTP theoretically represents a core linkage of contiguous land areas in terms of the Memorandum of Understanding of November 2000 and the Establishment Treaty of December 2003, in reality the only areas that have been truly integrated and jointly managed are the 1 900 000-ha KNP (including the Makuleke community contractual area) and the 1 100 000-ha LNP. Linkage with Gonarezhou National Park in Zimbabwe depends on the establishment of a Sengwe Community Wildlife Corridor, complicated by veterinary concerns about the spread of foot-and-mouth virus disease as well as bovine tuberculosis from KNP into the beef-exporting areas of Zimbabwe. The basic soundness of a wildlife linkage —with associated tourism benefits— will surely result in an appropriate solution being found through zonation of the relevant area.

However, perhaps the greatest challenge of all lies in finding a socially acceptable solution for the more than 15 000 tribal people who live as a sparse scattering along the Shingwedzi and Limpopo Rivers in the LNP of Mozambique. Here they eke out a subsistence existence, having done so for many decades, surviving droughts and civil war, and having little interest in being relocated to alternate areas, no matter how attractive. No one intends to force them to leave, but their presence does pose a challenge to wildlife managers intent on reintroducing ele-

phants, buffalo, lions, and other animals to this area so heavily impacted by decades of war and wildlife poaching. A solution must be found and will require mutual understanding and compromises on all sides. If the GLTP can involve these communities effectively in demonstrating, considering, understanding, and experiencing that the GLTP offers a secure and sustainable future in the area, then it will have been successful. There can be no question of local communities becoming the victims of macro-economic policy implementation. In the GLTP, as in any TBCA worldwide, it is the local people who have the greatest stake in the area, despite the high level of negotiation and diplomacy that such initiatives demand. It is incumbent upon the proponents of an initiative, such as the GLTP, to ensure that local interests and security are paramount.

Another challenge remains a successful conclusion to the discussions around a wildlife corridor through the Sengwe Community, essential if the Makuleke Region of KNP and Gonarezhou are to be linked. This issue is further complicated by the presence of bovine tuberculosis within the buffalo population of Kruger, and the reluctance of veterinary authorities in Zimbabwe to allow free entry of wildlife from Kruger northwards across the Limpopo River. Innovative solutions to this challenge also need to be developed, probably by zoning combined with veterinary interventions in the northern part of Kruger to ensure a bovine tuberculosis-free area south of the Limpopo.

Africa today is littered with "paper parks," conservation areas in name only, and subject to high tolls through rampant poaching, tree-felling for fuel-wood, and permanent settlement as people move away from war-ravaged areas, and areas heavily overgrazed by too many cattle, drought, or expanding populations. Governments are faced with huge challenges presented by chronic poverty, job creation, health provision, housing, education, water provision, and the AIDS pandemic, in addition to the fact that most countries simply do not have sufficient resources to effectively manage their biodiversity assets. This is reality in Africa today, and it makes the few real success stories all the more worthy of praise, respect, and support. The GLTP represents a mix of these successes and failures, but the synergy of the mix and the solid political commitment to jointly manage the various component areas so as to pool the strengths for common good bodes extremely well. Those with an understanding of the region, who are aware of the strong technical base resident within many of the current staff, the existing resources, goodwill, and political impetus know that the GLTP will not be a case

On the opposite page, a mother hippopotamus (Hippopotamus amphibius) and her offspring, with basking Nile crocodiles (Crocodylus niloticus) in the background. Amazingly, these two imposing species coexist with little conflict in the rivers of the Greater Limpopo system.

Above, a male nyala (Tragelaphus angasi), one of the common antelope species found in the Greater Limpopo region.

On pp. 98-99, a leopard (Panthera pardus) asleep on a branch. This elusive predator spends much of its day resting, often hidden away in the canopy of large trees. All photos,
© *Patricio Robles Gil/Sierra Madre*

of dragging the integrated whole down to the lowest common denominator, but rather harnessing together all the multiple opportunities to reach a new elevated economy of scale which will benefit the entire region. How will this be achieved?

The first visitors into KNP entered through its gates in 1927 (a total of three cars the entire year bringing in a revenue of three-pound sterling), and it is now one of the most well-known and most-visited national parks in the world, having achieved that fine balance of rendering itself economically viable without sacrificing its core values. But there are additional attractions and opportunities to be had in the Mozambican and Zimbabwean components of the GLTP, broadening and deepening the already rich range of experiences available in Kruger. Some of the biggest challenges have already been met, that of attaining political commitment for a regional biodiversity and tourism initiative, that of gaining official and public support, and that of reaching consensus and accepting a Joint Management Plan with a Joint Management Board. What remains now is to harness the private investment and public support to realize its development opportunities so that lodges, roads, bridges, and people can not only move through KNP into the adjoining areas, but for international visitors and local visitors to also flow from Maputo and Harare into these magnificent areas. The overall tourism vision exists, and governments are establishing roads and border posts to enable this vision to unfold. The real challenge now is to attract investment into the tourism infrastructure in Mozambique and Zimbabwe, and then to market and manage the region as an integrated and complementary world-class destination. The degree to which an optimal balance of benefits to people and wildlife is achieved will determine the ultimate long-term viability of the GLTP initiative, but all the signs so far are good.

LEO BRAACK

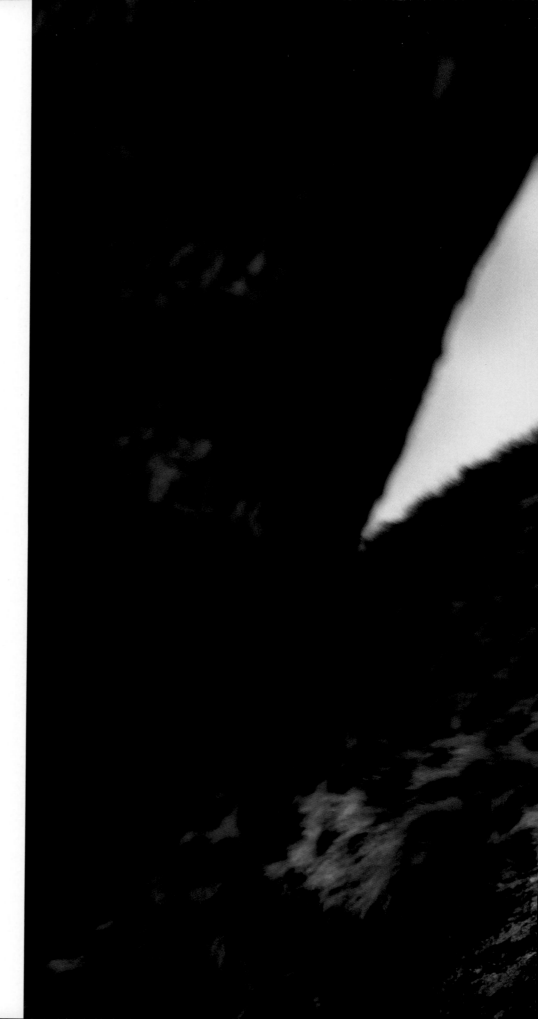

EL CARMEN-BIG BEND: AN EMERGING MODEL FOR PRIVATE PUBLIC PARTNERSHIP IN TRANSBOUNDARY CONSERVATION

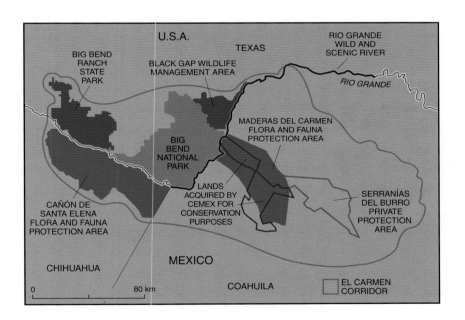

One of the most interesting transboundary areas in the Americas, and indeed in the world, is in the process of being developed on the border between the American state of Texas and the states of Coahuila and Chihuahua in Mexico. It covers one of the most diverse areas in the great Chihuahuan Desert, and spans the international border along the Rio Grande. South of the Rio Grande and at the center of this ecoregion is El Carmen, located in northern Coahuila, a magnificent area that extends north and eventually connects with the extensive Santiago range in western Texas. In Mexico, the Área de Protección de Flora y Fauna Maderas del Carmen covers 208 421 ha, has 32 km of frontage on the Rio Grande, and consists of 64% *ejido* land and 36% private land. Recently, CEMEX, an international corporation and one of the world's three largest cement companies, acquired important tracts of land both within and adjacent to the protected area. El Carmen is "a vast sky island" that rises from the Chihuahuan desert floor (1 000 m) and culminates in fir forest (over 2 700 m). It can be divided into two parts, a limestone portion in the north and an igneous portion in the south, and it is characterized by five major vegetation associations: desert shrub, chaparral, grasslands, pine-oak forest, and fir forest. Water is abundant in rushing mountain streams, springs, breathtaking waterfalls, and desert *tinajas*. Towering rugged peaks dominate the landscape, a complex canyon system with drainages that carry floodwaters to the desert floor, and ultimately to the Rio Grande. Here, a rich archaeological history provides evidence of occupation by several Native American tribes, adding further to the international interest of this region.

To the east of El Carmen is the Serranías del Burro, which connects to Maderas del Carmen by a broad valley of Chihuahuan Desert grasslands —a rugged region where lands are privately-owned cattle ranches, with conservation-minded landowners. It covers nearly 300 000 ha and exhibits unique biological characteristics due to its complex topography, with several elevation gradients and a large system of canyons with wide biodiversity.

To the west of El Carmen is a series of connecting desert mountains covering 277 220 ha across a vast expanse of desert, the Área de Protección de Flora y Fauna Cañón de Santa Elena, Chihuahua, that lies adjacent to Big Bend National Park and Big Bend Ranch State Park in the U.S. Here, ownership of land is 56% *ejidos*, 35% private land, and 6% communal lands. The primary reason for establishing the Santa Elena Canyon Protected Area was to protect the Rio Concho watershed.

To the south is a vast landscape incorporating the Sierra la Encantada in the center, which links to El Carmen through a narrow pass known as the Cuesta Malena. To the east is the Sierra Santa Rosa, which joins the Sierra La Encantada, and to the west, the Sierra del Pino is linked to El Carmen by a series of small desert mountains.

On the U.S. side of the border, the Rio Grande Wild and Scenic River (RGWSR) was officially designated on November 10, 1978. It includes 313-km river frontage and a land corridor extending 400 km inland from the river's edge. The land corridor includes federal, state, and privately-owned lands. Federal lands within the RGWSR are managed by the National Park Service, and State lands are within the Black Gap Wildlife Management Area and are managed by the Texas Parks and Wildlife Department. Private lands are cooperatively managed through agreements as established in the Rio Grande Wild and Scenic River Management Plan.

In the center is Big Bend National Park (324 165 ha), established in 1944 and managed by the National Park Service. It has long been famous for its magnificent scenery, biodiversity, and especially as a bird watcher's paradise for Chihuahuan Desert species. The Chisos Mountains are a focal point, and a hike into the high country from the surrounding desert is a treat for park visitors. Big Bend National Park has been designated part of the Chihuahuan Desert Biosphere Reserve. Elevations range from 450 to 2 600 m, although lower elevations are typical of the Chihuahuan Desert, with a diversity of cactus and native desert plants, while the highlands contain pine-oak woodland, with springs and complex canyons. The Deadhorse Mountains of Big Bend National Park are the northern geologic extension of the Sierra del Carmen of Coahuila, separated only by an incision made by the Rio Grande known as Boquillas Canyon. Thus, the Deadhorse Mountains are often referred to in the U.S. by their geologically more correct name, Sierra del Carmen.

To the east of Big Bend National Park is the Texas Parks and Wildlife's Black Gap Wildlife Management Area (47 600 ha), where the Serranías del Burro reach their northern limit and the Sierra del Carmen enters Texas. Black Gap is typical desert country, with some of the lowest elevations found in the Chihuahuan Desert. The area has rough desert mountains, an intricate canyon system, while the higher elevations support several canyons with mixed oak forests.

To the west of Big Bend National Park is Big Bend Ranch State Park (113 316 ha), managed since 1988 by the Texas Parks and Wildlife Department. It includes remote, rugged country, rich in archaeology, culture, and history dating back some 10 000 years. The area includes two mountain ranges, the most famous one being the Solitario Dome.

Overall the area represents one of the largest, wildest, and biologically richest and most diverse areas in North America. It is managed collectively by a varied combination of private, federal, and state-owned conservation agencies, but with a common objective. In Mexico, there is collaboration between protected area management and CEMEX and other private ranchers. In the U.S., the state agencies are cooperating with their Mexican counterparts, paying attention to the socioeconomic differences between both countries.

The geographical location and varied topography give rise to the biological diversity in the region, and the varied landscape sustains healthy populations of the regional megafauna. Over 80 species of mammals have been recorded for this region, several of them endemic or very rare; Miller's shrew (*Sorex milleri*), also known as the Carmen shrew, is an endemic species that inhabits the higher woodland elevations. The cliff chipmunk (*Tamias dorsalis carminis*) is a small striped chipmunk that dwells in the higher elevations and is found in only a few isolated mountain ranges in Coahuila. The Carmen mountain white-tailed deer (*Odocoileus virginianus carminis*) is another endemic taxon that is named after the region. A second specimen of the Coahuila mole (*Scalopus aquaticus montanus*), described first in 1950 in El Carmen, was found in 2003. A species that has apparently extended its range northward is the eastern fox squirrel (*Sciurus niger*), which is a common resident in the pine-oak woodland. Long-tailed weasels (*Mustela frenata*) are a rare species in the lower desert elevations. The bat fauna is diverse with 20 species currently documented, and includes the Mexican long-nosed bat (*Leptonycteris nivalis*), the red bat (*Lasiurus borealis*), the southern yellow bat (*Lasiurus ega*), and the ghost-faced bat (*Mormoophs megalophylla*).

Medium and large mammals are well represented: the puma (*Puma concolor*), bobcat (*Lynx rufus*), coyote (*Canis latrans*), gray fox (*Urocyon cinereoargenteus*), and ringtail (*Bassariscus astutus*) are common residents. The coati (*Nasua narica*) is a rare resident and little is known of the ecology of this species in northern Mexico. Three other species of cats —the ocelot (*Leopardus pardalis*), the jaguarundi (*Herpailurus yagouaroundi*) and the jaguar (*Panthera onca*)— have also been sighted, but not yet officially documented.

Three big mammal species deserve special attention: the desert bighorn sheep (*Ovis canadensis mexicana*), undoubtedly

one of the most emblematic species of the region; the black bear (*Ursus americanus*), a keystone, flagship, and umbrella species that is an indicator of the well-being of the environment, and the pronghorn antelope (*Antilocapra americana*) that, thanks to the efforts of ranchers and NGOs, was re-established in the region.

Over 450 species of birds have been documented, and the region is an important migration corridor during spring and fall for neotropical birds as well as shorebirds and waterfowl. The mosaic of vegetation associations, water and food availability, vegetable covering, and protected nesting areas provide a veritable oasis for birds. Some Mexican species, like the Colima warbler (*Vermivora crissalis*), reach their northern limit in Big Bend National Park. Several species deserve special mention. Wild turkeys (*Meleagris gallopavo*) maintain an excellent population in several areas. The American peregrine falcon (*Falco peregrinus anatum*) is a common resident and its nest sites are found on well-protected high cliffs. The solitary eagle (*Harpyhailaetus solitarius*), a Mexican species, was discovered to be a summer resident. Black-capped vireos (*Vireo atricapillus*) are summer residents and nest in the mid-elevation chaparral habitat. Finally, the golden eagle (*Aquila chrysaetos*) is another resident and its nest sites are also totally protected.

The reptile fauna comprises nearly 70 species. Several are listed as "Threatened" in Mexico, such as the Texas desert tortoise (*Gopherus berlandieri*), the Texas horned lizard (*Phrynosoma cornutum*), and the Mexican racer snake (*Coluber constrictor oaxaca*). Amphibians are also diverse with many species of frogs and toads.

Plant life is remarkably diverse, with over 1 200 species documented. The vast pine-oak woodland contains 16 species of oaks, including sandpaper oak (*Quercus pungens*) and the endemic Chisos oak (*Q. graciliformis*). Coahuila fir (*Abies coahuilensis*) is common in the high forest. Desert grasslands are scattered with sotol (*Dasylirion leiophyllum*) and up to five species of yucca, with beaked yucca (*Yucca rostrata*) and giant white yucca (*Y. carnerosana*) representing the most common species. Other desert plants include shrubs, with creosostebush (*Larrea tridentata*) as dominant species, in addition to over 20 cactus species, several orchids, and an incredible array of desert and mountain wildflowers. Agaves are well represented in the region, the most unusual being the red-flowered or Carmen agave (*Agave potreana*). Deciduous and evergreen trees, pines, vines, succulents, grasses, and firs all combine to make this area highly representative of the overall Chihuahuan Desert flora.

This region is one of the most diverse in North America, and the pine-oak forests of northern Mexico and western Texas have recently been listed as a new global hotspot —the Madrean Pine-Oak Woodlands— by Conservation International (Mittermeier et al. 2004). It is a vast land with very few inhabitants and one of the few remaining wild places in the mid-latitudes, and requires effective conservation management to maintain its wilderness values. In particular, the expansion of populations of desert bighorn sheep and black bear, both of them important flagship species, is highly dependent on maintenance of effective biological corridors in this landscape.

Efforts to re-establish the desert bighorn sheep began in the 1950s in the Black Gap Wildlife Management Area, and populations of bighorns found today in Big Bend National Park and neighboring ranches are the result of these efforts. In 2000 and 2001, CEMEX, in collaboration with Agrupación Sierra Madre and Unidos para la Conservación, began the now highly successful desert bighorn sheep restoration program that has resulted in 100 sheep in a breeding facility and nearly 30 sheep in the wild in Maderas del Carmen, the first free-roaming herd in Coahuila since their extinction in the late 1940s.

Black bears are another good example of sustained conservation commitment. Their numbers began declining in Mexico during the 1940s and 1950s and they were totally extirpated from much of their historical range. A few surviving populations remained in isolated mountain ranges in northern Coahuila, mainly in the Maderas del Carmen, Santa Rosa, and Serranías del Burro. In the Serranías del Burro, where cattle ranching is the main economic activity, dedicated ranchers and their families (notably Guillermo Osuna, Marcial Llano, David Garza Lagüera, and Elizabeth Spence de Sellers) began a conservation initiative to protect important species such as the black bear. It is through the efforts of these local ranchers that the black bear population has begun to recover and slowly expand to adjacent mountains, not only in Coahuila and Nuevo León, Mexico, but also in Big Bend National Park and Black Gap Wildlife Management Area. Research on black bears is currently being conducted in the region, with support from CEMEX. The study, which focuses on the dispersal of black bears and the protection of dispersal corridors, is complemented by similar previous work in Big Bend National Park, the Black Gap Wildlife Management Area, and the Caesar Kleberg Wildlife Research Institute in the Serranías del Burro.

The presence of committed private ranchers and NGOs has advanced conservation efforts for the re-establishment of the

Above, a male northern cardinal (Cardinalis cardinalis), a widespread and common North American species.
© Patricia Rojo

On the opposite page, Spanish dagger (Yucca gloriosa) and lupines in Big Bend National Park, Texas.

On pp. 108-109, a rain-swollen river in the usually dry river bed of Cañón de San Isidro, in the heart of the Sierra del Carmen. Both photos,
© Patricio Robles Gil/Sierra Madre

pronghorn antelope in Coahuila, emulated by ranchers in the grasslands of Valle Colombia, in the Sierra La Encantada. In association with the Mexican NGOs Agrupación Sierra Madre and Unidos para la Conservación, this effort has resulted in a small herd of this charismatic species in the valley.

Starting in the early 1800s and up until the late 1970s, there was severe abuse of natural resources in Maderas del Carmen. Overgrazing, mining, logging, hunting, and the harvesting of the *candelilla* plant (*Euphorbia antisyphilitica*) was widespread. Concern for the conservation of El Carmen was voiced by Agrupación Sierra Madre, whose persistence resulted in CEMEX purchasing land in the Maderas del Carmen complex in the year 2000. This was the beginning of a rebirth for this great mountain ecosystem, and this has been followed by long-term commitment of resources by CEMEX. With this support, the first scientific baseline inventory of the flora and fauna of El Carmen began, and proactive habitat and wildlife restoration programs were launched.

There has also been a proud tradition of research and management in the U.S. component areas, starting in Big Bend National Park in 1944. A wide variety of studies have been completed, ranging from work on individual species (e.g., peregrine falcon, black bear, puma, bats) to work on rare plant communities, reptile and amphibian research, air quality monitoring, GIS mapping, history, paleontology, and river water quality. In addition, there have been sponsored international workshops, and the provision of interpretative programs and opportunities for public recreation, especially on the Rio Grande.

Likewise, the Black Gap Wildlife Management Area has hosted research on threatened species, in addition to its main objective of demonstrating habitat and wildlife management practices to landowners. This has been complemented by a range of activities, including workshops on desert survival, photography, and a host of interpretative programs, such as the longhorn cattle drive in Big Bend State Ranch Park. Despite this experience of effective management in the respective component protected areas, wide-ranging species and essential habitats are not completely secure and success of local conservation efforts is dependent upon cooperative management of all the protected areas, both north and south of the Rio Grande, and the participation of both private and public neighbors, landowners, and other stakeholders well beyond protected area boundaries.

Initiatives to secure this international cooperation have experienced varying levels of progress over the years since Big Bend National Park was established in 1944, at which time it was also proposed that a sister park be established in Maderas del Carmen on the Mexican side. However, it was not until November 7, 1994 that Mexican President Carlos Salinas de Gortari declared Maderas del Carmen an Área de Protección de Flora y Fauna, and Cañón de Santa Elena an official protected area. This enabled the development of a management plan for the Mexican components, including implementation of programs for animal husbandry, vegetation inventory, alien plant control, mapping, research on soil erosion, and recovery and use of *candelilla* plants. Environmental education in *ejidos* is focused on water development, soil erosion management, and educational materials for schools, with emphasis on the "Endangered" black bear and other high profile species.

While there remains much potential for improving cooperative efforts between the partners in this transboundary region of the Chihuahuan Desert, the first steps were undertaken when the U.S. Secretary of the Interior and the Mexican Secretariat of Environment, Natural Resources, and Fisheries signed in 1997 a Letter of Intent to Cooperate on transboundary environmental and conservation issues. This was followed by a Memorandum of Agreement in 2000 between the National Park Service, the Mexican Protected Areas Department, and the Texas Parks and Wildlife Department that specified the development of international conservation projects.

Although high-level officials and priorities in both the U.S. and Mexico have changed over time, local and grassroots efforts have continued to grow, evolve, and adapt to setbacks, and they are now demonstrating the fruits of their labor. Among other things, there has long been social and economic friction over the presence of large protected areas. From early conflict due to the perception that these areas harbored livestock-damaging predators and detracted from the local culture of family ranches, to concerns that local tax coffers would suffer due to lack of economic development of protected lands, the areas and, to some degree, the adjacent lands, have been viewed by some with skepticism.

While these concerns have not vanished, there has been an increased appreciation of the role of tourism as a pillar of the local economy, especially during times of economic hardship in the agricultural sector and other traditional industries of the region. The intact natural landscapes, with their resources for public recreation, stand in contrast to the general trend of rural decline. Numerous studies have demonstrated that property values in areas adjacent to protected areas are consistently higher than elsewhere, and communities with access to these resources

On the opposite page, the Cañón de Santa Elena at one of its narrowest points. The left wall is in Mexico, the right wall in the U.S.
© Patricio Robles Gil/Sierra Madre

Above, one of the 150 desert bighorn sheep (Ovis canadensis) that have been reintroduced to the CEMEX reserve in El Carmen, Mexico.
© Jaime Rojo

have greater prospects than those without them. Furthermore, the closing regulations of cross-border activities, which virtually brought to a halt generations of traditional trade based on the sale of handicrafts and other products to visitors, can now be replaced by legitimate trade governed by the closer working relationship between the two countries.

However, since the declaration of NAFTA (North American Free Trade Agreement), there has been no allocation of resources to conservation programs. Economic subsidies to stimulate this economy would undeniably help to stabilize the currently unstable situation. Despite a positive outlook, one of the biggest problems faced by conservation management in Mexico is that lands are still privately-owned ranches or communal *ejidos* with locked gates, which hampers cooperative management. This might be remedied in time with the efforts and assistance of NGOs to facilitate greater collaboration among private and state agencies. Rather than relying on a single management solution to the whole region, the currently diverse management arrangements have demonstrated the value of a variety of approaches and styles in an effort to achieve an agreed overall goal and point the way to cooperative transboundary management in the future.

The Chihuahuan Desert, like most of the semi-arid areas in the world, is a fragile land, very sensitive to impacts and requiring long periods of recovery following damage. Erosion and soil loss are probably the biggest threats to the region, accelerated by the removal of vegetation and the compacting of soils by overuse. Impacts caused by overgrazing in the past are being gradually reversed, but continued human use, especially by visitors, could become the most serious new threat. Poor land management also poses a threat to water resources. Reduced infiltration caused by loss of vegetable covering and compaction affects the replenishment of ground water, especially under the low rainfall climate. Furthermore, pollution of water supplies affects the entire riverine ecosystem.

Other threats include:

• the increasing problem of atmospheric pollution, which not only results in acid rain but also the visual impacts of haze, yielding a negative effect on the region's uncluttered large landscape views, one of its greatest assets;
• the uncontrolled expansion of populations of exotic animals, which in some areas have entirely replaced native species and which are extremely difficult to control, especially in a mosaic of state and private land;

• the sub-division of larger private properties into "ranchettes," resulting from changes in the agricultural sector, increased land values, and restrictive inheritance laws.

This vast transboundary landscape encompasses approximately 2 000 000 ha under a variety of protection mechanisms, with many opportunities for expansion, as the Mexican Government is planning to incorporate the area between Santa Elena and Maderas del Carmen as part of this complex. This remarkable mosaic of protection mechanisms carries the hope of a multi-agency and transboundary institutional model which will require innovative new policies and working relationships among federal and state agencies in both countries, enabling them to work together with NGOs and private ranchers. With the presence and support of CEMEX, which is planning to expand its commitment on both sides of the border, there is now an opportunity to consolidate the relationship between both countries, involving a full partnership with a common goal; namely, the protection of a highly diverse mega-corridor that constitutes one of the last wilderness areas of North America.

BONNIE REYNOLDS McKINNEY
PATRICIO ROBLES GIL
RAYMOND SKILES
JONÁS A. DELGADILLO
JAIME ROJO

AMERICA

THE ALASKA-YUKON-BRITISH COLUMBIA BORDERLANDS: THE WORLD'S LARGEST CONTIGUOUS PROTECTED AREA COMPLEX

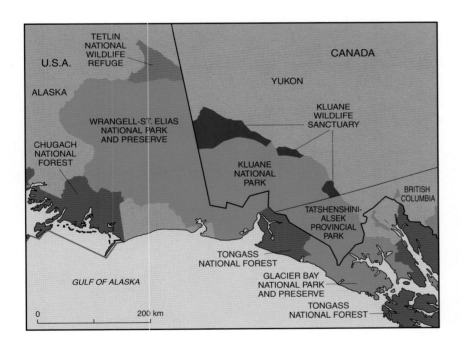

The greater St. Elias region bridges Canada and the U.S., spanning southwest Yukon, south-central and southeast Alaska, and northwest British Columbia. It is a remarkably diverse landscape, ranging from the high ice fields and mountain tops of the St. Elias ranges at 4 000 to 6 000 m to the boreal spruce forests of interior Yukon and Alaska, to the tidewater glaciers and temperate rainforests of coastal Alaska. Forests and wetlands are generally found only at low elevations, rapidly giving way to large expanses of alpine meadows and tundra at around 2 000 m. The landscape is tectonically and geomorphologically active, and subject to extensive periglacial and permafrost processes. It includes many small lakes and numerous creeks and rivers, most of them glacially fed. The most famous of these waterways are the Copper, Alsek, and Tatshenshini Rivers, which act as the major regional linkages between the interior and the Gulf of Alaska, and Kluane Lake and the Tanana River, which feed the massive Yukon River drainage.

The core of the region includes a series of large protected areas: Kluane National Park and Reserve (2 200 000 ha) and Kluane Wildlife Sanctuary (630 000 ha) in Yukon, Wrangell-St. Elias National Park and Preserve (4 900 000 ha), Glacier Bay National Park and Preserve (1 300 000 ha), and Tetlin National Wildlife Refuge (290 000 ha) in Alaska; and Tatshenshini-Alsek Provincial Park (960 000 ha) in British Columbia. In addition, Tongass National Forest contains two adjacent wilderness areas totaling 180 000 ha. Although Glacier Bay was first protected in 1925, and Kluane Wildlife Sanctuary in 1942, most of these protected areas date from the late 1970s or early 1980s and Tatshenshini-Alsek was not established until the early 1990s. The major protected areas together are an international World Heritage Site, and Glacier Bay is a UNESCO Biosphere Reserve. The total area covers 10 499 800 ha, or 11 021 800 ha if private inholdings are included.

At a regional scale, the greater St. Elias straddles two broad ecozones: a coastal-maritime belt that includes areas sloping towards the Gulf of Alaska and an interior-boreal area that incorporates the rest of the region. Strong altitudinal zonation occurs across much of the region, resulting in the montane-sub-alpine-alpine progression typical of many mountainous areas. There are, however, also some significant lowlands and wetlands in each ecozone, like the boreal wetland complex of Tetlin National Wildlife Refuge and the intertidal mosaic of the Copper River Delta.

In addition to the coast and interior forests, wetlands, and tundra, there are several unique plant communities supporting a number of rare and endemic species. Many well-drained, south-facing slopes in the region's interior support steppe-like plant communities, possibly relict grasslands linked to the Beringian refugium. Other communities are associated with unique landforms and lithologies, including grasslands found on saline floodplains, sand dunes, and volcanic ash deposits. Also of note are archipelagos of arctic-alpine communities on isolated *nunataks* rising above the region's immense glacial ice fields. From a scientific perspective, communities found on recently deglaciated terrain are particularly interesting as they provide a rare opportunity to observe and study primary succession.

These diverse and relatively untouched ecosystems are home to substantial wildlife populations, from marine mammals on the coast, to large carnivores and ungulates, small mammals, birds of prey, and migratory waterfowl, and songbirds. Many of these exhibit characteristics well-suited to use as focal species in biodiversity conservation. They include the grizzly bear (*Ursus arctos*), the glacier bear (*U. americanus emmonsii*), the wolverine (*Gulo gulo*), the gray wolf (*Canis lupus*), the Dall sheep (*Ovis dalli dalli*), the mountain goat (*Oreamnos americanus*), caribou (*Rangifer tarandus*), the tiny shrew (*Sorex yukonicus*), the snowshoe hare (*Lepus americanus*), and the collared pika (*Ochotona collaris*). Among the birds, the golden eagle (*Aquila chrysaetos*), the bald eagle (*Haliaeetus leucocephalus*), the trumpeter swan (*Cygnus buccinator*), the peregrine falcon (*Falco peregrinus*), the gyrfalcon (*F. rusticolus*), the harlequin duck (*Histrionicus histrionicus*), the timberline sparrow (*Spizella breweri*), and the snow bunting (*Plectrophenax nivalis*). And finally, in the case of fish we have the Anadromous salmon (*Oncorhynchus* spp.) and the Kokanee salmon (*O. nerka*).

In combination, Kluane, Wrangell-St. Elias, Glacier Bay, and Tatshenshini-Alsek parks, Tetlin Refuge, and Tongass Wilderness Area cover a total area of 10 500 000 ha and constitute the largest internationally-adjoining protected area complex in the world, second only to Greenland National Park (which occurs within the borders of a single nation) as the world's largest contiguous area managed for the purposes of ecosystem or wilderness protection. Superlatives abound to describe the global significance of the region. It is among the most geologically diverse and active areas in the world. Some of North America's largest recorded earthquakes have been registered in the region, which contains several dormant volcanoes and an active one, as well as a number of unusual features like mud volcanoes. It also contains the highest coastal mountain range and the largest subpolar ice field in the world, in addition to 10 of North America's 15 highest mountains, the continent's longest valley and piedmont glaciers, and one of the world's largest concentrations of surging glaciers. Coastal areas receive as much rainfall in one year as portions of Amazonia, and annual snowfall in the Ice Field Ranges is higher than anywhere else in North America. The region contains more than one-quarter of the global population of Dall sheep and provides the only habitat in the world for the glacier bear. Several rare, threatened, and endangered plant and animal species inhabit the region, and populations of large mammals are among the largest and densest in North America.

The area has been home to aboriginal peoples for millennia. Land claims in the Alaska part of the region were settled in the early 1970s, resulting in the formation of large regional corporations, including Ahtna Inc., Chugach Alaska, Doyon, and Sealaska Corps. Land-claim settlement began in Canada with the Yukon Umbrella Final Agreement in 1990. The Champagne-Aishihik First Nation approved their final, local agreement in 1993; and the Kluane First Nation in 2003. Pending claims in northwestern British Columbia are entirely unsettled. Subsistence harvesting by indigenous people is permitted in many of the protected areas, though not extensively. European exploration and settlement began with the Russians in Alaska's Copper River Valley in the late eighteenth century, but did not spread much until mineral exploration in the late nineteenth century, and especially the Klondike gold rush. Much of the St. Elias region was not readily accessible until the completion of the Alaska Highway in 1942. The total regional population today is still under 10 000.

Big-game hunting and guiding are major past and present activities, now limited to areas outside the national parks, if not necessarily to the other protected areas in the region. Minerals, particularly placer gold, but also hard rock copper, nickel, and a range of related metals are or could be mined in or near the parks. Indeed, Tatshenshini-Alsek Provincial Park came about as the result of efforts to halt the Windy-Craggy mine project within what is now the park. Tourism grew steadily through the mid-1990s, then leveled off and may have declined slightly in the last few years. Cruise ships, and more local marine excursions, are a major source of activity in coastal towns such as Juneau and Skagway, with associated bus tours going north on the Haines and Alaska Highways. Science has been a major activity in the region since at least the late-nineteenth century

On p. 116, aerial view of dunes in El Pinacate and Gran Desierto de Altar Biosphere Reserve.

On p. 118, the mountains of Wrangell and St. Elias are in one of the most pristine wilderness areas left on Earth. Both photos, © Patricio Robles Gil/Sierra Madre

On pp. 120-121, a bald eagle (Halaeetus leucocephalus), national symbol of the U.S., seeks refuge in this large coastal protected area. © Art Wolfe

On the opposite page, moose (Alces alces), such as this male in Kluane National Park, feed on algae and other aquatic vegetation in the many lakes formed when snow melts in the spring.

Above, one of the most important populations of dall sheep (Ovis dalli) is found in the St. Elias Mountains. In this photograph, a young calf in Kluane National Park. Both photos, © Patricio Robles Gil/Sierra Madre

123

and it has included many ethnographic, geological, and ecological studies.

There have been efforts to cooperate between the parks in the past, particularly in areas of enforcement. Overall, however, cooperation here is informal and depends on initiatives by local protected-area managers with higher government approval. Areas of cooperation include rafting and mountaineering management, interpretation, joint search and rescue in the past, wildlife management and enforcement, and cooperative publications. Most cooperation and collaboration efforts have been simple and informal, largely consisting of data and information sharing. More formalized efforts tend to be regional in scale, such as national park-territory/state wildlife management and joint management boards deriving from land claims (e.g., Alsek Renewable Resources Council, Kluane National Park Management Board in Yukon). World Heritage Site and biosphere reserve designations might have potential, but political and funding issues for now make them difficult to build on or introduce.

Although this region is large and remote, and includes many protected areas, threats do exist. There are strong desires for economic development at local and higher levels in the region. There are prospective mines in the region, awaiting various combinations of mineral price changes, power supply improvements, or various assessments. Tourism is considered by many as the main or best alternative to mining development. Yet demands for more tourism attractions could increase activities with potentially negative effects, such as those from flight-seeing, spatially concentrated day and overnight hiking, and other motorized forms of tourism. Forestry activities range from substantial on the Alaska coast to tentative and doubtful in the Yukon interior. But their effects are well known. And the intensive spruce beetle infestations in much of the region are complicating forestry and fire management choices. The ecological and physiographic complexity of the region also complicates forecasts of the potential impact of climate change —but they are likely to be substantial over the longer term.

Several current issues and trends have been at the forefront of change in the St. Elias area in the last five years, including economic development, subsistence and devolution, land claims, and local participation, especially in the Canadian parts of the region. These may augur well for the achievement of deeper coordination and integration in the future. Since the late 1980s, in the Canadian part of the St. Elias area, there has been much more cooperation between national and territorial inter-

ests, and both First Nations and other local interests. As of early 2003, the Canadian Federal Government completed devolution of land and resource management to the Yukon Territorial Government, and that has combined with the establishment of the final land-claims-based assessment processes to create a window for integrated management. A new territorial protected area in the ecologically significant Klutlan area to the north of Kluane National Park and Reserve also appears increasingly likely. Local co-management of protected areas, wildlife, and even other resources is increasing in the Canadian part of the St. Elias, but this may complicate large-scale management, at least initially. The comparative lack of transboundary cooperation and collaboration in the St. Elias has clearly several fairly obvious roots. The international border with the U.S. is significant, as is the fact that the region is physically difficult to cross as well. Possibly, the key obstacles in the St. Elias include issue-driven and own-land driven perspectives, the lack of resource management and science staff equivalents in Canadian versus American national park agencies, and concerns over loss of control by agencies. Nonetheless, all things considered, the prospects for long-term survival of this magnificent region are as good as for any described in this book.

SCOTT SLOCOMBE
RYAN K. DANBY

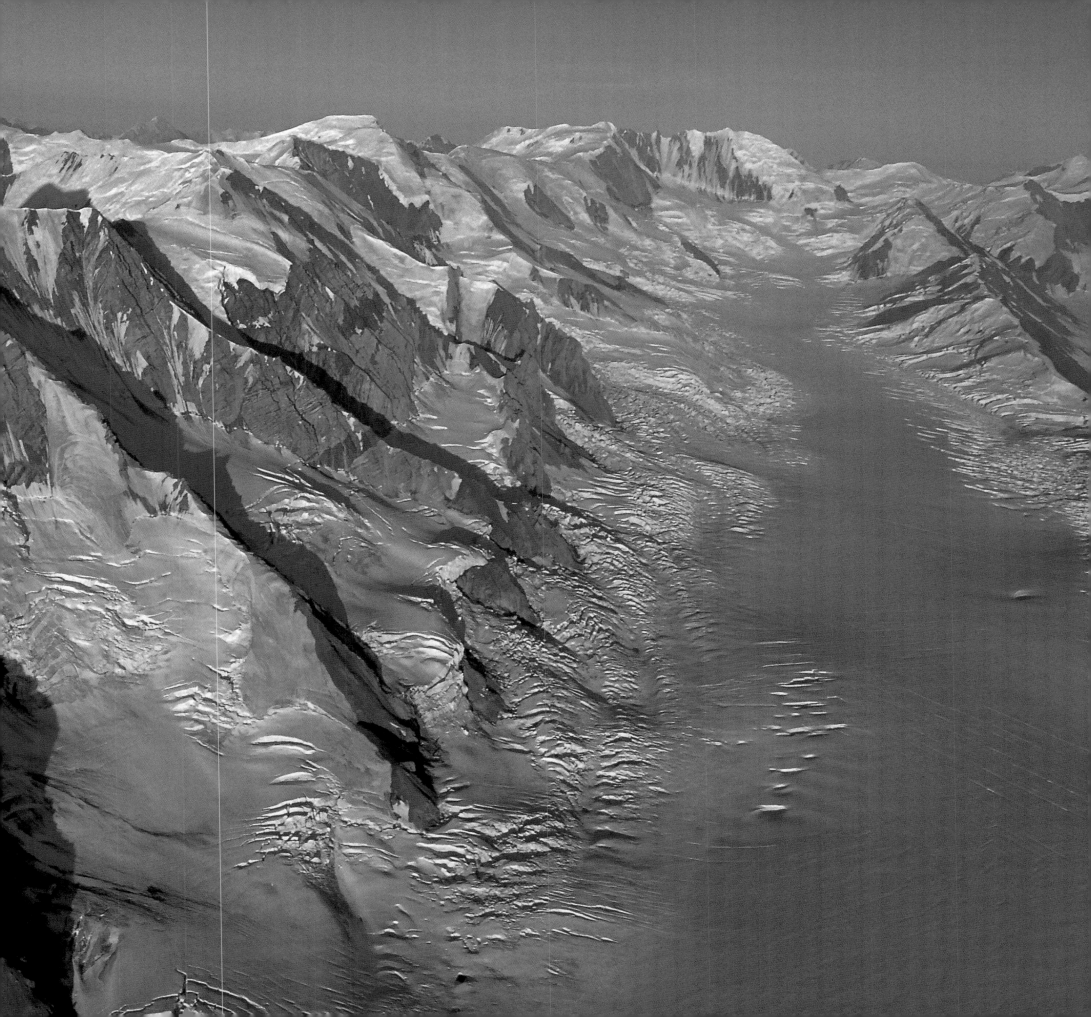

DRY BORDERS: LINKING NATURE RESERVES ACROSS THE SONORA-ARIZONA BORDER

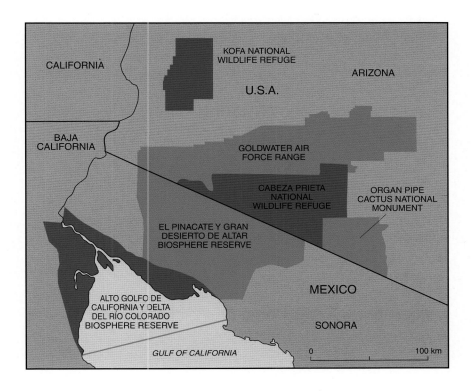

The "dry borders" region straddling the boundary between the U.S. and Mexico is too immense and too lightly settled to have been given a common name. Parts of it have been called the Gran Desierto, El Pinacate, Cabeza Prieta, the Old Caborca-Yuma Trail, or the Delta. Some early explorers called it Western Papaguería or Western Pimería Alta, but even those broad strokes failed to do justice to its grandeur, its native peoples, or natural wonders. Because the region covers about 250 of the 400 km where the Sonoran Desert overlaps the most arid Mexico-U.S. border, it might be referred to as the "Dry Borders region," although "The Sonoran Corridor" may also be an appropriate name to reflect its role as a refuge and movement corridor for wildlife.

From an aerial perspective, on a course from Mexicali to Sonoyta, the northern end of the Gulf of California and the Baja California peninsula is visible. Fractal-patterns of tidal wetlands fringe the coastline, and in the southeast, dried cracked mud spreads across the expansive delta of the Colorado River. Bordering the delta is the driest, harshest part of the Sonoran Desert. Inland across the Gran Desierto dunes, the biggest sand sea in North America, is El Pinacate, with snarled black and red lava flows, countless cinder cones, and some of the world's most spectacular steam blast (maar) craters. In all directions the heart of the Sonoran Desert is visible, with arid mountains emerging like islands from the desert flats. The newer volcanoes are interspersed among range after range of jagged granitic sierras in their northwest-southeast trend. Towards the north-east, the tops of the highest desert mountains, the Ajos, Sand Tanks, and Table Tops, form the biological roof of the desert, where there is an elevated "island ecosystem" of mixed yucca, juniper, scrub oak, and rosewood in a flora that includes more than 156 plant species not found in the lowland desert.

What is not obvious from the air are the geo-political boundaries. Four great protected areas run contiguously from the upper gulf into Arizona. These are the Alto Golfo de California y Delta del Río Colorado Biosphere Reserve and the El Pinacate y Gran Desierto de Altar Biosphere Reserve in Mexico, and the Organ Pipe Cactus National Monument and Cabeza Prieta National Wildlife Refuge in the U.S. Bordering Organ Pipe and Cabeza Prieta is the Barry M. Goldwater Range in Arizona, not a formally protected area, but generally managed as one throughout its 200-kilometer span, and bisected by only one paved roadway. Adjoining the Goldwater Range is the

Sonoran Desert National Monument, just southwest of the sprawl of urban Phoenix. These six areas cover the Dry Borders region, an immense unspoiled wilderness covering 3 million ha and spanning 350 km from San Felipe, Baja California, to Phoenix, Arizona, forming the largest zone of contiguous protected desert anywhere in the Americas. Although the administration and management of the protected areas is undertaken independently in each country, there has been extensive transboundary collaboration over many decades regarding management, recovery of endangered species, and collaborative research.

In terms of wildlife, the northern gulf is biologically rich and more than 1 000 species of macro-invertebrates and 400 species of fish are known from the Alto Golfo Reserve. The delta of the once mighty Colorado River supported great gallery forests of cottonwoods and willows fringed with mesquite trees, screwbean, impenetrable thickets of arrowweed, and probably more than 200 to 400 now extirpated plant species. Steamboats regularly plied the river in the days before the transcontinental railroad. Among the various Alto Golfo species still at risk of imminent extinction are the delta clam (*Mulina coloradoensis*), the totoaba (*Totoaba macdonaldi*), and the vaquita (*Phocoena sinus*). The little delta clam used to number in the trillions. Like various other Colorado delta species, it requires adequate freshwater flow for its survival. The totoaba, weighing up to 100 kg, was one of the mainstays of early commercial fishing in the northern gulf. Loss of spawning habitat and overfishing has led to its demise. The vaquita, the smallest and most endangered cetacean in the world, occurs only in the northernmost reaches of the gulf. Only a few hundred survive. These little porpoises display darkly outlined lips, like lipstick on an ever-smiling face. In spite of legal protection, unacceptable numbers are drowned every year in fishing nets.

Tides at the delta are extreme, often rising and falling 10 m twice daily, flooding and exposing thousands of hectares of nipa (*Distichlis palmeri*), a saltgrass endemic to the northern gulf. Its stronghold is the delta where it thrives on seawater, producing a wheat-sized grain that was once a staple of the indigenous Cucapah people. Nipa has the potential to become a major world crop and is one of the great biological treasures of Mexico in need of serious conservation efforts.

Other endemic animal and plant species are scattered across the Dry Borders. Some such as the Pinacate groundsel (*Senecio pinacatensis*) and a yet unnamed shrubby mint (*Salvia* sp.) in Cabeza Prieta are known from only a single mountain. Sand endemics like the dune croton (*Croton wigginsii*), Gran Desierto camphor-weed (*Heterotheca thiniicola*), dune creosotebush (*Larrea divaricata* var. *arenicola*), and the fringe-toed lizard (*Uma notata*) are bound to the dunes by evolution and geologic history, and cannot live in any other environment. The behavioral and evolutionary adaptations of *Uma notata* for exclusive dune living include a dislike of stable substrates and fringed toes for running on the sand. To keep sand out of their eyes, nose and mouth, they have interlocking eyelash-like scales on their eyelids, a countersunk lower jaw, and a unique nasal passage architecture. Their dorsal coloration matches the sand (different for each population), and their white ventral coloration deflects sunlight reflected off sand, while an internal melanin sheath around the body cavity blocks UV.

About 10 frogs and toads and 60 reptile species inhabit the Dry Borders region, which is also host to more than 500 bird species and 85 mammals. By comparison, more than 600 bird species are known for the Sonoran Desert, almost two-thirds of the avifauna from northern Mexico to Canada. The Dry Borders region encompasses a unique community of desert birds, with distinctive specialties such as Le Conte's thrashers (*Toxostoma lecontei*), Abert's towhees (*Pipilo aberti*), Lucy's warblers (*Vermivora luciae*), and rufous-winged sparrows (*Aimophila carpalis*). Common and characteristic species of this region include Gila woodpeckers (*Melanerpes uropygialis*), cactus wrens (*Campylorhynchus brunneicapillus*), phainopepla (*Phainopepla nitens*), and greater roadrunners (*Geococcyx californianus*). The fragile wetland and riparian areas often harbor distinct, often threatened, subspecies or populations such as the Yuma clapper rail (*Rallus longirostris yumanensis*), the southwestern willow flycatcher (*Empidonax traillii extimus*), the western yellow-billed cuckoo (*Coccyzus americanus*), and the Sonoran yellow warbler (*Dendroica petechia sonorana*). The region forms a desert bridge between the Nearctic and Neotropical realms in western North America, which is critical for migrations of both landbirds and waterbirds. Millions of birds, including rufous hummingbirds and white-winged doves and other migratory pollinators must journey through, stopping at key places to rest and refuel. Dominant migratory landbirds include Wilson's warbler, the Pacific-slope flycatcher, Swainson's thrush, and the western tanager.

Sonoran pronghorn antelopes (*Antilocapra americana sonorensis*), once ranging over most of the region, now struggle to survive despite protection by both the U.S. and the Mexican legislation. Current estimates place the population in Mexico at 220, but there are only 25 to 40 in the U.S., down from 250

On p. 128, forest of saguaro
cactus (Carnegiea gigantea)
at dusk in the Goldwater
Air Force Range.

On pp. 130-131,
the desert in bloom in
El Pinacate and Gran Desierto
de Altar Biosphere Reserve.
Both photos,
© Patricio Robles Gil/Sierra Madre

On the opposite page, El Elegante
Crater, a spectacular natural
feature in El Pinacate and Gran
Desierto de Altar Biosphere
Reserve that measures 1.5 km
in width and is 250 m deep.
© Jack Dykinga

Above, the desert primrose
(Oenothera deltoides)
is one of the most characteristic
species of this desert region,
carpeting the desert floor as soon
as winter ends.
© Patricio Robles Gil/Sierra Madre

133

several years ago. Severe drought has limited their food supply, and human infrastructure, such as highways and fences, including the international border, has curtailed their movement patterns.

The Dry Borders region supports at least 840 vascular plant species, one-third of the total flora of the entire Sonoran Desert. Quite apart from its species-richness, a particular characteristic of the region is the elegant simplicity of its landscape quality. The vast and shadeless creosotebush (*Larrea divaricata*) flats contrast with the linking veins of green vegetation along dry watercourses, down bajadas and valley plains, and becoming bigger and greener at the draining bottoms. Most of this green ribbon is made up of small gallery trees formed by the three woody legumes, namely mesquite, palo verde, and ironwood (*Prosopis, Parkinsonia* and *Olneya*). This ever-changing and complex ecosystem of endlessly intersecting mosaics and gradients defies simple description. Its epithet, "mixed desert-scrub," belies a beautiful potpourri of hundreds of plant species and habitats, including the chaparral-like mountain tops, the shifting sands, playas, and porous flats, while the oases, wetlands, and big canyons have their own and often highly diverse floras.

Most significantly, the environment remains in a surprisingly intact, natural state. Some extinctions or near-extinctions and extirpations have occurred, but thousands upon thousands of species across a broad spectrum of ecosystems are alive and well. Where losses have occurred, at least some restoration is still possible. There are, however, threats to the continued persistence of habitats and species, arising from unsustainable land-use practices in the region. The Dry Borders region is severely impacted by the depredations of smugglers and migrant jobseekers, resulting not only in the loss of human life, but damage to plants and other wildlife. Increased human settlement, trampling by livestock, damage by vehicles, pollution by pesticides, alien plant invasions, as well as a falling water table, are taking their toll. The tightening of border control measures is also impacting previously undamaged areas. In addition, despite the fact that only three highways run through the Dry Borders region, the towns at the periphery are poised to boom, and can be expected to generate negative impacts on the region. Solutions must be found, and it has been suggested that a transboundary conservation program, endorsed by both countries, would be a good starting point. The histories, cultures, and future of the people of the region are so intertwined that transboundary conservation areas aimed at both effective conservation management, sustainable development, and peaceful relations are a logical route to follow. Key to success will be to ensure the support of government, and awareness and involvement of the people of the region. The area demands that action is taken to secure its future and the livelihoods of the people that live there. The Dry Borders region, "the Desert Sisters," can be the cornerstone of conservation efforts in the region, including conservation projects in western Mexico and a rallying point for conservation in western North America. The Sonoran Desert Sisters cap an arch of actual and potential reserves and protected places through the greater Sonoran Desert and the Gulf of California, and form a staircase of protected areas, the "Escalera Ecológica del Golfo de California." But that begins with sister protected areas embracing the complex but valuable borderland desert. Our call to action is: "Go to the Dry Borders. Walk the ground. Talk with the Sonoran Desert Sisters. Smell the ethereal queen-of-the-night blossoms. Touch the cool night sand. Smell the desert pungent from creosotebushes on a dewy dawn. Hear the trilling nighthawk and dream of tomorrow."

RICHARD S. FELGER
BILL BROYLES
EXEQUIEL EZCURRA

Above, Gambel's quail (Callipela gambelii) *is a well known, very visible species of the Sonoran Desert.*

On the opposite page, pair of desert bighorn sheep (Ovis canadensis) *in El Pinacate. This magnificent desert dweller is the region's most important flagship species. Both photos,* © Patricio Robles Gil/Sierra Madre

On the opposite page, the Sierra del Rosario in the Gran Desierto de Altar, Sonora, Mexico.

Above, the Sonoran pronghorn antelope (Antilocapra americana sonorensis) *is the most endangered of the five subspecies of this wide-ranging North American species. Both photos,* © Patricio Robles Gil/Sierra Madre

LAGUNA MADRE: A MAJOR TRANSBOUNDARY WETLAND ON THE TEXAS-TAMAULIPAS BORDER

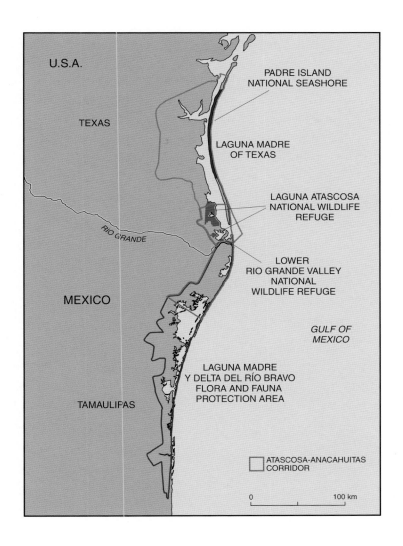

The Laguna Madre is a world-renowned coastal, hypersaline lagoon ecosystem. It is the largest such system in the world and traverses the boundary between the U.S. and Mexico. Divided by the Rio Grande Delta, the Laguna Madre is comprised of two almost mirror-image, shallow elongate lagoons along the Gulf of Mexico coastlines of Texas and Tamaulipas. The lagoons are both divided by vast tidal flats. The upper and lower Laguna Madre in Texas are separated by the land-cut tidal flats, and the northern and southern Laguna Madre in Tamaulipas are separated by the El Carrizal tidal flats. Likewise, both lagoons are protected on the east by barrier islands and peninsulas, and bounded on the mainland by vast cattle ranches, farmlands, and the brush country of the Tamaulipan Biotic Province. In Texas, the Padre Island National Seashore, the Laguna Atascosa National Wildlife Refuge, and the famous Kenedy and King ranches afford almost complete protection to most shoreline areas. In Tamaulipas, the lagoon's remoteness, along with the lack of paved roads and utility infrastructure, have similarly protected the shores and waters of this unique ecosystem.

These two lagoons are best known for their hypersalinity, large overwintering redhead duck (*Aytha americana*) population, numerous protected species, vast seagrass meadows and tidal flats, and great fishery productivity. Hypersalinity of the ecosystem is caused by the regional semi-arid or subtropical steppe climate, which is characterized by extreme variability in precipitation and evapotranspiration that is two to three times higher than precipitation. In addition to climate, the lack of freshwater inflow is also an important factor. There are no rivers that flow into the Texas lagoon, only the Arroyo Colorado, a heavily modified and channelized creek that drains into the lower Laguna Madre. Only one small river, the Rio San Fernando, drains into the Mexican lagoon. Historical salinities of over 100 parts per thousand (ppt) (more than double the salinity of normal sea water) in both systems have been moderated in recent decades due to changes in water circulation caused by the Gulf Intracoastal Waterway (GIWW) and Mansfield Pass in Texas, and four passes connecting the Gulf of Mexico with the lagoon in Tamaulipas.

In Texas, almost 80% of all seagrass beds in the state are found in the Laguna Madre, and although still productive, the historically highly productive commercial fisheries have now largely given way to some of the best recreational fishing for red drum, black drum, and spotted sea trout in North America. In Tamaulipas, a "boom and bust" cycle of great fishery production alternated with

briny, almost sterile waters before the 1970s. The cycle included a highly productive lagoon for several years after a wet hurricane, then dwindling fisheries and species diversity as the barrier island passes closed and the completely enclosed lagoon became more and more saline. During extended droughts, or long periods between hurricanes, the lagoon would begin to dry up and salinities increased due to evaporation. When salinities reached 150 ppt, only brine shrimp survived, and at the highest recorded salinity of 295 ppt, salt precipitated along the shoreline and in the bottom of the lagoon. Then, another hurricane would open the Gulf passes, flush the system with floodwaters from rain, and the cycle would begin again. This cycle was demonstrated in Tamaulipas after the major hurricanes in 1909, 1933, and 1967. A similar cycle probably existed in Texas before hypersalinity was moderated as a result of completion of the GIWW in 1949 and stabilization of Mansfield Pass with jetties in 1962.

In contrast to their remoteness and the unique natural hallmarks just described, recent concerns have arisen about increased population pressures in some areas, brown tide impacts, the effects of maintenance dredging on seagrass habitat, nonpoint source pollution (contaminated run-off), and other issues in Texas, focusing attention on the long-term health of the ecosystem. In Tamaulipas, environmental concern was recently raised over the possibility of extending the GIWW through the Rio Grande Delta and into the state's Laguna Madre from Brownsville, Texas, to Tampico, Tamaulipas. Although considered by scientists as a complete ecosystem, the Laguna Madre of Texas and Tamaulipas are managed separately by the two separate states and countries where they are located.

Aquatic biodiversity in the Laguna Madre appears to be only 35 to 45% of the normal or positive estuaries to the north due to the harsh hypersaline conditions, as well as temperature extremes in the very shallow waters. By comparison, 938 species have been recorded in the upper Laguna Madre and Baffin Bay, 706 in the Laguna Madre of Tamaulipas, and 2 043 species in the Texas Coastal Bend (three estuaries) just north of Laguna Madre. The Tamaulipan lagoon may have considerably more species, but there have been few studies to document its biodiversity.

In contrast to the relatively low biodiversity in the Laguna Madre, some very important, extensive habitats (seagrasses and tidal flats) support amazing populations of very important birds. Together, the two lagoons host over 77% of the North American overwintering population of redhead ducks. In addition, protected bird species, such as piping and snowy plovers, reddish egret, brown pelican, and peregrine falcon, are found in both lagoons, while colonial waterbird rookeries abound.

Thirty-eight waterfowl species have been documented along the lower Texas coast. Like the redhead duck, many use the seagrass meadows in the lagoon as primary wintering habitat, but they also use coastal freshwater and brackish ponds in the uplands adjacent to the lagoon and in the Rio Grande Delta. Thirty-four colonial waterbird rookeries are found on islands of the Texas Laguna Madre, and 23 species of herons, egrets, ibises, pelicans, terns, gulls, and skimmers nest on vegetated and unvegetated shorelines in Texas. The only major coastal colony of American white pelicans is found in the upper Laguna Madre of Texas, and a smaller nesting population has also been documented in the Laguna Madre of Tamaulipas.

The Laguna Madre in Texas and Tamaulipas contains some of the largest expanses of undisturbed wetland complexes in the Western Hemisphere, and it is one of the most significant coastal areas for aquatic bird life on the entire Gulf of Mexico coast. Large numbers of migratory and wintering shorebirds use wind-tidal flats and barrier beaches. Probably most of the threatened Great Plains population of piping plover winter in Laguna Madre, and both barrier islands and tidal flats appear to be essential wintering habitats. Snowy and Wilson's plovers are the most abundant species nesting on tidal flats and related habitats, such as washover passes in South Texas and Tamaulipas. Lastly, the largest concentration of reddish egrets in the world is found in the western Gulf of Mexico, and they are the most common wading bird on tidal flats in Laguna Madre.

The Laguna Madre is a bar-built coastal lagoon, extending along 445 km of Gulf of Mexico coastline from Corpus Christi, Texas, to Rio Soto la Marina, Tamaulipas. Geomorphically, the Rio Grande Delta divides the lagoon into two separate systems, each approximately 185 km in length and between 7 km and 12 km in width. Averaging 1 m in depth, the Laguna Madre in Texas covers 1 235 km^2 at mean sea level and in Tamaulipas 2 028 km^2. Seagrass beds and tidal flats are the predominant habitats in Texas and although bare bottom predominates in Tamaulipas, considerable amounts of seagrasses and tidal flats are also found.

The Laguna Madre is characterized as a negative estuary or hypersaline lagoon. The food web of the Laguna Madre is predominantly based on seagrasses and algae, rather than on the phytoplankton typical of most positive estuaries.

In addition to the best-known features of the Laguna Madre mentioned above, there are other unique lesser-known, but important characteristics, such as: the most extensive wind-tidal flats and clay dunes in North America; the only strain of high-salinity-adapted oysters in North America; the only natural rocky (coquina) shoreline in Texas; the only serpulid worm reefs

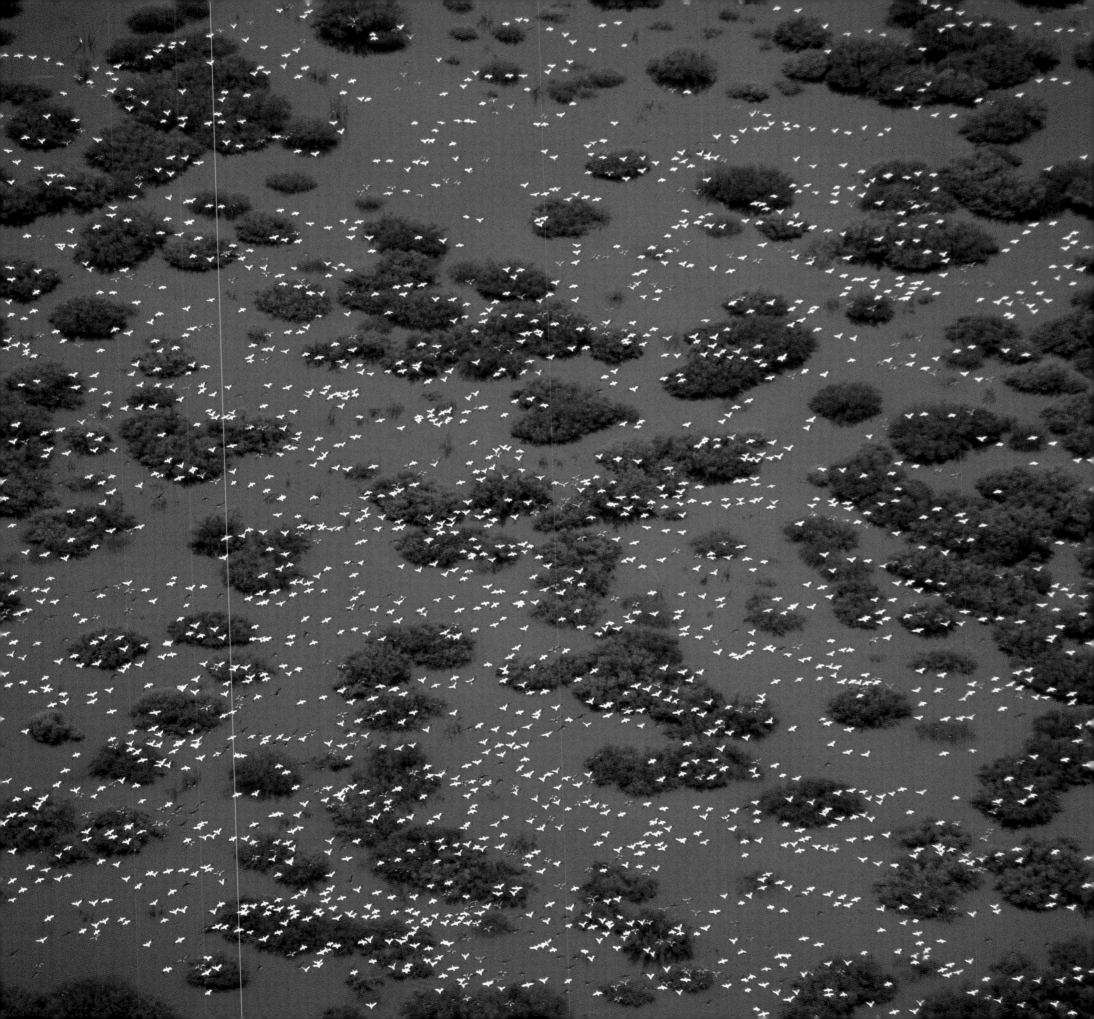

in Texas, and the only locality of oolite (calcium carbonate) and gypsum crystal formation in Texas.

The Laguna Madre, the largest coastal lagoon in both Mexico and U.S., is important in commerce, transportation, oil extraction, and recreation. It is also the most important commercial and sport fishery area in the northwestern Gulf of Mexico.

The Laguna Madre represents 50% of the Tamaulipan coastline and contributes about 15% of shrimp, 13% of blue crab and 40% of mullet landed commercially in Mexico. The resources of the lagoon provide a living resource for as many as 13 500 artisanal and commercial fishers. In 2003, $88 million of revenue from fishing activities was generated in Tamaulipas, largely from Laguna Madre.

The Texas Laguna Madre system provided 62% of the finfish (primarily black drum) landed commercially between 1997 and 2001 and generated about $220 million of annual revenue from sport fishing and other recreational and tourism activities. World-class fishing for red drum, black drum, and spotted sea trout brings sport fisherman from all over the world. Corpus Christi, Port Mansfield, South Padre Island, and Port Isabel are centers of recreation and tourism on the Texas Laguna Madre. Travel and tourism in the Laguna Madre in both Texas and Mexico have increased significantly in the past decade.

The shallow, productive waters of the Laguna Madre are threatened by changes in freshwater inflow, overfishing, water quality, habitat destruction, and coastal development. Some of the most serious threats to the health of the Texas Laguna Madre are related to dredge material disposal associated with maintenance dredging of the GIWW. Dredging often results in release and resuspension of contaminants in the water, as well as decreased water clarity that can starve seagrasses of sunlight. In addition, dredge material disposal may destroy seagrass beds and other submerged or intertidal habitats through burial. In the past decade, a proposal to extend the waterway from its termination at Port Isabel to Tampico, through the entire length of the Mexican lagoon, was nearly approved.

Untreated sewage from San Fernando and some of the other nearby small cities and villages is discharged into the Laguna Madre in Mexico. Concentrations of lead, cyanide, cadmium, and hydrocarbons that exceed permitted levels have been found in every water analysis conducted by Semarnat (Secretaría de Medio Ambiente y Recursos Naturales), the Mexican Government's environmental protection agency. The Arroyo Colorado in Texas receives municipal and residential wastewater, as well as agricultural runoff. The impact of these sources on water quality in Arroyo Colorado has resulted in its designation as "impaired" water body by the Texas Commission on Environmental Quality. Damming and channelization of creeks that flow into the Mexican lagoon for irrigation have modified freshwater inflow. Water quality in these channels and creeks is usually poor, and constitute a threat to water quality in the Laguna Madre of Tamaulipas.

In Tamaulipas, fishery production has declined since 1994. Part of the decline can be attributed to a lack of organizational capacity in the artisanal fishery. However, illegal industrial fishing techniques, like trawling, have brought the shrimp in the Laguna Madre "close to the limit of sustainability," according to the National Institute of Statistics, Geography, and Information (INEGI).

Since the early 1940s, governmental programs have promoted extensive agricultural expansion in northern Tamaulipas. However, improper soil conservation techniques have resulted in almost 120 000 ha of bare soil between October and March. Winds now cause sand and dust storms that have resulted in declines in the air quality of Reynosa and other cities and towns adjacent to Laguna Madre and on the Texas-Mexico border.

The conservation of 600 000 ha of the Mexican Laguna Madre through its designation as a Natural Protected Area by the Federal Government and the state of Tamaulipas will help assure long-term resource protection, enforcement of fishing and other regulations, and community involvement and outreach. Nature tourism is the fastest growing segment of the tourism industry. Sustainable activities, such as bird watching, are becoming more and more popular, and the Laguna Madre is becoming a premiere birding destination in both the U.S. and Mexico. As communities become aware of the potential of ecotourism to grow their economies without compromising the integrity and natural beauty of the area, the protection afforded by conservation areas in the lagoons in both countries, as well as by the large, undeveloped tracts of ranchland in Texas, bode well for the future of this unique ecosystem.

JOHN W. TUNNELL
ROSARIO ÁLVAREZ

Above, a white-tailed deer (Odocoileus virginianus) in Laguna Atascosa National Wildlife Refuge. This widespread species is one of the most common mammals in this region.

On the opposite page, a typical scene in Laguna Atascosa National Wildlife Refuge, Texas. Both photos,
© Patricio Robles Gil/Sierra Madre

THE MAYA TROPICAL FOREST: SAVING A THREATENED TRI-NATIONAL BIOLOGICAL AND CULTURAL HERITAGE

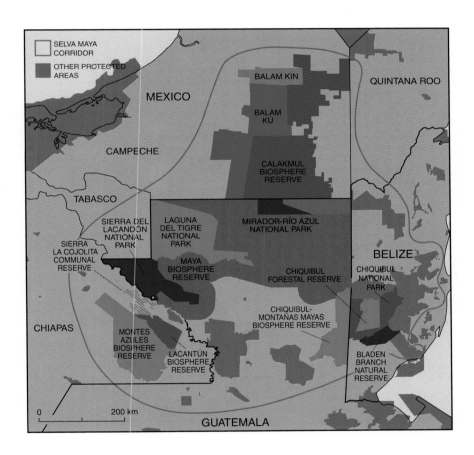

The Maya Tropical Forest spreads across the midriff of Meso-america, where Mexico and Central America bring together a biological cornucopia produced by the conjunction of the northern and southern parts of the American continent. The region is a mosaic of high and low tropical forests, grassland savannahs, seasonally flooded scrub forests called *bajos*, pine savannahs, and the largest freshwater wetland in Central America. The region stretches from the eastern lowlands of Chiapas across northern Guatemala, into the Yucatán Peninsula, and across Belize. Human history has divided the Maya Tropical Forest into three sovereign nations, but on the ground, the flora and fauna of the region are remarkably similar.

The Maya Forest is one of the largest blocks of continuous tropical forest in the Western Hemisphere, covering more than 4 400 000 ha, although only 2 500 000 ha of this expanse are under protected status (Nations et al. 1998). It is also one of the most biologically diverse regions on the planet, providing a home for more than 3 400 species of vascular plants, 60 species of fresh water fishes, 42 amphibians, 121 reptiles, at least 571 birds, and 163 mammals (Conservation International 2003).

One of the Maya forest's elemental features is its plant diversity, both in types of forest and in the variety of plant species within those forest types. The region includes a true rainforest in extreme southeastern Chiapas and southwestern Petén and a semi-deciduous tropical forest in northern Petén and the southern Yucatán Peninsula. In Chiapas, the Selva Lacandona is mostly lower montane tropical rainforest lying between the pine and oak forest of the Chiapas highlands and the lowland swamp forests of the State of Tabasco. The Selva Lacandona itself harbors various ecological zones, including moist tropical forest and even pine forest on mountains reaching 1 000-m altitudes (Breedlove 1973).

Among the most charismatic flagship species found in the region are the jaguar (*Panthera onca*), Baird's tapir (*Tapirus bairdii*), the spider monkey (*Ateles geoffroyi vellerosus*), the scarlet macaw (*Ara macao*), the harpy eagle (*Harpia harpyja*), and the jabiru stork (*Jabiru mycteria*). The area is also critical for migratory birds, with up to one billion flying through every year.

The 330 000-ha Montes Azules Biosphere Reserve in the Selva Lacandona region of Mexico was established in 1978, and in 1992 the Mexican Government added 55 000 ha in adjoining protected areas. Montes Azules and its adjacent protected areas are 85% overlapped with the indigenous territory called the Communal Wealth Region of the Lacandon Zone, home to more

than 15 000 inhabitants of the Tzeltal Maya, Chol Maya, and Lacandon Maya communities. Internal boundaries have been controversial, but the three indigenous groups have cooperated to defend their lands against outside encroachment (Nations 1994). One positive outcome has been the Communal Reserve Sierra La Cojolita, which serves to connect the Montes Azules Biosphere Reserve with Guatemala's Maya Biosphere Reserve through a narrow corridor of natural forest rich with wildlife.

The Maya communities —Tzeltal from Nueva Palestina, Chol from Frontera Corozal, and Lacandon from Najá, Mensabak, San Javier, Betel, and Lacanjá-Chansayab— and others have been working with Conservation International (CI) for more than 13 years on several conservation and development programs, including the Forest Fire Prevention Campaigns, which build capacity to prevent forest fires; responsible tourism projects, which focus on community-based ecotourism enterprises; and sustainable natural resource management projects, focused on non-timber forest products like *xate* palm and *pita* bromeliad. CI also works with local indigenous communities to develop management plans for the region's protected areas, since a large portion of these protected areas include indigenous communal lands. CI is also working to conserve the Communal Reserve Sierra La Cojolita, a 50 000-ha corridor managed by indigenous Maya.

In 1990, Guatemala created the 1 600 000-ha Maya Biosphere Reserve, which connects with the 700 000-ha Calakmul Biosphere Reserve in Campeche, Mexico on its northern border, and to the east with the Rio Bravo lands of the Programme for Belize. Farther south along the border between Guatemala and Belize are two protected areas next to the international boundary established by Belize in 1991 —Chiquibul National Park and Chiquibul Forest Reserve, which protect the watershed of the Chiquibul River. In 1995, Guatemala followed suit by declaring the Chiquibul-Montañas Mayas Biosphere Reserve an adjacent protected area. Today, 80% of the border between Belize and Guatemala's Petén is under protected area status, although the Guatemalan side is under serious threat from logging and illegal colonization.

Mechanisms have recently been created by the governments of Guatemala and Belize to help diminish these threats, such as the Good Neighbors' Policy, implemented to improve quality of life in local communities, many of which are supported by ACICAFOC (Asociación Coordinadora Indígena y Campesina de Agroforestería Comunitaria Centroamericana) and ACOFOP (Asociación de Comunidades Forestales del Petén).

The complex of protected areas in the Maya Tropical Forest provides at least legal, if not actual, protection for more than 2 500 000 ha of tropical forest and related natural ecosystems. The building blocks for conservation of the Maya Tropical Forest are the various national parks and the five biosphere reserves (Montes Azules, Lacantún, Maya, Calakmul, and Chiquibul). The Mexican reserves are managed by the Federal Government in cooperation with state governments and local communities. National non-governmental organizations, including Defensores de la Naturaleza, ProPetén, and Belize Audubon, co-manage the Guatemalan and Belizean reserves in coordination with Federal Government agencies. This remarkable constellation of protected areas also creates a natural corridor that supports the largest population of jaguars north of the equator (Swank and Teer 1989).

The countries are also linked by the rich cultural roots of the Maya peoples who have lived in this forest for millennia. The forest hides the ruins of the cities of the pre-Classic and Classic Maya —a group that flourished here for a thousand years, between 100 B.C. and 900 A.D. As early as the pre-Classic Period, the Maya began to turn the biological wealth of this forest into the ecological foundation for one of the most developed civilizations of its time, with sophisticated mathematics, astronomy, water control, art, a calendar that measured time more accurately than our modern Gregorian version does, and the only invented indigenous written language in the Western Hemisphere (Nations, in press).

When the civilization fell around 900 A.D., they left behind a forest filled with species useful to modern human communities —rubber, timber, copal incense, fruits, and medicinal plants. Today, this forest has become one of the world's premier ecotourism attractions. The forest, in fact, is largely a human artifact, the result of centuries of selective clearing and manipulation by the Maya people who lived in this region for thousands of years, then watched it reclaim the land when their civilization collapsed.

At its population peak around 700 A.D., the Maya Tropical Forest was home to as many as five million people. Today there are fewer than one million people in the region, yet the forest is rapidly being transformed to pastures and wasteland with little benefit to the local people, many of whom continue leading lives of poverty and desperation.

One of the promising responses in the region today is the expanding economic force of tourism, drawn to the Maya Forest by the region's rare combination of ancient Maya cities and diverse wildlife. Activities such as the Waka/El Perú Project, which is designed to incorporate local communities into the management and financial benefits of ecotourism, are turning

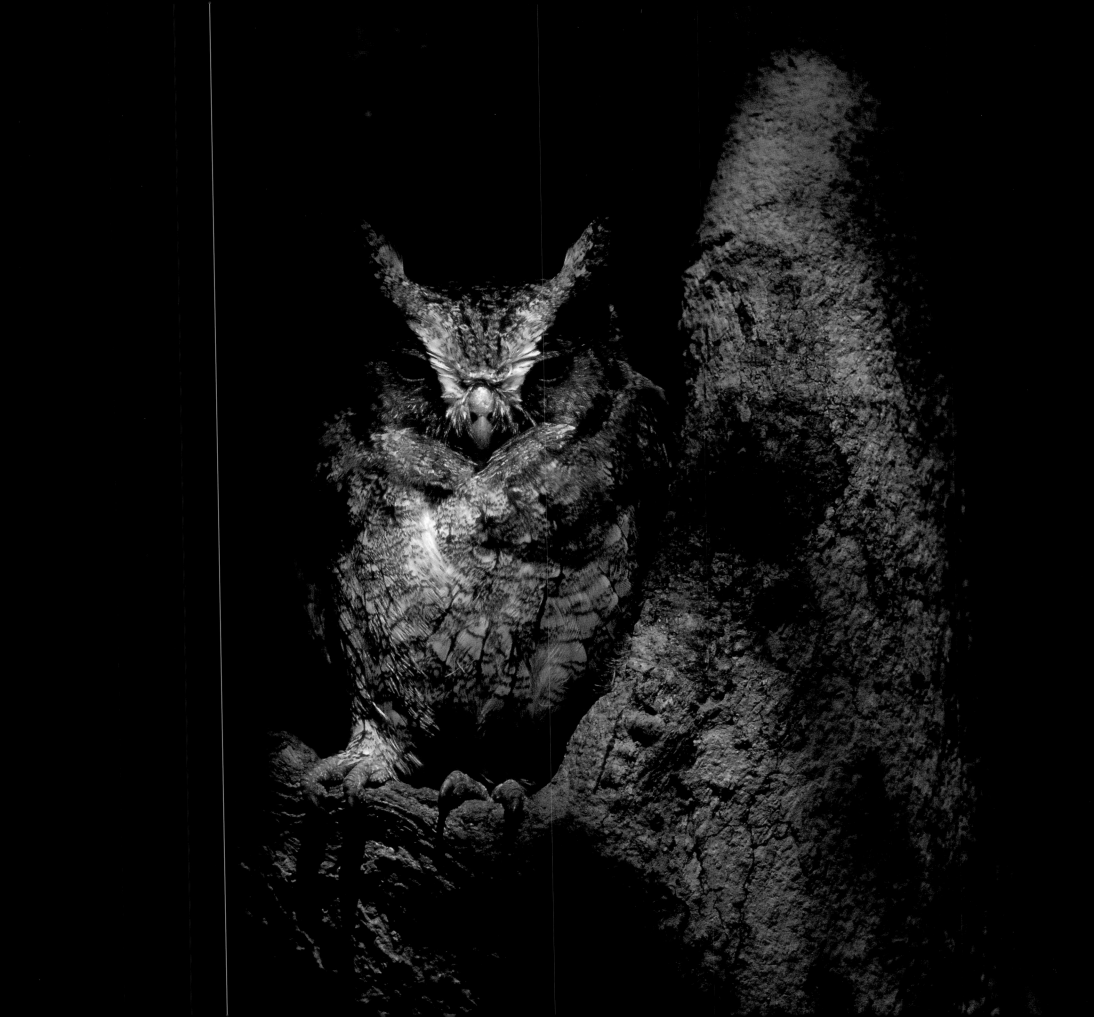

archaeological and biological resources into long-term economic forces for positive change in the region.

While the ancient Maya cleared the forest exclusively for food production, modern deforestation has been the result of commercial logging, oil exploration, road construction, colonization, slash-and-burn agriculture, and cattle ranching. Today, deforestation is driven by over-consumption of natural resources within the developed countries and by one of the most rapidly growing human populations anywhere in the world.

A 2005 satellite image of the area shows huge blotches of deforestation spreading out from human settlements in concentric rings of destruction. In Mexico's Selva Lacandona, roads that originally were meant for forestry and oil exploitation, but nowadays are used by local communities, spread across the forest like spider webs. Population in the Guatemalan Petén is growing at 7 to 10% per year, bringing new waves of land-hungry colonists. The case of Laguna del Tigre is the best example due to the high degradation of this park, more than 70% caused by illegal invasions and a lack of authority in recent years. This issue, which is now under the supervision of the Guatemalan Government, through the National Council for Protected Areas (CONAP) and with the collaboration of CI and the Kanteel Alliance, represents one of its major conservation challenges. In Belize, Salvadoran refugee farmers, citrus plantation entrepreneurs, and Mopan and Q'eqchi Indians clear the forest for subsistence agriculture, while Mennonite farmers rip out hectare after hectare of trees to plant monoculture food crops such as sorghum maize, corn, and rice in full-scale agribusiness style, with silos, barns, and barbed wire fences. As a result, the current rate of destruction in the Maya Tropical Forest exceeds 50,000 ha per year.

The expansion of this agricultural frontier is enabled by the construction of roads that, in many cases, benefit only oil companies or timber industrialists. As their products flow out of the forest on newly constructed roads, farm families flow into the forest seeking new land for exploitation.

Creating and defending protected areas and developing viable economic alternatives for thousands of pioneer farm families have become the most important activities in the survival of the Maya Tropical Forest. Today, conservationists are working to keep alive this unique ecosystem by ensuring the stability of its protected areas, eliminating destructive get-rich-quick schemes, intensifying agricultural production in deforested areas, and creating economic alternatives through micro-enterprises, ecotourism, and sustainable harvesting of renewable forest products. Successful examples are forest concessions managed by communities and by the responsible tourism effort of Alianza Verde,

a group of communities and business that promotes ecotourism activities in the Petén region (with support from the U.S. Agency for International Development, USAID). Similarly, ECAO (Equipo de Consultoría en Agricultura Orgánica) is a community-based group working in the region on the commercialization of vegetables and fruits through organic agriculture.

Conservation organizations at work in the region include the Guatemalan organizations Defensores de la Naturaleza, ProPetén, Proselva, Asociación Balam, and Trópico Verde, a Guatemala-based organization that assesses and evaluates government activities in the region. CONAP is in charge of Laguna del Tigre National Park and also works with the Kanteel Alliance in order to promote the conservation of this park.

Also in Guatemala, a community group, Guardianes del Bosque Maya, has requested a mandate for co-management of one of the biological corridors in Petén. On the Mexican side, Unidos para la Conservación (UPC) and international organizations, such as CI and The Nature Conservancy (TNC), are the main facilitators of conservation efforts.

These and other undertakings help demonstrate the growing political will to face common threats and improve management of the mosaic of protected areas in the Maya Tropical Forest. These efforts are enhanced by proposed international agreements, including the Memorandum of Understanding (MOU) for the conservation of protected areas between Mexico, Guatemala, and Belize, and the "Jaguars without Borders" and "Macaws without Borders" strategies. The MOU includes joint actions to safeguard the natural and cultural heritage shared by these areas and joint responses to environmental contingences. "Jaguars without Borders," initiated by UPC and Agrupación Sierra Madre in Mexico, is based on a 10-year study on jaguar ecology carried out in collaboration with the Universidad Nacional Autónoma de México (UNAM), Ecosafaris, a professional wildlife management and capture team dedicated to ecotourism activities, and Duke University. This effort has benefited from the active participation of governments, NGOs, and specialists from Mexico, Guatemala, and Belize, with support from USAID, CI, the National Fish and Wildlife Foundation, and the Safari Club International Foundation. The groups' efforts have produced an exemplary transboundary strategy that will soon be signed by the ministries of the three countries involved.

In Mexico's Selva Lacandona and in Sierra del Lacandón National Park in Guatemala a recently integrated multidisciplinary team formed by CI, PRONATURA-Chiapas, Defensores de la Naturaleza, and the Kukulkan Foundation will begin complementary actions so that Guatemala's efforts will match those in

*On the opposite page, a jaguar (*Panthera onca*) peers out from the forest at Caobas, Quintana Roo, Mexico.*

*Above, the lineated woodpecker (*Drycopus lineatus*) is a species in which both parents take turns to feed the two to three chicks in their nest. Campeche, Mexico.*

On pp. 154-155, the Chicaná archeological site in Campeche, Mexico. In many sites like this in Mexico and Guatemala, protection is afforded to both the ruins and the forests that have kept them hidden from the outside world for hundreds of years.

*On pp. 156-157, the ornate hawk eagle (*Spizaetus ornatus*) is a powerful and agile raptor that inhabits tropical forests in the Americas. All photos,*
© Patricio Robles Gil/Sierra Madre

Mexico with support from USAID. The team will address monitoring, responsible tourism, and the development of productive programs for the Usumacinta River Basin. Another valuable initiative is being led by TNC and the Promote Commission —a trinational group constituted by both NGOs and government institutions— for the development of eco-regional planning for the Selva Maya, and the Zoque and Olmeca areas, to define conservation priorities for the region.

Among the most promising sites for the long-term conservation of natural ecosystems in the Maya Tropical Forest are:

• the Bladen Branch Nature Reserve in Belize, a property with no permanent human communities either inside or along its edges, but which still requires boundary delimitation and ranger stations;

• the Columbia River Forest Reserve, in Toledo District, Belize, a priority area for neotropical migratory birds and, according to CI's Rapid Assessment Program, the most species-rich district in Belize (Parker et al. 1993);

• the Tzendales region of the Montes Azules Biosphere Reserve and adjoining Lacantún Biosphere Reserve, considered the best preserved section of the Selva Lacandona, and,

• the Mirador-Calakmul region, the largest block of contiguous forest in the Maya region, which is protected from spontaneous colonization by the lack of road access and surface water.

What all of these surviving areas have in common is isolation from human settlements. They represent the centers of larger blocks of protected areas in the Maya Tropical Forest. Preventing road construction and ensuing colonization and cattle ranching are the most important factors in keeping these areas alive.

JAMES D. NATIONS
CARLOS MANTEROLA
CARLOS RODRÍGUEZ
RICARDO HERNÁNDEZ

LA AMISTAD:
A LONG HISTORY OF
TRANSBOUNDARY
FRIENDSHIP
IN CENTRAL AMERICA

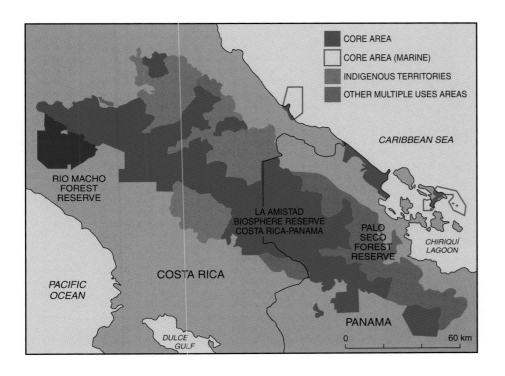

CORE AREA
CORE AREA (MARINE)
INDIGENOUS TERRITORIES
OTHER MULTIPLE USES AREAS

CARIBBEAN SEA

RIO MACHO
FOREST
RESERVE

LA AMISTAD
BIOSPHERE RESERVE
COSTA RICA-PANAMA

PALO
SECO
FOREST
RESERVE

CHIRIQUÍ
LAGOON

PACIFIC
OCEAN

COSTA RICA

DULCE
GULF

PANAMA

0   60 km

La Amistad Biosphere Reserve and binational World Heritage Site is located in the Talamanca-Tabasara Mountain Range. Stretching from southern Costa Rica to western Panama, it is a conservation and multiple-use area acting as a backbone and linking these two countries.

La Amistad covers approximately 1.3 million ha in both countries, and is one of the largest and richest ecosystems in Central America. Its system of protected natural and cultural areas includes approximately 633 000 ha in Costa Rica (12.4% of the country) and 655 000 ha in Panama (8.5% of the country). The protected areas in the Costa Rican portion of La Amistad include La Amistad International Park/Costa Rica Sector, Chirripo, Barbilla and Macizo de la Muerte National Parks, Hitoy Cerere Biological Reserve, Río Macho Forest Reserve, Las Tablas, Ujarras, Salitre, Cabagra, Talamanca, Taini, Telire and Chirripo Indigenous Territories, and the Wilson Botanical Gardens. The Panamanian protected areas of La Amistad include La Amistad International Park/Panama Sector, Baru National Park, Bastimentos Marine National Park, Palo Seco Forest Reserve, Fortuna Forest Reserve, and the San San and Volcan wetlands.

La Amistad ("friendship" in Spanish) was officially declared a symbol of binational cooperation on the Costa Rican side in 1982 and on the Panamanian side in 1998. This biosphere reserve has a large core zone in La Amistad International Park, declared a World Heritage Site by UNESCO.

La Amistad sits on the narrow land bridge between North and South America, where two distinct biotas, extreme ranges of temperatures, rainfall, altitude, slope, and exposure converge, making it one of the most biologically diverse protected regions in the Western Hemisphere. This diversity is evident not only in the high levels of endemism (between 20 to 50% for all groups, i.e., 21% of the 12 000 species of vascular plants, 40% of the 521 species of mammals), but also in the total numbers of species present within the biosphere reserve (from 80 to 100% of all of Costa Rica's and Panama's flowering plants, non-vascular plants, moss, lichen, and orchid species).

This binational reserve contains a great expanse of pristine forest, including the largest portion of cloud forest in Central America, and provides a unique refuge for native wildlife species, whose populations depend upon large tracts of land. Close to 70% of the fauna of both countries and 75% of all known reptiles and amphibians reside in this complex area.

On p. 158, a resplendent quetzal (Pharomachrus mocinno), one of Central America's most important flagship species.
© Art Wolfe

Above, a male golden-browed chlorophonia (Chlorophonia callophrys) in a cloud forest in Costa Rica.

On the opposite page, a female anole (Norops biporcatus) perched on a heliconia frond (Heliconia irrasa) in a Costa Rican forest.
Both photos,
© Michael and Patricia Fogden

Insect diversity is even more impressive. La Amistad has the second most diverse butterfly fauna in the world (De Vries 1987, 1997). Populations of large mammals thrive within this complex of protected areas, including the tapir (*Tapirus bairdi*), the giant anteater (*Myrmecophaga tridactyla*), six species of cats —most notably the jaguar (*Panthera onca*)— and three of the four species of monkeys found in Costa Rica: the Central American spider monkey (*Ateles geoffroyi*), the mantled howler monkey (*Alouatta palliata*), and the white-faced capuchin (*Cebus capucinus*).

Nearly 70% of Costa Rica and Panama's bird species inhabit the core zones of the biosphere reserve. As an example, 50% of the high-altitude Costa Rican bird species are found only in the steep ranges of La Amistad, which harbor the largest populations of quetzals (*Pharomachrus mocinno*) in both countries. The national bird of Panama, the harpy eagle (*Harpia harpyja*), a magnificent predator whose highly restricted distribution is a direct consequence of extensive deforestation, is also found here. Furthermore, the reserve is the convergence point for 75% of all migratory birds in the Western Hemisphere.

For millennia, this mountain range has provided a land bridge that, to this day, allows the exchange of North and South American biota (Gómez 1989; Alvarado 1988). Habitats range from lowland rainforests to cloud forests and subalpine meadow/scrub (Andean paramo) at higher altitudes. At lower elevations, the wet and moist tropical forests and premontane wet forests support great biodiversity. The floristic complexity of these forests is evidenced by the large number of species per unit area and the tall and well-formed trees covered with epiphytes, reflecting high temperature, humidity, and rainfall.

More than 80% of all Holdridge life zones in Costa Rica and Panama are found in La Amistad. High-elevation zones include the premontane, lower montane, and montane rainforests. These areas, dominated by oak species (*Quercus* spp.), are the most extensive forest type found in La Amistad, and the largest stands of this type of forest in both countries. The floristically-rich and visually-stunning lower montane wet forest, found only in Las Tablas protected zone in the southwestern sector of the reserve in Costa Rica and in the western sector of La Amistad International Park in Panama, is believed to be the last remaining natural forest stand of its type in either country. The only undisturbed subalpine ecosystems in the region are found at elevations above 3 100 m on the mountain peaks of Durika, Utyum, Kamuk Echandi, and Fabrega. These ecosystems include associations of paramos and swamps.

In 1979 Costa Rica and Panama established their first transboundary cooperation agreement for the purpose of jointly developing investment and assistance projects. Presidential declarations issued both in 1979 and 1982 with reference to the establishment of La Amistad International Park emphasized two important arguments: the need to conserve their joint natural and cultural heritage, and the importance of having a model for peace and friendship between neighboring countries.

Over the years, governmental and non-governmental agencies in both countries have engaged in coordinated efforts to foster joint plans and binational cooperation under the transboundary agreement signed 25 years ago. A binational commission formed by the two ministries of environment coordinates and implements joint terrestrial and aerial patrolling against hunting, illegal poaching, land invasion, and deforestation. It also conducts training activities for staff and seeks to integrate the two recently elaborated management plans into a binational and executive plan.

Equally important are the efforts of development agencies and the non-governmental community at the local and international levels to ensure that binational initiatives are developed. Since the early 1990s, the Organization of American States (OAS) and Conservation International (CI), along with governmental agencies, formulated an institutional development strategy for La Amistad, operational in both countries (OAS/CI 1990, 1994). Based on the strategy's recommendations, international funding was secured over the subsequent years for sustainable development projects in the buffer zones of the two countries and binational exchange of civil society groups. Support came from bilateral European Governmental agencies, NGOs including CI, The Nature Conservancy, the Global Environmental Facility, the United Nations Environmental Program (UNEP), and foundations such as the MacArthur Foundation.

More recently, The Nature Conservancy, CI, and the Critical Ecosystem Partnership Fund (CEPF) jointly promoted binational integration for protection control and implementation of priority actions identified in management plans. CI and the CEPF also provide support to local groups for the development of conservation coffee projects, with a strong component in binational coordination amongst the groups. Other initiatives have supported binational assessments on ecotourism, agro-forestry, and others (USAID through PROARCA).

This region is of great cultural importance, as shown by the numerous archaeological sites discovered within the biosphere reserve, silent testimony to more than 12 000 years of human

history that spans millennia of occupation from the first settlers, who were hunter-gatherers, to the complex, agriculturally-based tribal societies encountered by Europeans in the sixteenth century. To date, research conducted by archaeologists has shown that pre-Columbian societies were once widespread throughout the area that now constitutes La Amistad.

This area also encompasses the ancestral lands of the two largest indigenous groups in Costa Rica: the Bribri and the Cabecar. Their combined population of 26 000 (Guevara 2000) represents nearly two-thirds of the country's total number of indigenous people. Three ethnic groups live in and around the Panamanian side of the biosphere reserve: the Guaymi or Ngobe, the Naso, and the Bribri. Their population is much higher than on the other side, numbering about 75 000 individuals. Through traditional practices of shifting agriculture (corn, beans, plantain, and rice), hunting, fishing, and utilization of forest products, these groups have maintained a relatively sound relationship with their natural environment.

La Amistad is important biologically and economically to these two countries. The high annual rainfall of 2 000-7 000 mm, combined with the short and steep watersheds common to the region, creates both serious flood hazards and a potential for hydroelectric energy production. Half of Costa Rica's freshwater flow originates from catchments in La Amistad and over 25 sites for potential hydroelectric development have been identified within the protected area. In Panama, the land surrounding La Amistad is vital to the country's economy, producing 80% of the country's fruits and vegetables. Several potential hydroelectric development sites have been identified within the Panamanian part of La Amistad as well. The two rivers in Panama with highest hydroelectric potential, the Teribe and the Changuinola, arise in this same area (MIPPE 1992). Currently, both Costa Rica and Panama have major hydroelectric projects inside or adjacent to La Amistad (e.g., the Fortuna dam that produces a significant portion of Panama's energy, and the Cachi dam that produces energy for the Costa Rican economy).

The great potential for hydroelectric production in and around La Amistad has generated much controversy over the years. Many potential sites for dam construction identified by some governmental and private agencies are considered a serious threat to biodiversity conservation. This is particularly true in sites inside of La Amistad International Park and indigenous territories, given that loss of habitat and displacement of indigenous groups are the common consequences of these types of development projects. In Costa Rica, there is strong opposition

for the development of some new sites outside the protected areas (i.e., Pacuare and Boruca dams), and this is also a more tremendously sensitive issue inside protected areas.

The Talamanca region has undergone little development compared with the rest of Costa Rica and Panama. While the majority of land within the core of the Talamanca remains relatively pristine and legally protected, adjacent areas have suffered severe changes from improper land use. Two decades after its declaration, land tenure within La Amistad still represents a source of conflict for the conservation unit. As an example, indigenous territories are progressively losing land to non-indigenous settlers, particularly on the Pacific side of the reserve. Encroachment is severe in the Panama sector of La Amistad International Park, which is not only the major core zone of the complex in that country but also a key part of the Mesoamerican Biological Corridor.

Habitat destruction driven by poverty is the single greatest threat to La Amistad. The region has the lowest socioeconomic standards in either country, suffers from inadequate health care, transportation, and education facilities, and has the highest infant mortality, malnutrition, and illiteracy rates. In the buffer zone surrounding the protected area, and even in its core zone, land is being cleared for cattle ranching and subsistence farms, threatening to overwhelm the social infrastructure and the ecosystems of the region.

The geographic, cultural, and biotic complexity of the Talamanca region requires a broad range of institutional involvement. Full support from national entities, governmental agencies, and international organizations is needed to ensure the success of La Amistad as a transboundary protection area. Only coordinated action between these entities will generate the required level of integrated management and development fundamental to the long-term survival of the biosphere reserve. Finding common ground between these and local landscape users remains a difficult task. Nonetheless, local and regional civil society groups and international agencies now recognize that working together is the only way to achieve desired outcomes. Building strategic alliances, at least within the environmental community, will be the first solid step to a coherent and practical action plan to prevent resource deterioration and enhance protection of the biodiversity wealth of this biosphere reserve. Several of these working alliances are now underway and are coordinating joint actions and projects.

The recognition that conservation of biodiversity and its entire ecosystems is of economic benefit to both countries has

On the opposite page, two male strawberry poison dart frogs (Dendrobates pumilio) wrestling over territory.

Above, a male three-wattled bellbird (Procnias tricarunculata) calling from its display perch. Both photos, © Michael and Patricia Fogden

On pp. 164-165, a rainforest stream flows through La Amistad National Park in Panama. In addition to its many other values, this transboundary region is a major watershed for Costa Rica and Panama. © Dr. Sevcik/SILVESTRIS

created a renewed interest in the coordinated management of the La Amistad ecoregional complex. There is a growing awareness of the binational and regional ecosystem services that the area provides, particularly in terms of the role of conserving forest cover in the upper watersheds of rivers originating in the La Amistad complex to ensure continued water supplies to population centers, hydropower, and other economic activities. Clean air, biodiversity, and scenic beauty values for ecotourism are also beginning to be appreciated, all of which bodes well for the future.

La Amistad is a place of intrinsic beauty and very high biodiversity. Within and around the reserve there are human communities that must reconcile their social and economic aspirations with the integrity of the environment that supports them. Hopefully, the many local, national, and international efforts now underway will help to preserve this area and ensure its long-term survival.

MANUEL RAMÍREZ

VILCABAMBA-AMBORÓ: TRANSBOUNDARY COLLABORATION FROM ANDEAN PEAKS TO THE AMAZON BASIN

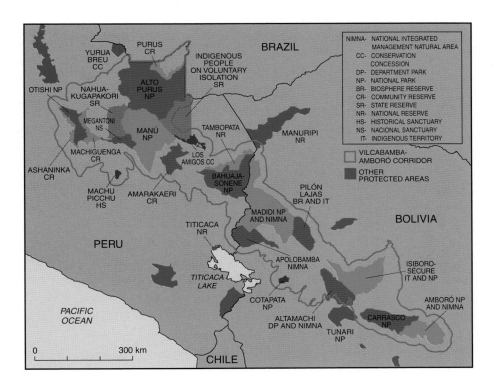

A blue haze hangs in the background, shrouding majestic mountains carpeted in lush vegetation. Their snow-capped peaks rise above the mist and loom over the deep valleys, which drop away towards endless forests on the plains stretching out at their feet. This is the image imprinted on the mind of any first-time traveler to the Tropical Andes. The relief is one of dramatic contrasts brought about by the collision of the great tectonic plates of Nazca and South America. This caused the emergence of the Andes along the South American Pacific coastline during the Tertiary, and formed the planet's second highest mountain range after the Himalayas. This massive range, over 7 000 km long, forms a barrier to the humid winds from the Amazon, which deposit vast quantities of rain on the Andean slopes, making this one of the greatest sources of fresh water on the planet.

The confluence of geographic, climatic, and altitudinal factors, along with the complex morphology of the land, has created a laboratory of evolution in the Andes, generating an extraordinarily high diversity of species and levels of endemism. The area's natural wealth supported the development of important cultures, such as the Incas and Aymara, who inhabited a large part of the Andes in pre-Columbian times. In fact, the last refuge of the Inca Empire before the Spanish Conquest was within the Urubamba basin, which is in the Peruvian part of the Vilcabamba-Amboró Conservation Corridor. The Corridor covers an area of some 300 000 km^2, stretching south to the so-called "elbow" of the Andes in central Bolivia, near the modern city of Santa Cruz de la Sierra, and taking in the Inca fortresses of Samaipata and Sacsayhuaman and the lost city of Machu Picchu. It is a wilderness of vibrant natural beauty, its history colored by the coming and going of peoples who have left their mark along the way. It is also a land of contrasts, from the permanent snows of Ancohuma, at 6 427 m the corridor's highest summit, to the calm waters of the Madre de Dios River, snaking slowly towards the Amazon. In less than 200 km, as the crow flies, water from the snowcaps of the Central Andean peaks drops to a mere 200 m above sea level, before crossing to the east of the continent in majestic rivers, which are up to a kilometer wide. The conservation of the huge Amazon biodiversity needs an ecosystem approach, and ecological corridors are one suitable tool (Suarez de Freitas et al. 2000; Conservation International 2004).

Forests dominate the corridor, but the landscape is marked by steep-sided ridges and valleys, breathtaking glaciers, lakes, rivers, and stretches of savannahs, producing a mosaic of ecosystems. According to the World Wildlife Fund's ecoregion classification (2004), the majority of the corridor comprises Southwest Amazon moist forests, Peruvian *yungas*, and Bolivian *yungas*. The highest parts of the *yungas*, over 3 500 m, comprise mostly thickets and scrublands, but the rest, right down to 400 m, is tropical and sub-tropical moist forest. Particularly spectacular is the cloud forest, with its abundance of ferns, orchids, bromeliads, and other epiphytes. Endemism is high, including many threatened species of birds, such as the southern helmeted curassow (*Crax unicornis*) and Royal Cinclodes (*Cinclodes aricomae*). The *yungas* also support threatened, wide-ranging mammals, such as the spectacled bear (*Tremarctos ornatus*) and the pacarana (*Dinomys branickii*).

Below 400 m the *yungas* give way to the Southwest Amazon moist forests, which occupy much of the northeastern part of the corridor. Here the forest composition is greatly influenced by past and present patterns of flooding, since flooding brings nutrient-laden sediments that enrich the soils. Some areas are dominated by bamboo or, in the swamp forests, palms. Most of this ecoregion, however, consists of tall, dense forest, perhaps rather uniform in appearance, but in reality extraordinarily diverse due to the variety of soils, topography, geology, and climatic history. Flagship species of the region include the giant river otter (*Pteronura brasiliensis*), giant anteaters (*Myrmecophaga tridactyla*), and woolly monkeys (*Lagothrix lagotricha*). The opossums are also of special interest, as this region of the corridor supports the water opossum (*Chironectes minums*), the Aceramarca gracile mouse opossum (*Gracilinanus aceramarcae*), the agile mouse opossum (*G. agilis*), and the entire known range of Anderson's mouse opossum (*Marmosa andersoni*). A new genus, *Cuscomys* (represented by the species *Cuscomys ashanika*), was discovered by Louise Emmons in January 1998, during the Conservation International's Vilcabamba Rapid Assessment Program (RAP) Expedition (Alonso et al. 2001).

A fourth ecoregion, the Beni savannahs, also occurs at the eastern edges of the corridor on the Bolivian side. These flat plains are subdivided by numerous rivers and streams and dotted with lakes, marshes, and forest patches. Seasonal flooding affects most of the savannah and, together with human activities, such as agriculture, livestock grazing, and burning, determines the patterns of vegetation. Endemic to the Beni savannahs is the blue-throated macaw (*Ara glaucogularis*), which is "Critically Endangered." In general, however, the savannah is noted not so much for endemism as for its unique assemblages of wildlife, including the marsh deer (*Blastocerus dichotomus*), the maned wolf (*Chrysocyon brachyurus*) and, in the rivers, the boto river dolphin (*Innia geoffrensis*), the caiman (*Melanosucus niger* and *Caiman yacare*), the giant Amazon river turtle (*Podocnemis expansa*), the anaconda (*Eunectes murinus*), and numerous wetland birds.

In this short description we have named a few, outstanding species, but it is the sheer numbers of species that are so staggering —the mosaic of ecosystems in the Vilcabamba-Amboró corridor is among the richest on the planet. For example, Manu National Park in Peru is home to more than 1 000 species of birds, or 10% of the world's avifauna. Carrasco National Park in Bolivia has more than 600 species of fern, while in the Tambopata National Reserve, which covers a little over 5 km², 1 200 butterfly species have been recorded. The Peruvian *yungas* contain over 3 000 species of plants, including over 200 orchids, while in the southwest Amazon moist forest ecoregion, mentioned above, tree diversity can reach up to 300 species in one hectare. In Upper Madidi, renowned botanist Al Gentry found more than 200 species of tree in one tenth of an hectare (Universidad Nacional Agraria La Molina 1995).

Fortunately, there exists an extensive network of protected areas to ensure the survival of this variety of ecosystems, which covers the full altitudinal range of the eastern slopes of the Andes and the wealth of species they contain. For example, in the part of the conservation corridor that straddles the Peru-Bolivia border, there is a complex of five protected areas (three in Bolivia, two in Peru) that covers 40 000 km². Thus, the central challenge in the Vilcabamba-Amboró Conservation Corridor is to enable its many protected areas to be effectively managed and to promote compatible land uses around them, maximizing connectivity between areas. Of special importance is the maintenance of connectivity across the altitudinal range, as this is critical for the continuation of seasonal migrations, as well as for the survival of biological communities through climate change.

Responding to an analysis of gaps in the protected area network, the Peruvian Government has set out to create a series of new protected areas (Otishi National Park, Alto Purus National Park, Megantoni National Sanctuary) and community reserves

(Amarakaeri, Machiguenga, Ashaninka and Purus) in the 2002-2004 period. The principal outstanding gaps in the network are at higher altitudes, especially in the Peruvian *yungas*. In Bolivia, by contrast, the *yungas* have better protected area coverage.

Indigenous communities are very important partners in the conservation efforts, for their lands contain some of the most biologically valuable forest, both within and outside reserves (GEF/UNDP/UNOPS 1997). Aymara and Quechua people live in the mountainous part of the Corridor, while the Amazonian forests are home to approximately 40 different ethnic groups. Indeed, the cultural diversity of the Corridor matches its biological diversity.

This landscape of priceless biodiversity is the setting for increasingly intensive development, based on both renewable and non-renewable natural resources. In the Conservation Corridor —on both sides of the border— there are major hydrocarbon reserves, especially gas reserves. The Camisea Project, which involves the extraction of gas and its transport through a gas pipeline built right across the Conservation Corridor, has been the subject of much controversy, with Peruvian civil society mobilizing to defend environmental and social values of the area. The project is surely just the first of many, as the two countries seek to utilize their gas reserves. Mining activities, in particular gold mining in the Apolobamba mountain range, have led to the discovery of large primary reserves in the highlands, as well as river-borne minerals in the valleys. The region is also a center for agriculture, in which coca-growing still plays a major role; for the exploitation (often illegal) of timber and other forest products (such as the Brazil nut in Puerto Maldonado); for fishing and tourism, as well as for all the resulting trade. All this economic development has led to a population boom in the Corridor and the border region, which has in turn created a demand for roads, river transport, and air connections. The transport routes are the driving force behind changes in patterns of land use. They are increasingly important in the eyes of local residents and authorities, and are beginning to have geopolitical significance for both countries. Mega-projects for transport infrastructure involving these two countries and Brazil have strong governmental endorsement (Suarez de Freitas et al. 2000).

The patterns of development are changing the landscape and making ever more important the role of protected areas as sanctuaries for biodiversity. Already, 67 species of vertebrate present in the corridor have been classified as "Threatened" on the IUCN *Red List*. Over the course of history, as people have defined their territories, they have subdivided landscapes which would otherwise have provided uninterrupted habitat for large, wide-ranging animals, such as the spectacled bear or *jucumari*, the only South American bear. These open lands would also have allowed natural ecosystems to function unhindered and evolutionary processes to continue. In short, fragmentation and increased human access, associated with infrastructure development, are threatening biodiversity. Ideally, this growing conservation versus development conflict would be addressed by constructing a mosaic of different uses of space and ecosystems in which the needs of local residents and the countries' aspirations for development can be satisfied in a planned manner, without jeopardizing the natural resources and biodiversity which support all these processes. It is with this aim that the Vilcabamba-Amboró Conservation Corridor was created.

Reflecting ecological patterns, the Corridor straddles the Peru-Bolivia border. Thus it is that, over a hundred years after their national territories were defined, the institutions of these two countries are coming together again to conserve the biodiversity of their shared ecosystems. The managing bodies of the five protected areas along the international border meet frequently and draw into the discussions high-ranking authorities, such as mayors, provincial governors, and foreign office representatives. Over the last four years significant progress has been made in harmonizing approaches to protected area management and sustainable land use. Multidisciplinary groups, along with members of local communities, discuss problems, identify opportunities, and propose mutually beneficial solutions.

This cooperation between governments, NGOs, grass roots organizations, local governments, and other actors has spawned a culture of support for sustainable development in the common border areas, with several projects under way or in preparation. Cooperation on biodiversity conservation has also found its way into the official bilateral agenda of the two countries. First, in 1999, a meeting of ministers in Cuzco signed a Letter of Intent to cooperate for the conservation of the Corridor and the cross-border region. This was followed by a participatory process to produce a basic strategy document for the Vilcabamba-Amboró Conservation Corridor. Most recently, in August 2004, bilateral cooperation on biodiversity conservation received high-level

On the opposite page, in spite of its name, the Brazilian tapir (Tapirus terrestris) is found in all of the northern countries of South America. Here one walks along the shore of the upper Rio Madidi in Bolivia's Madidi National Park, with a giant cowbird (Scaphidura oryzivora) perched on its back.
© André Bärtschi

Above, the bizarre hoatzin (Opisthocomus hoazin) is still common in this region, and is often seen perched on waterside vegetation in swamps and oxbow lakes.

On pp. 174-175, a pair of red-bellied macaws (Orthopsittaca manilata) peer out of a nest hole in the lowland rainforest of Peru. Both photos,
© Patricio Robles Gil/Sierra Madre

endorsement, through its explicit inclusion in the Economic Cooperation and Integration Treaty, which was signed by Presidents Carlos D. Mesa of Bolivia and Alejandro Toledo of Peru. The vision of the heads of state thus encompasses the conservation of biodiversity as part and parcel of integration between the two nations.

The conservation challenge is as daunting as the rugged border scenery separating the two countries, but the steps already taken give us an optimistic outlook for the future of biodiversity in this spectacular transboundary corridor. A stable binational coordination of corridor planning and management is already functioning. The idea of creating a huge biosphere reserve —surely the largest so far on the planet— incorporating the five protected areas along the border is even being contemplated. And yet threats still loom over this fascinating area, and it will require the skill of institutions, the political determination of decision-makers, and the hard work of local community members to ensure that this jewel will remain for future generations to enjoy.

EDUARDO FORNO
CARLOS PONCE
ANTONIO TELESCA
LUIS ESPINEL
EDDY MENDOZA
ROBERT BENSTED-SMITH

174

PANTEPUI: THE RORAIMA AND NEBLINA REGIONS OF BRAZIL, VENEZUELA, AND GUYANA

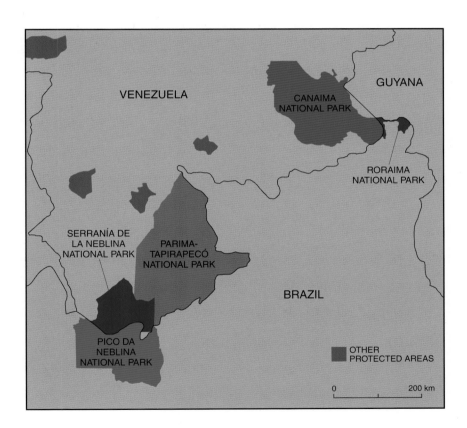

The border area between the countries of Brazil, Venezuela, and Guyana is marked by a rugged landscape with extraordinary, flat-topped sandstone mountains of over 2 000 to 2 500 m, encircled by steep cliff-lined walls of 300 to 1 000 m, locally known as *tepuis*.

Tepuis are the remnants of an ancient pre-Cambrian plateau that eroded away. This region, defined by Mayr and Phelps (1967) as the Pantepui, remains one of the most remote areas of the continent, as well as one of the most pristine.

Geographically, the Pantepui can be subdivided into eastern and western portions (Mayr and Phelps 1967; Maguire 1979). The eastern *tepuis* are found on the "Gran Sabana" area of Venezuela, Guyana, and Brazil. The area is moderately elevated (500 to 1 300 m) and is covered by impoverished savannah vegetation with highly seasonal rainfall. Mount Roraima (2 875 m) deserves special attention for its high elevation and large area, and it forms a natural divide between Brazil, Guyana, and Venezuela.

The western *tepuis* are found in the Amazonian area of Venezuela and Brazil and form a much steeper altitudinal gradient, since the elevation of the adjoining lowland is only 100 to 200 m above sea level. The area is one of the rainiest in South America. The lowland is covered by a dense mosaic of evergreen tropical rainforest, campinas, campinaranas (Prance and Schubart 1978), igapós, and várzea-like forests (Boublie 2002 and in prep). Among the western *tepuis* and sitting on the border between Brazil and Venezuela is Neblina, the highest of all *tepuis* (3 014 m) and also the highest mountain in South America outside of the Andes.

Both Neblina and Roraima have produced a unique set of organisms adapted to the harsh environmental climatic and soil conditions present on their summits. They were once referred to as "lost worlds," as it was imagined that evolution had taken an independent course on their tops (Doyle 1912). We now know that, due to climatic changes (e.g., glacial periods) and alternating orographic erosion processes, there has been an interchange in biotas between the *tepuis'* summits and the surrounding uplands and lowlands (Huber 1995). Because Neblina and Roraima have large plateaus (above 2 500 m), they harbor high numbers of plant species endemic to the Pantepui Province of the Guayana Shield (Brewer-Carías 1988; Gentry 1986; Huber 1995; Steyermark 1986).

Since their first exploration in 1884 (Roraima) and 1952 (Neblina), scientists have described a large number of new animal

and plant species from these two distant Guayanan Mountains (Brown 1901; Tate 1930; Brewer-Carías 1988). Alpha diversity, especially amongst animals, has been considered to be low, but beta diversity, on the other hand, seems to be relatively high due to the existence of a great variety of habitats in a dense mosaic of different landscape types. The most striking feature of the biota, however, is the unique vegetation and associated fauna found above 2 000 m.

The Neblina area probably holds one of the highest levels of biodiversity of the entire Pantepui region, due to its low latitude, high rainfall, and accentuated altitudinal gradient (100 to 3 014 m). Neblina is home to such endangered species as Humboldt's black uakari monkey (*Cacajao melanocephalus melanocephalus*), the giant armadillo (*Priodontes maximus*), the harpy eagle (*Harpia harpyja*), and the cock-of-the-rock (*Rupicola rupicola*), to mention only a few. There are more than 1 500 plant species known from the upper parts of Neblina, including a dozen endemic genera.

In contrast, the flat, rocky, and windswept summit of Mount Roraima —over 2 800 m— harbors fewer than 100 species, most of them endemic to the eastern section of *tepuis*. The frog genus *Oreophrynella* and the small mammal *Rhipidomys macconnelli* are both endemic to the Pantepui, and have now been found on Roraima.

Given the ecological importance of these areas, national parks have already been created by the governments of Brazil and Venezuela —and Guyana is in the process of doing so— forming two large transboundary protected areas in this border area of South America. The Neblina transboundary preservation area consists of one of the largest protected areas in South America with a total of 3 560 000 ha (2 200 000 ha in Brazil and 1 360 000 ha in Venezuela). The Brazilian Pico da Neblina National Park and the Venezuelan Serranía de la Neblina National Park were created in 1979 and 1978, respectively, to protect the Pico da Neblina massif, its endemic flora and fauna, as well as a large area of the surrounding lowlands (Huber 1995).

At present, the Roraima Transboundary Protected Area has a total size of 3 116 000 ha, including Canaima National Park in Venezuela (3 000 000 ha) and Roraima National Park in Brazil (116 000 ha). Guyana is committed to including its section of Mount Roraima in its National Protected Area System as well. Venezuela's Canaima National Park was also declared a World Natural Heritage Site in 1995 by UNESCO, together with Cerro Roraima. Although the boundaries between Guyana and Vene-

zuela were settled through international arbitration in 1897, under the impartial intervention of the U.S., Venezuela subsequently sought to nullify this settlement. Resolution of this issue is currently being addressed at the level of the Secretary General of the United Nations.

A good flagship species for the Pantepui is Humboldt's black uakari monkey. This primate is possibly the only medium-sized mammal restricted to the Neblina transboundary area and is already under threat from over-hunting by the Yanomami Indians, who hunt them with shotguns.

In the case of Mount Roraima, one possible threat is increased trekking tourism to its summit (approx. 3 000 visitors per year), which may harm some local plant and animal communities along the trails on the slopes and the plateau. Access to the summit of Roraima by helicopter-borne tourists from Guyana, Brazil, and Venezuela is unregulated, and the impact of tourists on trails, biodiversity, and the fragile ecosystem of the summit has not been as yet determined. On the other hand, although a large number of tourists have scaled Neblina in the last eight years, experienced and environmentally conscious local guides from São Gabriel da Cachoeira have escorted all groups, thus minimizing impact.

Indigenous peoples have inhabited the areas around Roraima and Neblina since prehistoric times, subsisting on hunting, gathering, and the cultivation of manioc and bananas. In Neblina, however, the present occupants, the Yanomami, are recent arrivals, having settled there in the early 1940s. There are no records of human occupation prior to their arrival, except for a handful of archeological artifacts found by gold miners that suggest an ancient human presence.

The greatest threat to Roraima and Neblina is small-scale mining carried out along the tributaries flowing off these mountains. This activity contaminates waterways with mercury (used in the recovery of gold), dumping of fuel oil, lubricants, and solid waste, and with noise from dredges, generators, and aircraft.

In Neblina, fires set by gold miners have also been a major problem. Until a few years ago, setting fire to vegetation on the summit's tepui vegetation was a common practice by prospecting gold miners. As a result, huge areas on the Neblina Plateau have been wiped out by fire, causing serious damage to the original ecosystem (Boublie 2002). Tourism, as well as mining activities, has produced increasing dependence on a money economy, contributing to a change in their traditional ways of life.

The impacts of the influx of miners and tourists are of concern, but of greater importance is the inadequate level of monitoring and enforcement of compliance regulations. To date, no management plan exists for Neblina or Roraima, and there is an urgent need for the establishment of collaborative management systems on a tripartite basis, involving the governments of Guyana, Brazil, and Venezuela. The core issues that need to be addressed through institutional collaboration include scientific research to establish base-line data; vulnerabilities and negative impacts on biodiversity; the integrity of the ecosystem and the sustainability of the indigenous communities based on traditional use of resources; environmental monitoring and enforcement to deter and to counter those activities which pose a threat to the integrity of the area and its human inhabitants; development of a shared vision for the management of this unique transboundary area; implementation of regulatory mechanisms for tourism and establishing benchmarks for the other economic activities and, finally, a public information and awareness strategy that will ensure public support for the implementation of a transboundary vision in all three countries.

These two South American transboundary areas include some of the world's richest sites in biodiversity and they are fortunately still in very good condition. Hopefully, the future will see increased collaborative efforts to conserve them and to ensure that their wonders will still be there for future generations to behold.

JEAN PHILIPPE BOUBLIE
OTTO HUBER
JOE SINGH

THE BORDERLANDS OF BRAZIL AND THE GUIANAS: THE WORLD'S MOST INTACT TROPICAL RAINFOREST

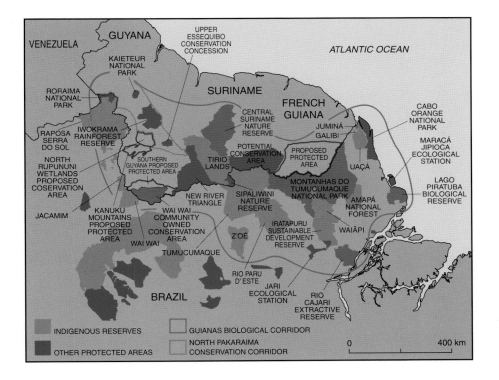

The Guianan Region of South America is one of the world's last great wild places. Occupying roughly the northeastern third of Amazonia, it is noteworthy for its exceptionally pristine state, its unique ecosystems, its levels of endemism, and its cultural diversity. It covers an area of 2 500 000 km², roughly equivalent to the American states of Alaska, Texas, and California combined, or five times the size of France, and accounts for more than 25% of the world's remaining tropical rainforest, yet its human population of only 1.5 to 2 million people or 0.6 to 0.8 people/km² is the lowest population density of any tropical rainforest region on Earth. Not surprisingly, it also has the highest percentage of intact tropical rainforest, with some 80 to 90% still in pristine condition. Indeed, the Guianan Region is one of the few places left on Earth where the opportunity exists to develop strategies for future conservation and sustainable development without having to undo the impacts of previous mistakes. Nonetheless, given the many proposals that now exist for natural resource exploitation in the region, it is urgent that the right path be chosen now, before the same poor decisions made in so many others parts of the world wreak havoc here as well.

This region lies mainly on the Guayana Shield, one of the oldest geological formations on Earth. In biogeographic terms, however, its borders extend beyond the limits of the Shield itself —as far as to the lower Rio Amazonas in the southeast, the Rio Japurá-Caquetá in the southwest, the Serranía de Chiribiquete in Colombian Amazonia in the far west, the Rio Guaviare and the Rio Orinoco to the northwest, and the Atlantic Ocean to the east and northeast. It includes the entire area of the countries of Suriname and Guyana, all of the French Overseas Department of French Guiana, all of Venezuela south of the Rio Orinoco (states of Amazonas, Bolívar, and Delta Amacuro), southeastern Colombian Amazonia between the Guaviare and the Caquetá, and a large portion of northeastern Brazilian Amazonia, including all the states of Amapá and Roraima, and the northern portions of the states of Amazonas and Pará.

The biodiversity of this region is particularly rich, with an estimated 20 000 vascular plant species, of which about 35% (7 000) are endemic, making it one of the three richest tropical wilderness areas on Earth. Avian richness is estimated at 975 species (175 more than all of the U.S. and Canada combined), with 150 endemics and 25 near-endemics; 282 mammals

(27 endemics), 280 reptiles (76 endemics), 272 amphibians (127 endemics), and 2 200 freshwater fish (700 endemics). Amphibians are especially concentrated in some parts of the region. For example, although the Guayana Shield Highlands cover only 17 000 km^2, less than 0.1% of South America, they exhibit a concentration of endemics seven times higher than anywhere else on the continent. Invertebrate diversity remains very poorly known, but certainly numbers in the hundreds of thousands of species. Invertebrate groups for which figures are available include 900 ants (with 300 endemics and 1 500 species expected), 150 termites (with 10 endemics and 225 species expected), 120 earthworms (with 2 000 expected, of which 1 900 are likely to be endemic), 210 dragonflies (with two endemics and 240 species expected), 95 moths with 16 endemics, 70 stingless bees (with 10 endemics and 90 species expected), and 200 social wasps (with 10 endemics and 250 species expected).

The Guianan Region also has a great variety of ecosystems —some found nowhere else on Earth. These include the sandstone *tepuis* or table mountains of the Guayana Highlands, with their highly specialized endemic flora and fauna and their unusual non-gramineous meadows and shrubby and herbaceous communities; the vast expanses of white sand vegetation with a flora highly adapted to low nutrient conditions; large savannahs, extensive coastal swamp forests, riparian flooded forests, and, of course, a wide variety of tropical rainforest systems.

In terms of flagship species, most of the better known large mammals and birds of Amazonia, notably the jaguar (*Panthera onca*), the giant otter (*Pteronura brasiliensis*), the giant armadillo (*Priodontes maximus*), and a host of monkey species, are common here and are far less threatened than anywhere else in their ranges. Perhaps the best flagship for this region is the blue poison dart frog (*Dendrobates azureus*), a species restricted to a few isolated mountains in the Sipaliwini Savannah of extreme southern Suriname, right on the Brazilian border. In spite of the remoteness and tiny extent of its range, this beautiful little blue and black frog is well known, is exhibited in many zoos, and is frequently depicted in publications, toys, and other paraphernalia sold in gift shops dealing with natural history.

The Guianan region is also extremely important in terms of global and regional ecosystem services. It includes major portions of the Amazon, the largest river system on Earth, the Orinoco, which is the third largest, and also a series of important watersheds in the Guianas. The Amazon is so large that several of its major tributaries themselves (e.g., the Rio Negro, almost entirely contained within the Guianan Region) rank among the world's largest rivers. Indeed, this region accounts for as much as 10 to 15% of the world's freshwater, and has the largest number of pristine or near-pristine river basins left on Earth. There are immense stocks of carbon in the living biomass of the forest, accounting for about a quarter of the total carbon pool in tropical forests. Its importance to global climate is difficult to assess, but there would undoubtedly be significant impacts if much of this forest, which generates 50% of its own rainfall, were to be destroyed.

The Guianan Region provides many opportunities to develop conservation initiatives at a scale that is no longer possible in Tropical Asia or Africa, and is rapidly becoming difficult elsewhere in South America. One example of an important transboundary area is the Pantepui region, also described in this book. In this chapter, we focus on another portion of this vast region —what we refer to as the Brazil-Guianas Borderlands, where the three Guianas (Guyana, Suriname, and French Guiana) meet northern Brazil. This borderland area is the most pristine portion of the entire Guianan Region, is actively engaged in the creation of globally significant protected areas at a national level, and offers many opportunities for transboundary conservation. Much of this region is entirely pristine or is sparsely populated by Amerindian tribes living in villages that rarely exceed 1 000 individuals, and by some 50 000 people of African origin known as Bushnegros or Maroons (mainly in Suriname but also extending into French Guiana). In all, only about 20 000 people live in this area of at least 25 to 30 million ha, more than half the size of France or two-thirds of California.

The Brazil-Guianas Borderlands have long been protected by their remoteness and low population density, and until recently had only a handful of formal protected areas. Beginning in the early 1990s, however, and partly in response to threats from Asian loggers in Suriname and gold mining in many parts of the region, more attention began to be focused on protective measures. Suriname, which was already the most advanced in protected area coverage dating back to the 1960s (Mittermeier et al. 1990), took the first major modern step in 1998, creating the 1.6 million-ha Central Suriname Nature Reserve. These globally important areas joined and dramatically expanded three smaller interior reserves, protected the entire middle and upper drainage of the Coppename River, supplemented the 100 000-ha Sipaliwini Nature Reserve on the Brazilian border, and brought protected area coverage for Suriname to 14%.

This was followed by Brazil's 2002 establishment of the 3 867 000-ha Montanhas do Tumucumaque National Park in the state of Amapá, creating the largest rainforest protected area on Earth. Since then, the Governor of Amapá has been actively engaged in creating a series of corridors linking other protected areas in his state and covering a total of 9 485 536 ha, or 66% of the state's land area —an unprecedented commitment. Montanhas do Tumucumaque National Park is immediately adjacent to the 3 071 067-ha Tumucumaque Indigenous Reserve in northern Pará State, bringing the Brazilian portion of these borderlands to an incredible 12 556 603 ha —an area slightly smaller than the state of New York.

At the request of the Wai Wai community of Masakenyari in southern Guyana, Guyana began shortly thereafter to take steps to establish a 600 000-ha community-owned conservation area. In less than two years, the government of Guyana bestowed an Absolute Grant of ownership of the area (the Kanashen District) to the Wai Wai community. The Wai Wai, through the government of Guyana, requested Conservation International's (CI) assistance in developing their capacity to manage their lands sustainably and to integrate them into Guyana's new National Protected Area System. In 2004, the Government, the Wai Wai, and Conservation International-Guyana signed a Memorandum of Cooperation, providing a framework for the delivery of the assistance requested. It is hoped that an agreement will be reached so that the Wai Wai Owned Conservation Area may be expanded eastwards and northwards to the proposed Kanuku Mountains Protected Area, to the north Rupununi Wetlands proposed Ramsar Site, and to the existing 371 000-ha Iwokrama Project, to achieve a total area of nearly 4 million ha in Guyana.

The effective partnership between CI and the government of Suriname is a solid basis for considering ways to connect the Central Suriname and Sipaliwini Nature Reserves and to extend them eastward and adjacent to the Montanhas do Tumucumaque National Park in Brazil, including another 1 to 2 million ha of protected land. Additionally, the Trio (or Tareno) Indians, whose territory straddles the Suriname-Brazil border, could par-

ticipate on the basis of their traditional land-use in an area of nearly 4 million ha on the Suriname side, supplementing the portion of their territory covered in the above-mentioned Tumucumaque Indigenous Reserve in Brazil.

Lastly, French Guiana has had ambitious plans for over a decade to create the Parc National Forestiere in the southern part of this Overseas Department, but this has not yet materialized for a variety of reasons.

These areas are depicted in the map accompanying this chapter, which also includes a number of other areas in Brazil that connect with or come very close to the borderland reserves and parks.

In addition to these efforts to create and link protected areas, CI and the World Wildlife Fund (WWF) have had active programs in Guyana and Suriname dealing with many other issues. WWF works in French Guyana as well, and both organizations, together with a wide range of Brazilian partners, have also been involved in a major way on the Brazilian side of the borders.

One excellent example of international collaboration was The Guyana Shield Conservation Priority-Setting Workshop held in Paramaribo in April 2002. Organized by CI, IUCN-Netherlands, and the United Nations Development Program (UNDP), this exercise brought together more than 100 of the world's leading experts on the region's biodiversity, supplemented by a group of specialists on the socioeconomic dimensions of this part of the world. The workshop highlighted the global importance of the biodiversity of the Guyana Shield, and produced both a unified vision and a series of recommendations for its conservation.

In terms of threats, the factors that have greatly reduced or eliminated tropical forests around the globe are now reaching the Guianan Region as well. Unsustainable logging, poor mining practices, and hydroelectric projects have already impacted significant areas, and could increase dramatically in the next few years. Monoculture agriculture (e.g., oil palm, soybeans) is now starting to make inroads as well, though still at a small scale. Bushmeat hunting and wildlife trade are also threats, although, if sustainably managed, could provide an alternative use of the forests.

The countries of the Guianan Region have a unique opportunity to learn from the experiences and mistakes elsewhere in the world, to define a new development path that takes

Above, Trio Indian child from Kwamalasemutu village with a pet black spider monkey (Ateles paniscus). Kwamalasemutu is located in extreme southern Suriname near the Brazil border, and is the largest village in this part of the borderlands.
© Mark J. Plotkin

On pp. 186-187, the interior of a tropical rainforest in Suriname. Huge old lianas, like the one seen here, are a good indicator that this forest has never been logged.
© Russell A. Mittermeier

Above, the attractive rainbow boa (Epicrates cenchria) is a common and widespread species in the Guianas, and is sought after for the pet trade.

On the opposite page, the Potaro River flowing through pristine rainforest below Kaieteur Falls, Guyana. Both photos,
© Russell A. Mittermeier

advantage of their unique position, and to engage in truly sustainable activities that improve livelihoods while maintaining healthy, functioning ecosystems. One opportunity has been created by the unresolved border disputes of the region. For example, the New River Triangle area is claimed by both Suriname and Guyana, but is used almost exclusively by the very small indigenous populations of the region and is still entirely intact and largely pristine. By engaging one another in the establishment of a formal transboundary conservation area, this controversy could perhaps be resolved to the benefit of all concerned.

Fortunately, the importance of the Brazil-Guianas Borderlands is beginning to be recognized by the international community as a very high global priority. This has already resulted in technical support and the beginnings of serious financial support as well. One example is the creation of the Suriname Conservation Foundation (a trust fund) that was started with a gift of $1 million from CI in 1998 and has now been fully capitalized at $15 million. This has included funds from the Global Environment Facility (GEF)/United Nations Development Program (UNDP) ($7.9 million), the Dutch Government ($3.6 million in a sinking fund running parallel to the endowment), $1.5 million from the United Nations Foundation (including $500 000 from CI), and a further $1 million from CI (Huber and Foster 2003).

Another example is the Iwokrama Project in Guyana, which was created in 1993 to demonstrate that a tropical rainforest could be conserved while simultaneously contributing to local and national economic development. This program has received more than $11 million of international support to date.

Yet another example is the 80 000-ha Upper Essequibo Conservation Concession, only the second such concession in the world and another initiative of CI, this time with the government of Guyana. Although relatively small, it is quite significant in terms of its political and socioeconomic impact within Guyana, where the government has integrated conservation concessions into its national forest policy and has plans to market them as a tool for conservation and income-generation.

The biodiversity resources and ecological services of this transboundary region represent an enormous competitive advantage to its people, especially as such intact resources become an ever scarcer global commodity. In the past, tropical forests were perceived as economically beneficial only if they were unsustainably logged, mined, or converted to agriculture or pasture. There is now a need to reach consensus on a vision to ensure the sustainable use of this area through activities like ecotourism, generation of non-timber forest products, sustainable fisheries, research, training, conservation concessions, creation of long-term funding mechanisms (e.g., trust funds), and traditional protection activities (e.g., park management, guard training, enforcement) —all of which should result in a flow of benefits commensurate with real needs and at least an order of magnitude beyond what has been provided in the past.

Although all four countries in this borderland region have made great strides, much more needs to be done to ensure that this vision becomes a reality. We believe that the time is now ripe to look beyond the borders of the individual nations involved and engage in a series of transboundary initiatives that would surely increase funding and technical assistance, to resolve existing border disputes, and to demonstrate to the global community the unique qualities of this very special part of the world. If this can be achieved, and we have every hope that it can, then it is likely that the Brazil-Guianas Borderlands will continue to be the world's most intact tropical rainforest region for a long time to come.

RUSSELL A. MITTERMEIER
JOE SINGH
JOSE MARIA CARDOSO DA SILVA
WIM UDENOUT
LISA FAMOLARE

IGUAÇU-IGUAZÚ: ONE OF THE WORLD'S GREATEST NATURAL WONDERS

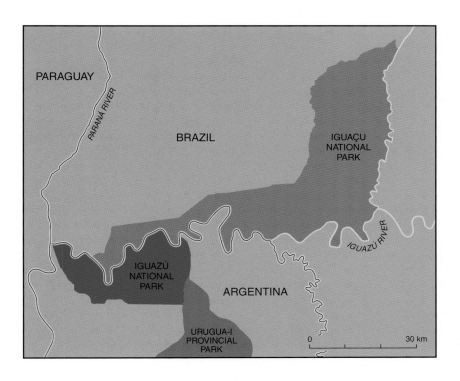

One of the world's greatest natural wonders and one of the two most impressive series of waterfalls on Earth is found at the border between Brazil and Argentina. There, separated by this border, along the final stretch of the Iguaçu River, where it joins the Paraná River, are the adjoining national parks of Iguazú on the Argentinian side and Iguaçu in Brazil. Most of the region presents an even, slightly undulating relief, covered almost exclusively by semi-deciduous forests and, to a lesser extent, by transitional *Araucaria* forests. The area represents a large forest fragment, surrounded by widespread agricultural areas (mostly soybean) and extensive cattle raising, forming a mosaic of land uses, and is one of the best known and most important tourist attractions on the South American continent, with over 1.5 million visitors a year.

Both national parks (declared World Heritage Sites by UNESCO in 1985) resulted from the first attempts to establish protected areas in Argentina and Brazil. Created in 1934 and 1939, respectively, their main objective was to protect the scenic potential of the binational Iguaçu Falls (Cataratas do Iguaçu). Based on available biological inventories, compiled mostly through the Argentinian territory (Chebez 1995), it is clear that the two protected areas hold vast species-richness, although only a small portion of the local flora and fauna has been adequately studied or researched. The avifauna presents close to 350 species (Seibene et al. 1996; Straube and Urben-Filho 2004; Straube et al. 2004), including the harpy eagle (*Harpia harpyja*), the Guiana crested eagle (*Morphnus guianensis*), the orange-breasted falcon (*Falco deiroleucus*), the Brazilian merganser (*Mergus octosetaceus*), the black-fronted piping-guan (*Aburria jacutinga*), the fasciated tiger heron (*Tigrisoma fasciatum*), the purple-winged ground dove (*Claravis godefrida*), the silky-tailed nightjar (*Caprimulgus sericocaudatus*), the helmeted woodpecker (*Dryocopus galeatus*), the russet-winged spadebill (*Platyrinchus leucoryphus*), and the strange-tailed tyrant (*Alectrurus risorius*). About 100 species of mammals are estimated to inhabit the protected areas, and some of the larger ones are already rare in the southernmost portion of their distribution, such as the jaguar (*Panthera onca*), the tapir (*Tapirus terrestris*), the howler monkey (*Alouatta guariba*), the giant river otter (*Pteronura braziliensis*), and the bush dog (*Speotthos venaticus*), in addition to other less known species like the thick-tailed opossum (*Lutreolina crassicaudata*), the Ipanema fruit bat (*Pygoderma bilabiatum*), and the spiny rice rat (*Abrawayaomys ruschii*). Over 40 species of reptiles have been confirmed

On p. 190, great dusky swifts
(Cypseloides senex) *cluster
in the mist on the Argentine side
of Iguazú Falls.*
© Günter Ziesler

192

to occur in the region, including William's South American side-necked turtle (*Phrynops williamsi*), a species of international interest for conservation, and the broad-snouted caiman (*Caiman latirostris*), which deserves special attention due to the high hunting pressure it suffers locally. Other taxa, like the South American opisthoglyph snake *Clelia plumbea* and the iguanid lizard *Urostrophus vautieri*, which are significant indicators of pristine habitats, are also found in both parks. The icthyofauna is also noteworthy with high levels of endemism, mostly due to the degree of biogeographic isolation created by the Iguaçu Falls.

The Argentine and Brazilian Iguazú-Iguaçu Parks are part of the most important forest transboundary conservation area (TCBA) in the southern cone of South America. Together they cover almost 253 000 ha (respectively ca. 67 000 and 185 000 ha) and form a large network of protected areas that covers over 690 000 ha, including the Itaipu Binational Biological Reserve on the margins of the Paraná River in Brazil and Paraguay (40 000 ha), regional conservation units in Misiones, Argentina (400 000 ha), and state and private protected areas in Paraná State, Brazil (500 ha), vastly increasing the potential for conservation of the regional biota.

The level of species-richness of the better-studied groups indicates the biological relevance for conservation of these seasonal forests of central-southern Brazil. A total of 83 species endemic to the Atlantic Forest can be found in the two parks, representing over 40% of the endemism of this biome. In addition, the parks are home to 105 species of high conservation interest, including 21 listed by the IUCN and 35 by Birdlife International, while the remaining, such as the Brazilian merganser, the fasciated tiger heron, the purple-winged ground dove, the vinaceous parrot (*Amazona vinacea*), and the strange-tailed tyrant make up the "Threatened" species list of both countries.

The two parks contribute significantly to the economy, mostly through the tourism generated in both countries. Although the areas open to the public are small, they are well organized and have high-quality infrastructure. Visitors from all over the world come to the parks, attracted by the unique scenery of the falls, the first-class accommodations, the interest in conventional ecotourism, and the excellent bird-watching opportunities. The TBCA is the main source of financial resources, both from tourism and from public subsidies, in the form of "ecological royalties," particularly for the municipalities where the attractions are located.

Threats to these protected areas reflect ongoing conservation challenges in southern Brazil and neighboring countries.

Although the parks' borders are not under pressure from real estate ventures, they are affected by obvious and frequent incursions by locals, mostly to hunt and collect native plants, especially heart of palm (*Euterpe edulis*). In an expedition conducted in March 2004 to monitor the Brazilian park, 26 hunting camps and three heart of palm harvesting sites were detected (Straube and D'Amico 2005). Hunting devices, such as traps and other destructive equipment, and a substantial number of recently killed animals, including pacas (*Agouti paca*), red brocket deer (*Mazama americana*), Azara's agoutis (*Dasyprocta azarae*), fasciated tiger herons, red-breasted toucans (*Ramphastos dicolorus*), and a variety of fish, were also encountered. On occasion, residents of local communities conduct excursions to hunt big cats, especially jaguar and puma (*Puma concolor*), both inside the parks and in the surrounding areas, alleging attacks on their cattle and sheep.

A relevant and ongoing threat is the Estrada do Colono, an unpaved 16-km road that cuts through the center of Iguaçu National Park in Brazil. This road once connected the towns of Serranópolis do Iguaçu and Capanema, but since the 1980s it has been frequently closed and reinstated, due to legal disputes that place national interests at odds with local social interests, with the local population claiming the right to use the road (Bergallo and Conde 2001; Rodrigues 2003). Similarly, the highly-politicized agrarian reform "Landless Movement" (Movimento Sem-Terra) chose this southern region of Brazil as a principal theater of action, creating social instability around the parks.

In addition, a Federal highway, BR-277, which borders a significant portion of the Brazilian park, has clearly had a strong negative impact on the region, causing innumerable road kills near the park (Cândido-Jr. et al. 2002). Accidents caused by animals and road kills are also frequent, both on the highway around the park and on the smaller access roads inside the protected area, and are the source of great concern for administrators of both parks, although little has been done to minimize such occurrences.

Another conservation issue relates to invasive species, including the Cape hare (*Lepus capensis*), the house mouse (*Mus musculus*), the black rat (*Rattus rattus*), and particularly the European bee (*Apis mellifera*), which is already completely adapted to the region and occurs widely and in large populations. Feral cats and dogs occasionally raid the forest as well, causing severe impacts on populations of small and medium-sized animals.

*On the opposite page,
a toco toucan
(Ramphastos toco),
largest of the toucan species.
© Staffan Widstrand*

*Above, a coati (Nasua nasua)
on the Argentine side of
the falls. This species has
become well-habituated,
along most tourist paths
in the region.*

*On pp. 196-197,
butterflies of several different
species seeking nutrients along
a river bank in Iguazú
National Park, Argentina.
Both photos, © Günter Ziesler*

To address these threats, a number of priority conservation measures are needed, including education, monitoring, and research. It is critical to expand the existing environmental education activities inside and around the parks, generating greater involvement of local communities in conservation actions. Similarly, the need to conduct more wildlife research is clear, especially biological inventories and a focus on more specific research to strengthen management plans. Particular attention should be given to the primitive zone (protected from any human intervention) of Iguaçu National Park, located in the Rio Floriano basin, where preliminary assessments show unprecedented levels of species diversity for southern Brazil, especially for birds, mammals, and plants (e.g., stenoic/restricted range plants of the Podostemaceae family). This virtually unknown area could potentially be a baseline reference for the study of environmental issues in the region (Straube and D'Amico 2005). Studies on the transitional *Araucaria* forest are needed to improve the knowledge of this forest type.

If existing management programs can be strengthened through actions such as the permanent closure of the Estrada do Colono road, a program to restore original vegetation, and activities to monitor and protect key species living in the region, it is likely that this globally significant natural wonder will be maintained intact for future generations.

FERNANDO C. STRAUBE
ALBERTO URBEN-FILHO

EUROPE

THE PYRENEES-MOUNT PERDU: A SHARED GEM ON THE FRENCH-SPANISH BORDER

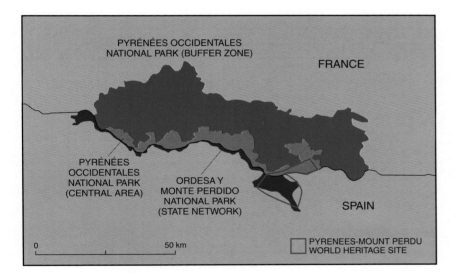

Adjoining each other on the border between Spain and France in the Central Pyrenees mountains are two national parks, the Parque Nacional de Ordesa y Monte Perdido (15 608 ha), originally established by Spain in 1918, and the Parc National des Pyrénées Occidentales (45 705 ha), established by France in 1967. The core zones of these parks, as well as some buffer zones in each country, constitute the Pyrenees-Mount Perdu World Heritage Site (31 189 ha), listed in 1997. Of great significance is that the area is listed on both natural and cultural criteria, making it one of only 23 sites worldwide that enjoy this distinction. Included among the qualities that were recognized as being of outstanding universal significance to humanity are the calcareous massif of Mount Perdu, which displays classic geological land forms, including deep canyons and spectacular walls; the outstanding landscape with its meadows, lakes, caves, and forests on mountain slopes; and the exceptional cultural landscape which combines scenic beauty with a socioeconomic tradition that illustrates a rare mountain way of life. At the time of its inscription, the World Heritage Committee also noted the "beauty of the spirit of *entente cordiale*" which exists between the communities on either side of the border. In Spain, the park, together with the Viñamala National Hunting Reserve, was recognized by UNESCO as the Ordesa-Viñamala Biosphere Reserve (51 396 ha) in 1977, while in France the area is extended by the Gavarnie, Troumouse, and Estaubé *Site Classé* (Classified Reserve).

From a landscape point of view, the limestone massif is centered on Mount Perdu (3 352 m) and includes about 20 km of the Pyrenean mountain range, part of the 400-km range stretching from the Mediterranean Sea to the Cantabric Sea. It has spectacular lakes, waterfalls, rocky outcrops, glacial cirques, and canyons. The World Heritage inscription refers to its superlative natural phenomena and exceptional beauty. The mountain peaks, cliffs and valleys, with their roaring waterfalls and lush forests, are visually emphasized by the frequent violent storms and rain. This natural beauty was perhaps aptly captured by the naturalist and writer Ramond, who in 1802 described the "simple solemn shapes, these bold clear-cut sections, these rocks, so unyielding and so untouched whose wide foundations align themselves barrier-like, forming semicircles, of tier-like amphitheatres thrusting upwards like towers which giants seem to have erected as straight as a die," and Victor Hugo, who called them "Nature's colossus" (de Bellefon 2002).

The diversity of landscape and biodiversity is a product of climate and topography, as the area straddles two major climatic

On p. 198, three snow-covered peaks, Monte Perdido, Cilindro, and Soum de Ramond, in Ordesa y Monte Perdido National Park, Spain.

On p. 200, the Cascada de la Cueva in the Valle de Ordesa of Spain's Ordesa y Monte Perdido National Park, one of the most important protected areas in the Pyrenees.

On the opposite page, the Cañón de Añisclo is the habitat of the lammergeier (Gypaetus barbatus), one of the region's most important flagship species. Aragón, Spain.
All photos, © Francisco Márquez

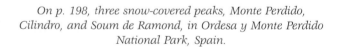

regimes, namely the oceanic climate to the north and a continental sub-Mediterranean climate to the south. Temperatures average –1°C in winter, rising to 12°C in summer, whereas rainfall varies from 900 mm to 2 000 mm, with an annual mean of 1 600 mm.

The peaks are the result of limestone deposition in a vast sea, and subsequent folding about 50 million years ago that formed the current Pyrenees. Glaciation during the Quaternary molded this landscape. Today, the remnant glaciers are protected due to their fragility and scarcity, and especially because of their rapid retreat in the past 100 years. During the last glacial period, many species that occurred in the area become extinct, including furry rhinoceros, lions and even the marmot (*Marmota marmota*). Other species, such as the alpine ptarmigan (*Lagopus mutus pyrenaicus*) dispersed, while still others, such as the Pyrenean ibex (*Capra hispanica pyrenaica*), found a refuge in these mountains.

The vegetation is characterized by five main types, namely sub-Mediterranean, collinean, montane, subalpine, and alpine (IUCN 2000). In the south the sub-Mediterranean type is dominated by oaks (*Quercus ilex* and *Q. rotundifolia*) in rocky sites, and *Q. faginea* on deep soils, while the collinean vegetation is dominated by the durmast oak (*Q. sessiliflora*). The montane areas support beech (*Fagus sylvatica*), silver fir (*Abies alba*), and Scotch pine (*Pinus sylvestris*) forests, and this is where the endemic "oreja de oso" or bear's ear (*Ramonda myconi*) is found. The subalpine vegetation is dominated by black mountain pine (*Pinus uncinata*), (*Vicia argentea*, R), and the endemic "Dioscorée des Pyrénées" (*Borderea pyrenaica*). The alpine area contains a high proportion of species endemic to the Pyrenees, including *Saxifraga iratiana* and *Androsace pyrenaica* (AMPPM 1995). The flora includes more than 1 500 species, of which 50 are Pyrenean endemics (Spain-France 1997).

Similarly, the area supports a diverse fauna. A flagship species is the bearded vulture or lammergeier (*Gypaetus barbatus*), which prospered in the area because of the widespread pastoralism practiced in the past, but which, as a result of changes in land use, is in decline throughout most of its European range unless supported by artificial feeding. Another Pyrenean flagship species was the Pyrenean ibex, which used to roam freely on these peaks, but which is now extinct as a result of uncontrolled hunting beginning in the middle of the nineteenth century. Competition with the abundant Pyrenean sheep did not make things any easier. Reduced to critically low numbers, the last individual died in January 2000. A similar fate may befall the brown bear (*Ursus arctos pyrenaicus*), as there are currently

very few bears left in the Pyrenees, almost all of which are restricted to the dark forests of Valle D'Ossau on the French slope, or in the valleys of Hecho, Ansó, and Roncal on the Spanish slope.

Other mammals found in the area include the Western roe deer (*Capreolus capreolus*) and the Pyrenean chamois (*Rupicapra pyrenaica*), and the insectivorous Pyrenean desman (*Galemys pyrenaicus*), which occurs at lowland elevations. The avifauna includes Bonelli's eagles (*Hieraetus fasciatus*), rock ptarmigans (*Lagopus mutus*), hazel grouses (*Bonasa bonasia*), capercaillies (*Tetrao urogallus*), yellow-billed choughs (*Pyrrhocorax graculus*), marsh tits (*Parus palustris*), tree creepers (*Certhia familiaris*), wall creepers (*Tichodroma muraria*), wheatears (*Oenanthe oenanthe*), black redstarts (*Phoenicurus ochrurus*), alpine accentors (*Prunella collaris*), water pipits (*Anthus spinoletta spinoletta*), and white-winged snowfinches (*Montifringilla nivalis*). Reptiles include the montane lizard (*Archaeolacerta bonnali*), restricted to higher elevations, while among the amphibians, species of interest include *Euproctus asper*, a brown frog that lives in mountain torrents right up to the subalpine zone, and the Pyrenean stream frog (*Rana pyrenaica*). Other noteworthy fauna include cave-dwelling species of insects, such as a collembolan (*Tricanthella frigida*), an endemic found in the Gavarnie Cirque at 2 500 m, and the coleopterans *Tipnus unicolor* and *Speonomus bolivari* (AMPPM 1995).

Species that survive the harsh winters are very characteristic, including the alpine ptarmigan which, with its white winter plumage, blends into the snow, as does the ermine (*Mustela erminea*) which, although usually nervous and jumpy, goes unnoticed in the snow. Marmots, on the other hand, are very evident. Re-established in the French portion from source populations in the Alps and the Carpathians, they have been highly successful opportunistic invaders.

Human occupation has been evident since the Palaeolithic (40 000-10 000 BC), and even now the strikingly similar human-made terraces indicate close ties among the peoples on either side of the current international border, symbolizing the long-standing occupation of the area. Humans occupied land from the mountains and transformed the forests and the grasslands. They cut forests and ploughed the land even in the most remote areas. This led to a seasonal migration of herders from one side of the Pyrenees to the other in search of seasonal grazing, necessitating the traverse of a most inhospitable landscape. Humans made their mark on the landscape by opening up paths and passes, building bridges, terraces, and other structures. Grazing by cattle and sheep had its impact on habitats and biodiversity. Overall

On the opposite page, the chamois (Rupicapra rupicapra)*, another well-known Pyrenees flagship species, seen here in Ordesa y Monte Perdido National Park.*
© Patricio Robles Gil/Sierra Madre

Above, one of the most important populations of griffon vulture (Gyps fulvus) *is found in the Pyrenees.*

On pp. 206-207, a lammergeier (Gypaetus barbatus) *surveying its domain. The Spanish name for this striking bird —"quebrantahuesos" (bone-breaker)— refers to its habit of dropping bones onto rock to break them open and obtain the rich marrow inside. Both photos,*
© Francisco Márquez

the knowledge of the mountains and their resources were passed from generation to generation, enabling the spatial and seasonal exploitation of the diverse landscape, elements of which persist to this day. The shared history created a unique cultural landscape, supported by a number of transboundary agreements over the timing and nature of resource use. For centuries, the people living in these mountains have had bonds and exchanges united by a community of interests, with little sharing or contact with the surrounding lowlands. These bonds and agreements, intended to maintain peaceful relationships among the mountain communities, are still relevant today, and form the basis for the wider transboundary relationship between Spain and France. A Cooperation Charter between France and Spain was signed in September 1988.

The landscapes of the area "speak of this magnificent and ancient alliance between man and his mountain; passes, lanes, hospices, refuges, sheds, low walls... this site as a whole mirrors the way of life that used to be widespread in European mountain areas, but here it is remarkable for the perfection of its development" (de Bellefon 2002).

It is not surprising that the wilderness character endures and is a major attraction for visitors to the region. In addition, there are local NGOs that maintain a high level of interest in the region and in promoting its significance and values. The Mont Perdu Patrimoine Mondial Association (AMPPM) is one of these, set up initially to promote the listing of the area as a World Heritage Site, but which maintains ongoing activities to ensure that the area is managed properly and to promote local development without compromising the integrity of the site. In addition, it has taken on the role of promoting public awareness of the area. Building on the transboundary linkage, the chairmanship of the AMPPM alternates between the mayors of French and Spanish villages associated with the site. With this active local support and with high level involvement of the two countries in terms of their cooperation charter, there is every reason to indicate that the future of the area lies in capable hands, and that the threats that resulted in the extinction of the Pyrenean ibex will not also result in the loss of other vulnerable species in the region.

RICARDO VILA
TREVOR SANDWITH

THE EUROPEAN GREENBELT: FROM VISION TO REALITY

One of the most important political barriers to affect Europe in the last half of the twentieth century was the Iron Curtain, which ran for approximately 6 800 km between Finland and Russia, through Germany and into South Eastern European countries, spanning some of the continent's most impressive and fragile landscapes. The Iron Curtain's presence was strongest on the Eastern side of the barrier and created a "forbidden zone" where no activity was allowed. The only positive result of this separation was that nature was given a 40-year respite from the intensive agricultural and development practices that were taking place almost everywhere else. Today this border region contains many of Europe's endangered species and important habitats and has been named the "European Greenbelt." It is also a region that is extremely important to the livelihoods of many rural communities.

The European Greenbelt will become an important component of a pan-European ecological network, with the many protected areas that are located along its route as its core zone. Although this core zone contains some of the last wilderness areas in Europe, these do not exist in isolation and are surrounded by landscapes that are also important for biodiversity. By linking these areas, it is hoped that plant and animal species will have a biological corridor for migration and dispersal. The grand vision is for the Greenbelt to become not so much a thin strip running through Europe, but a "backbone" to which surrounding areas will be connected.

The area covered by the Greenbelt is extensive; it incorporates most of Europe's distinct biogeographical regions and much of its biodiversity. The Greenbelt also provides a history of the relationship between humans and the managed agricultural and forested landscapes in which they have lived. It is perhaps easiest to survey the remarkable biodiversity of the Greenbelt by looking at the different regions in turn.

In the Scandinavian region between Norway, Finland, and Russia, some of Europe's few wilderness areas still remain, containing important examples of old growth forest and mire habitats. The Greenbelt runs through the western limits of the boreal taiga forest types and is home to many of the species that are dependent on this forest, including birds, such as great grey owls (*Strix nebulosa*), Siberian jays (*Perisoreus infaustus*) and three-toed woodpeckers (*Picoides tridactylus*), and also a number of Europe's threatened mammal species, including wolves (*Canus lupus*), wolverines (*Gulo gulo*), and brown bears (*Ursus arctos*). The region is important for its bogs and mires, which have not

*On p. 208, old growth forest near
Lusen Mountain in Germany's Bayerischer
Wald National Park, part of
the European Greenbelt.*
© Norbert Rosing

*In the Scandinavian region between
Norway, Finland, and Russia,
lie some of Europe's few remaining
wilderness areas, containing important
examples of old growth forest, like this
one in Posio, Finland.*
© Hannu Hautala/FLPA

been modified over time, and still harbors rare species of plant and lichen.

The Greenbelt then moves along the Baltic Sea coast, which is rich in valuable habitats and constitutes a very important region for migrating birds. As it advances into Western Europe through Germany, it passes through the most strongly guarded border region —the former Iron Curtain between East and West Germany. Here the strip of land forbidden to humans is clearly visible in the surrounding landscape. Further south at the heart of the Greenbelt lie the neighboring regions of Sumava National Park (Czech Republic) and the Bavarian Forest National Park (Germany), which are predominantly forested and home to the European lynx (*Felis lynx*). As the Belt continues between Austria, the Czech Republic, and Slovakia, it moves into a region rich in biodiversity and with a long history of transboundary cooperation for nature protection. Here Thayatal National Park (Austria) borders Podyji National Park (Czech Republic), surrounding the Dyje River Valley. This area is the meeting point between two continental climatic systems and contains a diversity of geomorphologic features, which combined create a species-rich area, with almost 3 000 species of plants. Animal species such as the great crested newt (*Triturus cristatus*), the smooth snake (*Coronella austriaca*), the black stork (*Ciconia nigra*), the white-tailed eagle (*Haliaeetus albicilla*), and the otter (*Lutra lutra*) are all found here.

At the border between Hungary and Austria lies the transboundary protected area, biosphere reserve, and World Heritage Site of Fertő-Hanság (Hungary) and Neusiedler-See (Austria) national parks. These national parks, which surround the shallow lake Fertő (Neusiedler-See) and its extensive reed beds, also contain important Pannonian *puszta* (meadows), which are used as grazing ground in part by Hungarian gray cows, a now rare breed of domestic cattle of Asian origin.

As the Greenbelt snakes through important wetland areas, such as the Drava-Mura River Basin, which is bordered by four countries (Austria, Croatia, Hungary, Slovenia), it moves into South Eastern Europe. The Drava-Mura River Basin encompasses some 380 km of river corridor, covers approximately 60 000 ha of floodplains, and is one of Europe's riverine gems, providing a range of habitats for many species, including the white water lily (*Nymphaea alba*) and the swamp frog (*Rana alvaris*).

In South Eastern Europe, the Greenbelt moves between the border regions of Romania, Bulgaria, and Serbia and Montenegro, passing through Djerdap National Park (Serbia), a transboundary protected area together with Iron Gates National Park (Romania). The Iron (Djerdap) Gorge around the Danube River is the gate-way to the Carpathian Mountains, home to the largest populations in of mammals Europe, such as the brown bear, the wolf, and the lynx.

At its base, the Greenbelt splits and travels west along the Greek border to and around Albania, and east to the Black Sea. One core zone in this part of the Greenbelt is Shkodor (or Skadar) Lake, which lies across the border between Albania and Montenegro. Shkodor is one of Europe's largest freshwater lakes, with an average area of 475 km^2 and a drainage basin of 5 490 km^2. The lake is an important breeding site for birds, and is home to rare avian species, such as the Dalmatian pelican (*Pelecanus crispus*) and the pygmy cormorant (*Phalacrocorax pygmaeus*). Nonetheless, the number of breeding birds is dropping rapidly with the increasing use of the lake.

Although continuous human habitation has altered much of its wild areas, Europe has some of the most developed nature protection legislation and international conventions in the world. Within the European Union (EU), each country must designate a proportion of their land under the Natura 2000 Network of Protected Areas. Outside the EU, there is a network of protected areas called the "Emerald Network," established under the Bern Convention. Work is also underway at the pan-European level to create a Pan-European Ecological Network, linking protected areas to migration corridors and buffer zones. In other words, the different political frameworks are in place, even if implementing them can sometimes be very difficult.

The Greenbelt is being built on the principle of increasing the connection among protected areas with their surrounding landscapes. As the above brief tour along the route of the Greenbelt shows, it encompasses some of Europe's most important regions for biological and cultural diversity. As the initiative becomes realized it will hopefully become a tool to implement many of the ecological network plans developed for Europe and will be used to improve the level of transboundary cooperation at the community level.

The Greenbelt travels along the migration routes of many bird species and crosses the migration routes of many mammals. It also provides a sample of the different latitudinal zones in Europe, making it a sort of ecological "laboratory" to study the effects of changes in species compositions with changing climates.

The Iron Curtain was one of Europe's most divisive barriers and touched the lives of all the people in that region. An incredible opportunity exists to promote and enhance cooperation between the people who currently reside alongside this corridor by capitalizing on its infamous reputation and turning this once negatively perceived barrier into a symbol of cooperation for

On the opposite page, a European lynx (Lynx lynx) *in Germany's Bayerischewald National Park.*
© Günter Ziesler

Above, a male black grouse (Tetrao tetrix) *performing his characteristic "rookooing" call to show off fully its white undertailed coverts.*
© Konrad Wothe

213

nature and sustainable development. By utilizing a bottom-up approach in the implementation of the many nature conventions agreed upon at high political levels in Europe, great strides can be made in regards to local community involvement and participation —actions that will only serve to strengthen the simultaneous goals of biodiversity conservation and sustainable development.

Within the Greenbelt, there are a number of possible socio-economic benefits to local communities. For example, there are many funding sources within the EU for structural and regional development and transboundary cooperation, which could be better utilized through the Greenbelt. The Greenbelt could be used to raise awareness and share good and bad examples of cooperation between private and public interests.

One of the main focuses for the Greenbelt in the coming years will be South Eastern Europe, where geopolitical boundaries have become increasingly complex and the demand on the region's natural resources much greater. It is within this region in particular that the Greenbelt can help advance positive relationships among all stakeholders involved in the use and protection of natural resources.

With an initiative as large as this, it is not difficult to imagine that threats are many and varied, although they can be generally grouped under two main categories: increasing demand for and use of natural resources, and development associated with transportation corridors and other infrastructure expansion. Accordingly, old growth forests in Fennoscandia are threatened by logging, while biodiversity in agricultural landscapes is threatened by large-scale industrial agricultural practices and land abandonment in Central and South Eastern Europe. In the latter case, however, recent changes to the EU's policies on agriculture offer a chance for improvement. In general, the economies of many of the countries have been subjected to recent changes either through transition from centralized control or with accession to the EU. These changes have involved both pressures and opportunities for the Greenbelt.

In Central and South Eastern Europe there has been a rapid increase in the development of infrastructure projects. For example, the development of large-scale transport networks that run North-South and East-West in Europe with financing from the EU threatens many fragile ecosystems. Also, because people's growing interest in visiting different regions has increased the pressure on these fragile ecosystems, sustainable tourism will become an important focus for Greenbelt activities.

The Greenbelt's immediate future will see the development of field projects in different parts of its route. These projects will be used to focus attention on the Greenbelt and to stimulate further donor interest. One of the first tasks will be to generate a detailed map of the entire route, showing the different protected areas and land-use practices. With this tool it will be possible to identify areas which require project attention in the future. In Germany, for example, some large-scale conservation projects are already underway or have been planned for upcoming years. Additionally there are plans to set aside most of the area of the Greenbelt for nature conservation purposes only.

Although the Greenbelt has seen its beginnings in the countries surrounding the former Iron Curtain, it will not stop there. The master vision is for the Greenbelt to develop a set of tools and methodologies that can be transferred to other regions of transboundary cooperation in Europe and around the world. The Greenbelt will thus become an example for initiatives in similar regions that have been sites of conflict and division. In Europe, two regions in particular could be important future developments for the Greenbelt: the border regions between Poland and Belarus and Ukraine, and the region between Ukraine and Russia. Both regions are major storehouses for European biodiversity, including one of Europe's two biodiversity hotspots, the Caucasus region, and both have had their natural heritage dramatically affected by changes in political systems. It would be a truly inspiring vision to see such initiatives constituting a network of "green arteries" running through Europe.

ANDREW TERRY
UWE RIECKEN
KARIN ULLRICH

Above, a European representative of the wide-ranging moose (Alces alces).
© Günter Ziesler

On the opposite page, a male red deer (Cervus elaphus) *calling.*
© Konrad Wothe

On the opposite page, a mountain creek in
the Bayerischewald National Park after a heavy spring rainfall.
© Norbert Rosing

Above, an Arctic fox (Alopex lagopus) *carrying its whelp.*
© Konrad Wothe

AFRICA

WEST AFRICA'S UPPER GUINEA FOREST REGION: TRANSBOUNDARY CONSERVATION IN A CONFLICT ZONE

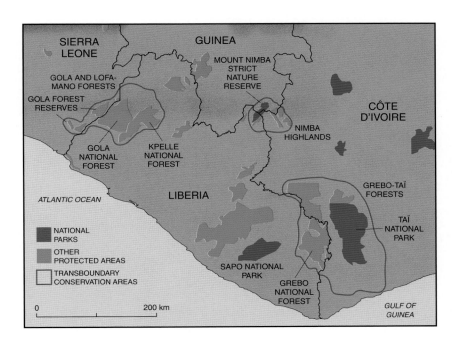

The Upper Guinea forest region covers an area of about 420 000 km^2, extending from southern Guinea into Sierra Leone, through Liberia and southern Côte d'Ivoire, into Ghana and western Togo. As a result of centuries of human influence, the original forest covering has been drastically reduced to less than 25% of the region. Today, the major conservation challenge in the Upper Guinea forest ecosystem is extreme habitat fragmentation, which has major implications for safeguarding wildlife populations and harmonizing land uses in the matrix. The remaining fragments in each of the six countries are islands in a sea of subsistence and commercial agriculture. Until recently, political instability had kept conservation from achieving a level of national priority in Liberia and Sierra Leone. In 2003, that instability extended into Côte d'Ivoire, where erstwhile rebels now occupy more than half of the country.

In spite of these challenges, West Africa as a whole, and the Upper Guinea forest in particular, continues to benefit from increased attention in the global conservation and donor community. A Regional Conservation Priority-Setting Workshop in 1999 identified 41 priority areas for biodiversity conservation in the Upper Guinea forest ecosystem, of which 25% are contiguous across national boundaries (Bakarr et al. 2001). These contiguous areas comprise a number of existing and targeted forest protected areas, including Taï National Park in Côte d'Ivoire and the Mount Nimba World Heritage Site in Guinea. Several contiguous forest areas in West Africa, which include the Gola and Lofa-Mano forests (Liberia and Sierra Leone), the Grebo-Taï forests (Côte d'Ivoire and Liberia), and the Nimba Highlands (Côte d'Ivoire, Guinea, and Liberia), offer great potential for transboundary conservation based on biodiversity patterns of political, economic, and social importance.

The Gola and Lofa-Mano forests include several significant blocks of forest in the Liberia-Sierra Leone transboundary area, such as three Gola Forest Reserves in Sierra Leone, and the Gola and Kpelle National Forests in Liberia. One of the many reasons for focusing on this area is the long-standing rationale and potential for its transboundary conservation, based on possible elephant movements across the Mano River (Mertz 1986). On the other hand, until the civil wars in both countries during the 1990s, these forests were targets for a range of wildlife surveys and ecological research (e.g., Davies 1987). Although parts of the forest blocks in both countries were logged at various times prior to the civil war outbreaks, areas of relatively undisturbed habitat

On. p. 218, wildebeest
(Connochaetes taurinus)
and zebras (Equus quagga
boehmi) *in the Masai Mara
Reserve in Kenya. Together with
the Serengeti, this is the site
of one of the world's greatest
wildlife migrations.*
© Günter Ziesler

*On p. 220, aerial view
of the Taï Forest, Côte d'Ivoire.*
© Michael Nichols/National
Geographic Image Collection

West African chimpanzees
(Pan troglodytes verus)
sharing fruit in Taï National
Park, Côte d'Ivoire.
© Michael Nichols/National
Geographic Image Collection

223

Above, elephants in the Guinean Forest region may represent a distinct subspecies, but this remains to be confirmed.
© Patricio Robles Gil/Sierra Madre

On the opposite page, the pygmy hippo (Hexaprotodon liberiensis) *is a highly elusive rainforest species that is among the most endangered large mammals of this region.*
© Roland Seitre

remain and represent major opportunities for transboundary conservation.

The Grebo-Taï forest contains the largest contiguous blocks of forests remaining in the Upper Guinea region (Sayer et al. 1992). The transboundary area brings together the Grebo National Forest in Liberia and the Taï National Park, the N'zo Faunal Reserve, and the Cavaly-Goin and Haute Dodo Classified Forests in Côte d'Ivoire. Of these, Taï National Park, including its adjacent forest reserves, is the most intensively studied and widely recognized (Martin 1991). On the other hand, the Grebo National Forest across the border in Liberia has been poorly studied, even in the years prior to the civil conflict. Taken together, the Grebo-Taï forests offer great opportunities for sustaining viable populations of numerous endemic and threatened species in the Upper Guinea forest ecosystem. Liberia's only formally gazetted protected area, Sapo National Park, lies further away from the transboundary area, but this important forest protected area could conceivably be linked to a Grebo-Taï transboundary conservation area (TBCA) through an effective landscape conservation strategy for the whole of southeastern Liberia. Indeed, the potential for a biodiversity corridor extending from the Cestos River in Liberia, eastward into Taï National Park in Côte d'Ivoire, would be greatly enhanced by the establishment of a TBCA.

The Nimba Highlands straddle the border between Guinea, Liberia, and Côte d'Ivoire, and are part of a series of mountain chains in southeast Guinea that form what is known as "Dorsal Guineénne." The highlands together contain the headwaters of a number of major rivers including the Niger, which flows through several Sahelian countries before heading to the Atlantic coast in Nigeria. Mount Nimba rises to 1 752 m and is characterized by distinct vegetation types ranging from lowland and montane forests to savannahs and upland grassland formations. Whereas the forests and other habitats on Mount Nimba have been extensively studied in Guinea, the biodiversity on the Liberia and Côte d'Ivoire sides is much less documented. The declaration of Strict Nature Reserves on the Côte d'Ivoire and Guinea sides has long established the Nimba Mountain Range as a global priority for conservation in the Upper Guinea region, and the Mount Nimba Strict Nature Reserve in Guinea (14 000 ha) is already both a Biosphere Reserve and Natural World Heritage Site. The Côte d'Ivoire side has a Strict Nature Reserve; at 500 ha it is much smaller but nonetheless reinforces the conservation significance of the transboundary area. Much of the Liberian portion of Mount Nimba has been highly degraded after decades of iron-ore

mining, but the conservation significance of remaining forests led to the recent designation of a Nature Reserve by the government, which includes two separate National Forests covering approximately 26 000 ha, as well as the Mount Nimba Nature Reserve, which was declared in 2003. Given the tri-national nature of this globally important mountain range, a transboundary conservation approach is necessary to ensure full protection of existing biodiversity.

The Upper Guinean forest region is part of West Africa's Guinean Forests Hotspot, one of the world's biologically richest and most endangered ecosystems (Mittermeier et al. 1999, 2004). The biodiversity is characterized by high species-richness and endemism, especially for birds and mammals. The entire Upper Guinea region is an Endemic Bird Area (EBA), with 15 restricted range species occurring exclusively in this forest (Stattersfield et al. 1998). Important bird flagships in the target transboundary areas include the white-breasted guineafowl (*Agelastes meleagrides*), the Gola malimbe (*Malimbus ballmanni*), the rufous fishing owl (*Scotopelia ussheri*), the white-necked picathartes (*Picathartes gymnocephalus*), the spot-winged Greenbul (*Phyllastrepus leucolepis*), the Nimba flycatcher (*Melaenornis annamarulae*), and the yellow-throated olive greenbul (*Crineger olivaceus*).

The targeted TBCAs also have several restricted-range subspecies of primates and antelopes with ranges extending across borders. For the primates, notable flagships in the Gola-Lofa-Mano and Grebo-Taï areas include the western red colobus monkey (*Piliocolobus badius badius*), the Diana monkey (*Cercopithecus diana diana*), the black-and-white colobus monkey (*Colobus polykomos polykomos*), and the western chimpanzee (*Pan troglodytes verus*). The western chimpanzee has its largest population in the Grebo-Taï forest, especially in the Taï National Park, where it numbers about 4 500 individuals (Kormos et al. 2004). For the antelopes, two endemic Upper Guinean species, Jentink's duiker (*Cephalophus jentinki*) and the zebra duiker (*Cephalophus zebra*) are important flagships. The forest elephant (*Loxodonta africana cyclotis*) and the pygmy hippopotamus (*Hexaprotodron liberiensis*), though highly reduced in numbers, are also important. Another notable mammal flagship species includes the rare Kuhn's mongoose (*Liberiictis kuhni*) and the Nimba otter shrew (*Micropotamogale lamottei*). The former occurs only in the Grebo-Taï forests, while the latter appears to be restricted to the Nimba Mountains. Among the herps, the viviparous toad (*Nectophrynoides occidentalis*) of the Nimba Highlands is particularly noteworthy. Mount Nimba is also known for its rich and diverse butterfly community.

All three targeted TBCAs have been given highest priority for safeguarding forest biodiversity in West Africa (Martin 1991; Bakarr et al. 2001), based primarily on the conservation significance of existing forest blocks that straddle national borders. The Gola Forest Reserves constitute the largest remaining blocks of contiguous Upper Guinea lowland forest in Sierra Leone, covering nearly 75 000 ha in the Eastern Province. The forests occur in three major blocks —Gola North (45 800 ha), Gola East (22 800 ha), and Gola West (6 200 ha)— all lying between the Moa and Mano/Moro River Basins on the border with Liberia. The three blocks are separated by settlement and cultivation enclaves, which are mainly associated with industrial-scale logging activities in Gola East and West. The Lofa-Mano forests are located in the Mano and Lofa River Basins in neighboring Liberia, and cover an area of about 380 000 ha. Together, the Golas and Lofa-Mano more or less constitute a continuous block of lowland rainforest habitat extending across the two countries.

Davies (1987) conducted a detailed biological assessment of the Gola Forest Reserves in the mid- to late-1980s, and concluded that the Gola North forest offered the best opportunity for protecting unique Upper Guinea flora and fauna. In 2004, BirdLife International and the Royal Society for the Protection of Birds secured full commitment of the government to dedicate the entire Gola Forest to biodiversity conservation, pending formal agreements with chiefdom authorities, and Conservation International (CI) agreed to support this endeavor as well, through its Global Conservation Fund. This will serve as major step in the establishment of a future TBCA that will link the Golas to the Lofa-Mano forests in Liberia, resulting in the protection of more than 450 000 ha of relatively intact Upper Guinea forest between the two countries.

The Grebo-Taï forests are associated with at least one major drainage basin, that of the Cavally River, which has its headwaters in the Nimba Highlands and forms most of the national border between Liberia and Côte d'Ivoire. According to Diamond and Hamilton (1980), the forests of southeastern Liberia and western Côte d'Ivoire may have been the center of a Pleistocene refuge, and are noted for having high concentrations of Upper Guinean flora and fauna. Taï National Park (350 000 ha) is the single largest protected area in the Upper Guinea forest region. The N'zo Faunal Reserve (95 000 ha) and Haute Dodo Classified Forest (200 000 ha), to the north and south of Taï, respectively, also add important habitat areas that further reinforce the regional and global significance of Taï as a potential anchor for transboundary conservation. Expanding these into a TBCA that includes the Cavally-Goin Classified Forest (189 000 ha) and the Grebo National Forest (260 000 ha) will ensure long-term viability of numerous endemic and threatened animal species of the Upper Guinea region.

The coastal region of West Africa has been engulfed in civil strife and political turmoil for the last decade and a half. The Upper Guinea region at one point was the site of four of Africa's civil wars, involving Côte d'Ivoire, Guinea, Liberia and Sierra Leone, and it is believed that forests along national boundaries have played a major role in cross-border incursions among these countries (Richards 1996). Due to tribal overlaps across national borders, populations around cross-border forests tend to be linked by family ties and informal commercial activities. As a result, there are major footpaths connecting villages on both sides of the border, which allow access to these otherwise remote forests.

Prior to the eruption of the Liberian civil war in the late 1980s, socioeconomic and political relations with Sierra Leone were strong. A bridge across the Mano River made trade and movement of citizens between the two countries efficient. At the height of the Liberian civil war, during the early 1990s, it was alleged that rebels infiltrated Sierra Leone across the Mano River, probably through the Gola and Lofa-Mano forests. Sierra Leone's civil conflict, which lasted through the entire 1990s, was blamed on this initial infiltration. This led to a strained relationship that still persists between the countries, even as peace and reconstruction efforts get underway on both sides of the border. A similar situation also exists between Liberia and its other two neighbors, Côte d'Ivoire and Guinea.

The major threat to biodiversity in the Upper Guinea forest region is extreme habitat fragmentation resulting from logging, shifting cultivation, and mining. In addition, overexploitation of wildlife for bushmeat is a major factor in the decline of large mammal populations. Human settlement, farming, and commercial bushmeat hunting typically follow the pathways opened up by logging operations. In Côte d'Ivoire, cocoa production by smallholder farmers is a source of enormous pressure on forests. Furthermore, human pressure, intensified by the arrival of thousands of Liberian refugees during the 1990s, continues along the border region. The growing population has increased the demand for bushmeat and small-farmer agricultural production. Illegal logging has also been reported around the fringes of Taï National Park.

These threats cannot be addressed solely by the creation of a TBCA because some are driven by practices that play a major

*On the opposite page,
a West African rainforest seen
from the ground level up.*
© Patricio Robles Gil/Sierra Madre

*Above, a West African
black and white colobus
monkey* (Colobus polykomos
vellerosus).
© Roland Seitre

227

role in sustaining livelihood habits for local communities in the cross-border region. Nevertheless, establishment of TBCAs will help create viable economic alternatives for both local communities and national development. For example, options to engage commercial hunters must be developed in parallel if the supply chain is to be disrupted.

With recent commitment from the government of Sierra Leone to allocate the entire Gola Forest Reserves to biodiversity conservation, potential threats from industrial scale logging are no longer likely on that side of the border. In Liberia, however, large-scale logging operations remain a major threat since large blocks of forests are already in the hands of concessionaires.

Despite years of iron-ore extraction on the Liberian side, mining remains the single most important threat to biodiversity in the Nimba Highlands. The Nimba Range is believed to contain an estimated 800 million tons of iron-ore deposits worth in excess of $11 billion. For many years prior to the early 1980s, iron-ore mining in the Nimba Highlands was a major source of revenue for the government of Liberia, and the government of Guinea is now looking to this resource as a primary source of economic growth —mining concession agreements with a consortium of mining companies are already in the final stages of discussion. Although mining in Liberia resulted in a significant loss of forests, the government of Guinea is working closely with the mining companies and several international conservation groups to develop strategies for safeguarding the forests and other habitats from major destruction.

In Guinea, the forests surrounding the Strict Nature Reserve are under threat from small-scale timber operations. In addition, the civil conflicts in Sierra Leone and Liberia have resulted in a flood of refugees to the cross-border area. Threats from these two factors recently led to inscription of the Reserve on the List of the World Heritage Sites in Danger.

Establishment of TBCAs as "Peace Parks" will be a major step toward restoring socioeconomic ties among the local communities in the cross-border areas between Côte d'Ivoire, Liberia, Guinea, and Sierra Leone. Furthermore, it will enhance post-conflict bilateral economic development prospects through eco-tourism. The Mano River Union, which brings together Guinea, Liberia, and Sierra Leone in an economic and political alliance, could serve as a forum for Liberia and Sierra Leone to explore the Gola-Lofa-Mano TBCA as a symbol of peace between the two countries.

The urgent threat to Liberia's forests posed by timber extraction has prompted a major engagement from international conservation groups, which have developed the Liberia Forest Initiative (LFI) to find practical options that will stave off complete destruction and protect key biodiversity areas. Through the LFI, CI and Fauna and Flora International (FFI) are working with government agencies, major donors, and civil groups to strengthen forest conservation in the country. With the Sapo and Taï National Parks already serving as crucial anchors for trans-boundary conservation, the creation of additional protected areas will help scale-up conservation impacts across the entire cross-border area. A TBCA will ensure connectivity between the core-protected zones, provide alternative livelihoods to local people, help build an economy around conservation, and symbolize peace and cooperation among these countries.

Since 2001, various efforts aimed at protecting Mount Nimba by the governments of Guinea, Liberia, and Côte d'Ivoire have been underway, including a workshop in February 2002 to plan the establishment of a transfrontier conservation area. International conservation groups, such as CI, FFI, and Birdlife International, are providing technical support to facilitate dialogue among the three governments. These efforts will likely make a TBCA for the Nimba Highlands a reality in the near future.

MOHAMED BAKARR

THE TRI-NATIONAL DE LA SANGHA: TRANSBOUNDARY CONSERVATION IN THE WESTERN CONGO FOREST

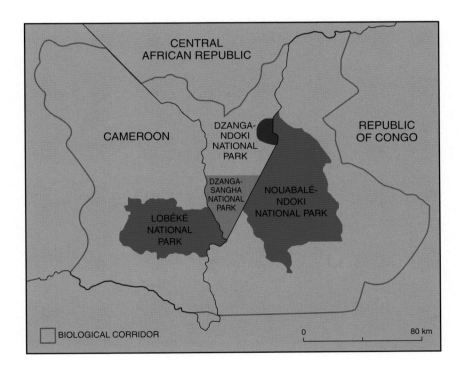

The Tri-National de la Sangha is located in the second largest block of tropical forest left on the planet, the Congo Forests of Central Africa, one of the world's five high biodiversity wilderness areas (Mittermeier et al. 2002) and also part of World Wildlife Fund's Northwestern Congolian Lowland Forests Ecoregion (Burgess et al. 2004). The Tri-National de la Sangha covers a total area of some 2 800 000 ha of dense moist semi-evergreen forests shared by three countries, Cameroon, the Central African Republic, and the Republic of Congo, and is considered one of the most important conservation areas in western Central Africa (Kamdem-Toham et al. 2003). One of its most interesting features are the large natural forest clearings covered with wet grasslands that are very attractive to a number of large mammal and bird species, and are locally known as *bais*, the Ba'Aka Pygmy name. While much of the habitat is natural, logging over the past 30 years has contributed to the opening of the canopy in several parts of this region. The importance of this transborder forest block was first recognized about a decade ago, and conservation activities are now being carried out by World Wildlife Fund (WWF) and the German Gesellschaft für Technische Zusammenarbeit (GTZ) in two of the Tri-National de la Sangha sites, Lobéké (Cameroon) and Dzanga-Sangha (Central African Republic), and by the Wildlife Conservation Society (WCS) in Nouabalé Ndoki (Congo), all of them working closely with the government conservation agencies of Cameroon, the Central African Republic, and the Republic of Congo.

The dense semi-deciduous forest is characterized by a patchwork of high forest, secondary forest, and low-lying swamp interwoven with a mosaic of Maranthaceae/Zingiberaceae forest, mono-dominant stands, and forest clearings. The vegetation is categorized as "swamp/transitional (moist evergreen and semi-deciduous) closed forest." Dominant tree species include *Gilbertiodendron dewevrei*, *Guibourtia demeusii*, *Entandrophragma* spp., *Terminalia superba*, *Ceiba pentandra*, *Lophira alata*, *Berlinia grandiflora* and, in degraded areas, *Musanga cecropioides*, a common pioneer tree species.

The patchwork of different forest types promotes an unusually high diversity and abundance of mammals in the Tri-National de la Sangha, including charismatic flagship species such as forest elephants (*Loxodonta africana cyclotis*, VU), western lowland gorillas (*Gorilla gorilla*, EN), chimpanzees (*Pan troglodytes troglodytes*, EN), bongos (*Tragelaphus eurycerus*), sitatunga (*T. spekei*), forest buffaloes (*Syncerus caffer nanus*), and giant forest hogs (*Hylochoerus meinertzhageni*). Other important primate species include the

231

crowned guenon (*Cercopithecus pogonias*) and the agile mangabey (*Cercocebus agilis*). Sizeable populations of a number of species internationally recognized as "Endangered" still thrive in this forest, although they are increasingly threatened by uncontrolled commercial hunting. Moreover, the zone includes a significant area of primary forest, one of the few remaining unlogged areas in Central Africa. Birds are also quite diverse and include a species of forest robin (*Stiphornis sanghensis*, DD) just described in 1999 (Beresford and Cracraft, 1999), an important population of the Dja River warbler (*Bradypterus grandis*, NT) in the extensive sedge marshes dominated by *Rhynchospora corymbosa*, and another restricted range bird species, the Gabon batis (*Batis minima*, NT) (Fishpool and Evans 2001) (IUCN 2004).

The 2 800 000 ha Tri-National de la Sangha includes the national parks of Lobéké (210 000 ha) in southeast Cameroon, Dzanga-Ndoki (122 000 ha) in the southwest of the Central African Republic, and Nouabalé-Ndoki (400 000 ha) in northwestern Congo, as well as their buffer zones. The three parks are contiguous and are surrounded by extensive buffer zones that include the Dzanga-Sangha Dense Forest Special Reserve (315 900 ha) in the Central African Republic, forests around Lobéké (about 70 000 ha), and the "peripheral zone" in Congo with almost 1 200 000 ha of logging concessions. This large area protects typical forest types of the region, including some forests that have never been logged —an increasingly rare phenomenon in Central Africa.

Of the many *bais* in the area, the Dzanga Bai is particularly special and already attracts tourists from around the world. Since 1990, more than 2 500 individual forest elephants occurred there, and every day up to 100 of them can be observed. Indeed, this and the other *bais* in this landscape have great ecotourism potential because of the ease of seeing otherwise highly elusive species like forest elephants, gorillas, forest buffaloes, and bongos. The tourism program in Dzanga-Sangha is especially innovative because tourism fees are divided among different stakeholders, with 90% of entry fees (which totaled $9 000 in 2002) directly benefiting local populations, an unprecedented situation in Central Africa.

The core conservation areas that constitute the Tri-National de la Sangha are also ranked as Important Bird Areas by BirdLife International (Fishpool and Evans 2001).

In March 1999, the heads of state of Cameroon, the Central African Republic, Chad, Congo, Equatorial Guinea, and Gabon signed the Yaoundé Declaration that included 12 points on conservation and sustainable use of forests in the region. One of the commitments included was promotion of a transborder conser-

vation initiative in Central Africa by adopting a regional approach and promoting coordinated policies in forest management. Since then, the Yaoundé Declaration has been considered the way forward by governments, conservation partners, and all other stakeholders involved in biodiversity conservation and forest-resource management.

After Yaoundé, a regional group named COMIFAC (Commission des Ministres des Forêts d'Afrique Centrale) was created at the ministerial level to implement the resolutions of the declaration. This group has been leading the process of promoting forest conservation, resulting so far in a total of 4 060 700 ha of new protected areas (Burgess et al. 2004).

The Tri-National de la Sangha is the most advanced site in Central Africa in terms of transboundary natural resource management, as evidenced by the signature of the Sangha Tri-National Cooperation Agreement by all three governments in December 2000 that created this initiative and gave it its name. The Tri-National de la Sangha is thus not only a regionally and globally important area for biodiversity conservation, but also a testing ground for assessing and enhancing the effectiveness of collaborative approaches to the conservation of wildlife and wild places.

The main ethnic groups in the Tri-National de la Sangha are Bantus and Ba'Aka pygmies, the latter being the original indigenous people of this region. All of the other ethnic groups, referred to as Bilo by the Ba'Aka, arrived relatively recently. Ba'Aka are now being employed by logging companies, and ecotourism, research, and conservation projects. Some of them, however, have retained their ancestral traditions of hunting and gathering, and hunting with nets is still common practice. This practice takes place not far from settlements and involves the entire community. Nets, made of the kosa liana (*Manniophyton fulvum*), are used to capture the blue duiker (*Cephalophus monticola*) and the African brush-tailed porcupine (*Atherurus africanus*). Bow hunting is practiced by men and targets arboreal creatures such as monkeys. Spear hunting is used to kill forest elephants, western lowland gorillas, red river hogs (*Potamochoerus porcus*), and forest hogs. Trapping is also a common activity and involves snares aimed at capturing rodents (Christy 2002).

This region was once quite remote and had a low human population density, but this began to change in the 1970s with the commencement of logging activities. The possibility of finding employment attracted hundreds of families into the area. With the rise of human population, pressure on the natural resources also increased. Today, hunting activities are no longer limited to small species like duikers taken for local consumption, but has now also been extended to the forest elephant, the

On p. 230, a view of the Sangha River in the Central African Republic.

*On pp. 232-233, forest elephants (*Loxodonta cyclotis*) in the Dzanga Bai in Ndoki National Park, Central African Republic.*

On the opposite page, a chimpanzee (Pan troglodytes) in Nouabale-Ndoki National Park, Republic of Congo. This amazing park still has populations of naïve chimps and gorillas living in pristine conditions.

Above, a great blue touraco (Corythaeola cristata) eating a fig in Cameroon. All photos, © Michael Nichols/National Geographic Image Collection

235

bongo, and apes and other primates for commercial trade. Elephant hunting for ivory is another common practice. Illegal settlements for gold panning and diamond exploitation have also impacted the forest. Logging companies in the area have not yet fulfilled their legal obligation to develop and implement management plans for the concessions, meaning that promises of low-impact logging are rarely fulfilled. One example of the extent of the impact is the fact that some 5 000 km of road network were opened for forest exploitation in southeast Cameroon, in the process facilitating illegal access to large tracts of previously inaccessible forest. Insufficient control of transborder poaching activities for commercial purposes has become a major threat. Finally, some animals are also hunted for fetishes and the pet trade, one of the best examples being the African gray parrot (*Psittacus erithacus*).

The Tri-National de la Sangha concept has been in development for more than 10 years. A legal framework for this initiative was established when the three countries signed the Sangha Tri-National Cooperation Agreement. This framework acts as a coordinating mechanism for addressing transboundary issues that cannot be addressed solely by complementary management and jurisdictional structures of the individual countries. The Comité Trans-national de Planification et d'Exécution is the primary organizing body of the Tri-National de la Sangha and the main mechanism for coordinating transboundary activities. It is composed of representatives from the four conservation projects that are the primary actors in the Tri-National de la Sangha: the Projet Dzanga-Sangha (WWF/GTZ) in the Central African Republic, the Unité Technique Opérationnelle WWF/GTZ/Ministère des Eaux et Forêts in Cameroon, the Parc National Nouabalé-Ndoki (WCS), and the Projet de Gestion Ecologique dans la Zone Périphérique du Parc Nouabalé-Ndoki, a project involving WCS, the Ministère de l'Economie Forestière et de l'Environnement, and the Congolaise Industrielle de Bois, a private timber company in the Republic of Congo that started activities in 1999. The Comité Transnational de Planification et d'Exécution meets roughly once every six months at one of the parks' headquarters and has established four technical commissions. These commissions work collaboratively during and between regular meetings of the committee, and each commission is tasked with developing guidelines and activities that support the Tri-National de la Sangha.

The four established commissions are the Anti-Poaching Commission, which coordinates cross-border law enforcement activities; the Institutional Commission, which focuses on issues such as coordination, constituency building, and improvement of cross-border travel regulations; the Socioeconomic Commission, which addresses transnational issues, including human movements, alternative protein sources, and cross-border subsistence hunting; and the Ecological Monitoring Commission, which seeks to establish standards for ecological monitoring across the three reserves and will also provide guidelines for sharing information.

To guarantee the success of this transboundary conservation initiative, it is imperative that the governmental agencies of the three countries involved continue to cooperate on the development of a shared landscape plan and agree on common protocols for conservation management. It is also essential that the nongovernmental organizations involved on different sides of the national borders continue to collaborate and develop common systems for landscape planning, monitoring, and data sharing, ensuring that a region-wide landscape plan be rooted in the national laws of each country involved. Of particular importance in this regard is that the judicial systems of each government be sufficiently empowered to regulate hunting in logging concessions and elsewhere.

Fortunately, a lot of this is already starting to take place under the leadership of WWF. This includes a Landscape Master Plan that will provide broad-based guidelines for managing the Tri-National de la Sangha, including both the core protection zone and the peripheral zones; shared approaches to policy and law enforcement which aim to have the three governments work towards harmonization of policies on law enforcement; timber trade, and overall management framework for the transfrontier area; shared approaches to capacity building, exploration of alternative livelihoods, including controlled subsistence of bush meat hunting and development of ecotourism as a source of income; development of a shared monitoring system to track critical parameters in the region and, finally, investigation of sustainable financing mechanisms. The conservation partners have already initiated a trust fund mechanism for the Tri-National de la Sangha.

If this ambitious and pragmatic agenda can be fully implemented, then the likelihood that this magnificent region will be protected in perpetuity will be greatly enhanced.

OLIVIER LANGRAND
RICHARD W. CARROLL

THE VIRUNGA VOLCANOES TRANSBOUNDARY CONSERVATION AREA: HOME OF THE MOUNTAIN GORILLA

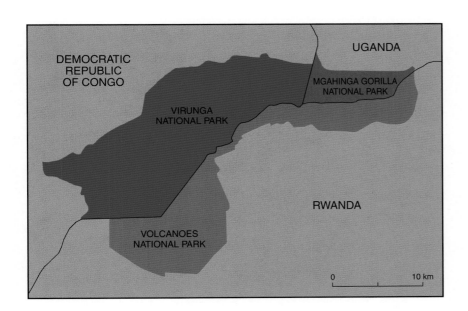

The Virunga Volcanoes Transboundary Conservation Area (TBCA) is arguably the best known, most studied, and widely supported transboundary conservation area in Tropical Africa. It covers 43 400 ha at altitudes of 2 300 to 4 511 m and is situated where the international borders of Uganda, Rwanda, and the Democratic Republic of Congo (D.R.C.) meet. Three national parks make up this area, Mgahinga Gorilla National Park in Uganda (3 400 ha), Volcanoes National Park (16 000 ha) in Rwanda, and the southern (volcanoes) portion of Virunga National Park (24 000 ha) in the D.R.C. The Virunga Volcanoes TBCA lies in the watershed between the Nile River and the Congo River Systems. Dominated by six extinct and two active volcanoes, it is comprised of rugged, often steep terrain. Due to its considerable altitudinal gradient, the vegetation varies from montane forests (ca. 2 400 to 2 500 m), to bamboo *Arundinaria alpina* and *Hagenia-Hypericum* forest (ca. 2 500 to 3 600 m), to subalpine ericaceous vegetation (ca. 3 500 to 4 000 m), to Afro-alpine vegetation (over 4 000 m). In addition, there are high-altitude crater-lakes, swamps, and moorlands. Mean annual rainfall is about 2 200 mm.

Virtually all that remains of the Virunga Volcanoes Ecosystem falls within the three national parks and, as such, what happens in one of the national parks impacts the conservation and ecological processes of the entire Ecosystem. Until recently, these three contiguous protected areas were managed independently by the three national parks' authorities: the Uganda Wildlife Authority, the Office Rwandais de Tourisme et des Parcs Nationaux, and the Institut Congolais pour la Conservation de la Nature. This, in spite of the fact that they share common borders and, therefore, threats from outside any one border can affect the entire Virunga Volcanoes TBCA. Under these circumstances, achieving effective transboundary management to help ensure the long-term survival of this TBCA has been a major conservation objective for the past 25 years or so.

"The benefits of establishing a regional framework for collaboration and transboundary natural resource management can be demonstrated by the fact that most of the threats to the natural resources [of the Virunga Volcanoes TBCA] are from people living all around the shared ecosystem. Threats from one side will impact the entire ecosystem. The potential and real benefits of the forest ecosystems, from an ecological, cultural, as well as economic perspective, are also similar on all sides of the border. The incentive, therefore, to protect the ecosystem, and to benefit from its various functions, is comparable within the three

*On p. 238, Mount Mikeno at sunset from
Mount Visoke, Virunga Mountains, Rwanda.* © Gerry Ellis / ENP Images

On the opposite page, the mountain gorilla (Gorilla beringei beringei)
*is one of Africa's most important flagship species. It is found only
in the Virungas, with a second population in the Bwindi (Impenetrable)
Forest of Uganda, which may represent a distinct subspecies.*
© Konrad Wothe

countries. The costs of effective management and protection are also comparable." (Lanjouw et al. 2001).

In the case of the Virunga Volcanoes TBCA, the transboundary managers are moving towards adopting and implementing a common regional framework and array of activities as they strive to manage the TBCA as one shared conservation area. These range from simple non-opposing national-level management activities to complex, fully collaborative, transboundary activities. The choice of actions is based on current needs, opportunities, and constraints. To date, the emphasis has been on harmonizing conservation approaches and actions on the ground, while slowly formalizing and institutionalizing support for transboundary legal, policy, and management mechanisms (particularly protection) at the highest political levels (Kalpers 2001; Lanjouw et al. 2001).

The montane and Afro-montane habitats of Africa are of particular importance as sites for the conservation of biodiversity. This is because they cover but a small portion of Africa's land surface while supporting a disproportionately high number of endemic and threatened species. Mammals are represented by 86 species, of which 18 are endemic and six are on the IUCN *Red List*. These include some high profile flagship species, of which by far the best known is the endemic "Critically Endangered" mountain gorilla (*Gorilla beringei beringei*). Other high-profile mammal species present are the near-endemic "Endangered" golden monkey (*Cercopithecus mitis kandti*) and the "Endangered" bush elephant (*Loxodonta africana*).

In terms of birds, all three of the national parks of the Virunga Volcanoes TBCA are classified as "Important Bird Areas." This TBCA holds at least 258 species and 20 of the 37 species of birds endemic to the Albertine Rift Endemic Bird Area. Four of these bird species are threatened. The Virunga Volcanoes TBCA is particularly important as a site for the conservation of Lagden's bush-shrike (*Malaconotus lagdeni*), the Kivu ground-thrush (*Zoothera tanganjicae*), Grauer's swamp-warbler (*Bradypterus graueri*), and Shelley's crimson-wing (*Cryptospiza shelleyi*) (Fishpool and Evans 2001).

Reptiles are represented by 43 species, seven of them endemic, and amphibians by 47 species, 16 of which are endemic and nine are on the IUCN *Red List*. In all, the number of non-fish vertebrates (mammals, birds, reptiles, amphibians) known to be present in the Virunga Volcanoes TBCA is 434, of which 61 are endemic to the Albertine Rift Region and 19 are listed as "Threatened" on the IUCN *Red List* (Plumptre et al. 2003).

Of the 880 species of plants recorded for the TBCA, 185 are endemic to the Albertine Rift Region and four are threatened (Plumptre et al. 2003).

As home to endemic and threatened taxa of plants and animals, maintenance of the biodiversity of the Virunga Volcanoes TBCA is necessary if loss of biodiversity within the Albertine Rift Region is to be prevented. Virtually no forest survives on the densely populated land beyond the boundaries of the TBCA. One result is that the farmlands of the region lose roughly 11 tons of soil/hectare/year through erosion (Waller 1996) —this in a region where more than 16% of the people are already landless and where more than 50% do not have enough land to meet basic needs (IGCP 1996). In contrast, the TBCA maintains a lush, dense, natural vegetation covering over those parts of the Virunga Volcanoes that are above ca. 2 300 m. This plant covering is not only critical to the maintenance of ecological and hydrological processes over the Virunga Volcanoes, but also essential as it provides enormous indirect benefits to the millions of people who depend on the clean water that flows from this catchment.

The vast majority of the people of the region around the Virunga Volcanoes TBCA have few livelihood alternatives to subsistence agriculture. As such, the promotion of jobs in conservation and tourism in and around the TBCA is not only a strategy for enhancing livelihood security and for promoting a culture of peace in the region, but also a strategy for halting habitat and biodiversity loss.

The Virunga Volcanoes TBCA is the most famous site in the world for gorilla viewing by tourists. Gorilla-based tourism can promote government and public conservation support, increase foreign exchange earnings, generate employment, and attract financial support and investment capital. By helping to integrate protected areas into the local and national economies, gorilla-based tourism can provide economic incentives and justification for supporting the conservation of gorillas and their species-rich habitats (Butynski and Kalina 1998; Butynski 2001). Revenues from gorilla-based tourism can be considerable. For example, in Uganda, from 1994 to 1999, gorilla-based tourism generated net foreign exchange earnings of ca. $7.7 million and supported nearly 1 700 person-years of jobs (Yakobo and Uwimbabazi 2000). Some of the funds generated have been used to support the activities of the national parks authorities. In Uganda (but not in Rwanda or the D.R.C.), 20% of the park entrance fees go directly to local communities to support small-scale development projects.

*On the opposite page,
in mountains long protected by
thick vegetation, giant heather
trees in the Virungas
of the Democratic Republic of
Congo cast bizarre shapes
against a morning sky.*
© Michael Nichols/National
Geographic Image Collection

*Above, the gray parrot is
a common, widespread
African species (Psittacus
erithacus) renowned for its
ability to mimic human speech.*
© Günter Ziesler

Much of the Albertine Rift Region was once covered with forest. However, deforestation for agriculture and pasture over the last 800 years or so, particularly over the past century, has destroyed all but a tiny portion of the original forest cover. What remains is an array of small islands of forest, one of which is the Virunga Volcanoes TBCA. It is today an ecological island completely surrounded by a dense human population (more than 400 people/km^2), intensive cultivation, poverty, and frequent political and social insecurity. The growth rate of the human population around the Virunga Volcanoes TBCA is over 3% per year. The number of people living within a few kilometers is estimated to be well over one million, more than 90% of which are subsistence farmers and pastoralists. As such, the TBCA is under considerable threat from agriculturalists, pastoralists, hunters, and politicians (Butynski and Kalina 1993; Kalpers 2001; Lanjouw et al. 2001; Plumptre et al. 2003). The main problems are the constant pressures to degazette parts of the Virunga Volcanoes TBCA for agriculture and the illegal and unsustainable extraction of forest products, including fuel wood, timber, bamboo, medicinal and food plants, honey, water, and meat.

The national parks' authorities (and other government agencies responsible for environmental management) of Uganda, Rwanda, and the D.R.C. are limited by their weak political position, finances, technical and managerial capacity, information-base, and interagency coordination. In none of the three countries is there strong political will or political priority for the sustainable use of natural resources (Lanjouw et al. 2001). Rapid population growth, inappropriate agricultural practices, corruption, insecurity, interference for political gain, and outdated or nonexistent national environmental strategies and action plans are additional constraints towards the long-term effective management of conservation sites such as the Virunga Volcanoes TBCA (IGCP 1996; Kalpers 2001).

Through conservation efforts over the past 25 years, the population of the flagship species of the Virunga Volcanoes TBCA, the mountain gorilla, has increased slowly but steadily from a low of ca. 260 individuals in 1981 to ca. 385 individuals in 2003. On the other hand, the number of elephants has declined over this period and some species have apparently been extirpated. For example, it has been several decades since the owl-faced monkey (*Cercopithecus hamlyni*) or the alpine chat (*Cercomela sordida*) have been observed in the Virunga Volcanoes TBCA. Many other species are now in low numbers and localized (e.g., the yellow-crested helmet-shrike, *Prionops alberti*).

Although gorilla-based tourism can provide economic benefits to people living in the vicinity of protected areas, such tourism is not without its risks. This applies particularly to the Virunga Volcanoes TBCA, where the number of visitors is greatly affected by the dynamic security situation. Perhaps more important from a conservation perspective are the risks that tourism poses to gorillas. The frequent close proximity to habituated gorillas of large numbers of tourists, guides, and security personnel brings with it a number of risks. These include behavioral changes among the gorillas, increased incidence of disease transmission between gorillas and humans, and higher levels of conflict between gorillas and those people living near gorilla habitat (Butynski and Kalina 1998; Homsy 1999; Woodford et al. 2002). These increased threats, in turn, raise a number of ethical questions as concerns gorilla-based tourism (Butynski 2001).

Today, the national parks authorities in Uganda, Rwanda, and the D.R.C. all recognize the importance of multi-national cooperation for the management and sustainable utilization of their shared ecological treasure —the Virunga Volcanoes. Although many opportunities for enhanced public and private cooperation, cost-sharing, information exchange, and partnership building remain untapped, the three national parks' authorities responsible for the management of the Virunga Volcanoes TBCA are well on their way towards demonstrating to a skeptical world that they are able to shake off their dependency upon international assistance and interventions as concerns the conservation of the Virunga Volcanoes Ecosystem.

The main argument put forth in support of the transboundary approach to the conservation of the Virunga Volcanoes TBCA is that the 385 mountain gorillas and threatened biodiversity of the Virunga Volcanoes can only be conserved in perpetuity through a high level of international collaboration and cooperation. To this end, the considerable progress made over the past 25 years towards the transboundary management of the TBCA gives cause for optimism, as does the recent proposal to establish it as an International Peace Park.

THOMAS BUTYNSKI

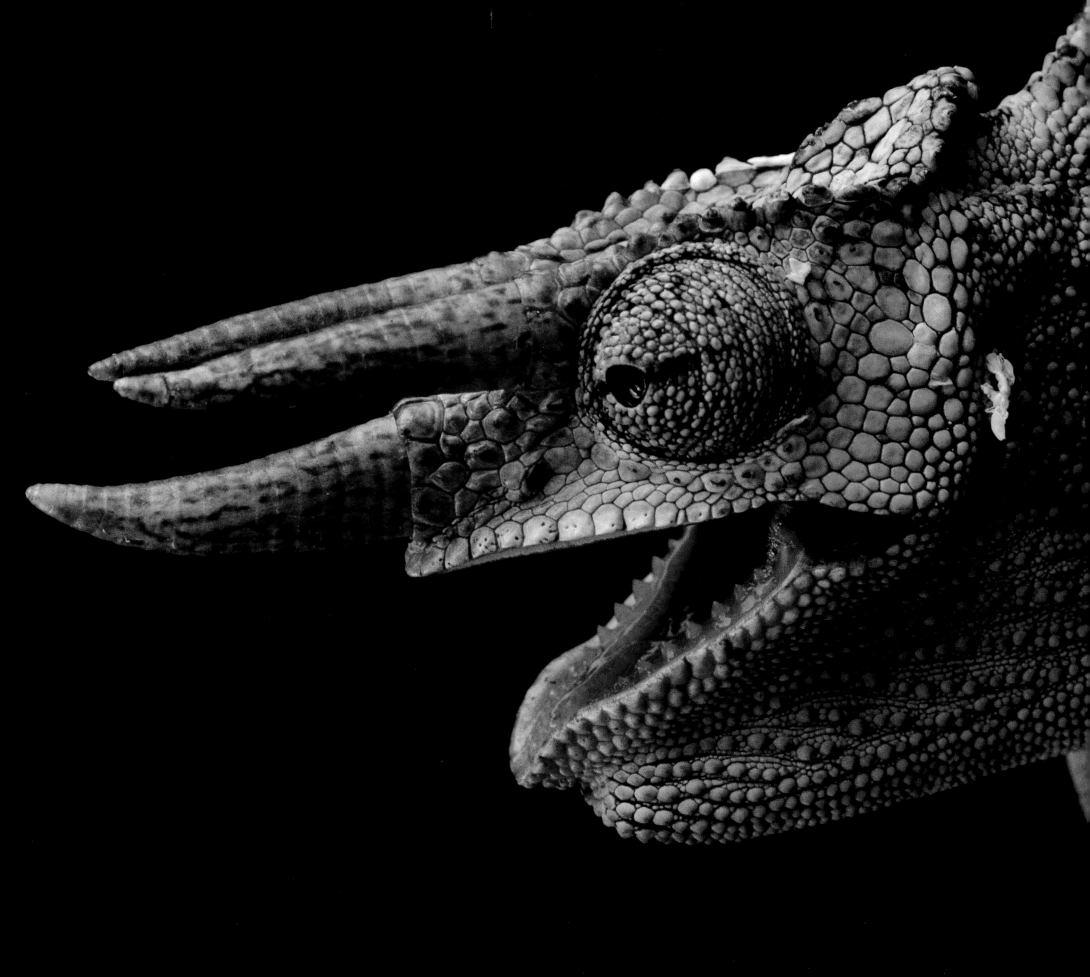

SERENGETI-MASAI: LAND OF THE GREAT MIGRATION

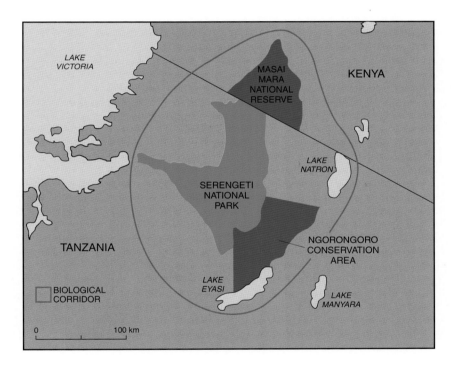

LAKE
VICTORIA

KENYA

MASAI
MARA
NATIONAL
RESERVE

LAKE
NATRON

SERENGETI
NATIONAL
PARK

TANZANIA

NGORONGORO
CONSERVATION
AREA

LAKE
EYASI

LAKE
MANYARA

☐ BIOLOGICAL
CORRIDOR

0   100 km

If the presence of large, charismatic creatures are one's measure, East Africa's Serengeti is certainly the planet's most spectacular wilderness. Herds of animals totaling in the hundreds of thousands —even the millions— crisscross the region's seemingly endless plains each year in an event known worldwide as the Great Migration. These mind-numbing congregations of hoofed mammals sometimes span the horizon and are a global attraction for the transboundary protected area formed by Tanzania's Serengeti National Park and the adjoining Masai Mara National Reserve of Kenya and adjacent lands.

In ecological terms, these two units represent one continuous ecosystem, broadly defined by the wildebeest migration route (Iwago 1987). The Masai Mara National Reserve is actually an integral component of the Serengeti Plains ecosystem, extending across the border of Tanzania and Kenya. The transboundary protected area is also at the heart of the 70 000 km^2-Serengeti Wilderness Area (Christ and Konstant 2002) and is composed of the Serengeti Volcanic Grasslands Ecoregion and the Southern *Acacia-Commiphora* Bushlands and Thickets Ecoregion (Olson et al. 2001).

Fascination with this region began more than a century ago when German and English explorers returned from expeditions with tales of extraordinary natural wonders such as Mount Kilimanjaro, Lake Tanganyika, Lake Victoria, and the Ngorongoro Crater, yet serious threats of disease kept many from following in their footsteps. The first wildlife protection efforts came in 1929 when the British Colonial Government designated an area of about 230 km^2, including the Serengeti plains and adjacent regions near Lake Victoria, as a lion sanctuary. The Serengeti National Park was created in 1951 and, at 14 763 km^2, is among Tanzania's largest protected areas. IUCN declared it a World Heritage site in 1981 and, in the same year, UNESCO included the Serengeti-Ngorongoro complex in its Man and Biosphere Program (Baker et al. 1995; UNESCO 2002). The biosphere reserve adds Tanzania's Ngorongoro Conservation Area and the Maswa Game Reserve to the Serengeti grasslands. On the Kenyan side, the 1 510-km^2 Masai Mara National Reserve was established in 1961 and completes the transboundary protected area. No formal transboundary agreement exists between the neighboring countries, and in the 1970s, political tensions between Kenya and Tanzania led to a complete border closure, in part led by conflict over access to the Serengeti for tourism. Today, however, officials on both sides of the border collaborate closely with regard to law enforcement, wildlife management, and ecotourism activities. On the Tanzanian side these activities are undertaken at the

national level, while across the border in Kenya they are handled by local government authorities of the Maasai. In a further sign of peace and cooperation between the two countries, officials in Kenya and Tanzania are exploring opening the border directly between the Serengeti and the Masai Mara to promote more effective tourism management and mutual economic benefit.

Grassland is the dominant habitat of the Serengeti ecosystem, and plants derive their nourishment from a bed of rich volcanic soil and respond to the peaks and lows of strongly seasonal rainfall. Couch grass (*Digitaria macroblephara*) predominates among the seven or eight most common species, sedges are more characteristic of low wet terrain, acacia woodlands occur both in the valleys and the hill country, and sparse gallery forests follow rivers and streams. During periods of severe drought, the grasslands appear almost denuded of vegetation, but flourish again when precious moisture eventually arrives. Approximately 1 200 species of vascular plants are native to the region, of which less than 2% are believed to be endemic (Jon Lovett, pers. comm., 2002).

Faunal diversity varies widely among the terrestrial vertebrates. Amphibians are represented by a mere 22 species, none of which are endemic. Reptiles, with 87 species present, are four times more diverse but only Grzimek's dwarf gecko (*Lygodactylus grzimeki*) is unique to the region. By comparison, bird diversity is high. The entire wilderness area is reported to harbor 552 different kinds of birds, of which more than 350 are reported from the transboundary protected area (Zimmermann et al. 1996). Raptors make up about a tenth of these, with other prominent species including the ostrich (*Struthio camelus*) and the lesser flamingo (*Phoenicopterus minor*). According to BirdLife International, the gray-breasted francolin (*Francolinus rufopictus*) is a Serengeti endemic of conservation concern (Stattersfield et al. 1998).

It is clearly the large mammals, however, that have set the Serengeti apart from the rest of the world. The wildebeest (*Connochaetes taurinus*) is by far the dominant species, with its numbers approaching 1.5 million in peak migration years. Zebras (*Equus burchelli*) and Thomson's gazelles (*Gazella thomsoni*) join its ranks at approximately 200 000 and 300 000 individuals, respectively, and all combine to form an enormous food base for what are believed to be the largest remaining populations of African lions (*Panthera leo*) (Campbell and Borner 1995; Hanks and Charlton 2004). The remaining list of large charismatic mammals seems almost as endless as the plains themselves: buffalo (*Syncerus caffer*), bushbuck (*Tragelaphus scriptus*), cheetah (*Acinonyx jubatus*), eland (*Taurotragus oryx*), elephant (*Loxodonta africana*), giraffe (*Giraffa camelopardalis*), golden jackal (*Canis aureus*), Grant's gazelle (*Gazella granti*), hippopotamus (*Hippopotamus amphibius*),

leopard (*Panthera pardus*), oryx (*Oryx gazella*), reedbuck (*Redunca redunca*), sitatunga (*Tragelaphus spekei*), spotted hyena (*Crocuta crocuta*), striped jackal (*Canis adustus*), topi (*Damaliscus lunatus*), waterbuck (*Kobus ellipsiprymus*), and warthog (*Phacochoerus aethiopicus*). Wild dogs (*Lycaon pictus*), once found in great numbers on the plains, have experienced a serious decline due to outbreaks of canine distemper, and black rhinoceros (*Diceros bicornis*), which used to be a common sight in the Serengeti, have virtually disappeared from the park, having been the victims of organized poaching for the illegal trade in rhino horn. Today, the black rhino can most easily be found within the Ngorongoro Crater, one of the last safe refuges for black rhino in all of Africa.

A great deal of seminal biological research has been conducted in the Serengeti. In the early 1950s, ornithologist Herbert Friedmann documented the unusual behavior of the greater honey guide (*Indicator indicator*), a small bird whose Latin name recognizes its talent for locating bee nests. In payment for being guided to stores of wild honey, the Maasai reward their avian "partners" with small pieces of the waxy comb (Friedmann 1954). In the early 1960s, Hans and Ute Klingel pioneered field techniques for identifying hundreds of individual zebras within large herds, a key to understanding wild equine social behavior (Moss 1975). Later that same decade, George Schaller conducted the first study of the Serengeti lions (Schaller 1973), and soon thereafter, Colombian biologist Carlos Mejía spent several years studying giraffes, learning that young animals are typically left unattended by their mothers in groups known as "kindergartens" (Moss 1975). The Serengeti is also where Jane Goodall and Hugo van Lawick first observed Egyptian vultures (*Neophron percnopterus*) using stones as tools to crack open ostrich eggs (van Lawick and Goodall 1968) and where the behavioral mysteries of lesser-known predators, such as cheetahs, hyenas, jackals, and crocodiles, continue to be revealed.

A critical contribution of the transboundary protected area is the sanctuary it affords to the many species of animals. This point was hammered home nearly a half-century ago by the father-and-son team of German zoologists, Bernhard and Michael Grzimek. Their classic film and book, *Serengeti Shall Not Die*, put forth the most effective arguments for increasing wildlife protection efforts in East Africa and laid the foundation for international cooperation. The two million plus animals that reside in or annually traverse the Serengeti ecosystem neither recognize nor respect national borders. Consequently, the joining of Tanzania's Serengeti National Park with Kenya's Masai Mara National Reserve upholds the concept of Transboundary Protected Areas and represents the most practical method of dealing with species that migrate across international borders.

On p. 246, topis (Damaliscus lunatus topi) *at sunrise in Kenya's Masai Mara Reserve.*
© Günter Ziesler

On pp. 248-249,
the migration of the wildebeest (Connochaetes taurinus) *in the Serengeti-Mara ecosystem is one of the most spectacular wildlife events on Earth.*
© Anup Shah

On the opposite page, a lioness (Panthera leo) *growling at her cub in the Masai Mara Reserve in Kenya.*
© Günter Ziesler

Above, a male lion (Panthera leo). *Tanzania has the world's largest remaining population of this magnificent big cat.*

On pp. 252-253,
different species of ungulata, such as the cape buffalo (Syncercus caffer), *live in the Serengeti and Ngorongoro regions. Both photos,*
© Anup and Manoj Shah

Of equal importance is the balance that this park may help to strike between the needs of wildlife and human cultures. The Maasai people came to this region millennia ago from the north, and today are among the last indigenous peoples still practicing a traditional way of life in Kenya and Tanzania. They are pastoralists and nomads whose subsistence on livestock requires lands also used by native species. Maasai county councils were responsible for turning the Mara region of southwestern Kenya into a game sanctuary in 1948, and today this area constitutes the national reserve, the northernmost extent in the annual migration. The Mara is also at the core of debate regarding human-wildlife interactions. Field biologists are taking a very close look at the ways in which pastoralism affects wildlife numbers, noting that the Maasai have traditionally coexisted peacefully with wild animal populations. But in the last three decades, wildlife has increasingly moved outside protected area boundaries, leading to increased conflict with the human population surrounding the Mara, which has essentially doubled. At the same time, local peoples, including the Maasai, have begun to diversify their livelihoods to include ecotourism, small-scale agriculture, and mechanized cultivation (Lamprey and Reid 2004). It is hoped that ongoing research efforts will identify land management practices that will benefit wild animal populations and local communities alike.

In the meantime, conservationists continue their quest to stop poaching, which remains a serious problem in certain areas, despite growing levels of public awareness and law enforcement. Snares, arrows, spears, and rifles regrettably are still in use, yet wildlife remains relatively abundant and international tourists continue to flock to East Africa to witness the great migrating herds. Visitors spend millions of dollars each year for the nature experience of a lifetime, representing enormous contributions to the Kenyan and Tanzanian economies and insuring that infrastructure will continue to develop to accommodate such a lucrative industry. As field and industry studies demonstrate that certain areas are being over-utilized and becoming noticeably less pristine, Kenyan and Tanzanian authorities are responding to calls for a more sustainable tourism industry that brings direct benefits to local peoples and protects the natural heritage of the region for future generations. Effective management, including transboundary cooperation and a combination of sustainable tourism practices, conservation, research, and effective law enforcement will ensure the persistence of this unique ecosystem.

WILLIAM R. KONSTANT
COSTAS CHRIST

*On the opposite page, a Nile crocodile (Crocodylus niloticus)
attacking a wildebeest calf as the herd crosses a river
during its migration.*

*Above, a pair of Masai ostriches (Struthio camelus)
in the Masai Mara Nature Reserve in Kenya.
Both photos,* © Anup Shah

255

|AI-|AIS-RICHTERSVELD-SPERRGEBIET: TRANSBOUNDARY CONSERVATION IN AN ARID HOTSPOT

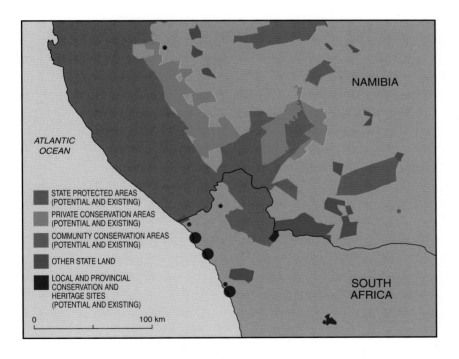

ATLANTIC OCEAN

NAMIBIA

SOUTH AFRICA

STATE PROTECTED AREAS
(POTENTIAL AND EXISTING)

PRIVATE CONSERVATION AREAS
(POTENTIAL AND EXISTING)

COMMUNITY CONSERVATION AREAS
(POTENTIAL AND EXISTING)

OTHER STATE LAND

**LOCAL AND PROVINCIAL
CONSERVATION AND
HERITAGE SITES**
(POTENTIAL AND EXISTING)

0   100 km

A spectacular transboundary conservation and development area is emerging in the winter-rainfall |Ai-|Ais-Richtersveld-Sperrgebiet region of Namibia and South Africa, spanning roughly 56 000 km² of arid wilderness. This is the northernmost reach of the Succulent Karoo, the world's only entirely arid biodiversity hotspot that extends to the Nama Karoo. The newly agreed, but yet to be proclaimed, Sperrgebiet National Park (2 600 000 ha) in Namibia will greatly bolster the existing 604 500-ha |Ai-|Ais-Richtersveld Transfrontier Park, and is likely to be supplemented by a mosaic of private and communal conservancies and reserves (see map). The overall area is likely to be known as the Greater !Gariep Transfrontier Conservation Area (TFCA), derived from a name in the Nama language.

The |Ai-|Ais-Richtersveld-Sperrgebiet TFCA is a harsh landscape of mountain, inselberg, gravel, and sand, flanked by a foggy and windy shore. The mountains are formed of ancient sediments —some deposited 2 600 million years ago— metamorphosed by intrusive granites and violent folding. Their sculptured slopes and jagged peaks are best exposed in the deep and dramatic valley along southern Africa's largest river, the !Gariep (formerly Orange). Elsewhere, windswept plains of gravel and mobile sand predominate. Meager rainfall —ranging from 30 to 300 mm a year— is unusually reliable for an arid system, and precipitation from fog and dew during the dry summer months may explain how so many species evolved and persist in this arid area. Moving east and away from the influence of the cold Atlantic Ocean, one enters a true land of extremes, where temperatures can soar up to 53°C, or be bitterly cold, damp, and windy —sometimes both in a single day.

The number of species supported in the TFCA is unknown. The Gariep Center of Plant Endemism, which roughly coincides with the TFCA, includes some 2 700 plant species, more than 560 of which grow nowhere else, and a startling 28 endemic plant genera (van Wyk and Smith 2001). With its abundance and diversity of tiny-bodied succulents, including mesembs, crassulas, tylecodons, and asclepiads, and their brightly-colored spring blooms, the region supports between four and six times the number of plant species of other global deserts and, in fact, rivals figures for some tropical rainforests (Cowling et al. 1998).

An obvious flagship plant species for the region is the half-mens ("half human") (*Pachypodium namaquanum*), an endemic tree succulent that grows on the steep, poleward-facing slopes of the Richtersveld and Sperrgebiet. These curious plants have

northward-leaning stems topped with a whorl of green leaves that local folklore claims are the frozen forms of Nama people, banished south and staring forlornly to their northern homeland (Rundel et al. 1995). The rare bastard quiver tree (*Aloe pillansii*) is another bizarre and beautifully-shaped tree succulent restricted to the rugged mountainsides of the area, endangered by over-collecting and in some areas by the depredation of baboons (Midgley et al. 1997). Its main Namibian population of about 1 200 individuals may be further threatened by dust from the adjacent Rosh Pinah zinc mine (Loots and Mannheimer 2003). In South Africa, its main Richtersveld population at Cornellskop is limited to only 21 individuals (Pierce and Cowling 1999).

The botanical richness of this region often overshadows its rarely-glimpsed fauna. Mammals include several red data species: oryx (*Oryx gazella*), brown hyaena (*Hyaena brunnea*), grey rhebok (*Pelea capreolus*), African wild cat (*Felis sylvestris lybica*), cheetah (*Acynonix jubatus*), and aardwolf (*Proteles cristatus*) (Pallett 1995; Barnard 1998). More easily seen but less well-known are invertebrates, including a bountiful array of scorpions and insect mutualists. Monkey beetles (Scarabaeidae: Melolonthinae: Hopliini) are an important flagship pollinator group, and numerous range-restricted endemics are crucial for pollination of Asteraceae and Mesembryanthemaceae (J. Colville, in litt.; J. Irish and E. Marais, in litt.). The area is also home to numerous endemic reptiles, particularly tortoises, including the highly restricted Namaqualand tent tortoise (*Psammobates tentorius trimeni*) and several endemic species of girdled lizards (*Cordylus* spp.) (Simmons et al. 1998; Pierce and Cowling 1999). Despite relatively low bird diversity, the coastal plain, offshore islands and !Gariep River Mouth support high densities of wetland and seabirds, including the near-threatened Damara tern (*Sterna balaenarum*) (Simmons, in press).

The conservation significance of this region cannot be overestimated. At a national scale, the area shelters the highest levels of endemic biodiversity in Namibia (Burke 2004) and has long been regarded as a major conservation priority in southern Africa, also owing to its high concentration of endemic plants (WWF and IUCN 1994). The region protects the !Gariep centre of diversity and endemism (van Wyk and Smith 2001), which includes the Richtersveld, Sperrgebiet, and extends eastward to incorporate the !Gariep valley as far as Augrabies, as a northern realm of the globally recognized Succulent Karoo hotspot (Driver et al. 2003). It is one of the few areas in the world where vast wilderness can still be found in a threatened hotspot ecosystem.

This area has the potential to evolve into a truly massive transboundary conservation corridor, from south to north encompassing Richtersveld National Park in South Africa, the |Ai-|Ais-Hunsberg Reserve Complex, Sperrgebiet National Park, Namib-Naukluft and Skeleton Coast Parks in Namibia, and Parque Nacional do Iona in Angola. Although this may seem like an impossible dream, the consolidation of the Sperrgebeit and the |Ai-|Ais in Namibia can be realized by the integration of a few intervening land parcels and will bring Namibia's protected area coverage to more than 17% (Barnard and Frazee 2002). Linking three countries through parks, conservancies, and other conservation categories, this corridor would form the largest conservation area in Africa, enabling long-term protection to be achieved.

The component protected areas (Richtersveld National Park in South Africa, and the |Ai-|Ais and Sperrgebiet National Parks in Namibia) have extremely different land-use histories. There has been little human access to much of the Sperrgebiet for most of the past century as a result of its status as a concession to diamond interests. Although the overburden of much of its coastal strip has been completely removed and processed by diamond mining, the mining activities have minimally impacted spectacular arid plains and inselbergs, and sites of high geological, palaeontological, historical, and archaeological value have remained pristine (Pallett 1995). The nearby |Ai-|Ais-Hunsberg Reserve Complex was established between 1969 and 1988 from sparsely populated and stocked rangelands (Barnard et al. 1998). In contrast, the contractual Richtersveld National Park (162 445 ha) is the result of a 1991 arrangement between local communities and the state, which allows continued livestock grazing, fuelwood collection, and honey gathering, and has opened doors for tourism-related enterprises and employment for the previously landless communities.

Final proclamation of a Greater !Gariep TFCA will depend on a bilateral agreement over a lingering border dispute that deprives Namibia of significant water rights from the !Gariep River. Its success, however, will also depend on uncommon partnerships between mining and conservation in Namibia, and between local pastoral communities, conservation, and mining in South Africa. Proclamation of conservation areas in this region seeks to unlock development opportunities for adjacent rural communities, including biodiversity-based enterprise development, community-based tourism, and wilderness education. Realization of benefits from these opportunities is essential

*Of all flightless birds, the ostrich
(Struthio camelus) is the best-adapted for running,
reaching speeds of 70 km per hour.*
© Gerald Cubitt

to overcome the challenges of historic marginalization and widespread poverty.

Mining and agriculture are prevalent throughout the region. While diamond mining has helped maintain large areas of the region in pristine condition, the intensively mined coastline may require many decades to recover from damage, if it recovers at all (Burke 2002). Exploitation of base metals and small-scale prospecting continue to threaten the region's biodiversity, as enforcement of regulations over this vast area is extremely difficult. Along the !Gariep River, fields of cotton, lucerne, and table grapes are rapidly expanding. Unsustainable growth in agricultural activities in the upper reaches of the !Gariep may drastically impact the ecology of this arid system (Bohensky et al. 2004). As local populations and visitor numbers increase, overharvesting of fuelwood, game poaching, illegal harvesting of the charismatic species, and overgrazing by livestock will increasingly threaten this unique vegetation and wilderness landscape. Additionally, as with most of the world's deserts, the environment of the TFCA is fragile, and global climate change is endangering many of the restricted range endemics (Midgley and Millar, in press). This looming threat emphasizes the need for holistic design and management of the Greater !Gariep TFCA (Driver et al. 2003).

Political and local support for conservation of this unique region is increasing. In Namibia, recommendations from the Sperrgebiet Land Use Plan (Sperrgebiet Consortium 2000) were taken up by the Namibian Ministry of Mines and Energy, successfully containing the rapid diversification of mineral prospecting activities and restricting activity to large corporations with strong environmental track records. Namdeb Diamond Corporation and its predecessors, which have protected most of the Sperrgebiet in a pristine state, established a strong conservation partnership ethic with the government mining and environment regulatory authorities. In South Africa, the Richtersveld communities secured their land tenure and reaffirmed their commitment to conservation as a vehicle for development. In 2003, the South African and Namibian Governments committed themselves to holistic co-management of |Ai-|Ais-Richtersveld Transfrontier Park, acknowledging both its importance for regional economic development and the need to establish other cross-border conservation initiatives along the !Gariep River. Several transboundary and regional conservation programs, including a bilateral working group on the !Gariep River Mouth Ramsar Site, the Millennium Ecosystem Assessment of the !Gariep Basin, and the Succulent

Karoo Ecosystem Programme (SKEP), are harmonizing their action plans. Significant national and international funding has been obtained, and local project implementers are actively coordinating their activities and helping partners reap the conservation and socioeconomic fruits of this investment (http://www.skep.org).

With the Sperrgebiet National Park as a groundbreaking partnership between mining and conservation and the contractual park in the Richtersveld, where the local community retains rights to economic activities in the area, conservation efforts in the future Greater !Gariep transfrontier conservation areas have the potential to promote new models of peace and co-management between two states. The acid test will be how well these approaches conserve these stark landscapes and their subtle but astonishing biodiversity.

SARAH R. FRAZEE
PHOEBE BARNARD
RICHARD M. COWLING

Above, the eastern rock elephant shrew (Elephantulus myurus) *is a member of an entire mammalian order, Macroscelidea, endemic to Africa.*
© Ingrid van den Berg/Ardea.com

On the opposite page, landscape in the Fish River Natural Reserve in Namibia, sister reserve to the Richtersveld National Park in South Africa.
© Gerald Cubitt

KAVANGO-ZAMBEZI: THE FOUR-CORNERS TRANSFRONTIER CONSERVATION AREA

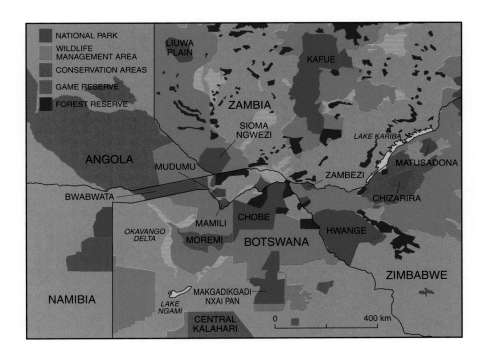

One of the great advantages of transboundary conservation areas (TBCAs) is that two or more countries can share a wide range of species and natural resources, and in certain cases they can also share major rivers and river basins. A good example of the latter is the proposed Kavango-Upper Zambezi Transfrontier Conservation Area (KUZ-TFCA), which includes significant parts of the basins of the Okavango and Upper Zambezi Rivers. It is also known as the "Four-Corners TFCA," as the boundaries of Botswana, Namibia, Zambia, and Zimbabwe meet at Impalila Island in the middle of the proposed area, the only place in the world where four countries come together at one point.

This ambitious initiative is being supported in its first phase by the U.S. Agency for International Development (USAID) and the Swiss Agency for Development and Cooperation (SDC), with the potential of bringing together parts of Angola, Botswana, Namibia, Zambia, and Zimbabwe. Protected areas which should eventually be linked include the Hwange and Zambezi National Parks in Zimbabwe, the Mamili, Mudumu and Bwabwata National Parks in the Caprivi Region of Namibia, the Sioma Ngwezi and Kafue National Parks in Zambia, the Chobe and Makgadikgadi Nxai Pan National Parks, the Moremi Game Reserve in Botswana, and the Luiana Partial Reserve in Angola. The precise boundaries of the TFCA and the design and shape of the corridors joining protected areas together are yet to be defined.

The proposed TFCA embraces most of the Okavango River Basin, an integral part of an ecosystem that is connected to the Upper Zambezi River Basin, extending the regional links of this important area to five countries. It attracts large-scale migrations of mega fauna and several *Red Book* animal species, making this a wilderness of global biological significance. With parts still relatively untransformed, and a surprisingly high number of species recorded from the miombo woodland, it is anticipated that the TFCA will play a valuable role in the conservation of biodiversity not covered elsewhere in Africa and make a significant contribution towards the conservation of such threatened species as the African wild dog (*Lycaon pictus*), the wattled crane (*Bugeranus carunculatus*), the Nile crocodile (*Crocodylus nilotica*) and the cheetah (*Acinonyx jubatus*).

The Okavango Delta itself supports 128 species of mammals, with major populations of large mammals that are not well-represented in other parts of the continent, including the red lechwe (*Kobus leche*) and the sitatunga (*Tragelaphus spekii*). All of Africa's non-forest large predators are conspicuous, with the wild dog being present in significant numbers. Although at

least 450 species of birds have been recorded, as well as 36 species of amphibians, 86 species of fish, 89 species of reptiles, and over 1 000 species of plants, the only endemic species is the Makgadikgadi spiny agama (*Agama makarikarica*).

The KUZ-TFCA also embraces the largest contiguous population of African elephants (*Loxodonta africana*), one of the continent's most important flagship species. Recent estimates in northern Botswana alone are in excess of 125 000 elephants growing at 5% per year. Veterinary fences in northern Botswana and civil unrest in neighboring countries have almost certainly contributed to these high concentrations by posing restrictions to normal dispersal patterns. These elephants are part of a population linked with animals in northwestern Zimbabwe, the Caprivi Strip of northern Namibia, southwestern Zambia, and southern Angola. *Recent research has shown that there is considerable movement of the species between these five countries.*

In Botswana, the Department of Wildlife and National Parks is becoming increasingly concerned about the effects that this build-up of elephants is having on the riverine vegetation, particularly in Chobe National Park. Furthermore, several local communities adjacent to Chobe are also expressing concern about the escalating human-elephant conflicts, which have included crop-raiding (even total destruction of crops), damage to wild fruits and wild trees, impeded human activities and movement, and water depletion during the dry season. All of this has resulted in a growing demand and pressure to reduce the number of elephants, and a major culling program has been mooted.

As part of a program to address these concerns, Conservation International has been working in collaboration with the Botswana conservation agencies to determine the abundance, distribution, population structure, habitat needs, and movements of elephants in northern Botswana and on the transboundary movements of the species within the KUZ-TFCA. What has emerged from this important study is that there is considerable potential for elephants from Botswana to move north into Zambia and Angola once new corridors have been established, which should reduce the environmental and social pressures of their overabundance in Botswana and Caprivi.

When formally established, the KUZ-TFCA will represent the largest contiguous wilderness, wetland, and wildlife area in southern Africa (in excess of 12 000 000 ha), with the potential to become one of the world's leading tourist destinations. The Okavango Delta itself is the "crown jewel" of the KUZ-TFCA. Covering approximately 1 600 000 ha, it is one of the largest inland deltas and Ramsar Sites in the world, a highly variable and complex aquatic ecosystem, largely structured by the cli-

matic regime, the chemical and physical environment, and the biological interactions that occur within it. Three major biomes are represented, namely the permanent swamp, the seasonal swamp, and the drainage rivers, the latter creating a mosaic of aquatic habitats which forms the core of northern Botswana's highly successful tourism industry. Outside the river basin, the TFCA incorporates a complex mosaic of vegetation types, largely of significant areas of wet and dry miombo woodlands, comprising mainly members of the legume subfamily Caesalpinioideae (species in the genera *Brachystegia*, *Julbernardia*, *Isoberlinia*, *Burkea* and *Cryptosepalum*). The woodlands are interspersed with dambos and grasslands, mopane (*Colophospermum mopane*) woodlands, Kalahari acacia savannah, and woodlands of Zambezi teak (*Baikiaea plurijuga*) on Kalahari sand.

An increasing number of Africa's political leaders are embracing and promoting TBCAs, and it is most encouraging to see the support the KUZ-TFCA is receiving from local communities, governments, conservation and tourism organizations, including hunting groups, bilateral and multilateral aid agencies, the private sector, and a variety of NGOs. Broadly speaking, the attraction of TBCAs is generally related to the multi-faceted role the areas could play in dealing with the conservation of biodiversity, socioeconomic development through job creation in the tourism and hunting industry, and the promotion of a culture of peace through enhancing regional cooperation and development. The KUZ-TFCA qualifies in all sectors.

The establishment of this new TBCA received an important boost with the launching of the Okavango Upper Zambezi International Tourism Spatial Development Initiative (OUZIT-SDI), which grew out of a proposal for the establishment of a southern African wildlife sanctuary in the wetlands associated with the Okavango and Zambezi River systems. It is now an official project of the New Partnership for Africa's Development (NEPAD) with funding from the Development Bank of South Africa and other development assistance agencies. OUZIT-SDI was also approved by the Southern African Development Community (SADC) as an official regional project, and was launched as a Type II Partnership Project at the World Summit for Sustainable Development in 2002 in Johannesburg. Angola, Botswana, Namibia, Zambia, and Zimbabwe have all subsequently become signatories to the OUZIT-SDI, boding well for the conservation of biodiversity which will follow within the KUZ-TFCA.

In the Angolan part of the KUZ-TFCA, the status of biodiversity is largely unknown. Vast areas of the country have been inaccessible for the past 30 years as a result of civil unrest, and access is likely to be difficult for many years to come as a result

On p. 264, a wetland in the Moremi Wildlife Reserve in Botswana.
© Patricio Robles Gil/Sierra Madre

On pp. 266-267, elephants (Loxodonta africana) *in Botswana, sniffing the air for signs of danger.*
© Beverly Joubert/National Geographic Image Collection

Above, an African fish eagle (Haliaeetus vocifer), *a close relative of the American bald eagle and a conspicuous species in this part of Africa, here seen in the Moremi Game Reserve in Botswana.*

On the opposite page, male and female Egyptian geese (Alopochen aegyptiacus) *in Chobe Natitonal Park, Botswana. Both photos,*
© Patricio Robles Gil/Sierra Madre

On pp. 270-271, Zambezi lechwe males (Kobus hydrotragus)
fighting over a female that was on the border between their two
territories. Okavango Delta, Botswana.
© Patricio Robles Gil/Sierra Madre

On pp. 272-273, lion cubs (Panthera leo) moved
to a buffalo carcass by their mother.
© Beverly Joubert/National Geographic Image Collection

of wide spread landmines. The greatest threat to the ecological integrity of the whole area is poverty, with over half of the population living in a situation of absolute poverty. The recent collapse of the Zimbabwean economy and associated changes in land tenure have exacerbated the threats to biodiversity with more and more people throughout the region moving into subsistence agriculture with a concomitant acceleration of deforestation and habitat fragmentation leading inevitably to the loss of biodiversity, which at this stage is difficult to quantify.

The continued ecological functioning of the all-important Okavango Delta is dependent on not just the quantity of water reaching it but also on the timing of that water. The flood-pulse is vital to various ecological processes which take place. Any potential large-scale agricultural development upstream will need to take the income-generating capacity of the delta into account. If the delta is threatened through the construction of water-storage dams upstream, it is highly unlikely that the loss of tourism income will be compensated for by the production of crops.

The creation of the KUZ-TFCA is a mega-project requiring massive financing, political commitment and regional coordination, which cannot realistically be completed in one phase, particularly as the unequal levels of development between the states and the regions involved complicate integration efforts. Underdeveloped areas, such as southern Angola, will require a greater share of the resources to bring them on to a similar footing as the other countries involved. At this stage it is more realistic to concentrate on incremental projects, all aimed toward the long-term goal of forming the KUZ-TFCA. Nevertheless, the KUZ-TFCA is an outstanding example of how major protected areas —at present isolated from one another in five countries— could be joined together into a continuum. The economic opportunities associated with the growth of tourism centered on the Victoria Falls and embracing some of the continent's most exciting tourism destinations could transform large parts of the region. At the same time, a unique level of regional cooperation through the facilitation of transboundary movements of large mammals (especially elephants) and of tourists, and the marketing of a unified tourism destination, has the potential to promote peace and stability.

JOHN HANKS

THE ROOF OF AFRICA: TRANSBOUNDARY CONSERVATION IN THE MALOTI-DRAKENSBERG MOUNTAINS

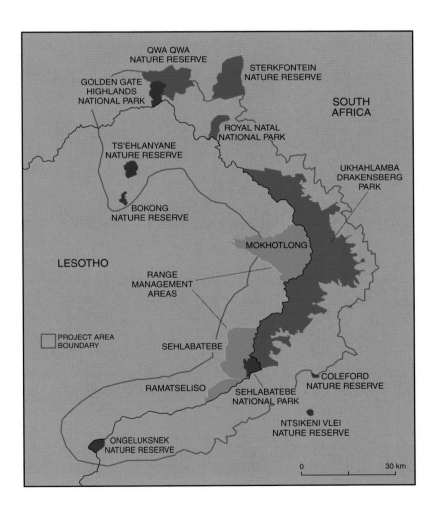

The Maloti-Drakensberg Transfrontier Conservation and Development Area straddles the boundary between Lesotho and South Africa. In the Kingdom of Lesotho, the Maloti Mountains dominate the eastern portion of the country, forming part of the Great Escarpment. From the perspective of South Africa, the Drakensberg mountain range consists of a spectacular barrier of sandstone and basalt rising above 3 400 m. Thabana-Ntlenyana in Lesotho, at 3 482 m, is the highest point in southern Africa and it is claimed that the uThukela Falls are the second highest in the world at 994 m. These sheer rock walls, buttresses, ramparts, spires, and high altitude grasslands are steeped in biological, archaeological, and historical value. Although they form an apparent boundary between the two countries, and a convenient political divide, biological, cultural, and ecosystem functions suggest otherwise.

As with other mountain ecosystems, the Maloti-Drakensberg Mountains are a fragile island of biodiversity, surrounded by monocultures and destroyed landscapes. In addition to their intrinsic value, which has been recognized by the global community through the listing of the Ukhahlamba-Drakensberg World Heritage Site on both natural and cultural criteria, the mountains are the primary source of water for the entire southern African sub-continent; the grasslands and wetlands a source of primary livelihoods for large numbers of people, and the scenic diversity, rock faces, peaks, rivers, and valleys a favorite tourism resort. These uses, whether they derive from economic exploitation or rural subsistence, threaten the persistence of the natural and cultural values of the area, unless they are carefully controlled, demanding in turn unique institutional and management arrangements, which span the boundary between the two countries.

The unique biological diversity of this mountain bioregion has evolved over geological time resulting from the interplay of complex biotic and abiotic conditions, including altitude, geology, topography, rainfall, and fire, creating numerous microhabitats. The area is species-rich, containing at least 2 153 plant species, 299 bird species, 48 mammal species, 48 species of reptiles, and 26 species of frogs. Such richness is also found in various invertebrate groups, and there is a vast diversity of several groups of ancient forms of insects associated with the alpine tundra vegetation that are also endemic to the site. These include 32 species of craneflies, 21 species of danceflies, and four species of lacewings. Some 119 of the plant and animal species occurring in

the area are threatened species listed in the international *Red Book* and include the Drakensberg cycad, and various lily, orchid, and bird species such as the Cape vulture and the locally "Vulnerable" lammergeier. The area is also distinctive because of its high degree of plant, bird, and invertebrate endemism, estimated at 30% for plants (a percentage occurring nowhere else on Earth). This area falls within one of Conservation International's seven biodiversity hotspots found in Africa, the Eastern Afromontane hotspot, and it also straddles two Endemic Bird Areas, the Lesotho Highlands and the Southern Africa Grasslands (Mittermeier et al. 2004; Birdlife International 2004).

Two main high altitude vegetation complexes occur, namely the Alti-Mountain Grassland biome, from 2 500 to 3 480 m above sea level, and the Afro-Mountain Grassland biome, from 1 700 to 2 500 m. Hidden from view, except for those who make the effort to climb into the higher reaches, are extensive wetlands, which are distinct, both structurally and floristically, from all other wetland systems in southern Africa. The wetlands provide a vital hydrological function, ensuring the delivery of high-quality water throughout the year, and are the habitat for a range of endemic plants and animals, such as the Maloti minnow (*Pseudobarbus quahlambae*), the rock catfish (*Austroglanis sclateri*), the Drakensberg frog (*Rana dracomontana*), and the submerged water-plant (*Aponogeton ranunculiformis*). One of the more cryptic creatures living in the high altitude wetlands is Sloggett's ice rat (*Otomys sloggettii*), invisible unless you sit quietly in the middle of one of the alpine bogs, when it will emerge from its hummock burrow and run. In the summer, these wetlands are a blaze of color with stands of flowering red-hot pokers (*Kniphofia* sp.) and irises (*Moraea* sp.). In recognition of the international importance of these wetlands, the entire Ukhahlamba-Drakensberg Park has been listed as a Ramsar Wetland.

Climatically, this is one of the few areas in southern Africa where long-term annual average precipitation exceeds evaporation. The mountains are strategically placed to deliver water to much of the region, and the Lesotho Highlands Water Scheme is currently providing 50% of the water needs of South Africa's economic hub, the province of Gauteng. It is further estimated that by 2030, 70% of the region will be relying on the water from the bioregion, which in turn depends upon the health and vigor of the biodiversity within it.

In addition to biodiversity values, the natural landscape contains many caves and rock-shelters, home to the largest and most concentrated group of paintings in Africa south of the Sahara, made by the San people over a period of at least 4 000 years. The rock paintings are considered to be outstanding in quality and diversity of subject and in their depiction of animals and human beings. They bear an exceptional testimony to the San people, who no longer live in the region, and represent their spiritual life and beliefs. This rock art heritage is of particular interest today as it is protected in the context of the very landscape which the artists inhabited. One can sit quietly in one of the painted shelters and look out onto a landscape, which is substantially the same as that in which the San people lived and worked, spot a herd of eland or a gray rhebuck (which occurs nowhere else) making its way up a steep grassy slope opposite the cave, and ponder this unique combination of natural and cultural heritage.

The biological and cultural resources of the bioregion are increasingly threatened by unsustainable land-use practices, alien invasive species, poverty, and illegal activities, many of which can be controlled or mitigated by harmonized transboundary management regimes.

In Lesotho, the soils are particularly fertile, but also shallow and very susceptible to erosion. The latter is also a factor of steep slopes and high intensity precipitation events. Although seasonally grazed according to a weak communal land tenure regime, the stocking rates far exceed the level of sustainability. Coupled with the injudicious use of fire as a range management tool, both biodiversity and basal cover are decreasing markedly with the related impact of accelerated soil loss. Although levels of fertility are not as high in South Africa, the same dynamics are prevalent, as are the consequences. In addition to unsustainable subsistence farming, large areas under intensive commercial farming have also caused significant losses of biodiversity.

Alien invasive species are found in many parts of the area. These have exerted pressure on other species and have displaced many natural communities. The problem of alien invasive species is particularly common in South Africa where alien species, such as the wattle (*Acacia mearnsii*), the Patula Pine (*Pinus patula*), and the American bramble (*Rubus cuneifolius*) have invaded and displaced the natural communities. Overgrazing of natural rangelands in Lesotho has led to the prevalence of the native but locally invasive and unpalatable woody shrub (*Chrysocoma oblongifolia*). Over-harvesting of biological resources for traditional and commercial purposes is also a major threat in the area, particularly in Lesotho, where access

is largely uncontrolled. Most of the harvested species are illegally exported to cities and towns in South Africa and Lesotho, where they are sold to the general public for medicinal or horticultural uses, e.g., the spiral aloe (*Aloe polyphylla*).

Poverty is both the source and a result of environmental degradation in the Maloti-Drakensberg bioregion, especially in Lesotho, where over 35% of mountain households belong to the lowest income quintile of less than one dollar per month. The hardships experienced by mountain inhabitants leave them with no option but to engage in unsustainable economic activities that destroy the rich mountain biodiversity. Unless the existing economic disparities resulting from marginalization of mountain communities are addressed, and the income sources of mountain communities are diversified, environmental degradation will continue indefinitely.

Common cross-border illegal activities along the Maloti-Drakensberg escarpment include stock theft, trafficking of marijuana, and smuggling of firearms. These problems have resulted in the loss of many lives. In addition, they have and will continue to have an impact on the implementation of conservation management strategies and may negatively affect ecotourism development in the area.

The need for a transboundary conservation initiative was recognized in the early 1980s with an interchange among authorities in the two countries. Despite the prevailing political climate, the initiative survived, gained momentum, and was enshrined in a "declaration" signed by both countries at Giant's Castle in 1997. This was in recognition of the fact that both countries share this strategically and globally significant bioregion and that collaborative management is essential to efficiently address the threats described above.

Of particular interest to the authorities was to address the issue of illegal cross-border activities, mainly in the theft and trafficking of cattle and marijuana, which inhibit range management programs and security in both countries. The extent and relative inaccessibility of the border area, together with the extreme climatic conditions —particularly in winter— make it very difficult to monitor and control the movement of people. In addition, there is the illegal movement of people in search of work, and problems associated with their indeterminate status in both countries, leading to exploitation of workers, competition, and conflict regarding employment and the associated dangers of firearms and violence. A coordinated transboundary approach to management of these issues is essential.

It has also been recognized that a more strategic approach to coordinated planning and management of the area, together with the development of a linked and compatible tourism industry, could hold the key to sustaining livelihoods and providing alternatives to destructive exploitation of the resource. To this end, a multi-faceted program was developed to consult and involve all stakeholders in the bioregion in developing a common vision, achieving international agreement, and implementing a cooperative management program.

A Memorandum of Understanding signed by the appropriate ministers of the two countries on June 11, 2001 established a Bilateral Steering Committee, which meets twice-yearly to guide and monitor progress. In each country there is a Project Coordinating Committee (PCC), representing key sectors and interests. In Lesotho, the PCC is a multi-departmental committee chaired by the Ministry of Tourism, Environment, and Culture, while in South Africa, the PCC is chaired by the National Department of Environmental Affairs and Tourism with representatives of the key implementing agencies from the three provinces in which the bioregion occurs.

Coordination of program activities is being undertaken by a Project Coordinating Unit in each country, with the main function to secure an integrated approach to transboundary activities. These units are working closely with the implementing agencies to ensure the mainstreaming of the project into their various organizational planning processes, while also ensuring the incorporation of related governmental role-players and other key stakeholders into project activities. The most important of the latter is the establishment and implementation of a bioregional planning process, which will be handed over to the implementing agencies at the end of the current phase of program development in 2007-2008.

Transboundary conservation programs around the world differ in the extent to which they attempt to achieve biodiversity goals, as well as social, economic, political, and institutional goals. In the case of the Maloti-Drakensberg program, there is no simple solution to achieving biodiversity conservation at the scale of a mountainous bioregion shared by two countries with sharp disparities in context and capacity. It is clear that solutions are likely to be found when it is understood that the underlying resource value is the most promising path to prosperity, and that if the two countries cooperate, they can share experiences and support one another to achieve significant progress. It is on this shared understanding that the interim institutional

On the opposite page, the black wildebeest or white-tailed gnu (Connochaetes gnou) was nearly exterminated by hunting, habitat loss, and periodic outbreaks of disease by 1900. Today, the total population is roughly 18 000 animals, most of it on private land.

Above, this appealing little ice rat (Otomys sloggeti) is endemic to the high plateau of Lesotho, where it is quite abundant and regularly seen peering out of its burrow. Both Photos, © Patricio Robles Gil/Sierra Madre

On pp. 280-281, lilies blooming in Sani Pass in the southern Drakensberg Mountains, KwaZulu Natal, South Africa. © Sycholt/SILVESTRIS

frameworks for cooperation have been built, despite the somewhat turbulent political history of the region. There is also a shared experience in the two countries of poor communities living on either side of the international boundary, whose future livelihoods are dependent on compatible management of the natural resource base and on the development of new economic opportunities. Two clear directions have emerged which augur well for the future. Firstly, the demand for large quantities of quality water creates a market for environmental services that can be provided by the mountains and the people who live in and manage them. Pilot payments for the delivery of water supplies, enhanced by effective soil erosion control and alien invasive plant management, have demonstrated that jobs can be created and community institutions built. Secondly, the World Heritage status and spectacular mountain environment can continue to be developed and marketed to support the growth of the region's tourism business and create not only a diversity of employment, but also the possibility for people to derive real benefits from this emergent biodiversity economy. This mainstreaming of biodiversity into the social and economic development of the region is likely to provide the most compelling case for the sustainability and persistence of the region's globally and locally significant value, while ensuring that the good relations developed between the countries by tackling joint concerns will continue to contribute towards lasting peace and security.

KEVAN ZUNCKEL
CHABA MOKUKU
TREVOR SANDWITH

ASIA/PACIFIC

WEST TIEN SHAN: AT THE CROSSROADS OF CENTRAL ASIA

Situated at a biological crossroads, the mountains of the West Tien Shan in Central Asia lie at the westernmost edge of the Himalayan Chain. The region covers a spectacular landscape with snow-capped mountain peaks rising to more than 3 000 m and towering above flat grassy steppes and river canyons. The West Tien Shan Transboundary Conservation Area (TBCA) covers a complex of montane habitat where the borders of Kyrgyzstan meet those of neighboring Kazakhstan and Uzbekistan and includes four long-established but non-contiguous protected areas in the transborder region. The three countries are collaborating on a World Bank/Global Environmental Facility (GEF) project to strengthen management of existing protected areas, to expand and connect the protected area networks across the national boundaries, and to develop a bioregional plan that will promote conservation in the broader production landscape outside the four protected areas. The West Tien Shan TBCA fits two of the working definitions used by the IUCN Transboundary Task Force. It can be described both as "a cluster of protected areas and the intervening land" and as "two or more contiguous protected areas across a national boundary." Discussions are underway between the three republics on an interstate agreement for a West Tien Shan transboundary conservation area.

Situated at the heart of Central Asia, the West Tien Shan mountains lie at the meeting point between the Palearctic and Indo-Himalayan bioregions, and support a mixture of Oriental and Palearctic species, with high levels of species endemism. The West Tien Shan region, including the outlier Karatau Range in Kazakhstan, is species-rich with some 3 000 recorded species of flora and fauna. The mountains boast 170 endemics and many species which are endangered elsewhere in their range and threatened globally. The region covers a range of climatic conditions from sub-tropical to tundra and glaciers, and from semi-arid steppe to mountain juniper forests and snow-covered peaks. The mountains harbor unique stands of walnut forest (*Juglans regia*) and wild ancestors of cultivated fruit trees such as apple, pear, pistachio, and almond, as well as endemic species of tulips, irises, crocus, and other native bulbs. Seven species of wild tulips are known from this region, ranging in size from delicate miniature tulips to tall-stemmed species which include Greig's tulip (*Tulipa greigi*), *T. ferganica*, *T. turkestanica*, *T. bifloriformis*, *T. dasystemon*, *T. anadroma*, and the rare Kauffmann's tulip (*T. kauffmanniana*), found even on the highest pastures above 2 500 m.

Rare and threatened animals include the snow leopard (*Uncia uncia*), the magnificent argali (*Ovis ammon*), and colonies

of the endemic Menzbier's marmot (*Marmota menzbieri*), which are unique to the high mountain pastures. Other characteristic mammals include the white-clawed bear (*Ursus arctos leucoryx*), the lynx (*Lynx lynx*), and the Central Asian mountain goat (*Capra sibirica*). Rare and endangered birds include golden eagles (*Aquila chrysaetos*), Eurasian eagle-owls (*Bubo bubo*), lammergeiers (*Gypaetus barbatus*), and the Himalayan griffon vulture (*Gyps himalayensis*). The mountain passes provide important flyways for migrating raptors moving south to escape northern winters. The West Tien Shan is a recognized center of agricultural biodiversity, home to medicinal plants, more than 220 herbs, pasture grasses and clovers, such as the lucerne, which originated here, wild grapes, tulips, and fruit trees. Many commercial and domesticated apple varieties originated in these mountains and the remaining wild relatives in the Tien Shan may offer potential for developing scab-resistant species.

The three-nation Central Asian Transboundary Biodiversity Project will assist the governments of Uzbekistan, Kazakhstan, and Kyrgyzstan to strengthen management in the protected areas of the West Tien Shan Mountains and to encourage more sustainable land-use management in the whole transboundary region. Initially the project will focus in and around four *zapovedniks* or strict nature reserves: The Aksu-Djabagly Reserve in Kazakhstan (85 574 ha), the Sary Chelek Reserve (23 868 ha) and Besh Aral (63 200 ha) in Kyrgyzstan, and the Chatkal Reserve (35 724 ha) in Uzbekistan. These relatively small sheltered areas protect a range of habitats, rising from river valleys through juniper and tugai forests, steppe and meadows to high peaks. Sary Chelek is also well known for its walnut forests and spectacular mountain lakes. Although these *zapodneviks* are characterized as strict nature reserves, most are managed for a range of uses including tourism, grazing, and hay making. Nested within a much wider mountain wilderness area covering more than 78 000 km^2, *zapovedniks* have considerable potential for conservation, especially for the wide-ranging predators and ungulates living in these mountain habitats.

Under the World Bank/GEF project, support is being provided to the four key protected areas through a mix of investments in capacity building (including training, transport, communications, and infrastructure), community awareness and education, and research and monitoring. The project has established new technical standards for protected area management and is involving local communities by providing incentives for conservation. A small grants' program provides financial and technical assistance to buffer-zone communities and community-based organizations to finance demand-driven activities in sustainable agriculture, alternative livelihoods, and alternative energy systems to reduce pressures on protected area resources.

In addition to these national-level activities, the project supports regional cooperation and planning, including the development of framework laws on protected areas and an interstate agreement for a West Tien Shan TBCA. The three countries are collaborating in joint planning efforts to designate wildlife corridors and appropriate land uses to maintain the reserves as a linked protected area network, as well as for the joint training, joint research, and monitoring of key wildlife species. These bioregional planning efforts have already led to the extension of the Chatkal and Besh Aral reserves and the creation of four new *zakazniks* or game reserves adjacent to Aksu-Djabagly in Kazakhstan: Boraldaiski (52 500 ha), Irus-Daubabinski (19 000 ha), Sairam-Ugamski (28 300 ha), and Berikkara (17 500 ha). Further proposals to include representation of key habitats within the protected area network include plans to link the Karatau Range and Aksu-Djabagly and connect some of the existing protected areas by creating a new large transboundary protected area in the Talas Range, between the Kara Bura and Uzun-Akmat *zapovednik*, adjacent to Besh Aral. The bioregional plan for conservation in the Greater West Tien Shan Ecosystem will integrate activities within the protected areas, their buffer zones, and the corridors and intervening lands that connect them. The plan is being developed using an integrated GIS platform for the three countries.

As part of the former Soviet Union, the three republics share Russian as a common language and an economic and conservation history. The main economic activity in the ecoregion is agriculture, especially livestock grazing. More than half of the population lives in poverty, and the situation is worsening due to problems associated with the transition from a centrally-planned economy to a market economy. During the Soviet era, a highly intensive regional (now international) system of livestock and pasture management was in use, which managed the seasonal movements of millions of sheep and goats between the mountain summer and winter lowland pastures. After the three republics' independence in 1991, livestock numbers dropped sharply as a result of the suspension of price controls and subsidized feed imports, and the collapse of intra-Soviet Union trade arrangements. Despite the decline in livestock numbers, the problem of overgrazing persisted, with overutilization of the more accessible pastures, while those furthest from settlements are undergrazed. A large part of the pasture resource is in poor condition, with low productivity, topsoil erosion, and occasional mudflows in highly degraded areas. The bioregional plan will attempt to address these and other socioeconomic issues, including

new ecotourism opportunities, as part of a holistic approach to economic development and nature conservation.

In addition to their biodiversity values, the mountains of the West Tien Shan are major water towers, producing water supplies for all three countries. Kazakhstan and Uzbekistan are especially reliant on water production from the Kyrgyz Mountains to maintain irrigated agriculture on converted steppe lands. In return for free access to water, Kazakhstan provides access to oil and energy supplies to Kyrgyzstan. The regional benefits and ecosystem services accruing from conservation and sustainable management of the natural habitats of the TBCA need to be better assessed so that appreciation of the mountains' role in water production can be embedded in the transboundary protocol.

Cooperation among the three countries has been historically strong, even before the Soviet Period, and the transboundary project has helped to strengthen approaches to conservation planning and land management in the Greater West Tien Shan Ecosystem. Nonetheless, the transboundary region is characterized by interdigitated national boundaries (a legacy of the Soviet era), with attendant border disputes and conflicts over managing water flows for agriculture and energy production. The bioregional plan for the Greater West Tien Shan Ecosystem will lead to more harmonized planning and will be integrated with other high level instruments for regional cooperation. Although the West Tien Shan has not been designated as a peace park, it is promoting cooperation between the three countries, and conservation efforts have led to a joint declaration of cooperation for management of the transboundary region.

The breakup of the former Soviet Union into independent republics and the worsening economic situation in the former republics has led to increasing pressure on natural resources, including a significant decline of forest covering (50% in the case of Kyrgyzstan) and excessive overgrazing of mountain pastures by livestock. This increased exploitation of natural capital to optimize revenues and offset economic pressure in the new republics has occurred simultaneously with a decline in law enforcement, and diminished institutional effectiveness and environmental monitoring. The new republics of Central Asia inherited a protected system of *zapovedniks*, *zakazniks*, and natural monuments that was common to the whole of the former Soviet Union and was once one of the best in the world. Now in Central Asia, as in Russia, economic difficulties and the strains of the transitional period have seriously undermined financing for nature conservation. At the same time, communities living adjacent to or within protected areas have increased their reliance on those areas' resources, especially through additional demands for pas-

ture, fuel wood, arable land, and game for immediate consumption or sale. Overgrazing of Kyrgyz mountain pastures, for instance, is associated with transhumance activities and seasonal herding of livestock from Uzbekistan for summer grazing, a practice that is neither ecologically nor economically sustainable. The Central Asia Transboundary Project will help to address some of these issues through improved planning and management for strengthened conservation and more sustainable land management.

In the context of Central Asia, the goal of transboundary cooperation is assisted by the fact that all three countries have inherited a common protected area network framework as a legacy from the former Soviet Union. The protected areas are managed at the national level, but the transboundary project is being implemented under the guidance of the Transnational Steering Committee and has fostered harmonization of legal frameworks and adoption of compatible management standards for all protected areas as well as for the bioregional plan. Joint planning, training, and research have allowed the countries to adopt a realistic landscape approach to ecosystem management in line with their obligations under the Convention on Biological Diversity. It also has enabled the countries to jointly address complex social issues that impact on the region's human inhabitants as well as on biodiversity. Currently these conservation efforts are receiving encouraging international support both for conservation and complementary local development. Activities to develop community-based tourism and rural livelihoods have been supported by the EU/Tacis, the Swiss Agency for Development and Cooperation, and the Dutch Government.

While regional projects are generally more complex to implement than national ones, there is demonstrated value in a regional approach to transboundary ecosystem management. One positive outcome of the project has been the trust and collaboration built between the three countries and the creation of the 1998 Tri-National Agreement, signed by the three presidents. This agreement and the Transnational Steering Committee provide a good institutional framework for future transboundary cooperation, joint work programs, and exchange of expertise in Central Asia and with other similar transboundary initiatives globally.

KATHY MACKINNON
PHILLIP BRYLSKI
AGI KISS

Above, a Himalayan snowcock (Tetraogallus himalayensis), *a widespread species in this region.*

On the opposite page, the ibisbill (Ibidorhyncha struthersii) *is a largish, pale gray wader very popular with bird watchers.*
Both photos, © Otto Pfister

MANAS: TRANSBOUNDARY CONSERVATION ON THE ASSAM-BHUTAN BORDER

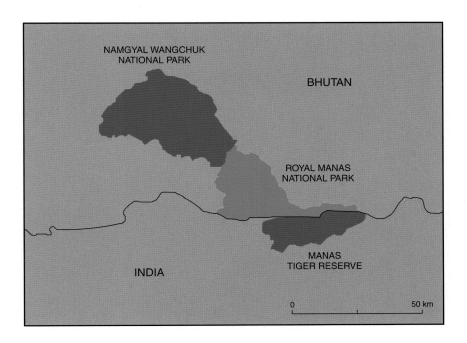

The Manas region (named after the goddess Manasa) on the border between Assam, India, and Bhutan consists of nearly 330 000 ha of protected forest separated by the Manas River. On the Indian side, the Manas Tiger Reserve lies at the foothills of the Bhutan Himalayas in the far eastern state of Assam, India. In Bhutan, the Royal Manas National Park (102 300 ha) and the adjacent Namgyal Wangchuk National Park (173 000 ha) form a contiguous complex with the Manas Tiger Reserve.

The Manas Tiger Reserve covers an area of 283 700 ha and its location at the confluence of the Indian, Ethiopian, and Indo-Chinese realms results in very high levels of biodiversity. Historically, the Raja of Gauripur and the Cooch-Behar royal family used Manas as their Royal hunting grounds. The Manas Reserve Forest was created in 1917, but even before the official designation in 1928 of the Manas Wildlife Sanctuary, hunting, shooting, and trapping of animals were prohibited in an area of 36 000 ha, initially known as North Kamrup. Today Manas incorporates Manas National Park and the Natural World Heritage Site of 52 000 ha, surrounded by a buffer zone consisting of 18 reserved forests in North Kamrup, Western Assam Wildlife Division, and Kachugaon, as well as Haltugaon forest divisions intertwined with revenue villages.

On the Bhutan side, the Royal Manas National Park covers 102 300 ha (IUCN Management Category II) and ranges in altitude from 200 m to 2 310 m, extending from the Aigunmari River on the east to the Sukutaklai River in the west. With about 92% of the park still under forest cover, the Royal Manas National Park is the richest of Bhutan's protected areas. In 1988, it was established as a National Park, based on a master development plan that recommended upgrading of the former Manas Wildlife Sanctuary and its amalgamation with the Namgyal Wangchuk Wildlife Reserve (Lahan 1986).

Together they form a transboundary conservation area (TBCA) of immense importance for the conservation of many endemic and endangered species (Blower 1986), and an important staging and overwintering area for waterfowl (Scott 1989). With support from Project Tiger, an initial joint Management Plan for the TBCA was prepared in 1974.

Lying in the foothills of the Outer Himalaya, the northern parts of Bhutan are forested hills, which give way to low-lying and flat areas in India to the south. In Bhutan, the area is well watered by the Manas River and various smaller perennial rivers flowing southwards through it. In the west, the Kanamakra River cuts through the northern hills as a deep narrow valley and emerges in the lowlands as a broad stony bed several hundred metres wide. The main geological formations are: the Siwalik series (Miocene-Pliocene), consisting of bedded sandstones and gray to green claystones along the southern boundary; the Phuntsholing series (mid-Palaeozoic), comprising mostly folded successions of purple phyllites, quartzites, and silicon limestones with epidiozite sills along the length of the park; and the Buxa series (Permic-Triassic), represented by isolated formations of feldspar, sandstone, phyllites, and slates with coal. Soil of the Bhabar formation lies over mixed layers of boulders and gravels along the foothills. Recent alluvial deposits cover the floodplain, beneath which are older soils of brown loam and sandy loam (Lahan 1986).

In India, the Manas River flows through the western portion of the sanctuary, where it splits into three separate rivers and joins the Brahmaputra some 64 km further south. These and other rivers running through the reserve carry an enormous amount of silt and rock debris from the foothills, resulting from the heavy rainfall and the fragile nature of the rock and steep gradients of the catchments. This leads to the formation of alluvial terraces, comprising deep layers of deposited rock and detritus overlain with sand and soil of varying depth, shifting river channels and swamps. The northern portion is represented by the Bhabar formation, which is very porous due to the deep deposits of coarse detritus overlain by sandy loam and then a thin layer of humus. The Terai tract in the south consists of fine alluvial deposits with underlying pans. The area of the Boki basin, in the west of the sanctuary, is sometimes inundated during the monsoon, but never for very long, due to the sloping relief. The altitude of the Manas Tiger Reserve in Assam ranges from 50 to 190 m. The tropical climate provides three distinct seasons. Most of the annual precipitation falls between June and September, and reaches up to 4 000 mm. The average recorded maximum temperature in summer and lowest in winter has been 36º and 5ºC, respectively.

As part of the Himalaya Hotspot, the Manas Tiger Reserve of India is extremely rich in biodiversity. It also has the unique distinction of having the highest number of endangered endemic species of any Indian protected area. These include the only viable populations of hispid hare (*Caprolagus hispidus*) and pygmy hog (*Sus salvanicus*), Indian rhinoceros (*Rhinoceros unicornis*) and clouded leopard (*Neofelis nebulosa*). The region is also the only habitat for the endemic golden langur (*Trachypithecus geei*), as well as the country's last population of wild water buffalo (*Bubalus bubalis*). The hispid hare and pygmy hog, habitat-specific species of the alluvial grasslands found in the area, were considered extinct until their rediscovery in 1971 in Bronadi and Manas (Mallinson 1971; Oliver 1984). In addition, the Indian elephant (*Elephas maximus*) attains its largest concentration anywhere in India, with approximately 2 000 individuals, of which 1 000 move freely between India and Bhutan. The Bengal tiger (*Panthera tigris*) population numbers over 120 individuals, second only to the Sunderbans population in West Bengal.

Other mammals include the capped langur (*Trachypithecus pileata tenbricus*), the hoolock gibbon (*Hylobates hoolock*), the leopard (*Panthera pardus*, V), the golden cat (*Catopuma temmincki*, I), the fishing cat (*Prionailurus viverrinus*), the leopard cat (*P. bengalensis*), the marbled cat (*P. marmorata*, I), the binturong (*Arctictis binturong*), the sloth bear (*Melursus ursinus*, I), the wild dog (*Cuon alpinus*, V), the Ganges dolphin (*Platanista gangetica*), the Indian rhinoceros (E), the pygmy hog (E), the swamp deer (*Cervus duvauceli*, V), the sambar (*C. unicolor*), the hog deer (*Axis porcinus*), the Indian muntjac (*Muntiacus muntjak*), the water buffalo (*Bubalus arnee*, V) —probably representing the only pure strain of this species in India—, the gaur (*Bos gaurus*, V), the giant squirrel (*Ratufa indica*), and the Indian pangolin (*Manis crassicaudata*).

Threatened bird species in Manas include the osprey (*Pandion haliaetus*), the swamp partridge (*Francolinus gularis*), the Bengal florican (*Houbaropsis bengalensis*), the great pied hornbill (*Buceros bicornis*), the Indian pied hornbill (*Anthracoceros malabaricus*), and the wreathed hornbill (*Aceros undulatus*). Threatened reptiles include the gharial (*Gavialis gangeticus*), the eastern hill terrapin (*Melanochelys tricarinata*), the swamp back terrapin (*Kachuga tecta*), the Chapant terrapin (*K. smithi*), the flapshell turtle (*Lissemys punctata*), and the Malayan box turtle (*Cuora amboinensis*). Most of these are "Scheduled Species" under the Indian Wildlife [Protection] Act of 1972.

In terms of plants, there are 374 species of dicotyledons and 139 species of monocotyledons recorded in the park, including some rare and important plants such as the yellow flax (*Reinwardtia indica*), the telegraph plant (*Desmodium motorium*), the moyan (*Pueraria subspicata*) the rare gentian (*Exacum teres*), the janum (*Pygmaeoprema herbacea*), the sal (*Shorea robusta*), the chamal (*Artocarpus chaplasha*), the jarul (*Lagerstromia parviflora*), and the elephant tree (*Mallotus phillippinensis*). The area also harbors a total of 43 species of grasses (29 genera) and 15 species of orchids (Singh and Singh 1994). An economically important species is agar (*Aquilaria agallocha*), which is valued as incense and medicine in the Middle East.

On p. 290, a scene along the Manas River.
© Gertrud and Helmut Denzau

Above, an Asian elephant (Elephas maximus) *in the Manas Forest Reserve, Assam, India.*
© Gerald Cubitt

On the opposite page, the Bengal tiger (Panthera tigris tigris) *is still to be found in the Manas region.*
© Patricio Robles Gil/Sierra Madre

In addition to the flagship tigers, rhinos, elephants, leopards and golden langur, the Royal Manas National Park in Bhutan also harbors populations of other mammals endemic to the Bhutan-India border region, including wolves (*Canis lupus*, V), wild dogs (V), golden cats (I), and the gaur or Indian bison (V). The Eurasian otter (*Lutra lutra*), the wild boar (*Sus scrofa*), the Indian muntjac, the hog, the spotted deer (*Axis axis*), the sambar, and the serow (*Capricornis sumatraensis*) are also present. The Ganges dolphin is still reported to occur in the Manas River. In 1988, thirty tigers were reported to be in the park. The golden langur population is estimated to total at least 100 individuals. Subject to seasonal movements, elephants occur in small groups and are probably to be found mostly in the hills to the north in the dry season (Blower 1986). The pygmy hog (E) has not been recorded (Blower 1986). The gharial or Indian alligator (E) used to be present but is now probably extinct.

The Manas TBCA is noted for its spectacular scenery, with a variety of habitat types that support a diverse fauna, making it one of the richest wildlife areas in the region. The protected area represents the core of an extensive tiger reserve that protects an important migratory wildlife resource along the West Bengal to Arunachal Pradesh and Bhutan borders. Its wetlands are of international importance (Scott 1989) for migratory waterfowl. It is also the single most important site for the future survival of the pygmy hog and hispid hare (Oliver 1984).

There is only one forest village in the core zone of the Manas Tiger Reserve in India but, within the buffer zone, there are 57 revenue villages under the administrative control of the District Revenue Authorities and not the Forest Department. Their population of approximately 29 000 (up from 17 300 in 1971) exerts intensive pressure in the form of collection of minor forest products, cattle grazing, encroachment for agriculture, and illegal hunting for both local use and commercial purposes. The eastern (Bhuyanpara) and western (Panbari) parts of the park are under constant threat from the encroaching human population attempting to make inroads. About 1 500 ha in the Panbari Reserved Forests of the core zone of the park have been illegally settled since 1973 and all attempts to remove the squatters have been futile.

Until recently, the biggest threat to the park had been from the Bodo agitation —a violent period in which most of the rhino population was poached and the Bodo community was blamed for the killings, although the real culprits might have been professional poachers and loggers. For this reason, in 1989 the Manas National Park World Heritage Site was placed on the list of World Heritage in Danger. Apart from this commercial poaching, consumption of deer meat during festivals is a tradition in many towns bordering Manas.

The next most alarming threat comes from the local human populations inhabiting fringe areas of the park and slowly encroaching upon forest areas to increase their arable land. On the hilly foothills of the Himalayas, these are the only flat areas available to sustain the local economy. The lack of alternative sources for fodder and fuel has also led to the felling of trees for firewood and timber, mostly along rivers.

In recent years, as of 1996-1997, an eco-development program has taken root and has become one of the integral parts of the Project Tiger. Under this scheme, villagers have been convinced to move away from forest and wildlife products, and various eco-clubs and the NGO Manas Bandhu Groups, which works on issues related to the welfare of Manas, have been formed with help from the Manas management. These groups are promoting wildlife awareness and concern for protection of flora and fauna.

Largely unknown until the late 1980s, human-animal conflicts are now a major threat to the park, with recent reports of tigers killing people and their livestock and conversely, of tigers being killed by people. Elephants raiding nearby crops are also quite common despite park management efforts to control the situation before it turns hostile.

Grazing is not a big problem, but people collecting fodder inside the park pose a major threat. The livestock population has increased from 15 912 in 1971 to 20 231 in 1991, and continues to grow. Human-induced fire is also a threat to grassland habitats of the park.

Tourism has been badly affected by threats to the security of the area. In 1989, tourism came to a grinding halt and remained suspended for seven years due to safety concerns. Today, however, Manas is once again on the path of development, with the formulation of a Master Plan for 10 years under the auspices of the Project Tiger Directorate of the Ministry of Environment and Forests of the government of India. The Management of Manas is collaborating with local activists and making efforts to stop wanton destruction of the park habitat. It is encouraging to see that local activist groups are now helping Management Patrol to keep poachers out and to prevent the illicit felling of trees.

On the Bhutan side, Manas was originally established as a Royal Hunting Reserve and as a free natural resource for local people prior to its declaration as a national park. About 20 000

On the opposite page, the Indian rhinoceros (Rhinocerus unicornis) survives in a number of parks and protected areas in northeastern Indian, Bhutan, and Nepal, including the Manas region.
© Patricio Robles Gil/Sierra Madre

Above, a wild water buffalo (Bubalus bubalis). It is widespread as a domestic animal, and wild populations are now few and far between.
© Gertrud and Helmut Denzau

On pp. 296-297, the golden langur (Presbytis geei) is the most important flagship species for the Manas region, and occurs on both sides of the border.
© Elio Della Ferrera/naturepl.com

villagers grew crops, collected fuel wood, grazed their livestock, and were allowed to kill wildlife in conflict situations. Since its proclamation, it has not been extensively exploited, apart from a degree of encroachment for clearing and sugarcane plantations which affected 500 ha of forest in the north.

Other problems include poaching (mainly from across the Indian border but also from a number of settlements around the park), the deliberate setting of fires, and theft of timber, particularly the valuable agar wood which is used in medicine and to make incense (Blower 1986). A proposal by the Indian Government to build two dams in the upper reaches of the Manas and Sankosh Rivers for flood control and electricity production has been rejected. This dam would have caused substantial damage to both the Indian and Bhutanese sides of this important transboundary region.

At this time, there is no formal program between the Indian and Bhutanese Governments for joint management of Manas. Cooperation is informal, and comes in the form of quarterly meetings between field directors to deal with enforcement issues, eco-development, and sharing of technical assistance (Thorsell and Harrison 1990). The inaccessibility of the Bhutanese part of Manas forces local people to detour through India to reach other parts of Manas. This discourages tourism to Bhutan Manas, but makes it easy for timber smugglers and poachers to take advantage of the porous border, an issue that can only be dealt with through joint management. Another important issue that requires international collaboration is smuggling endangered medicinal fauna and flora into China, something that will require the collaboration of the Chinese Government as well (Johnsingh and Yonten 2004).

ATUL K. GUPTA

THE LANJAK ENTIMAU/ BATANG AI/BETUNG KERIHUN COMPLEX: A HERITAGE AREA IN THE HEART OF BORNEO

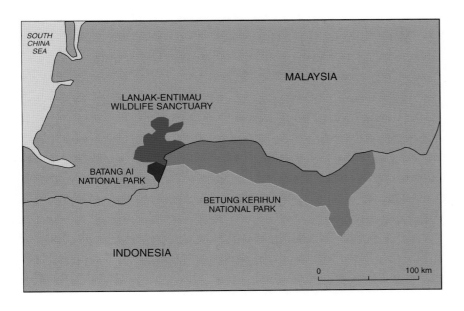

Rugged hills carpeted with magnificent dipterocarp forests straddle the boundary along much of the Indonesia-Malaysia border in the very heartland of Borneo. Most of the island's rivers originate as rocky, whitewater streams, maturing as they flow down into the lowlands, where they supply freshwater ecosystems throughout Borneo, as well as forming the waterways for the boats of Dayaks and other peoples. In this unspoiled part of Borneo, upriver longhouses nestle along riverbanks and a patchwork of traditional shifting cultivation disturbs the forest without destroying it. Here, the cry of the gibbon can still be heard through the early morning mist, eagles and hornbills still dominate the canopy, and the forests themselves retain their magnificent natural architecture across millions of hectares of the least accessible land.

West Kalimantan's Betung Kerihun National Park, Sarawak's Lanjak Entimau Wildlife Sanctuary, and Batang Ai National Park protect some 1 000 000 ha of this wonderland, one of the last bastions of Southeast Asian rainforest. It is a significant Heritage Area for Borneo, because the full diversity of the tropical forest cannot be maintained if it is reduced to a patchwork within an otherwise human-made landscape. Successful forest conservation requires the maintenance of very large blocks of inter connected forest, without which many species, especially those species with large ranges, become extinct.

Surveys conducted throughout the Heritage Area have established that there are well over 200 bird species, approximately 150 reptile and amphibian species, and nearly 100 different mammal species (WWF-Malaysia 1998). The area also represents the richest assemblage of primates in Borneo, including two macaque species (*Macaca* spp.), five leaf monkeys (*Presbytis* spp.), the Bornean gibbon (*Hylobates muelleri*), the slow loris (*Nycticebus coucang*), and the Horsefield's tarsier (*Tarsius bancanus*) (Supriatna and Warjono 2001).

Squirrels (at least 12 species) and tree shrews (five species) are strikingly abundant, as are at least seven species of hornbills, including the rhinoceros hornbill (*Buceros rhinoceros*) and the helmeted hornbill (*Rhinoplax vigil*). These species are important for the Iban, the dominant local tribal culture. Among other birds, pheasants are also well represented, including the great argus (*Argusianus argus*) and the shy and secretive Bulwer's pheasant (*Lophura bulweri*), endemic to the island. The area also holds high plant diversity. In Betung Kerihun National Park alone, for example, 1 216 species of trees have been identified, including 418 genera and 110 families. In addition, 75 of those are endemic to Borneo and 14 species are newly listed. Thirteen new species of palm have also recently been discovered (ITTO et al. 2000).

However, the area's best-known flagship species is the Bornean orang-utan (*Pongo pygmaeus*). The Lanjak Entimau/Batang Ai/Betung Kerihun complex is thought to hold approximately 2 500 animals (Singleton et al. 2004), a population that is not only critical to the species' survival, but also of sufficient size to be one of the few remaining viable populations. Local traditions help to effectively protect animals, often much more so than modern laws. The Ibans of the Ai Valley have a taboo on killing or disturbing orang-utans, and aerial surveys in the area have shown orang-utans to be relatively abundant in the area's forests (Kavanagh 1996; NPWO/WWFM 1983, 1984). On the other hand, over the ridge, in the physically similar Engkari Valley, there is no such taboo among the Iban people there and orang-utans have been exterminated.

The 168 758-ha Lanjak Entimau is Malaysia's largest wildlife sanctuary. Much of this area is mixed dipterocarp forest, as well as heath forest (*kerangas*), found mainly on exposed ridges and hilltops. Lanjak Entimau was set aside in 1983, mainly for the protection of the orang-utan. Batang Ai National Park, created in 1991, adds 24 040 ha of mixed dipterocarp secondary forests. The 800 000-ha Betung Kerihun National Park received official protected status in 1995. The result is a complex comprising almost 1 million ha of protection for the forests of northern Borneo. This is clearly one of the most important areas of conserved rainforest in the world —so large that it is considered to have a significant impact on the local climate, with the highland mossy forests acting as condensers that collect rainfall and release it gently into the upland streams.

Betung Kerihun falls within the Kapuas Hulu District of West Kalimantan, which includes the entire upper catchment of the mighty Kapuas River —the source of West Kalimantan's major life support system. Fifty-five percent of Kapuas Hulu lies within the Betung Kerihun and Danau Sentarum National Parks. The latter is a Ramsar Site, fed by these waters. These conservation areas provide ecological services to the whole province and dominate the administrative district.

The forests also have a practical value for the local people as living space for commonly hunted animals, such as the bearded pig (*Sus barbatus*). Furthermore, surveys in Lanjak Entimau have revealed more than 140 types of medicinal plants, plus a number of wild fruits and nearly 40 wild vegetables used by local people. There is every likelihood of more being discovered, given the enormous extent of the area.

Borneo has a rich mix of indigenous groups and cultures, with a diversity of languages and traditions. All are adapted to the forest environment in their different ways, and most of them are based on longhouses that form entire village-style communities in single buildings. The Heritage Area is the geographical centre of the culture of the Ibans, a proud people known for their tradition of *berjalai* —adventurous travel by young adults. Today, they maintain their culture and their attachment to their homelands, while looking for economic advancement through education, modern agriculture, and an increasing interest in tourism. Some of the indigenous groups are related across national borders, thus promoting cooperation.

Some Iban communities have moved, both to make way for a hydroelectric scheme on the lower reaches of the Batang Ai River and to take up a plantation lifestyle. Tourism has become a mainstay for some longhouses. Amid all this change, shifting cultivation and collection of forest products retain important positions in the local economies.

In Kapuas Hulu itself, the *Bupati* (head of the district administration) is undertaking an important initiative to meet the aspirations of local people through sustainable economic development as a "Conservation District." In April 2004, the District hosted an international workshop to launch and guide the process to implement development on the basis of sustainable use, protecting life support systems and conserving biodiversity. An action plan was drawn up and conservation NGOs are expected to join a multi-stakeholder working group to assist with planning and implementation, including helping to bring in technical and financial resources.

Sarawak's vibrant economy has brought palm oil plantations to the periphery of these lands, and created markets for forest products. Throughout Borneo, hunting and wildlife trade have escalated dramatically in recent years in the rush to exploit resources. New roads lead to forest fragmentation, and also open ways for hunters and traders to enter illegally in search of wild meat and other wildlife products. Enhanced access to the forests increases the rates at which local people hunt, since they often hunt for animals to sell in addition to their subsistence hunting. Surveys have revealed that these forests are quite poor in wildlife when compared to similar areas where hunting has not been allowed (M. Gumal, pers. comm.).

In Kalimantan, human population pressure is bringing the frontier of smallholder development close to Betung Kerihun National Park, but plantation agriculture and tourism have not yet had a real impact. Unfortunately, illegal logging has become a way of life, with timber being taken from wherever it is

On p. 298, the palm understory of a forest in Lanjak-Entimau, Sarawak.

Above, Hose's boradbill (Calyptomena hosii), a submontane species that is patchily distributed in Sabah and Sarawak, Malaysia and Kalimantan, Indonesia.

On the opposite page, a singing male long-fingered slender toad (Ansonia longidigita) in Bentuang-Karimun, Indonesia. Three photos, © Doug Wechsler

On pp. 302-303, rhinoceros hornbills (Buceros rhinoceros) in dipterocarp forest. © Tim Laman/National Geographic Image Collection

accessible, sold to collectors, and processed in huge sawmills before being openly trafficked across the border into Malaysia through Lubok Antu. In the absence of sufficient alternative economic development, this is an irresistible lure for the local communities and a thorn in the flesh for Indonesian-Malaysian relations. Illegal logging has become a political issue that damages not only the forests but also the ability of the two governments to cooperate on transboundary conservation issues.

Without question, Borneo's spectacular forests are a critical priority for global biodiversity conservation. The governments of Indonesia and Malaysia have proposed that Betung Kerihun National Park, Lanjak Entimau Wildlife Sanctuary, and Batang Ai National Park jointly receive World Heritage status, and this proposal is currently under consideration by UNESCO. This encouraging development could be enhanced if the linkages with adjacent forests could be protected in perpetuity through buffer zones (e.g., sustainably managed production forests) and the protection of other forests of high conservation value. If this proposal succeeds, it should strengthen the governments' abilities to apply resources to priority conservation activities, and focus the attention of the world's conservation community, including technical aid and development agencies, on the area's global importance. Adjacent human use also needs attention, otherwise it will harm these protected areas if not sustainably managed. Transboundary cooperation is essential for this, given the ease of moving across the international border. The initiative to develop Kapuas Hulu as a Conservation District could be of major significance, but its prospects depend upon the early support of the international conservation community and development agencies. The Kapuas Hulu District Government is being very forward in seeking to run the local economy on the basis of sustainable utilization, protection of life support systems, and maintenance of biological diversity. It remains to be seen whether or not the people there will receive the support and be able to coordinate the effort to make it a success.

MIKAAIL KAVANAGH
JATNA SUPRIATNA
SUSIE ELLIS

WASUR-TONDA: TRANSBOUNDARY CONSERVATION IN THE NEW GUINEA WILDERNESS

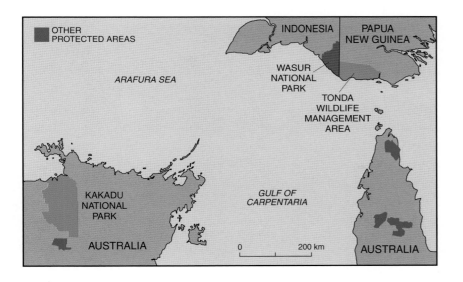

Although New Guinea is usually associated with intact tropical moist forests, the extensive savannahs, grasslands, and monsoon forests of the Trans-Fly stand apart from the rest of the island. The seasonally-dry climate is unusual for the island and more comparable to that of northern Australia. In fact, habitats and species are so similar between this region of Indonesia, Papua New Guinea (P.N.G.), and Australia, that the three countries have signed a Tri-National Wetlands Agreement to protect the Trans-Fly. Although this area is under pressure from a number of invasive species and changing land-use patterns, many of the habitats in the region are still relatively intact.

A large transboundary conservation area (TBCA) exists in the Trans-Fly of New Guinea, formed by Wasur National Park in Indonesia and the Tonda Wildlife Management Area in P.N.G.

Wasur, in the Indonesian province of Papua, is managed by the national Ministry of Forestry's Directorate of Forest Protection and Nature Conservation. A number of indigenous groups own customary land in the park, but they currently have no legal role in its management. A large thrust of conservation efforts in Wasur has entailed working with a local non-governmental organization, traditional community groups, and Park Management officials to develop a co-management program. In stark contrast, the Tonda Wildlife Management Area in P.N.G.'s Western Province is still customarily owned by the local indigenous groups, who control the protection and management of wildlife resources through management committees with legal status. The national and provincial governments play a very small role in the management of Tonda, and there is room for conflict over land ownership and related revenue generation. These two models of park management, seemingly representing the extreme opposite ends of the spectrum, are contrasted in one TBCA across the Indonesia-P.N.G. border.

Its extraordinary variety of habitats and its location between the extensive tropical moist forests of New Guinea and the savannahs of Australia, make the Trans-Fly transboundary area remarkable and distinctive. The area shares a rich and unique assemblage of spectacular species with other ecoregions in Australasia, including crowned pigeons, birds of paradise, cassowaries, echidnas, wallabies, pademelons, and flying foxes.

In terms of endemic species, the only mammal unique to the Trans-Fly is the bronze quoll (*Dasyurus spartacus*). Little is known about this elusive creature, which at only 1 kg is still New Guinea's largest living mammalian carnivore. Six restricted-

range bird species are found in the Trans-Fly Endemic Bird Area (Stattersfield et al. 1998). While three of the six are also found in other ecoregions, two finches, the grey-crowned munia (*Lonchura nevermanni*), and the black munia (*L. stygia*), as well as the Fly River grassbird (*Megalurus albolimbatus*, VU), are essentially confined to the Trans-Fly. The transboundary area also forms the heart of the Southern Fly Platform Centre of Plant Diversity (Davis et al. 1995) and is a critical habitat for several restricted-range amphibians and reptiles (Allison 1994). Until relatively recently, the pitted turtle (*Carettochelys insculpta*) was only known from the Trans-Fly. This unique species, in its own family, was found not so long ago in Arnhemland in northern Australia, further linking these regions (Cogger 2000).

The Wasur-Tonda TBCA protects approximately 10 000 km² of savannahs, grasslands, and monsoon forest. Wasur National Park, finally gazetted in 1997, contains 4 100 km², while Tonda, gazetted in 1975, contains 5 900 km². Efforts are currently underway to create three additional Wildlife Management Areas just north of Tonda, which will effectively double its size. Both Wasur and Tonda are Ramsar Sites.

While the island of New Guinea is an active tectonic area with a complex geologic history, the Trans-Fly itself is tectonically stable, and the transboundary area includes the flat coastal plain and the low-lying Oriomo Plateau (Bleeker 1983). These gentle plains stand in contrast with New Guinea's rugged central mountain ranges. The unique savannahs, grasslands, and monsoon forests of the Trans-Fly ecoregion are a result of its distinct seasonality (Paijmans 1975; MacKinnon 1997). Most precipitation occurs during the December-to-May wet season, when the combination of shallow topography and heavy rain results in extensive flooding. These highly interconnected wetlands are some of the largest in the Asia-Pacific region. The dominant trees in the savannahs include *Eucalyptus*, *Albizia*, and *Melaleuca* (Miller et al. 1994). The *Melaleuca* forest is indicative of areas that are submerged in up to one meter of water during the wet season. Locally, in the dry season, indigenous people have managed the vegetation with fire for many thousands of years.

Both the fauna and savannah vegetation have strong affinities with those of northern Australia. The wetland areas are of international importance as a migration point for avian migrants from New Guinea and Australia and as components of the larger East-Asian-Australasian flyway for waterfowl, waders, and other species. In addition to tens of thousands of waterfowl found in the region during the wet season, a significant proportion of the world's population of little curlews (*Numenius minutus*) congre-

gates in the Trans-Fly from September to December. This is one example of the strong ecological links to the nearby northern reaches of Australia, including the coastal fringes of the Gulf of Carpentaria (Beehler 1994; Bishop 2004).

In terms of cultural and linguistic diversity, the Trans-Fly is just as exceptional as the rest of New Guinea. The fact that dialects from at least three native language families and 60 cultural groups are found in the region (Wurm and Hattori 1981) has implications in the management of the transboundary protected areas. Despite some intense outside influences, cultural identity in the transboundary area remains very strong. The vast majority of the people living within the protected areas still rely on natural resources to sustain themselves. Customary or traditional land ownership is still the rule, with determination of boundaries understood (or disputed) only by the local people involved. These ownership patterns are rarely registered in any formal way, and land is passed through the generations, largely patrilinearly. In the border area, individuals may own land on one side of the border, yet live on the other, and there is constant low-level movement across the border by canoe or foot, regulated by the two governments in the form of a traditional border pass system.

While infrastructure and government services are generally poor on both sides of the border, they are somewhat more advanced on the Indonesian side due to the presence of the major town of Merauke, close to the west. There are currently approximately 3 000 people in 13 settlements located within Wasur and 1 500 people in 28 small villages in Tonda. Most roads connecting these within the protected areas are only passable during the dry season, so during much of the year the best method of travel is by canoe or boat.

Economic potential is quite limited. Legal and illegal trade to Merauke does occur, but a 32-km border quarantine zone for pests and livestock diseases stifles the cash cropping in P.N.G., and most attempted livelihood development projects have had limited success. Although the local people are keen to harvest and market the numerous biological resources available in the protected areas (deer meat, *Cervus timorensis*; barramundi, *Lates calcarifer*; crocodile skins, *Crocodylus novaeguinaea*, and *Crocodylus porosus*, etc.) —and this activity could be beneficial if tightly regulated— access to markets is still too difficult.

Transboundary conservation efforts have been facilitated by the World Wildlife Fund (WWF) since 1991. A general border agreement between Indonesia and P.N.G., the Basic Agreement between the government of P.N.G. and the government of the

Above, a partridge pigeon (Geophaps smithii) *in Kakadu National Park, across the straits from Wasur-Tonda.*
© Daniel Zupanc/Auscape

On the opposite page, bushland with speargrass, sand palm, Hibiscus meuzeliae, *and* Eucalyptus. *Kakadu National Park.*
© Jean-Paul Ferrero/Auscape

Republic of Indonesia on Border Arrangements, has helped structure a variety of activities, including the protection of flora and fauna. Visits between Wasur, Tonda, and Kakadu National Park staff began in 1993. The 20 000-km² Kakadu National Park in the Northern Territory of Australia also contains a wide variety of habitats which are quite similar to those of the Trans-Fly, despite being separated by the 1 000-km Arafura Sea. The intent of the exchanges is to share technical and management expertise, provide training, engage in collaboration and research, and generally increase awareness among communities, protected area managers, and government officials. These visits culminated in 2002 with a Tri-National Wetlands Agreement signed by Indonesia, P.N.G., and Australia to protect up to 30 000 km² in the Trans-Fly. This has been one of several agreements between the three governments to benefit these interconnected savannahs and wetland habitats.

Although the region is inhabited by a large number of sparsely-distributed tribal groups, population pressure is generally low, especially on the P.N.G. side. There are no roads connecting the Trans-Fly to the rest of P.N.G. and there is generally little disturbance. Over 90% of the original habitat is still intact in this ecoregion (MacKinnon 1997). On the Indonesian side, however, a government-sponsored transmigration program (now ended), which brought people in from overcrowded areas elsewhere in Indonesia, has threatened the protected areas from within and without. The result of these settlements is increased hunting, wildlife trade, agricultural conversion, and unsustainable forestry practices, some of which impacts Wasur National Park itself, and even extends across the porous border into Tonda. A proposed road from Sota in Indonesia to Daru in P.N.G. would cut right through Tonda. The municipal water supply for Merauke is drawn from the Rawa Biru wetland within Wasur, and the interconnected nature of the wetlands complex means that Tonda is also affected by this water extraction.

Perhaps the most pervasive and insidious threat across the transboundary area is that of invasive species. The list reads like a litany of almost intractable invasive problems, including the purposely introduced rusa deer (*Cervus timorensis*) that has had serious impacts on the grasslands (though its meat is highly valued), the water hyacinth (*Eichhornia crassipes*) in the countless interconnected waterways, the giant sensitive plant (*Mimosa pigra*) that invades grasslands, and numerous introduced fish species, including snakeheads (*Channa* spp.), which threaten to upset the fragile and valuable native fish fauna. The vast majority of these introductions has originated on the

Indonesian side, but because habitats, waterways, and cultures are continuous across the border, one side's problem quickly becomes the other's.

The work that WWF began in 1991 continues to this day, now in the form of a Trans-Fly Ecoregion Action Program for the larger ecoregion. Given that some of the most pervasive threats in the area, especially invasive species (deer, weeds) and the disconcerting encroachment (whether natural or not) of *Melaleuca* into important grassland habitats, do not respect the international border, the local people are well aware of the need to coordinate management activities in a cooperative way across the border.

Since 1998 the Indonesian Government has increasingly recognized traditional rights, and indeed Wasur was the first Indonesian park where such recognition was provided. In Tonda, assistance from the Australian Government and conservation organizations is slowly raising the technical capacity of the local people to organize and manage their resources. The Indonesian and P.N.G. National Governments maintain good relations, though both are handicapped by lack of resources. There is a high degree of goodwill among the local indigenous people on either side of the border, in large part because they are culturally the same. They have managed to adjust to colonial and now national political changes. As a result, over time, the management of Wasur and Tonda is converging to meet common challenges. Despite some difficult environmental problems, the habitats of Wasur-Tonda are in good condition and there is hope that the local people, who still rely on their environment, will insist on and enforce conservation of natural resources in the future.

JOHN MORRISON
MICHELE BOWE
ADAM TOMASEK

MARINE

THE MESOAMERICAN REEF:
A SHARED COMMITMENT
FOR THE CARIBBEAN JEWEL

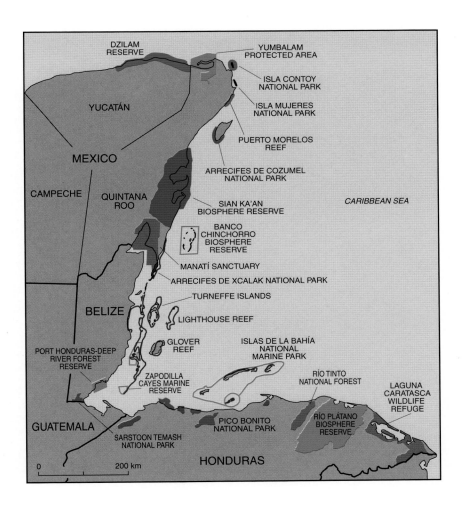

From just north of the resort city of Cancún in Mexico, throughout coastal Belize to the Bay Islands of Honduras, the Mesoamerican Reef threads its way through over 1 000 km of shallow Caribbean waters. Buffered from the sea by the reef, the protected navigable seaway has nourished important commercial and cultural links within the Maya world. The Mesoamerican Reef, the longest coral reef system in the Western Hemisphere and one of the healthiest, embraces the coasts of Mexico, Belize, Guatemala, and Honduras. From a series of isolated patch reefs, which occur south of Contoy Island on the northeast corner of the Yucatán Peninsula, this winding ecosystem makes its way southward past Cancún as fringing reefs along the coast of the Mexican state of Quintana Roo, and all the way south to San Pedro in Belize. From Punta Nizuc in Cancún to north of Akumal, a relatively wide but narrow continental shelf results in the reef crest where the waves break —the most highly developed feature of the reef. Southwards, this very narrow continental shelf fosters highly developed deep frontal reefs, where extensive spur-and-grove systems occur at the edge of the shelf before it plunges into much deeper water.

Arrowsmith Bank, Cozumel Island, and Banco Chinchorro are offshore components of this section of the coastline, which is notable for the lack of freshwater flow from rivers. South of San Pedro, the Mesoamerican Reef System enters Belize and becomes a true barrier reef at the edge of the underwater shelf, all the way south to the Zapodilla Cays. The wide continental shelf creates an extensive reef lagoon bordered inland by vast mangrove forests, which buffer the impacts from Belizean coastal rivers to the offshore reefs. Seawards are Glovers Reef, Lighthouse Reef, and the Turneffe Islands, the only geological features of this type in the Western Hemisphere, which harbor complex ecosystems of mangrove forests and coral formations.

In the Guatemalan portion of the Gulf of Honduras, the barrier reef is replaced by wide expanses of seagrass pastures and isolated reef patches. Landward, large remnants of mangroves, flooded forests, coastal lagoons, lowland rainforests, and riparian forests play an important role in the maintenance of the key ecological processes that link the reefs to these coastal ecosystems. Of particular significance are the forested mountaintops that reach over 1 000 m above sea level within 10 km of the coastline. The ecological gradients found in these mountains, particularly in Cerro San Gil and Pico Bonito, have created unique conditions for high levels of biodiversity and endemism

of flora and fauna. Unfortunately, some of the largest and most deforested watersheds, such as Rio Dulce and Motagua in Guatemala, and Ulua and Chamelecon in Honduras, also drain into the Gulf of Honduras, carrying sediment loads that pose a serious threat to the long-term health of the Mesoamerican Reef. Coastal ecosystems along the Gulf of Honduras are also vital corridors and wintering habitats for over 100 species of Neotropical migratory birds. Further east in Honduras, coastal reefs develop along Punta Sal and Punta Izopo and eventually become important fringing reef systems at Cayos Cochinos and the Islas de la Bahía or Bay Islands, an archipelago of approximately 200 minor islands and several larger islands that include Roatan, Utila, Guanaja, and Barbareta. Coastal Honduras is characterized by long expanses of sandy beaches interspersed with large rivers, bays, and coastal lagoons. Turbid water prevents substantial coral reef development near the coast.

The Mesoamerican Reef includes a wide variety of interlinked ecosystems, from near shore estuarine to offshore environments. The diversity and productivity of these ecosystems result from complex interactions that take place between shallow bays, mangrove forests, sea grass beds, patch, fringing and barrier reefs, and oceanic atoll-like formations. Colonies of beautiful corals with evocative names like elk horn, brain, and fire, thrive in the warm Caribbean waters where the Mesoamerican Reef is still rich in sea life. The largest populations of the West Indian manatee (*Trichechus manatus*) inhabit the waters of its coves, inlets, bays, and the reef lagoon. Coastal wetlands and some of the reef's larger atolls support populations of two species of crocodiles, the American crocodile (*Crocodylus acutus*) and Morelett's crocodile (*C. moreletti*). The "Endangered" hawksbill (*Eretmochelys imbricata*), the loggerhead turtle (*Caretta caretta*), the green turtle (*Lepidochelys olivacea*), and the leatherback turtle (*Dermochelys coriacea*) crawl across the sandy beaches to lay their eggs. Bird diversity is high, with over 400 species recorded, and tropical forest and wetland, marine, and migrant avifauna overlapping in this coastal region.

Along the Mesoamerican Reef, impressive fish spawning aggregations occur in highly unique sites, where currents, depth, and reef position create the ideal conditions for this rare natural phenomenon. Gladden Spit has been documented as one of the largest spawning aggregations in the region, and undoubtedly plays a key role in the replenishment of fisheries stocks throughout the region. The occurrence of these spawning aggregations has also been associated with regional migrations of the "Vulnerable" whale sharks (*Rhinchodon typus*).

The need to protect ecological linkages between mangroves, sea-grass beds, atolls, and coral reefs cannot be overemphasized. The permanent bidirectional flow of biomass between coastal and marine habitats is essential for the life cycles of many flagship and indicator species, many of which are not only important for economic and cultural reasons, but are also key players in the overall ecological stability of coral reef ecosystems. This is particularly true in the case of slow-growing and sedentary carnivores, such as groupers (*Epinephelus* spp.). The area supports productive near-shore commercial fisheries, including spiny lobster (*Panulirus argus*), queen conch (*Strombus gigas*), shrimp (*Peneaus* spp.), and fin-fish such as groupers (Serranidae), snappers (Lutjanidae), and barracudas (*Sphyraena barracuda*). Light tackle sport fishing takes place in calm sheltered waters, targeting species such as bonefish (*Albula vulpes*), permit (*Trachinotus falcatus*), tarpon (*Megalops atlanticus*), and snook (*Centropomus undecimalis*), while deep-sea sport fishermen seek marlin and sailfish.

Beyond the ecological functions of the Mesoamerican Reef are the economic, physical, and aesthetic protection values. These features are critical to the wellbeing of the coastal communities that call this region home. The recognition of two sites as World Heritage Sites, the Belize Barrier Reef Reserve System and the Sian Ka'an Biosphere Reserve in Mexico, emphasizes their outstanding universal value to humanity. The beauty of the reef attracts millions of visitors every year from all over the world and has made tourism the primary source of income. The reef protects the coastlines from erosion and from the direct impacts of waves and storm surges during hurricanes, which makes it a critical feature in the protection of coastal infrastructure. It is clear that for ecological, economic, and social reasons, the integrated protection of the Mesoamerican Reef is both desirable and, in view of the threats, urgent. Although there are over 60 coastal and marine protected areas in the Mesoamerican Reef, many of them exist only on paper and have little or no effective management.

On World Environment Day in the International Year of the Reef, June 5, 1997, heads of state of Belize, Honduras, Guatemala, and Mexico signed the Tulum Declaration, which launched the Mesoamerican Caribbean Coral Reef Systems Initiative, to express their commitment towards the protection and sound use of their shared coastal habitats, especially the coral reef. All four countries understand that this rich, diverse, and highly interlinked ecosystem constitutes the base for many of their industries, including tourism and fisheries. The Mesoamerican

On p. 310, squirrel fish (Sargocentron sp.) on reef. Cocos Island, Costa Rica.
© Flip Nicklin/Minden Pictures

On p. 312, an aerial view of the famous Blue Hole on Lighthouse Reef in Belize. This stunning dive site is actually a collapsed limestone cave, and has become a major tourist attraction.
© Kevin Schafer

On the opposite page, a manatee (Trichechus manatus) in the Laguna de Bacalar, Quintana Roo, Mexico.
© Patricio Robles Gil/Sierra Madre

Above, a cushion sea star (Orea reticulatus) in a bed of sea grass (Thalassia testudinum). Banco Chinchorro, Quintano Roo, Mexico.

On pp. 316-317, a southern stingray (Dasyatis americana). This species usually remains on the floor of the ocean, covering itself with sand and feeding on mollusks, worms, clams, and other creatures. Both photos,
© Claudio Contreras

Caribbean Coral Reef Systems Initiative provides a forum for all four nations to act and manage their coastal resources at a regional scale. The overall goal is to take advantage of growing opportunities for sustainable development, through the rational use and conservation of the coral reef and associated ecosystems shared by these four nations. Involvement and support by coastal communities, private companies, national and international non-profit organizations, and government officials is crucial to the success of this regional and integrated initiative. Some of the objectives include the establishment of protected areas, strengthening regulations, ecotourism planning, securing sustainable funding for conservation efforts, and encouraging coastal management to address the need for the sustainable use and conservation of this area. This initiative is providing unique opportunities for training, scientific research, and monitoring.

Having recognized the added value of ensuring uniformity of management in the transboundary area, the countries of the region have taken decisive steps to harmonize management planning for the whole transboundary conservation area. This harmonized approach is consistent with the ecosystem approach and overcomes the impact of political boundaries in the management of the Mesoamerican Reef. Efforts to manage shared fisheries are also progressing well.

The Mesoamerican Reef was largely protected from development pressures by its remoteness and the sparse habitation of the mainland. This is no longer the case as the rich coastal lands of Central America and Mexico are being overtaken by coastal development and agriculture. Currently, land-based activities have caused destruction or irreversible damage. Since the 1960s, the reefs have been subjected to intensive artisanal fishing effort, with impacts not yet evaluated. Since the mid 1970s, tourism has become an increasing reef-impacting activity. Impacts caused indirectly by tourism, such as urban growth and coastal water pollution, are becoming important and growing threats. But the most serious threats to the reef are derived from changes in land use and poor land management. The forests along the coast are being cleared for agriculture and development. When the rains come, mud pours down the bare hillsides and unpaved roadways and clouds the waters with eroded soil, thus shading the delicate corals and preventing photosynthesis from occurring within the tiny dinoflagellate algae that live inside the coral polyps. Improper urban sewage and garbage disposal, as well as agriculture and untreated sewage, deposit nutrients into the delicate reef system, promoting the growth of algae that chokes the corals and prevents further colonization.

Industrial shipping remains an ever-present and threatening possibility of a catastrophic oil or chemical spill. Without effective protection, the area's rich marine life has become an alluring target for commercial fishermen and unregulated tourism. Threats include shark finning, commercial fishing during key spawning periods, and cruise ships bringing increasingly larger groups of tourists who pay very little for their use of the area and are largely unsupervised.

The political will manifested through the Tulum Declaration has undoubtedly triggered much interest in the region by local and international participants. Since 1997, the region has benefited from a host of initiatives and investments aimed at securing change in attitudes and the policy-reform interventions needed for the conservation and sustainable use of the resources of the Mesoamerican Reef. A preliminary assessment of progress made to date has revealed encouraging results, but it is also evident that much more work is needed to ensure its long-term conservation. It is clear that the achievement of the desired sustainable use objectives will require more than just a change in attitudes. Ensuring fair and accessible benefits to local communities and exemplary reforms to sectoral policies for fisheries and tourism will determine to what extent we can achieve effective conservation and long-term benefits in the Mesoamerican Reef.

JUAN BEZAURY
MARCO VINICIO CEREZO
DAVID GUTIÉRREZ
NOEL JACOBS
CRISTINA G. MITTERMEIER

THE EASTERN TROPICAL PACIFIC SEASCAPE: AN INNOVATIVE MODEL FOR TRANSBOUNDARY MARINE CONSERVATION

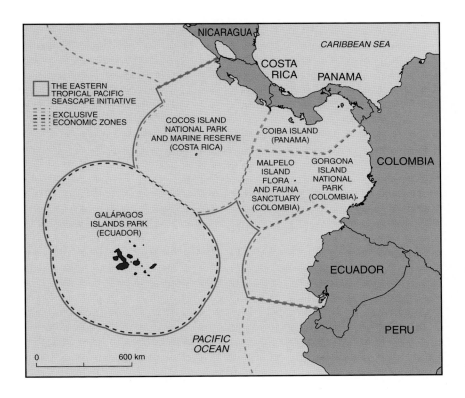

The Eastern Tropical Pacific Seascape Initiative, a transboundary marine ecosystem management initiative involving Ecuador, Colombia, Panama, and Costa Rica, is working towards the creation of a network of marine protected areas within the 211 million-ha region that covers the combined exclusive economic zones of these four countries. The Eastern Tropical Pacific Seascape (ETPS) features several flagship marine protected areas, including Ecuador's Galápagos Islands, Colombia's Gorgona National Park and Malpelo Island Flora and Fauna Sanctuary, Panama's Coiba Island, and Costa Rica's Cocos Island National Park and Marine Reserve and Las Baulas National Park. The initiative is working to develop a shared-ecosystem management approach within this large transboundary region, initiating program activities and research endeavors that are applying cutting-edge technologies to create innovative reserve models that will conserve and protect vulnerable species as they migrate across the open sea.

The Panama Bight, the islands and the waters surrounding them in the east central Pacific, comprise one of the most productive areas of the Pacific and belong to one of the world's most biologically diverse geographical provinces. This area has a high degree of ecological interconnection and complex oceanographic characteristics, mainly due to the convergence of major marine currents, which facilitate the dispersal of marine larvae and affect the migration, movement, and distribution of many species of regional and global significance. The Eastern Tropical Pacific is also affected intensely by the El Niño-La Niña climatic cycle, which causes dramatic swings in upwelling, sea temperature, and productivity.

The ETPS harbors unique and vulnerable habitats that support a rich marine biodiversity, including species that are endemic, in danger of extinction, or have ecological, economic, and aesthetic importance. Among them are "Endangered" great whales (the blue whale, *Balaenoptera musculus*, and the humpback whale, *Megaptera novaeangliae*), "Endangered" sea turtles (leatherbacks, *Dermochelys coriacea*; east Pacific greens, *Chelonia agassizi*; olive ridleys, *Lepidochelys olivacea*; loggerheads, *Caretta caretta*, and the hawksbill turtle *Eretmochelys imbricata*), tuna (yellowfins, *Thunnus albacares*; skipjacks, *Katsuwonus pelamis*, and bigeyes, *Thunnus obesus*), sharks (the silky, *Carcharhinus falciformis*; the scalloped hammerhead, *Sphyrna lewini*; the bigeye thresher, *Alopias superciliosus*, and the lemon, *Negaprion brevirostris*), rays (manta rays, *Mobula* spp., *Manta hamiltoni*, and the

pelagic sting ray, *Dasyatis violacea*), billfishes (swordfish, *Xiphias gladius*; striped marlins, *Tetrapterus audax*; shortbill spearships, *T. angustirostris*; blue marlins, *Makaira mazara*, and sailfish, *Istiophorus platypterus*), and sea birds (albatrosses, *Phoebastria* spp., and storm petrels, *Oceanites gracilis*, *O. castro*, *Oceanodroma tethys*).

Several of the marine protected areas within the ETPS, such as Cocos Island, Darwin and Wolf Islands, and Malpelo Island, are widely recognized for the vast migrations and large aggregations of hammerhead sharks, white-tip sharks (*Triaendon obesus*), whale sharks (*Rhincodon typus*), and other species that occur within and around these island habitats. In addition, several of the island habitats across the ETPS also harbor high levels of endemism. For example, over 300 species of coastal and pelagic reef fish have been observed at Colombia's Malpelo Flora and Fauna Sanctuary, including at least five endemics. Another 15 species are found only within Malpelo, Cocos, and the Galápagos Islands.

The Pacific leatherback sea turtle stands out as a conservation flagship for the ETPS. Populations of this species have declined from 90 000 nesting females in the Pacific Ocean in 1980 to less than 5 000 by 2002. Costa Rica's Las Baulas National Park currently hosts the largest remaining viable population of nesting female turtles in the Pacific Ocean. Although 15 years of ongoing hatchery efforts have improved recruitment, the population at Las Baulas National Park continues to experience significant declines, as evidenced by a reduction from over 1 300 nesting turtles recorded at Playa Grande in 1988-1989 to 59 nesting females recorded in 2002-2003. The Eastern Tropical Pacific Seascape Initiative aims to reverse this trend, and to demonstrate that it is possible to save wide-ranging, transboundary species that face enormous threats throughout their life histories and across their ranges.

As described, the ETPS, even though primarily oceanic, also includes numerous unique terrestrial and coastal marine habitats and ecosystems.

The oceanography of the ETPS is unique in that two cold highly productive eastern boundary currents enclose the warm eastern Tropical Pacific. These are the California Current to the north and the Humboldt or Peru Current to the south. Both currents flow towards the equator and form the North Equatorial Current and the South Equatorial Current, respectively. The currents are driven by the strong easterly trade winds that force surface waters away from the coast of South America,

creating surface flow and, in turn, upwelling of cold nutrient-rich waters. These nutrient-rich waters enable significant primary production in the region. Episodic fluctuations in upwelling, such as those associated with the *El Niño* and *La Niña* phases of the El Niño Southern Oscillation (ENSO), impose pressures upon many populations of marine and terrestrial organisms that depend upon the regions' high levels of productivity for survival. The presence and unpredictability of El Niño complicates attempts to plan and manage sustainable fisheries. Thus, intensive fishing or overfishing within the ETPS may increase the likelihood of lasting ecosystem impacts and further hinder or even obviate recovery from the El Niño-induced crashes.

Oceanic islands within the Seascape, such as Cocos, Malpelo, and the Galápagos Archipelago, represent the above-water outcroppings of undersea ridges and seamounts that extend up to 3 000 m from the ocean floor. These seamounts harbor a diverse and unique marine life, and serve as aggregation areas for various pelagic species that move throughout the Seascape region. The seamounts interact with nutrient-rich currents to create unique water-column properties and upwelling areas that act as "pelagic hotspots." These "hotspots" exist in various forms, ranging from persistent bathymetric environments, such as islands, seamounts, ridges, canyons, and reefs, to persistent hydrographic environments, such as currents and frontal zones.

New and innovative approaches are being applied to improve the definition, understanding, and management of important routes for species dispersal and migration within the ETPS. These routes afford ecological connectivity within and across a protected area network. Examples include migration routes for Eastern Pacific leatherback sea turtles that run along the Cocos Ridge from northwestern Costa Rica towards the Galápagos Islands, and northern routes that extend from the Galápagos towards the vicinity of Costa Rica, encompassing the oceanic islands of Cocos and Malpelo. These serve as migratory thoroughfares for large vertebrate species, such as sea turtles, swallowtail gulls, and sharks, as well as providing one of the primary routes for dispersal of plants and animals to the Galápagos (Edgar et al. 2004). Another important marine corridor runs eastward from the Galápagos towards continental Ecuador and Peru. This corridor, facilitated by the Peruvian Current, affords genetic connectivity for many temperate species in the Galápagos, including the tigris (*Oplegnathus insignis*) and goldspot sheepshead (*Semicossyphus darwini*). Migratory species that utilize this corridor include sperm

whales (Whitehead et al. 1997; Whitehead 2001) and waved albatrosses (Fernández et al. 2001; Edgar et al. 2002, 2004).

Although marine resources contribute significantly to the GDP and to the livelihood, economic well-being, and health of human populations across the ETPS, challenges such as illegal fishing, introduced species, immigration, pollution, habitat clearing and loss, and inadequate enforcement and monitoring have long compromised efforts to effectively manage shared marine resources within this region. An over-arching goal of the Eastern Tropical Pacific Seascape Initiative is to address these challenges within larger and more established marine protected areas, such as the Galápagos Islands, and within smaller, less developed areas, such as Cocos, Malpelo, Gorgona, and Coiba. These areas all experience common pressures, where interventions such as strengthening enforcement are shared priorities.

The ETPS area is particularly vulnerable to unsustainable fishing practices that impact fragile habitats and key species and the populations dependent on them. Artisanal fishing in the Galápagos Islands for sea cucumber, lobster, and other economically valuable species has been the subject of many intense local and national debates and conflicts. Fishermen from the mainland have immigrated to the islands to exploit fisheries resources. In so doing, they have created a significant human footprint on the Island's fragile terrestrial and marine habitats. Due to its incredible natural beauty and relatively pristine state, Coiba now faces similar challenges from the tourism and economic development sectors. The island's soon-to-be decommissioned prison has served as a barrier to human immigration, exploitation, and development. The fate of Coiba has also been a subject of intense debate at national and international levels. Like Colombia's Malpelo and Gorgona Islands, it is anticipated that ongoing efforts associated with the Eastern Tropical Pacific Seascape Initiative will eventually lead to global recognition of Coiba as a World Heritage Site, thus resulting in increased opportunities and funding for the island's conservation and management.

The ETPS provides an opportunity to demonstrate that, by cooperating to maintain a healthy marine environment, the four governments can improve the quality of life of coastal communities that depend upon marine resources. At the local and national level, the ETPS project will contribute to the food security of these populations. At the regional and international levels, the Eastern Tropical Pacific Seascape Initiative will work with existing institutions, such as the Inter American Tropical Tuna Commission, to help increase the sustainability of industrial fishing throughout this transboundary region. Fisheries across the ETPS constitute a significant source of employment. Within other parts of the world, history has demonstrated that these industries and their stakeholders will suffer if efforts are not undertaken to improve the long-term management of exploited species and the ecosystems upon which they depend.

Fishing-related threats to the biodiversity of the ETPS include overfishing, bycatch, illegal fishing, and indiscriminate, intensive, and destructive fishing techniques that produce high bycatch levels, compromise ecosystem processes, and destroy fragile habitats. Other threats include human-induced development pressures from poorly managed tourism. These activities contribute to increased pollution and habitat alteration, often degrading the unique natural attributes that attracted the tourism in the first place, and are not restricted to terrestrial environments. From a marine perspective, they include destructive interactions with marine life, coral destruction, and sea-bottom disruptions caused by anchoring, consumption, and extraction of marine resources and biota, and improper waste disposal. Perhaps one of the greatest pressures to the terrestrial habitats of the islands in the ETPS is the introduction of exotic species, including plants and animals, such as feral pigs, goats, dogs, cats, rats, donkeys, deer, and insects. Introduced species not only consume and out-compete native plants and animals, they alter critical habitats, cause erosion, spread disease and, once established, can continue to systematically colonize new environs without the assistance of human vectors.

The ETPS presents an extremely exciting and innovative model for marine transboundary conservation. The inception of the seascape benefited from the vision and invaluable support of government leaders. Now Conservation International and the governments are working to broaden the participation to include a wide range of institutions and stakeholders, so that the grand concept can become a reality. Through fortuitous geology and geopolitics, the island territories of Costa Rica (Cocos) and Ecuador (Galápagos) significantly extend the potential management influence of the ETPS beyond the typical 200-nautical miles Exclusive Economic Zone afforded to individual countries with coastal borders. These territorial extensions, coupled with the participation of the governments of Colombia and Panama, afford a unique opportunity to apply new marine management and conservation principles on a heretofore impossible scale,

On the opposite page, the Pacific leatherback sea turtle (Dermochelys coriacea schlegeli) *is one of the most endangered of all marine turtles, and has declined dramatically in recent years.*

Above, the Galápagos fur seal (Arctocephalus galapagoensis) *is endemic to these islands and can often be seen resting on rocky beaches. Both photos,*
© Patricio Robles Gil/Sierra Madre

On pp. 328-329, the Galápagos penguin
(Spheniscus mendiculus) *is the most northerly
occurring of all the penguins. Endemic to the Galápagos
Islands, with 90% of its population restricted
to the islands of Fernandina and Isabela.*
© Patricio Robles Gil/Sierra Madre

*On pp. 330-331, surrounded by creole fish, leather bass and
yellowtail surgeonfish, a male green turtle* (Chelonia mydas)
approaches a cleaning station. Wolf Island, Galápagos.
© Tui De Roy/Roving Tortoise

capturing significant portions of the ranges and habitats of the numerous important marine species that inhabit the Eastern Tropical Pacific. The ETPS is also noteworthy for its attempt to address the reality and importance of ecological interdependence. The vast, dynamic, interconnectedness of the ocean environment within the ETPS mandates a collaborative approach. Clearly, where multiple countries share ocean borders, it is impossible for any one country to protect its marine resources entirely. Among other elements, marine management plans must consider the maintenance of ecosystem processes, the protection of wildlife at critical life history points (migration, feeding, breeding, etc.), and the importance of long-distance larval dispersal and colonization. To accomplish these goals, it is imperative that countries with neighboring Exclusive Economic Zones work together to recognize ecological interdependence while respecting national sovereignty. Through the Eastern Tropical Pacific Seascape Initiative, the four neighboring governments of Ecuador, Colombia, Panama, and Costa Rica, will work to realize an array of regional activities, ranging from capacity-building and enforcement, to research, monitoring, fisheries management, tourism development, and conflict resolution.

GEORGE L. SHILLINGER

ANTARCTICA: THE LAST GLOBAL COMMONS

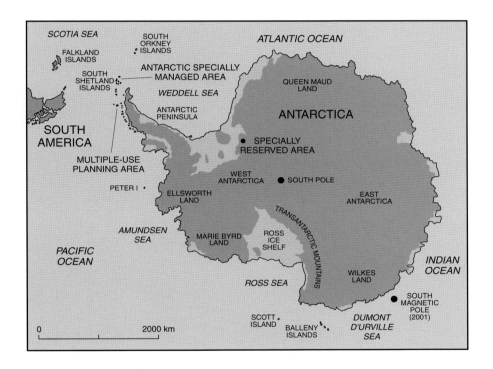

Among Earth's six continents, Antarctica is the fourth largest and is uniquely covered in a perpetual freshwater ice cap that averages 1 800 m in thickness. Antarctica holds 30 million km^3 of ice, which is about 90% of the ice on Earth and represents 70% of the surface freshwater (Pyne 1986). If this ice were to melt, the world's oceans would rise 60 to 65 m.

The actual land area of Antarctica is 13.9 million km^2 or 10% of Earth's surface, an area nearly double the size of Australia, or 1.5 times the size of the U.S. However, the seasonal freezing and thawing of the ocean surrounding the continent covers an additional 16 million km^2, further extending the effect of this region upon the ocean and the animals and plants that live in it. Antarctica plays an important role in the Earth's climate and weather patterns, and is of vital interest to science by providing clues about our planet's evolution and atmosphere. Separated from the rest of the world by the deep, cold, rough, and storied Southern Ocean, it has been called a Pleistocene relic.

Given its extreme isolation and freezing conditions, Antarctica was the last continent to be discovered (nineteenth century) and settled (twentieth century). Without indigenous people, its political structure has evolved rapidly over only the past 100 years. While some colonial-era attempts at land and ocean resource claims remain, it is global consensus that the region belongs to the "common heritage of mankind." This concept implies that the resources of Antarctica will be utilized and protected using the same broad multi-national frameworks, with the same advantages, limitations, and challenges as those used for other global commons, such as the high seas.

Endemic or near-endemic organisms, mostly invertebrates (protozoans, nematodes, tardigrades, rotifers, enchytraeids, arachnids, and insects) occurring with low diversity and existing in extreme environments, characterize the terrestrial biodiversity of Antarctica. The land habitats occur largely along the coastlines, but some are deep under the ice within the continent's interior. The terrestrial and freshwater biodiversity of Antarctica is by far the lowest of any continent, but also among the most unique (Mittermeier and Stone 2002).

Marine biodiversity is much richer, but still relatively low in diversity. Nonetheless, what the marine ecosystem lacks in species numbers it more than makes up for in biomass.

There are some 49 breeding marine bird species in Antarctica. The seabirds include six species of albatross, 17 typical petrels, prions, and shearwaters, three storm-petrels, two diving-petrels, one gull, two terns, two skuas, three shags and, of course,

On p. 332, reflection cast on the water during a late summer night
in Antarctica.
© Maria Stenzel/National Geographic Image Collection

Above, Emperor penguin (Aptenodytes forsteri) and chick.
© Frans Lanting/Minden Pictures

On the opposite page, Emperor penguin colony
seen through a window in the ice. Atka Bay, Weddell Sea, Antarctica.
© Pete Oxford/Minden Pictures

the seven species and eight taxa of penguins (BirdLife International 2000; Clements 2000). The diversity of birds may not be very impressive, but the number found in the region during the breeding season is staggering, with as many as 100 million individuals competing for nesting sites.

Antarctica has the highest marine mammal biomass in the world, with tens of millions of individuals representing 10 species of cetaceans (whales) and six species of pinnipeds (seals). For example, the crabeater seal is the most abundant seal in the world, numbering between 15 to 40 million and occurring only in Antarctica. Crabeaters account for one out of every two seals on Earth and are the most abundant large mammals in the world. Nonetheless, it remains one of the least studied and enigmatic of the pinnipeds.

The Antarctic marine system can support such large numbers of animal life because of the explosive growing season occurring each austral summer, when 24 hours of continuous daylight produces phytoplankton blooms that feed the Antarctic krill, the basis of the marine food chain. The Antarctic krill, one of the most abundant marine invertebrates on Earth, is channeled to higher predators, such as seals, birds, and whales.

There are two levels of conservation significance to Antarctica, one regional and the other global.

Regionally, Antarctica contains unique organisms and ecosystems. Since human impacts have been limited to the past century, the Antarctic ecosystem remains in relatively good condition with the oceans, supporting the most robust and productive ecosystem on Earth. The extreme Antarctic environments on land and in the sea greatly inform science about the limits of life on Earth.

Beyond its regional significance, the Antarctic is also a key part of the Earth's biosphere in regulating climate, maintaining ocean circulation, and producing oxygen from photosynthesis. For example, the Antarctic Circumpolar Current (ACC) is the largest current in the world, streaming more than 130 million m^3 of seawater a second as it flows around the Antarctic, driven by the fierce winds and cold of the continent. The ACC is 2 000 km and as deep as 3 700 m, and takes eight years to stream around the globe —the only ocean current to do so. In the course of its never-ending journey, the ACC influences weather throughout the planet, including the El Niño phenomenon in the Pacific, and is the only current to mix the Atlantic, Pacific, and Indian Oceans. If the integrity of the Antarctic ecosystem were to change —if the ice were to melt— ocean currents and global climate could be impacted through changes in the ACC (Gille 2001).

Antarctica is one of the most international and transboundary regions of the world. Unlike all other continents, no one "owns" Antarctica and there are no indigenous populations. United Kingdom, France, New Zealand, Norway, Australia, Chile, and Argentina have territorial claims that are not acknowledged by the international community, while the U.S. shrewdly maintains a permanent research base on the South Pole. Since all these claims are pie-shaped and join at the pole, the U.S. base essentially violates all the claims by overlapping each segment.

All Antarctic legal regimes can be traced to the International Geophysical Year (IGY) (1957-1958) when 12 countries (including all the nations making claims and the U.S., U.S.S.R., Japan, Belgium, and South Africa) engaged in a coordinated scientific project that established 55 research stations in Antarctica. This created the important precedent for international scientific collaboration that continues to this day. This paradigm of collaboration was codified with the signing of the Antarctic Treaty in 1959 by these 12 countries.

The Treaty was short and straightforward, determining that Antarctica should be used for peaceful purposes only and that scientists were free to continue to pursue research, as they did during the IGY. It also dealt with the sovereignty/ownership issue by indicating that nations did not have to relinquish their claims, but that they would not seek to enhance them while the Treaty was in force. Use of Antarctica for nuclear testing was prohibited.

Since the Treaty came into force, additional nations have been allowed to "accede" to it, or to join the original 12 as "consultative parties," with the result that there are now 26 consultative parties and 17 acceding parties. However, the Treaty has no Secretariat or other infrastructure. Parties simply meet and agree on measures and resolutions that they then pass on to their individual governments for ratification.

In the early 1960s, the consultative parties began the discussion of certain conservation issues that were less controversial than many others. This led to the 1964 Agreed Measures for the Conservation of Antarctic Flora and Fauna, which aimed at protecting Antarctica for scientific research, and the 1972 Convention for the Conservation of Antarctic Seals, which provided guidelines in the event that sealing should start again (which never happened). This was followed in 1982 by the Convention on the Conservation of Antarctic Marine Living Resources (CCAMLR), which focused on monitoring and regulating already-established commercial fisheries for krill and finfish.

In the 1980s, it became known that the consultative parties of the Treaty were secretly discussing mineral exploitation in Antarctica. This resulted in an outcry from environmental groups

On the opposite page, the gentoo penguin (Pygoscelis papua) is one of seven penguin species in Antarctica.
© Patricio Robles Gil/Sierra Madre

Above, an orca or killer whale (Orcinus orca). This amazing predator makes dives deep under the ice to hunt Antarctic cod.
© Todd Pusser

337

and also from the United Nations General Assembly, which wanted more equitable global sharing of any resources that might be extracted. This led to the 1988 Convention on the Regulation of Antarctic Mineral Resource Activities (CRAMRA). Attacks continued, with the Convention drawing strong criticism from both conservation organizations and non-Treaty members. As a result, the whole process foundered, and the question of mineral development in Antarctica was dropped. Today, mineral exploitation is specifically prohibited, and Treaty members are prevented from mining or drilling for oil and gas for at least 50 years from the Treaty's signing (Stonehouse 2000).

After the demise of CRAMRA, special Treaty meetings were held in 1990 and 1991 to develop a Protocol on Environmental Protection to add to the Antarctic Treaty. This provides for "...comprehensive protection of the Antarctic environment and its dependent and associated ecosystems," and requires that future activities neither increase risk to endangered and threatened species nor create hazards to areas of biological, scientific, historical, aesthetic, or wilderness significance. The Protocol also calls for the establishment of a Committee for Environmental Protection, and includes five annexes that cover environmental impact assessment, conservation of Antarctic fauna and flora, waste disposal and management, prevention of marine pollution, and protected area creation and management. Of particular note is the fact that the Protocol provides new categories of protected areas, Antarctic Specially Protected Areas (ASPAs) and Antarctic Specially Managed Areas (ASMAs). At least 17 ASPAs currently exist, covering everything from native vegetation to emperor penguin rookeries.

Historically, the hunting of whales and seals was the major threat to the region (Bonner 1985). Whaling has ended, with the exception of a relatively small annual Japanese minke whaling effort. It is possible that this minke whale fishery could be used as a beachhead for expanded whaling into other species if and when they recover. Therefore, careful monitoring of any further proposals for seal or whale hunting is necessary. A more immediate threat to Antarctica is overfishing of invertebrate species, such as krill, and vertebrate species, such as ice fish and Antarctic tooth fish. These fisheries must be studied and managed and conservation regimes enforced.

Tourism has grown dramatically in recent years, increasing from 3 000 passengers making 10 300 landings at 33 sites in 1989-1990 to 7 320 passengers making 58 417 landings at 117 sites in 1996-1997; over 10 000 passengers now stop at some 200 sites (Stonehouse 2000). The potential threat to fragile Antarctic ecosystems and wildlife is clearly present.

A further problem likely to affect both the flora and fauna is the continuing inadvertent introduction of alien species, whether via tourists or the activities of national research programs. Adélie and emperor penguin populations have already been affected by the incidental introduction of the Infectious Bursal Disease Virus.

Of perhaps greater long-term significance is the threat of oil, coal, iron, and other mineral exploitation. The Antarctic Treaty process has kept this in check for the foreseeable future, but the potential for future exploitation always exists.

Finally, of major significance is the potential impact of global warming on Antarctica and on the world. Ice is already melting and giant icebergs are forming at the greatest recorded rates (Stone 2003), while destabilizing changes have already been observed in Antarctic ecosystems as a result of this warming (Loeb et al. 1997). If temperatures continue to rise, a portion of the ice locked away in the Antarctic continent could begin to melt with drastic consequences for low-lying land areas everywhere on the planet, and with changes in ocean circulation, which would affect global climate systems.

Suggestions that Antarctica should be a "World Park," an "International Park," or perhaps an "International Wildlife Reserve," are all interesting concepts. In the meantime, it seems that the Antarctic Treaty and the 1991 Protocol on Environmental Protection have already had a truly positive impact on maintaining the Antarctic wilderness largely intact. A key ingredient in this success has been the international cooperation and progress, unhindered by a long history of human habitation and political structures. Antarctica, at least, seems likely to remain in its current state for many decades to come with the international regimes that have evolved to meet new challenges as they emerge.

GREGORY S. STONE
RUSSELL A. MITTERMEIER

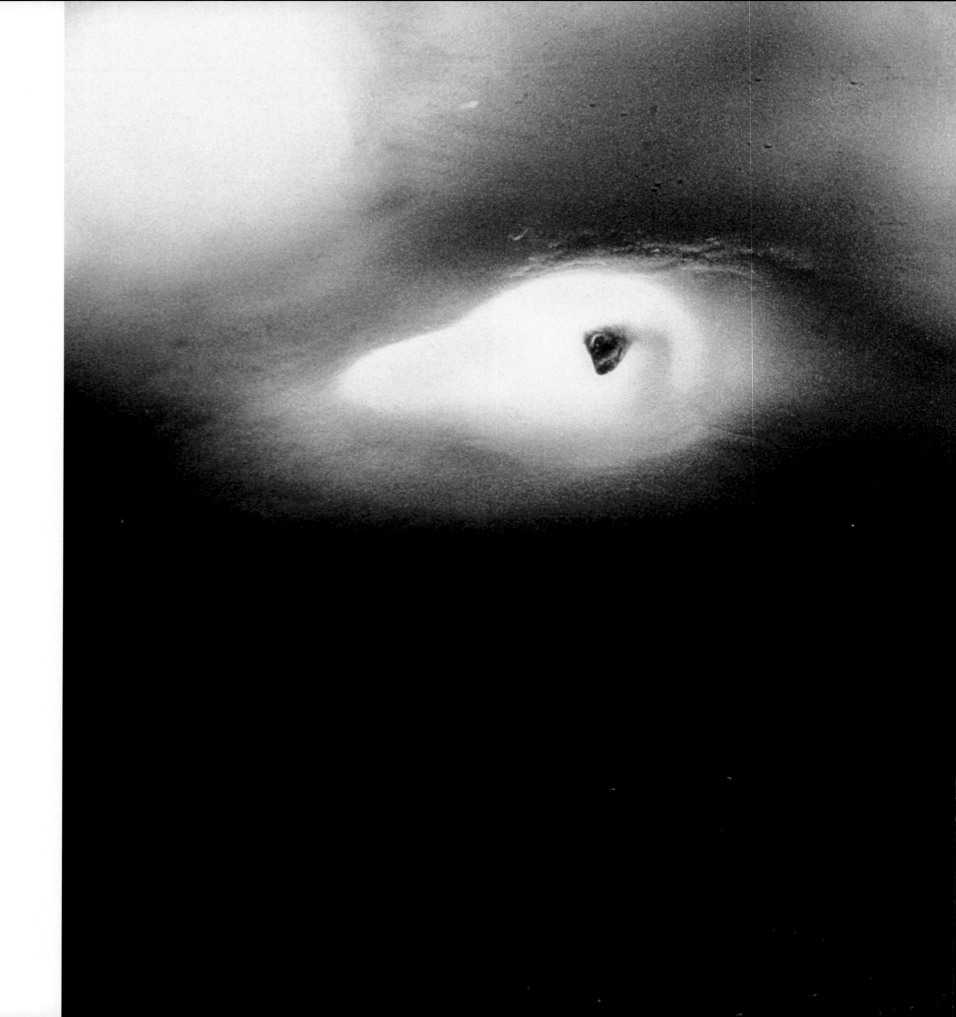

Introduction

Research conducted by Zbicz and Green (1997) identified protected areas that adjoined along international borders, which were termed internationally adjoining protected areas (IAPAs). The great value of this analysis was not only to identify, but also to promote opportunities for transboundary cooperation for conservation. Beyond direct biodiversity conservation applications, this study also identified places where transboundary conservation areas overlapped with zones of current or past conflict, and where conservation could offer an additional tool to support conflict resolution and to increase the sustainability of efforts for the preservation of regional peace.

A subsequent update of the list (Zbicz 2001) showed a large increase both in the number of IAPAs and in the total number of protected areas encompassed by these complexes, suggesting that transboundary conservation initiatives are an increasingly significant element on the global conservation agenda. As work has progressed on clarifying transboundary conservation concepts and tools, it has become useful to develop a standard methodology for identifying IAPAs as a basis for regular updates to the list.

Data sources and methodology

Due in large part to the efforts of IUCN, the World Conservation Union, and the UNEP-World Conservation Monitoring Centre to develop the World Database on Protected Areas (WDPA), the data available for updating the list of IAPAs has improved dramatically. The use of Geographic Information Systems (GIS) and the availability and coverage of protected areas have been increased and enhanced as more and more protected areas have been added to this large database (currently over 102 000 protected areas). This presented an opportunity to conduct the present analysis differently than has been done in the past. Rather than rely upon a global survey of protected area managers and other data sources to locate IAPAs, this analysis took the most recent data from the WDPA and identified protected areas that adjoin one another across international borders.

With the understanding that the WPDA itself is in a process of continual development, and that many existing protected areas have not been fully mapped, this analysis has been checked and supplemented with information from Zbicz and Green (1997), Zbicz (2001), as well as other reliable data sources.

Other data sources used in this analysis include data sheets available from the UNESCO World Heritage Centre and the Man and the Biosphere Programme sites. A significant difference in this analysis from previous ones is the inclusion of transboundary Ramsar Sites (Wetlands of International Importance). These data sets have been included not only because the component areas qualify as protected areas in both national and international law, but to highlight the broad utility of transboundary approaches to conservation.

To qualify for inclusion in this list the protected areas had to:

- conform to the IUCN definition of a protected area (IUCN 1994);
- be included in the World Database on Protected Areas as a mapped entity (polygon);
- be adjacent to an international boundary and adjacent to a protected area in a neighboring country.

In addition, protected areas that were *directly* adjacent to those identified above were included as part of the IAPA complexes.

Exceptions to the above criteria were evaluated on a case by case basis when these criteria conflicted with other datasets of IAPAs created by Zbicz (2001). Where past research showed there to be some level of cooperation between countries in managing these areas, the adjacency criteria were not enforced and these areas were included in the present analysis.

Some IAPA complexes included in previous lists were excluded here due to improved mapping techniques and, in particular, to the merging of some complexes and individual protected areas with nearby ones. Other complexes were excluded because boundary data do not yet exist or have not yet been incorporated into the WPDA. As information continues to improve, future analyses will certainly yield additional sites.

A note about naming: Most of the internationally adjoining protected area complexes identified in this list are unnamed. Generally, once an area becomes a focal point for international cooperation to protect biodiversity or for the promotion of sustainable development across borders, the area will be given a name through either a treaty, a Memorandum of Understanding, or other such international agreement. We indicate proper IAPA names from these international agreements by italicizing the name. In other cases, we list names that have been suggested by chapter authors in this book. These suggested names are not in italics.

The list that follows varies in significant ways from past work by Zbicz and Green (1997) and Zbicz (2001) due to methodological differences and use of different data sources. Comparisons between this list and former lists should therefore be made with great caution.

*On the opposite page,
zebras (Equus quagga) in Masai
Mara National Park, Kenya.
© Anup Shah*

A detailed listing of the methodology used in this analysis will be published on the Global Transboundary Protected Areas Network website (http://www.tbpa.net), the site maintained by the IUCN World Commission on Protected Areas Task Force on Transboundary Conservation.

Data Summary

The present analysis shows there to be 188 internationally adjoining protected area complexes and other transboundary conservation areas, including at least 818 protected areas in 112 countries. In many cases these protected areas overlap, especially in the case of World Heritage Sites (WH in the table), Biosphere Reserves (BR), and Ramsar Sites (RS), where the international designation often overlies nationally designated protected areas. This is of course by design, as the international designation would not be possible without the national governments first declaring their intent to protect these areas. We report size figures for each internationally adjoining protected area complex by describing its overall "footprint," thereby excluding many of the overlapping protected areas from these size figures.

The total size of all these protected area complexes detailed in the list that follows is little less than 3 169 000 km², representing approximately 16.8% of the global extent of protected areas (Table 1) and an area roughly equivalent in size to the country of India.

Nearly half of the total extent of IAPAs is located in North America. This is due in large part to the contribution of the Ellesmere Island/Greenland Transboundary Complex (101 million ha) and two complexes, each of about 14.6 million ha, that cross the border between Alaska, in the U.S., and Canada. These are the Kluane/Wrangell-Saint Elias/Glacier Bay/Tatshenshini-Alsek transboundary World Heritage Site and the unnamed complex involving Ivvavik National Park (Canada) and the Arctic National Wildlife Refuge (U.S.). Africa appears next in the list in terms of continents contributing the greatest number of hectares to the whole, dominated by the complex that comprises the Iona/Skeleton Coast TFCA between Namibia and Angola (12.5 million ha) and followed closely by the Okavango Delta and the Victoria Falls complexes that are contiguous to one another (12.9 million ha shared between Angola, Botswana, Namibia, Zambia, and Zimbabwe).

Countries with the greatest number of IAPA complexes on their borders include the Russian Federation (21), China (14), and Canada (12) (Table 2). Countries contributing most to the overall size of IAPAs include Greenland, the U.S., and Venezuela (Table 3).

Table 1. Internationally adjoining protected area complexes by continent

Region	2005 PAs	2005 Complexes	Size (km²)
North America	97	15	1 458 972.90
Africa	186	33	640 160.76
Central and South America	161	29	523 868.93
Asia	185	46	459 644.11
Europe	189	65	86 189.81
Total	818	188	3 168 836.50

Table 2. Countries ranked by number of IAPAs

Rank	Country	Complexes
1	Russian Federation	21
2	China	14
3	Canada	12
4	Poland	9
5	Finland	9
6	Ukraine	8
7	India	8
8	Argentina	8
9	Vietnam	7
10	United States	7

Table 3. Countries ranked by area in IAPAs

Rank	Country	Size (km²)
1	Greenland	974 523.90
2	United States	438 218.17
3	Venezuela	262 808.06
4	Russian Federation	166 670.51
5	Canada	139 587.42
6	Namibia	108 320.64
7	Zambia	100 963.53
8	Botswana	100 616.37
9	China	94 919.46
10	Bolivia	63 905.49

Discussion

This analysis shows protected areas throughout the world that straddle international borders. Identifying these areas is a useful first step to an understanding that transboundary conservation is a highly significant mechanism for conservation at a landscape scale. Maximizing the potential benefits of these areas requires that governments, national and international NGOs, and civil society engage with one another at many different levels to explore how this mechanism can lead to greater biodiversity conservation, increased benefits for local socioeconomic development, the implementation of sustainable development programs, and the engenderment of a culture of peace and cooperation between and among countries.

The analysis shows that these internationally adjoining sites constitute approximately 16.8% of the global extent of protected areas, a significant proportion of the global conservation estate. The analysis should, however, be considered a minimum set of all possible transboundary conservation areas. As a first step, improvements to the WDPA dataset will increase the number of qualifying protected areas. In addition, there are areas that do not conform to the current analysis or have not been mapped, such as Antarctica or several large marine protected areas that would markedly increase the global extent of IAPAs. There are also many areas that have been set aside as conservation areas by local communities and through other initiatives that have not yet been recognized in terms of the IUCN definitions. In addition, there are many transboundary conservation areas currently being developed that will result in IAPAs in the near future. This analysis is most certainly therefore an underestimate of the global extent of these areas.

Beyond simply identifying IAPAs, this analysis provides an important lens with which to view other global data sets. By overlaying this set of data with other known and mapped data sets including hotspots (Conservation International), ecoregions (World Wildlife Fund), and biological migratory pathways it will be possible to determine to what extent transboundary areas contribute to other conservation strategies, and particularly to the application of the ecosystem approach called for in the Convention on Biological Diversity, through the Programme of Work on Protected Areas adopted by the Seventh Conference of the Parties in 2004. A similar analysis could be conducted to determine the extent to which IAPAs fall within regions of current or past conflict and where transboundary conservation can be regarded as a mechanism for establishing and sustaining peaceful cooperation.

Large-scale conservation programs are complicated and expensive undertakings, and in a transboundary context they are even more so. Institutional commitment, adequate funding, and a sound rationale are necessary ingredients for any such initiatives; but the foundation must be good data. We hope that this analysis provides a starting point and roadmap for both accurate and replicable future analyses.

CHARLES BESANÇON
CONRAD SAVY

NO.	TBPA NAME[A]	COUNTRY[B]	PROTECED AREA NAME[C]	WCMC CODE[D]	IUCN CATEGORY[E]	SIZE (KM²)[F]	SUBTOTAL (KM²)[G]
NORTH AMERICA protected areas; total size of TBPA for this region: 1 458 972.90 km²							
1		Canada	Ellesmere National Park Reserve	13396	II	37 048.30	
	Ellesmere/Greenland Transboundary Complex	Greenland	North-East Greenland National Park	650	II	972 000.00	
			North-East Greenland Biosphere Reserve	2065	BR	972 000.00	
			Heden (Jameson Land)	67909	RS	2 523.90	
			Hochstetter Forland	67910	RS	1 848.20	
			Kilen	67911	RS	512.80	1 011 572.20
2	Roosevelt Campobello International Park	United States (Canada)	Roosevelt Campobello National Monument	300297	Unset	11.34	11.34
3		Canada	Ivvavik National Park	100672	II	9 720.07	
			Old Crow Flats Special Management Area	101594	IV	7 890.33	
			Vuntut National Park	100673	II	4 350.68	
			Old Crow Flats	67834	RS	313.91	
		United States	Arctic National Wildlife Refuge	2904	IV	79 328.18	
			Yukon Flats National Wildlife Refuge	10543	IV	44 503.32	146 106.49
4		Canada	Atlin Provincial Park	4178	II	2 051.11	
			Atlin Recreation Area	65094	II	418.87	
			Kluane National Park Reserve	612	II	22 062.01	
	Alaska-Yukon-British Columbia Borderlands (see Chapter 4)		Kluane Wildlife Sanctuary	18707	VI	6 557.82	
			Tatshenshini-Alsek Provincial Park	67406	Ib	9 405.39	
			Kluane/Wrangell-St. Elias/Glacier Bay/Tatshenshini-Alsek	12200	WH	32 038.27	
		United States	Chilkat State Park	68395	II	3 696.67	
	Kluane/Wrangell-Saint Elias/ Glacier Bay/Tatshenshini-Alsek World Heritage Site (1979) plus other areas		Glacier Bay National Park	1010	II	11 126.87	
			Misty Fjords National Monument	13041	IV	8 729.47	
			Tetlin National Wildlife Refuge	2956	IV	3 948.27	
			Tongass National Forest	13038	VI	4 898.86	
			Tracy Arm-Fords Terror Wilderness (Forest Service)	21254	Ib	20 813.21	
			Wrangell-St. Elias National Park	1005	II	52 364.48	
			Kluane/Wrangell-St. Elias/Glacier Bay/Tatshenshini-Alsek	2018	WH	72 143.52	146 073.03
5		Canada	Cascade Recreation Area	18628	II	175.72	
			Cathedral Provincial Park	4185	Ib	327.80	
			Chilliwack Lake Provincial Park	167270	II	92.44	
			Chilliwack River Ecological Reserve	18335	Ia	0.86	

NO.	TBPA NAME[A]	COUNTRY[B]	PROTECED AREA NAME[C]	WCMC CODE[D]	IUCN CATEGORY[E]	SIZE (KM²)[F]	SUBTOTAL (KM²)[G]
			Cultus Lake Provincial Park	65159	II	6.45	
			E.C. Manning Regional District Park	65177	V	663.78	
			International Ridge Provincial Park	18641	II	18.59	
			Liumchen Ecological Reserve	167403	Ia	21.76	
			Ross Lake Ecological Reserve	18404	Ia	0.61	
			Skagit River Cottonwoods Ecological Reserve	18410	Ia	0.90	
			Skagit River Forest Ecological Reserve	18411	Ia	0.75	
			Skagit River Rhododendrons Ecological Reserve	18412	Ia	0.65	
			Skagit Valley Provincial Park	101678	II	278.77	
		United States	Colville National Forest	101058	VI	4 721.53	
			Glacier Peak Wilderness (Forest Service)	21386	Ib	1 874.01	
			Lake Chelan National Recreation Area	2557	V	254.75	
			Mount Baker National Forest	101061	VI	5 383.40	
			Mount Baker National Recreation Area	75097	V	264.74	
			North Cascades National Park	979	II	2 783.27	
			Okanogan National Forest	101062	VI	6 192.02	
			Pasayten Wilderness (Forest Service)	21389	Ib	2 062.64	
			Ross Lake National Recreation Area	2991	V	512.18	
			Snoqualmie National Forest	101065	VI	6 237.11	
			Wenatchee National Forest	101067	VI	7 860.65	34 767.06
6		Canada	Akamina-Kishinena Provincial Park	21193	II	105.92	
			Waterton National Park	626	II	490.41	
			Waterton Glacier International Peace Park	93295	WH	563.43	
		United States	Bob Marshall Wilderness (Forest Service)	21330	Ib	4 052.21	
			Flathead National Forest	100967	VI	10 612.40	
			Gallatin National Forest	100968	VI	8 684.25	
	Waterton Glacier International Peace Park (1932) plus other areas (see Chapter 1)		Glacier National Park	973	II	4 063.35	
			Great Bear Wilderness (Forest Service)	21333	Ib	1 103.67	
			Helena National Forest	100969	VI	4 657.92	
			Kootenai National Forest	100971	VI	8 548.83	
			Lewis and Clark National Forest	100972	VI	8 036.50	
			Lolo National Forest	100973	VI	10 306.16	
			Mission Mountains Wilderness (Forest Service)	21334	Ib	293.07	
			Scapegoat Wilderness (Forest Service)	21336	Ib	959.21	
			Swan River National Wildlife Refuge	13845	IV	5.57	
			Flathead Indian Reservation	21468	Unset	5 233.30	
			Waterton Glacier International Peace Park	93296	WH	4 368.95	72 085.15
7		Canada	Quetico Provincial Park	66395	II	4 718.15	
		United States	Boundary Waters Canoe Wilderness (Forest Service)	21322	Ib	4 421.41	
			Cascade River State Park	68586	V	11.64	
			McCarthy Beach (Memorial) State Park	68594	V	10.92	
			Superior National Forest	100955	VI	13 235.27	
			Voyageurs National Park	988	II	790.54	18 766.52
8		Mexico	Alto Golfo de California y Delta del Río Colorado (Core Zone) Biosphere Reserve	306870	Ia	1 651.59	
			Alto Golfo de California y Delta del Rio Colorado Biosphere Reserve	101409	VI	9 373.07	
			El Pinacate y Gran Desierto de Altar (Core Zone) Biosphere Reserve	306855	Ia	2 278.43	
	Dry Borders (see Chapter 5)		El Pinacate y Gran Desierto de Altar Biosphere Reserve	306790	VI	7 146.74	
			Alto Golfo de California	198342	BR	16 446.03	
			Humedales del Delta del Río Colorado	145540	RS	3 216.92	
	Sonoran Desert Biosphere Reserve Network (1997)	United States	Cabeza Prieta National Wildlife Refuge	13771	IV	3 495.33	
			Cabeza Prieta Wilderness (Fish and Wildlife Service)	35472	Ib	3 272.58	
			Coronado National Forest	100881	VI	7 050.04	
			Coronado National Forest	100988	VI	294.30	
			Coronado National Memorial	22503	V	10.30	
			Organ Pipe Cactus National Monument	1020	III	1 322.06	
			Organ Pipe Wilderness (National Park Service)	35477	Ib	1 118.86	21 273.72
9		Mexico	Maderas del Carmen Flora and Fauna Protection Area	101431	VI	2 078.68	
	El Carmen-Big Bend Complex (see Chapter 3)		Cañón de Santa Elena Flora and Fauna Protection Area	101457	VI	2 797.81	
		United States	Big Bend National Park	976	II	2 791.41	
			Rio Grande (Texas) National Scenic River	2509	V	385.84	8 053.74
10		Canada (U.S.)	Creston Valley	95323	RS	71.78	71.78
11		Canada (U.S.)	Point Pélée	67850	RS	23.27	23.27
12		Canada (U.S.)	Long Point	67827	RS	110.66	110.66
13		Canada (U.S.)	Lac Saint-François	67843	RS	18.38	18.38
14		Canada (U.S.)	Cap Tourmente	67825	RS	25.81	25.81
15		Canada (U.S.)	Baie de l'Isle-Verte	67844	RS	13.75	13.75

NO.	TBPA NAME[A]	COUNTRY[B]	PROTECED AREA NAME[C]	WCMC CODE[D]	IUCN CATEGORY[E]	SIZE (KM2)[F]	SUBTOTAL (KM2)[G]
CENTRAL AND SOUTH AMERICA protected areas; total size of TBPA for this region: 523 868.93 km²							
16		Guatemala	Zona de Veda Definitiva Volcán Tacaná	302076	II	28.96	
		Mexico	Volcan Tacaná Biosphere Reserve	306853	VI	64.04	93.00
17	Maya Tropical Forest Complex (see Chapter 7)	Belize	Aguas Turbias National Park	61957	II	35.68	
			Bladen Branch Nature Reserve	12241	Ia	405.13	
			Caracol Archaeological Reserve	20229	IV	103.72	
			Chiquibul Forest Reserve	3306	VI	1 075.96	
			Chiquibul National Park	20230	II	600.04	
			Cockscomb Basin Wildlife Sanctuary	10579	IV	354.61	
			Columbia River Forest Reserve	3314	VI	602.02	
			Deep River Forest Reserve	3311	VI	314.84	
			El Pilar Archaelogical Reserve	301910	II	7.19	
			Fives Blues Lakes National Park	34313	II	16.49	
			Manatee Forest Reserve	12226	VI	446.96	
			Maya Mountains Forest Reserve	28850	VI	311.35	
			Mountain Pine Ridge Forest Reserve	3305	VI	494.03	
			Río Bravo Conservation Area Private Reserve	20224	IV	1 052.00	
			Shipstern Private Reserve	20226	IV	97.02	
			Sibun Forest Reserve	3307	VI	432.01	
			Sittee River Forest Reserve	12229	VI	382.36	
			Vaca Forest Reserve	116297	VI	240.01	
			Victoria Peak Natural Monument	301918	III	19.67	
		Guatemala	Cerro Cahuí Protected Biotope	12593	III	6.87	
			Chiquibul-Montañas Mayas Buffer Zone	315073	VI	829.38	
			Dos Lagunas Protected Biotope	102817	III	297.14	
			Laguna del Tigre Protected Biotope	115081	III	3 375.15	
			Mirador Río Azul National Park	30604	II	1 179.59	
			Reserva de la Biosfera Maya (RBM) Buffer Zone	315071	VI	4 669.12	
			Río Chiquibul-Montañas Mayas Biosphere Reserve	30614	VI	619.42	
			San Miguel la Palotada Protected Biotope	30606	III	355.36	
			Sierra del Lacandón National Park	30605	II	2 003.21	
			Tikal National Park	193	II	579.53	
			ZUM de la RBM (Multiple Use Zone)	315067	VI	7 815.02	
			Parque Nacional Laguna del Tigre	67982	RS	452.55	
			Tikal National Park World Heritage Site	197	WH	8 927.15	
		Mexico	Bonampak Natural Monument	67671	III	42.45	
			Calakmul (Core Zone) Biosphere Reserve	308529	Ia	1 482.70	
			Calakmul Biosphere Reserve	306780	VI	7 243.64	
			Yaxchilán Natural Monument	67672	III	26.41	
			Calakmul Biosphere Reserve	61401	BR	7 126.07	37 516.08
18		Belize	Bacalar Chico Marine Reserve	99651	IV	63.37	
			Bacalar Chico National Park	301985	V	51.06	
			Corozal Bay Wildlife Sanctuary	301909	V	733.15	
			Belize Barrier-Reef Reserve System	124383	WH	1 049.53	
		Mexico	Arrecifes de Xcalak National Park	306776	II	180.43	1 963.11
19	San Juan River Basin (Si-a-Paz)	Costa Rica	Barra del Colorado National Wildlife Refuge	12493	IV	812.11	
			Caño Negro National Wildlife Refuge	12488	IV	101.72	
			Cerro El Jardín Forest Reserve	102341	VI	14.27	
			Corredor Fronterizo National Wildlife Refuge	168129	IV	597.38	
			La Cureña Forest Reserve	102339	VI	60.07	
			Tortuguero Protective Zone	30599	VI	733.25	
			Caño Negro	67864	RS	74.75	
			Caribe Noreste Wetland	145525	RS	732.20	
		Nicaragua	Cerro Silva Forest Reserve	61075	VI	2 596.95	
			Los Guatuzos Wildlife Refuge	30630	IV	426.89	
			Río Indio-Maíz Biological Reserve	30628	Ia	4 129.75	9 472.39
20	Parque Internacional La Amistad (see Chapter 8)	Costa Rica	Barbilla National Park	19372	II	119.45	
			Chirripó National Park	163	II	509.19	
			Cuenca del Río Banano Protective Zone	61925	VI	92.48	
			Hitoy-Cerere Biological Reserve	156	Ia	99.50	
			La Amistad National Park	2553	II	1 991.49	
			Las Tablas Protective Zone	12491	VI	199.26	
			Río Macho Forest Reserve	3315	VI	756.98	
			Tapantí National Park	9636	II	51.55	
			Talamanca Range-La Amistad Reserves/La Amistad National Park	10903	WH	1 995.48	
		Panama	La Amistad National Park	2552	II	2 187.40	
			Palo Seco Protected Forest	17185	VI	1 157.08	
			Volcán Barú National Park	240	II	141.53	
			Lagunas del Volcán Wildlife Refuge	102253	IV	3.70	
			La Amistad Biosphere Reserve	198343	BR	2 187.39	7 309.61

NO.	TBPA NAME[A]	COUNTRY[B]	PROTECED AREA NAME[C]	WCMC CODE[D]	IUCN CATEGORY[E]	SIZE (KM²)[F]	SUBTOTAL (KM²)[G]
21		Costa Rica	Gandoca-Manzanillo National Wildlife Refuge	19402	IV	88.38	
			Gandoca-Manzanillo	145524	RS	62.90	
		Panama	Isla Bastimentos National Marine Park	16787	II	131.50	
			San San Pond Sak Wildlife Refuge	102254	IV	217.59	
			San San Pond Sak	68135	RS	132.90	437.47
22		Colombia	Darién and Colombia-Panama Boundary National Protective Forests Reserves	100764	VI	622.29	
			Los Katíos Natural National Park	142	II	767.25	
			Los Katíos National Park	61610	WH	64 748.00	
		Panama	Darién National Park	236	II	5 582.53	
			Darién National Park	2554	WH	5 537.63	
			Punta Patiño	95360	RS	389.76	
			Punta Patiño Private Reserve	102255	Unset	396.90	5 972.29
23		Colombia	Catatumbo-Barí Natural National Park	19993	II	1 658.12	
		Venezuela	Perijá National Park	318	II	2 954.73	
			Región Lago de Maracaibo and Sierra de Perijá Protective Zone	20068	V	2 452.37	
			San Rafael de Guasare Protective Zone	10775	V	3 049.40	10 114.62
24		Colombia	Tamá Natural National Park	144	II	558.42	
		Venezuela	El Tamá National Park	322	II	1 602.76	
			Rubio Protective Zone	20084	V	225.24	
			San Antonio-Ureña Protective Zone	30640	V	78.75	2 465.17
25		Brazil	Monte Roraima National Park	19762	II	1 299.83	
			Pico da Neblina National Park	54	II	22 994.03	
		Venezuela	Alto Orinoco-Casiquiare Biosphere Reserve	30029	VI	31 150.30	
			Canaima National Park	313	II	30 453.85	
			Delta del Orinoco Biosphere Reserve	30028	VI	9 902.02	
			Duida-Marahuaca National Park	4366	II	1 960.07	
			El Caura Forest Reserve	10780	VI	51 370.11	
			Formaciones de Tepuyes Natural Monument	30030	III	51 237.04	
			Imataca Forest Reserve	10779	VI	53 512.59	
			Jaua Sarisariñama National Park	4368	II	2 623.18	
			La Paragua Forest Reserve	10787	VI	7 948.15	
			Serranía de la Neblina National Park	4367	II	11 476.78	
			Yapacana National Park	317	II	2 811.21	
			Canaima National Park	61612	WH	30 413.44	276 738.68
26		French Guiana	Basse-Mana	94070	RS	643.02	643.02
		Suriname	Wane Kreek	12189	IV	454.00	
			Galibi Nature Reserve	282	IV	40.00	
			Wia Wia Nature Reserve	280	IV	360.00	1 497.02
27		Bolivia	Otuquis National Park	303883	II	9 050.77	
		Paraguay	Río Negro National Park	61556	II	297.94	
			Río Negro	145545	RS	3 164.92	12 215.69
28	Iguaçu-Iguazú (see Chapter 12)	Argentina	Iguazú National Park	15	II	468.18	
			Urugua-í Provincial Park	21217	II	832.57	
			Iguazú National Park	10901	WH	624.15	
		Brazil	Iguaçu National Park	60	II	1 700.36	
			Iguaçu National Park	12203	WH	1 921.92	3 001.11
29		Argentina	Lanín National Park	7	II	2 167.46	
			Lanín National Reserve	4330	VI	1 947.14	
			Nahuel Huapi 1 National Park	2497	II	3 067.64	
			Nahuel Huapi 1 National Reserve	61824	VI	1 489.74	
			Nahuel Huapi 2 National Park	97490	II	1 664.20	
			Nahuel Huapi 2 National Reserve	97491	VI	1 239.84	
		Chile	Huerquehue National Park	9418	II	66.73	
			Puyehue National Park	90	II	1 735.13	
			Vicente Pérez Rosales National Park	88	II	2 670.72	
			Villarrica National Park	91	II	1 019.73	
			Villarrica National Reserve	10706	IV	356.28	17 424.61
30	Glaciares-Torres del Paine-O'Higgins Complex	Argentina	Los Glaciares National Park	6	II	5 365.33	
			Los Glaciares National Reserve	61823	VI	1 877.84	
			Los Glaciares	2570	WH	7 170.34	
		Chile	Alacalufes National Reserve	9451	IV	3.15	
			Bernardo O'Higgins National Park	9414	II	2.96	
			Torres del Paine National Park	89	II	3 676.40	10 925.68
31	*Montecristo Trifinio Transboundary Protected Area Complex* (1991)	El Salvador (Guatemala, Honduras)	Montecristo National Park	9638	IV	20.00	20.00

NO.	TBPA NAME[A]	COUNTRY[B]	PROTECED AREA NAME[C]	WCMC CODE[D]	IUCN CATEGORY[E]	SIZE (KM²)[F]	SUBTOTAL (KM²)[G]
32		Honduras	Río Plátano Biosphere Reserve	5002	WH	4 380.05	
			Río Plátano National Park	41014	Unset	6 903.22	
		Nicaragua	Bosawas National Resources Reserve	12650	VI	7 300.98	11 681.03
33		Colombia	La Paya Natural National Park	9400	II	4 346.97	
			Yasuní National Park	186	II	10 383.42	
		Ecuador	Cuyabeno Faunal Production Reserve	2499	VI	6 033.80	20 764.19
34	Cordillera del Cóndor (1998 Peace Accord)	Ecuador	Podocarpus National Park	7912	II	1 470.15	
		Peru	Santiago-Comaina Reserved Zone	168280	Unset	16 425.67	17 895.82
35		Bolivia	Noel Kempff Mercado National Park	31	II	15 888.26	
		Brazil	Guaporé Biological Reserve	5126	Ia	6 181.93	22 070.19
36		Bolivia	Sajama National Park	33	II	267.43	
		Chile	Las Vicuñas National Reserve	9435	IV	2 066.92	
			Salar de Surire	145518	RS	92.52	
			Lauca National Park	86	II	1 393.23	3 820.10
37		Bolivia	Eduardo Avaroa National Reserve for Andean Fauna	36	IV	6 872.83	
			Laguna Colorada	67815	RS	193.58	
		Chile	Los Flamencos National Reserve	30043	IV	739.87	7 612.70
38		Argentina	Baritú National Park	11	II	1 863.85	
		Bolivia	Tariquía National Fauna and Flora Reserve	20041	IV	2 476.17	4 340.02
39		Argentina	Copahue-Caviahue Provincial Park	16873	II	299.75	
		Chile	Ñuble National Reserve	111	IV	691.74	991.49
40		Brazil	Pantanal Matogrossense	67816	RS	916.67	
			Pantanal Matogrossense National Park	2581	II	1 350.00	
		Bolivia	San Matías Integrated Management Natural Area	303891	Unset	29 156.44	30 506.44
41		Paraguay	Tifunque	145546	RS	2 238.81	2 238.81
42		Argentina	Río Pilcomayo	67759	RS	484.51	484.51
43		Uruguay	Bañados del Este y Franja Costera	68318	RS	3 981.45	3 981.45
44		Argentina	Reserva Costa Atlántica de Tierra del Fuego	95315	RS	315.65	315.65

EUROPE protected areas; total size of TBPA for this region: 86 189.81 km²

NO.	TBPA NAME[A]	COUNTRY[B]	PROTECED AREA NAME[C]	WCMC CODE[D]	IUCN CATEGORY[E]	SIZE (KM²)[F]	SUBTOTAL (KM²)[G]
45		Portugal	Ria Formosa Nature Park	4724	V	154.26	
			Sapal de Castro Marim e Vila Real de S. Antonio Nature Reserve	4723	IV	21.53	
			Ria Formosa	68146	RS	75.02	
			Sapais de Castro Marim	127885	RS	26.87	175.78
46		Portugal	Peneda-Gerês National Park	860	II	703.88	
		Spain	Baixa Limia-Serra do Xurés Nature Park	71215	V	279.70	983.58
47	Pyrenees-Mount Perdu World Heritage Site (1997) (see Chapter 13)	France	Adour et affluents Biotope Protection Order	147147	IV	1.86	
			Néouvielle Nature Reserve	1527	IV	23.16	
			Pyrénées Occidentales National Park (Buffer Zone)	103151	V	2 069.61	
			Pyrénées Occidentales National Park (Central Area)	662	II	456.83	
			Pyrénées-Mont Perdu	145592	WH	30.66	
		Spain	Aztaparreta Integral Reserve	142962	Ib	1.48	
			Larra Nature Reserve	20965	IV	27.20	
			Ordesa y Monte Perdido National Park (State Network)	893	II	101.11	
			Ukerdi Integral Reserve	142964	Ib	3.71	
			Pyrénées-Mont Perdu	145590	WH	145.16	2 684.96
48		France	Collet de Sen Biotope Protection Order	147168	IV	2.05	
			Mercantour National Park (Buffer Zone)	103154	V	1 467.25	
			Mercantour National Park (Central Area)	664	II	691.20	
		Italy	Alta Valle Pesio e Tanaro Regional/Provincial Nature Park	6020	V	24.48	2 184.99
49		France	Grande Sassière Nature Reserve	15140	IV	22.56	
			Hauts de Villaroger Nature Reserve	39809	IV	9.82	
			Mont Cenis et Vallon de Savine Biotope Protection Order	106753	IV	57.11	
			Plan de Tuéda Nature Reserve	39808	IV	11.15	
			Ruisseau de l'Eglise Biotope Protection Order	147142	IV	0.05	
			Tignes-Champagny Nature Reserve	15141	IV	11.05	
			Vanoise National Park (Buffer Zone)	103150	V	1 424.30	
			Vanoise National Park (Central Area)	661	II	534.72	
		Italy	Gran Paradiso National Park	718	II	663.61	2 724.55
50	Wadden Sea International Protected Region	Denmark	Fanoe Albuebugten mv Protected by Conservation Order	17665	II	39.00	
			Skallingen Protected by Conservation Order	17687	Ia	18.78	
			Vadehavet Nature Reserve	17703	II	1 167.97	
			Vadehavet (Wadden Sea)	67900	RS	1 239.39	

NO.	TBPA NAME[A]	COUNTRY[B]	PROTECED AREA NAME[C]	WCMC CODE[D]	IUCN CATEGORY[E]	SIZE (KM²)[F]	SUBTOTAL (KM²)[G]
		Germany	Hamburgisches Wattenmeer	67962	RS	122.10	
			Schleswig-Holstein Wadden Sea and adjacent areas	67963	RS	2 621.82	
			Wattenmeer Ostfriesisches Wattenmeer and Dollart	67936	RS	1 294.75	
		Netherlands	Waddenzee (Wadden Sea)	68102	RS	2 687.23	7 951.66
51		Czech Republic	Jizerske hory Protected Landscape Area	4272	V	372.45	
			Krkonose National Park	645	V	387.61	
			Krkonoská raseliniste (Krkonose mountain mires)	94067	RS	10.69	
		Poland	Karkonoski National Park	852	II	42.57	802.62
52		Poland	Pieninski National Park	857	II	24.68	
		Slovakia	Pieninsky National Park	646	II	22.97	
			Tatransky National Park	1975	II	762.86	
			Tatrzanski National Park	848	II	213.02	1 023.53
53		Poland	Bieszczadzki National Park	851	II	276.51	
	Eastern Carpathian Biosphere Reserve (1991)	Ukraine	Karpatskiy National Park	1745	II	610.81	
			Karpatskiy National Biosphere Reserve (Zapovednik)	1990	Ia	413.40	
			Nadsans'ki Regional Landscape Park	161272	V	192.96	
			Stuzhitsya State Reserve (Zakaznik)	161620	IV	48.49	
			Syanki Zapovedne Urotchische	161633	III	0.45	1 542.61
54		Lithuania	Kur_iø nerijos Nacionalinis parkas State Park	31552	II	116.26	
			Nemuno deltos regioninis parkas State Park	62285	V	119.81	
			Nemunas Delta	94075	RS	214.93	
		Russian Federation	Djunnyi Nature Sanctuary or Partial Reserve	203209	IV	63.31	
			Kurshskaya Kosa National Park	68348	II	85.47	384.84
55		Belarus	Belowezskaya Pushcha National Park	1985	II	882.32	
			Dikoe Nature Sanctuary or Partial Reserve	93916	IV	117.97	
			Porazauski Nature Sanctuary or Partial Reserve (Local)	146292	IV	87.98	
			Belovezhskaya Pushcha/Bialowieza Forest	67734	WH	1 291.44	
		Poland	Bialowieski National Park	854	II	44.93	
			Belovezhskaya Pushcha/Bialowieza Forest	2008	WH	41.62	1 133.18
56		Belarus	Radostovskiy Nature Sanctuary or Partial Reserve	93908	IV	79.91	
			Zvanets Nature Sanctuary or Partial Reserve (Local)	145850	IV	113.16	
		Ukraine	Zalukhivs'kiy Regional Reserve (Zakaznik)	161859	IV	11.42	204.48
57		Belarus	Prostyr Nature Sanctuary or Partial Reserve	101859	IV	42.78	
			Prypyatskiy National Park	1644	II	669.18	
		Ukraine	Prip'yats'kiy (3 Regional Reserves [Zakaznik])	161432	IV	9.38	
			Prypiat-Stokhid Regional Landscape Park	161439	V	499.31	
			Tsirs'kiy Regional Reserve (Zakaznik)	161666	IV	4.03	1 224.68
58		Belarus	Chyrvony Bor Nature Sanctuary or Partial Reserve (Local)	146316	IV	360.19	
			Osveyskiy Nature Sanctuary or Partial Reserve	93948	IV	226.29	
			Velikoe Boloto Nature Sanctuary or Partial Reserve	93927	IV	5.45	
			Ykhnovichskiy Nature Sanctuary or Partial Reserve	93943	IV	13.78	
		Russian Federation	Krasnaya luka Nature Monument	206111	III	5.64	
			Sebezhskiy Nature Sanctuary or Partial Reserve	206016	IV	173.67	
			Sebezhsky National Park	205993	II	496.93	1 281.95
59		Norway	Kvisleflået Wetland Reserve	9890	Ia	38.65	
		Sweden	Drevfjällen Nature Reserve	106835	Ib	330.04	368.69
60		Norway	Femundsmarka Landscape Protection Area	9906	V	61.28	
			Femundsmarka National Park	826	II	406.68	
			Grøvelsjøen Geological Reserve	31238	Ia	16.12	
			Gutulia National Park	833	II	20.45	
		Sweden	Långfjället Nature Reserve	106837	Ib	690.56	
			Töfsingdalen National Park	913	II	15.87	1 210.95
61		Norway	Børgefjell National Park	823	II	1 085.18	
		Sweden	Bjurälven Nature Reserve	10407	Ib	22.82	
			Korallgrottan Nature Reserve	106841	Ib	25.47	1 133.46
62		Norway	Rago National Park	829	II	170.10	
		Sweden	Padjelanta National Park	905	II	1 989.02	
			Pärlälvens fjällurskog Nature Reserve	174615	Ib	1 151.08	
			Sarek National Park	906	II	1 972.99	
			Sjaunja Nature Reserve	6907	Ib	2 788.38	
			Stora Sjöfallet National Park	3998	II	1 271.68	
			Laponian Area	124388	WH	9 466.59	
			Sjaunja	68221	RS	1 868.71	10 787.77
63		Finland	Käsivarren erämaa-alue Wilderness Area	64508	VI	2 181.15	
			Lätäsenon-Hietajoen soidensuojelualue Protected Mire	64542	VI	430.14	

NO.	TBPA NAME[A]	COUNTRY[B]	PROTECED AREA NAME[C]	WCMC CODE[D]	IUCN CATEGORY[E]	SIZE (KM²)[F]	SUBTOTAL (KM²)[G]
		Norway	Raisduottarhaldi Landscape Protection Area	31256	V	79.94	
			Reisa National Park	12297	II	765.88	3 457.10
64		Finland	Kemihaaran erämaa-alue Wilderness Area	64500	VI	298.11	
			Sompion luonnonpuisto State Nature Reserve	1518	Ia	177.47	
			Tuntsan erämaa-alue Wilderness Area	64499	VI	209.79	
			Urho Kekkosen kansallispuisto National Park	2561	II	2 531.51	
			Vaaranaavan soidensuojelualue Protected Mire	64529	VI	32.73	
			Värriön luonnonpuisto State Nature Reserve	7485	Ia	124.15	
		Russian Federation	Girvasskiy Nature Sanctuary or Partial Reserve	204570	IV	1 292.77	
			Nottinskiy Nature Sanctuary or Partial Reserve	204577	IV	297.69	4 964.23
65	*Pasvik Nature Reserve* (1993)	Finland	Vätsarin erämaa-alue Wilderness Area	64504	VI	1 598.74	
		Norway	Øvre Pasvik National Park	832	II	71.73	
			Pasvik Wetland Reserve	64472	Ia	19.10	
			Pasvik Nature Reserve	127876	RS	19.10	
		Russian Federation	Pasvik State Nature Reserve	62446	Ia	223.48	1 913.06
66		Finland	Oulangan kansallispuisto National Park	656	II	276.94	
			Sukerijärven luonnonpuisto State Nature Reserve	7486	Ia	20.65	
		Russian Federation	Paanayarvi National Park	68351	II	1 218.13	1 515.72
67	*Friendship Nature Reserve* (1991)	Finland	Elimyssalon luonnonsuojelualue State Nature Reserve	149666	VI	72.73	
			Ison-Palosen ja Maariansärkkien luonnonsuojelualue State Nature Reserve	149670	VI	38.97	
			Juortanansalon-Lapinsuon soidensuojelualue Protected Mire	102007	VI	37.91	
		Russian Federation	Kostomukshsky State Nature Reserve	13988	Ia	781.64	
		Finland	Ulvinsalon luonnonpuisto State Nature Reserve	1523	Ia	25.21	956.47
68		Russian Federation	Skripkinskiy Nature Sanctuary or Partial Reserve	201841	IV	37.08	
		Ukraine	Ostriv Regional Reserve (Zakaznik)	161316	IV	115.01	37.08
69		Russian Federation	Klevenskiy Nature Sanctuary or Partial Reserve	204103	IV	351.69	
		Ukraine	Shaligins'kiy State Reserve (Zakaznik)	161521	IV	28.45	380.14
70		Finland	Hammastunturin erämaa-alue Wilderness Area	64507	VI	1 814.74	
			Lemmenjoen kansallispuisto National Park	654	II	2 828.71	
			Pöyrisjärven erämaa-alue Wilderness Area	64503	VI	1 269.28	
			Pöyrisvuoman soidensuojelualue Protected Mire	64532	VI	42.79	
			Puljun erämaa-alue Wilderness Area	64501	VI	615.11	
			Saaravuoman-Kuoskisenvuoman soidensuojelualue Protected Mire	64541	VI	163.50	
		Norway	Øvre Anarjokka National Park	822	II	1 404.66	8 138.78
71	*Lake Fertö* (1991)	Austria	Neusiedlersee Seewinkel and Hanság	67801	RS	485.66	
		Hungary	Fertö-Hásági National Park	9566	II	114.38	
			Lake Fertö	68000	RS	12.01	600.04
72		Greece	Prespes National Park (Core Zone)	674	II	250.52	
			Lake Mikri Prespa	67978	RS	39.70	
		Macedonia	Galichica National Park	2516	II	215.25	
			Pelister National Park	1056	II	159.54	
			Lake Prespa	127887	RS	179.94	805.25
73	*Danube Delta/Green Corridor of Europe*	Romania	Danube Delta World Heritage Site	67728	WH	7 784.13	
			Danube Delta	68147	RS	6 263.59	
		Ukraine	Dunaiskiy/Danube Delta National Biosphere Reserve (Zapovednik)	160873	Ia	486.55	14 534.27
74		Italy/Switzerland	Stelvio National Park	717	V	1 347.56	1 347.56
75		Czech Republic/ Germany	Blansky les Protected Landscape Area	20517	V	218.91	
			Sumava CHKO Protected Landscape Area	4282	V	1 458.20	
			Sumavská raseliniste (Sumava peatlands)	67870	RS	17.75	1 677.11
76		Croatia/Hungary/ Serbia and Montenegro	Kopacki Rit	67867	RS	342.96	342.96
77		Serbia and Montenegro/ Bosnia and Herzegovina	Durmitor National Park	4326	WH	1 231.28	1 231.28
78	*Rhodope Mountains*	Bulgaria/Greece	Pirin National Park	9613	WH	271.95	271.95
79		Poland	Wolinski National Park	855	II	50.02	
		Germany	Insel Usedom Landscape Protection Area	20793	V	375.00	425.02
80	*West Polissya*	Belarus	Vygonoshchanskoe Nature Sanctuary or Partial Reserve	93914	IV	584.33	
		Poland	Poleski National Park	11147	II	76.69	
		Ukraine	Polesskiy Nature (Zapovednik)	1749	Ia	200.37	
			Shatskiy National Park	11580	II	334.55	1 195.94

NO.	TBPA NAME[A]	COUNTRY[B]	PROTECED AREA NAME[C]	WCMC CODE[D]	IUCN CATEGORY[E]	SIZE (KM^2)[F]	SUBTOTAL (KM^2)[G]
81		Finland	Itäisen Suomenlahden kansallispuisto National Park	7500	II	927.90	
		Russian Federation	Kurgalski Peninsula	95394	RS	534.87	1 462.77
82		Finland	Perämeren kansallispuisto National Park	40928	II	152.12	
		Sweden	Haparanda skärgård National Park	106872	II	73.57	225.69
83		France	Forêt de la Massane Nature Reserve	4042	IV	3.32	
		Spain	L'Albera Natural Landscape/s of National Interest	15419	V	40.68	44.00
84		France (Switzerland)	Rives du Lac Léman	67929	RS	30.86	30.86
85		Switzerland (France)	Le Rhône genevois-Vallons de l'Allondon et de La Laire	68237	RS	14.45	14.45
86		Switzerland (Germany)	Klingnauer Stausee	68238	RS	5.85	5.85
87		Germany (Switzerland)	Bodensee: Wollmatinger Ried-Giehrenmoos and Mindelsee	67943	RS	13.63	13.63
88		Austria (Germany, Switzerland)	Rheindelta Bodensee	67805	RS	37.65	37.65
89		Belgium (Netherlands)	Zwin	67811	RS	6.13	6.13
90		Belgium	Schorren van de Beneden Schelde	67810	RS	5.99	
		Netherlands	Westerschelde en Verdronken Land van Saeftinge	95358	RS	9.34	15.33
91		Belgium (Netherlands)	Kalmthoutse Heide	67813	RS	17.97	17.97
92		Germany (Netherlands)	Unterer Niederrhein	67961	RS	237.21	237.21
93		Netherlands (Germany)	Bargerveen	68110	RS	6.54	6.54
94		Slovenia (Croatia)	Secoveljske soline (Secovlje salt pans)	68162	RS	7.84	7.84
95		Slovakia (Ukraine)	Latorica	68161	RS	46.02	46.02
96		Hungary (Serbia and Montenegro, Romania)	Pusztaszer	67996	RS	28.24	28.24
97		Hungary (Croatia)	Szaporca	67990	RS	5.16	5.16
98		Croatia (Bosnia and Herzegovina)	Lonjsko Polje and Mokro Polje (including Krapje Djol)	67868	RS	577.09	577.09
99		Greece (Bulgaria)	Artificial Lake Kerkini	67976	RS	444.44	444.44
100		Greece (Turkey)	Evros Delta	67971	RS	193.57	193.57
101		Bulgaria (Romania)	Srébarna	67818	RS	9.21	9.21
102		Ukraine (Moldova)	Dniester-Turunchuk Crossrivers Area	166893	RS	366.29	366.29
103		Germany (Poland)	Unteres Odertal Schwedt	67955	RS	14.92	14.92
104		Poland (Germany)	Slonsk Reserve	68141	RS	26.60	26.60
105		Poland (Russian Federation)	Jezioro Siedmiu Wysp	68144	RS	19.67	19.67
106		Poland (Belarus)	Biebrza National Park	95369	RS	542.91	542.91
107		Estonia (Latvia)	Nigula Nature Reserve	134948	RS	32.27	32.27
108		Lithuania (Belarus)	Cepkeliai	94072	RS	97.19	97.19
109		Sweden (Norway)	Tjålmejaure-Laisdalen	68219	RS	62.04	62.04

AFRICA protected areas; total size of TBPA for this region: 640 160.76 km^2

NO.	TBPA NAME[A]	COUNTRY[B]	PROTECED AREA NAME[C]	WCMC CODE[D]	IUCN CATEGORY[E]	SIZE (KM^2)[F]	SUBTOTAL (KM^2)[G]
110	*Kgalagadi Transfrontier Park* (2000)	Botswana	Gemsbok National Park	7508	II	25 858.07	
		South Africa	Kalahari Gemsbok National Park	874	II	9 494.41	35 352.48
111		Angola	Iona National Park	347	II	15 315.71	
			Mocamedes Partial Reserve	2251	IV	5 316.58	
	Iona/Skeleton Coast Transfrontier Conservation Area (Angola and Namibia 2004) (see Chapter 19)	Namibia	Ai-Ais Hot Springs Game Park	8785	II	4 362.82	
			Namib-Naukluft National Park	883	II	50 817.15	
			National West Coast Recreation Area Recreational Resort	8786	V	7 471.14	
			Skeleton Coast Park Game Park	885	II	16 896.59	
			Sperrgebiet National Park	30369	Unset	22 679.24	
		South Africa	Richtersveld National Park	30851	II	1 612.19	
			Orange River Mouth	68172	RS	12.83	124 484.26
112		Angola	Luiana Partial Reserve	4493	IV	10 470.31	
		Botswana	Chobe National Park	600	II	10 583.24	
			Okavango Delta System	145516	RS	64 175.06	

NO.	TBPA NAME[A]	COUNTRY[B]	PROTECED AREA NAME[C]	WCMC CODE[D]	IUCN CATEGORY[E]	SIZE (KM²)[F]	SUBTOTAL (KM²)[G]
		Namibia	Caprivi Game Park	7442	VI	5 847.50	
			Mahango Game Reserve	23072	II	245.79	
			Popa Game Park	18001	III	0.41	
		Zambia	Mosi-Oa-Tunya National Park	2347	II	80.72	
			Sioma Ngwezi National Park	1087	II	4 467.32	
			Victoria Falls National Park	1993	III	26.56	
			West Zambezi Game Management Area	4081	VI	32 344.25	
			Zambezi National Park	2530	II	517.11	
			Mosi-oa-Tunya/Victoria Falls	20399	WH	73.16	
		Zimbabwe	Mosi-oa-Tunya/Victoria Falls	23172	WH	38.22	128 758.26
113		Zambia	Chiawa Game Management Area	62095	VI	1 520.45	
			Lower Zambezi National Park	7962	II	4 144.46	
			Luano Game Management Area	4095	VI	8 351.12	
			Rufunsa Game Management Area	303859	VI	2 790.42	
			West Petauke Game Management Area	4097	VI	3 184.61	
		Zimbabwe	Charara Safari Area	2524	VI	1 733.41	
			Chewore Safari Area	2525	VI	3 411.37	
			Dande Safari Area	2528	VI	499.70	
			Doma Safari Area	7429	VI	974.81	
			Hurungwe Safari Area	2527	VI	2 897.77	
			Mana Pools National Park	2531	II	2 129.51	
			Sapi Safari Area	2526	VI	1 197.96	
			Mana Pools National Park Sapi and Chewore Safari Areas	10907	WH	6 726.16	32 835.58
114		Mozambique	Limpopo Valley Wildlife Utilization Area	20295	VI	10 812.11	
			Banhine National Park	799	II	6 009.01	
	Great Limpopo Transfrontier Park (Mozambique and South Africa 2002) (see Chapter 2)		Zinave National Park	800	II	4 005.85	
		South Africa	Klaserie Private Nature Reserve	300443	IV	589.02	
			Kruger National Park	873	II	19 031.22	
			Letaba Ranch and other areas	39740	IV	67.20	
	Gaza/Kruger/Gonarezhou		Mala Mala Game Reserve	300599	IV	237.52	
	Transfrontier Conservation		Manyeleti Game Reserve	9072	IV	228.91	
	Area (2003)		Sabi Sand Game Reserve	300598	IV	249.53	
			Sabie Sabie Game Reserve	300602	IV	136.69	
	Dongola/Limpopo Valley		Timbavati Game Reserve	300447	IV	506.06	
			Umbabat Nature Reserve	300446	IV	201.38	
		Zimbabwe	Gonarezhou National Park	1104	II	4 935.51	
			Malipati Safari Area	30125	VI	171.50	47 181.51
115		Lesotho	Sehlabathebe National Park	7447	IV	68.05	
	Maloti-Drakensberg	South Africa	Cathedral Peak State Forest	300488	IV	241.51	
	Transfrontier Conservation		Monks Owl State Forest	300492	IV	177.99	
	and Development Area (2001)		Highmoor State Forest	300499	IV	176.33	
	(see Chapter 21)		Mkhomaze State Forest	300500	IV	273.71	
			Natal Drakensberg National Park	116328	II	76.24	
			Ukhahlamba Drakensberg Park	900006	WH	2 428.13	2 428.13
116		South Africa	Songimvelo Game Reserve	39744	V	404.14	
		Swaziland	Malolotja Nature Reserve	7445	IV	171.97	
		Mozambique	Maputo Game Reserve	4652	IV	780.44	
		South Africa	Greater St. Lucia Wetland Park	116275	II	499.72	
			Ndumo Game Reserve	116329	II	121.49	
			Tembe Elephant Park	39758	IV	305.85	
	Lubombo Transfrontier		Greater St. Lucia Wetland Park	198302	WH	2 326.08	
	Conservation Area (2000)		Kosi Bay	68173	RS	11.43	
			St. Lucia System	68168	RS	1 070.99	
			Turtle Beaches/Coral Reefs of Tongaland	68167	RS	331.22	
		Swaziland	Hlane Game Sanctuary	7444	VI	124.73	
			Mlawula Nature Reserve	7451	IV	187.53	5 493.21
117		Malawi	Kasungu National Park	780	II	2 349.59	
			Nyika National Park	779	II	3 130.07	
			Vwaza Marsh Wildlife Reserve	4648	IV	944.84	
		Zambia	Luambe National Park	1100	II	328.43	
			Lukusuzi National Park	1091	II	2 865.34	
			Lumimba Game Management Area	4101	VI	4 387.47	
	Vwaza Marsh (1994 2004)		Lupande Game Management Area	4100	VI	4 359.28	
	plus other areas		Munyamadzi Game Management Area	4104	VI	3 620.47	
			Musalangu Game Management Area	4102	VI	14 482.28	
			North Luangwa National Park	1088	II	4 527.87	
			South Luangwa National Park	1086	II	8 965.36	49 961.02
118		Kenya	Chyulu National Park	19563	II	343.70	
			Ngai Ndethya National Reserve	2595	VI	219.79	

NO.	TBPA NAME[A]	COUNTRY[B]	PROTECED AREA NAME[C]	WCMC CODE[D]	IUCN CATEGORY[E]	SIZE (KM²)[F]	SUBTOTAL (KM²)[G]
			Tsavo East National Park	752	II	13 051.92	
			Tsavo West National Park	19564	II	6 918.06	
		Tanzania	Mkomazi Game Reserve	1402	IV	3 161.66	23 695.12
119	*Kilimanjaro* (1997)	Kenya	Amboseli National Park	758	II	402.26	
			Loitokitok Forest Reserve	7633	Unset	27.74	
		Tanzania	Kilimanjaro National Park	922	II	755.75	
			Kilimanjaro Forest Reserve	301387	Unset	1 106.37	1 536.37
120		Kenya	Masai Mara National Reserve	1297	II	1 773.42	
	Serengeti-Masai (see Chapter 18)	Tanzania	Maswa Game Reserve	7437	IV	3 167.86	
			Serengeti National Park	916	II	13 308.99	
			Ngorongoro Conservation Area	2010	WH	8 308.21	
			Serengeti National Park	2575	WH	13 293.70	39 852.18
121		Rwanda	Akagera National Park	862		1 024.72	
		Tanzania	Ibanda Game Reserve	7884	IV	415.42	1 440.14
122		Burundi	Kibira National Park	9161	IV	375.22	
		Rwanda	Nyungwe National Park	9148	IV	4.29	379.51
123		Democratic Republic of Congo	Rutshuru Hunting Reserve	20331	VI	856.89	
			Virunga National Park	1081	II	6 231.38	
			Virunga National Park	2017	WH	7 780.82	
		Rwanda	Volcans National Park	863	II	457.67	
	The Virunga Volcanoes Transboundary Conservation Area, plus other adjacent areas (see Chapter 17)	Uganda	Gorilla (Mgahinga) National Park	18436	II	37.50	
			Bwindi Impenetrable National Park	61609	WH	320.92	
			Kazinga Animal Sanctuary	7934	VI	14.23	
			Kibale Forest Corridor Game Reserve	1442	IV	315.21	
			Kigezi Game Reserve	1443	IV	358.49	
			Kyambura Game Reserve	1446	IV	176.66	
			Rwenzori Mountains National Park	18438	II	2 082.46	
			Lake George	68242	RS	579.42	
			Rwenzori Mountains National Park	61608	WH	604.29	11 455.70
124		Kenya	Mount Elgon National Park	760	II	104.95	
		Uganda	Pian Upe Game Reserve	1435	IV	2 277.77	
			Sebei Controlled Hunting Area	9179	VI	1 694.29	
			South Karamoja Controlled Hunting Area	9178	VI	7 985.05	12 062.07
125		Cameroon	Campo-Ma'an National Park	1242	II	2 616.05	
		Equatorial Guinea	Río Campo Natural Reserve	313361	IV	338.51	2 954.56
126	*Tri-National de la Sangha Park* (2000) (see Chapter 16)	Cameroon	Lobeke or Lac Lobéké National Park	1245	II	2 184.45	
		Central African Republic	Dzanga-Ndoki National Park	31458	II	1 148.02	
			Dzanga-Sangha Special Reserve	31459	VI	3 448.36	
		Congo	Nouabalé-Ndoki National Park	72332	II	4 239.12	11 019.95
127		Cameroon	Korup National Park	20058	II	1 300.57	
			Takamanda Wildlife Reserve	20109	IV	620.84	
		Nigeria	Cross River National Park	20299	II	3 658.25	5 579.67
128		Cameroon	Faro National Park	1241	II	3 432.63	
		Nigeria	Gashaka-Gumti National Park	7873	II	5 892.95	9 325.58
129		Côte d'Ivoire	Mount Nimba Strict Nature Reserve	1295	Ia	47.14	
	Mount Nimba		Mount Nimba Strict Nature Reserve	20408	WH	47.14	
		Guinea	Mount Nimba Strict Nature Reserve	29067	Ia	146.23	
			Mount Nimba Strict Nature Reserve	2574	WH	146.23	193.38
130	*Niokolo Koba-Badiar* (1988)	Guinea	Badiar National Park	29069	II	279.25	
		Senegal	Niokolo-Koba National Park	865	II	8 455.93	
			Niokolo-Koba National Park	2580	WH	8 431.22	8 735.17
131		Mauritania	Parc National du Diawling	95349	RS	662.13	
		Senegal	Djoudj National Park	867	II	140.03	
			Djoudj	68151	RS	103.76	
			Djoudj National Bird Sanctuary	2578	WH	122.73	784.85
132		Egypt	Abu Gallum Protected Area	40978	VI	417.86	
			Nabq Managed Resource Protected Area	40977	VI	501.54	
			Ras Mohammed National Park	9782	II	786.75	
			St. Katherine Natural Area	12363	VI	4 719.38	
			Taba Natural Monument	312963	V	2 701.37	
		Israel	Hof HaAlmogim BeElat Nature Reserve	68390	IV	0.09	
			Massiv Elat Nature Reserve	14910	IV	391.69	9 518.69
133	*"W" Park*	Benin	Atakora Hunting Zone	2254	VI	1 328.63	
			Boucle de la Pendjari National Park	597	II	2 838.26	

NO.	TBPA NAME[A]	COUNTRY[B]	PROTECED AREA NAME[C]	WCMC CODE[D]	IUCN CATEGORY[E]	SIZE (KM²)[F]	SUBTOTAL (KM²)[G]
			Djona Hunting Zone	2252	VI	1 191.26	
			Pendjari Hunting Zone	2253	VI	1 830.79	
			"W" (Benin) National Park	12201	II	5 806.15	
		Burkina Faso	Arly Faunal Reserve	4488	IV	842.75	
			Arly Partial Faunal Reserve	9264	IV	1 059.62	
			Kourtiagou Partial Faunal Reserve	3226	IV	438.00	
			Madjoari Faunal Reserve	9265	IV	295.09	
			Pama Partial Faunal Reserve	3228	IV	2 340.91	
			Singou Faunal Reserve	3229	IV	1 935.65	
			"W" du Burkina Faso National Park	1048	II	2 438.58	
			Parc National du "W"	67824	RS	4 614.05	
		Niger	Tamou Faunal Reserve	2331	IV	791.59	
			"W" du Niger National Park	818	II	2 220.16	
			Parc National du "W"	17727	RS	2 205.05	
			"W" National Park	124385	WH	2 205.05	
		Togo	Kéran National Park	2339	II	1 200.95	26 558.40
134		Malawi (Mozambique)	Lake Chilwa	145538	RS	2 117.07	2 117.07
135		Uganda	Difule Animal Sanctuary	7933	IV	10.47	
			Mount Kei White Rhino Sanctuary	31276	IV	457.81	
			Otze Forest White Rhino Sanctuary	31275	IV	231.58	
		Sudan	Nimule National Park	904	II	410.00	1 109.86
136	Kidepo	Uganda	Kidepo Valley National Park	958	II	1 453.95	
		Sudan	Kidepo Game Reserve	1369	VI	1 200.00	2 653.95
137		Democratic Republic of Congo	Gangala-na Bodio Hunting Reserve	20327	VI	8 229.93	
			Garamba National Park	1083	II	4 998.65	
			Mondo Missa Hunting Zone	20326	VI	1 672.45	
		Sudan	Lantoto National Park		Unset	760.00	15 661.03
138		Central African Republic	Yata-Ngaya Faunal Reserve	2261	IV	5 427.26	
		Sudan	Radom National Park		BR	12 500.00	17 927.26
139	Delta du Saloum	Senegal (The Gambia)	Delta du Saloum National Park	866	II	695.71	
			Delta du Saloum	68153	RS	3 199.10	3 199.10
140		Cameroon	Kalamaloue National Park	609	II	67.22	
		Chad	Mandelia Faunal Reserve	5166	IV	1 321.29	1 388.52
141		Togo (Benin)	Reserve de Faune de Togodo	95398	RS	202.10	202.10
142		Kenya	Kiunga Marine National Reserve	3038	VI	243.36	
			Dodori National Reserve	2591	VI	732.73	
		Somalia	Juba Left Controlled Hunting Reserve	1371	Unset	—	
			Bushbush Game Reserve	13710	VI	3 340.00	
			Bushbush Controlled Hunting Area	13714	Unset	—	4 316.09

ASIA protected areas; total size of TBPA for this region: 459 644.11 km²

NO.	TBPA NAME[A]	COUNTRY[B]	PROTECED AREA NAME[C]	WCMC CODE[D]	IUCN CATEGORY[E]	SIZE (KM²)[F]	SUBTOTAL (KM²)[G]
143		Georgia	Ritsa Nature Reserve	1654	Ia	138.20	
		Russian Federation	Dahovskiy Nature Sanctuary or Partial Reserve	209683	IV	221.63	
			Kavkazsky State Nature Reserve	1696	Ia	2 741.72	
			Psebaiskiy Nature Sanctuary or Partial Reserve	200477	IV	379.17	
			Sochinskiy Nature Sanctuary or Partial Reserve	200480	IV	804.24	
			Sochinsky National Park	11577	II	1 219.21	
			Turinyi Nature Sanctuary or Partial Reserve	209685	IV	55.46	
			Western Caucasus	198301	WH	3 560.90	5 559.63
144		Azerbaijan	Zakatala State Nature Reserve	1984	Ia	247.71	
		Georgia	Lagodekhi Nature Reserve	1653	Ia	136.04	
		Russian Federation	Charodinskiy Nature Sanctuary or Partial Reserve	198927	IV	723.59	
			Tlyaratinskiy Nature Sanctuary or Partial Reserve	198920	IV	697.87	1 805.21
145		Armenia	Shikahogh State Reserve	20679	Ia	190.18	
		Azerbaijan	Arazboyu Nature Sanctuary or Partial Reserve	101830	IV	14.56	
			Basutchay State Nature Reserve	1641	Ia	8.72	
		Iran	Arasbaran Protected Area	17176	V	853.18	
			Arasbaran	2080	BR	836.72	1 066.63
146		Iran	Sarany Protected Area	313340	V	162.41	
		Turkmenistan	Guryhowdan Nature Sanctuary or Partial Reserve	167091	IV	106.22	
			Kopetdag State Nature Reserve	167106	Ia	507.57	776.19
147		Afghanistan	Hamun-i-Puzak Waterfowl Sanctuary	15498	IV	437.89	

NO.	TBPA NAME[A]	COUNTRY[B]	PROTECED AREA NAME[C]	WCMC CODE[D]	IUCN CATEGORY[E]	SIZE (KM²)[F]	SUBTOTAL (KM²)[G]
		Iran	Hamoun Protected Area	17131	V	3 016.07	
			Hamun-e-Puzak south end	17160	RS	172.16	
			Hamun-e-Saberi and Hamun-e-Helmand	17158	RS	1 766.49	3 453.96
148		Turkmenistan	Hodjapil Nature Sanctuary or Partial Reserve	167100	IV	149.93	
			Hordjaburdjibelend Nature Sanctuary or Partial Reserve	167101	IV	95.33	
			Kugitang State Nature Reserve	167107	Ia	312.15	
		Uzbekistan	Surkhanskiy State Nature Reserve	20683	Ia	328.91	886.32
149		Kazakhstan	Aksu-Dzhabagly State Nature Reserve	1671	Ia	740.89	
	West Tien Shan Conservation Area in Central Asia (see Chapter 22)	Kyrgyzstan	Besh-Aral State Nature Reserve	1675	Ia	1 237.16	
			Chandalash Wildlife Refuge	167075	IV	526.80	
			Manass Wildlife Refuge	167109	IV	434.29	
			Sary-Chelekskiy State Nature Reserve	1674	Ia	213.02	
	Western Tien Shan/Chatkal Mountains	Uzbekistan	Chatkalskiy State Nature Reserve	1761	Ia	580.17	
			Ugam-Chatkal National Park	101947	II	6 322.76	
			Chatkal Mountains Biosphere Reserve	134942	BR	573.60	10 628.69
150	*Taxkorgan* (1995)	China	Tashikuerganyeshengdongwu Nature Reserve	96118	V	16 349.07	
		Pakistan	Khunjerab National Park	836	II	3 333.04	19 682.11
151		China	Hanasi Nature Reserve	96123	V	4 376.74	
		Kazakhstan	Rakhmanovskie Kluchi Reserve (Zakaznik)	16253	IV	545.07	
		Mongolia	Altai Tavan Bogd National Conservation Park	99844	II	6 303.91	
			Sylkhemyn nuruu National Conservation Park	313187	II	1 552.38	
			Uvs Nuur Basin Strict Protected Area	93566	Ia	7 487.22	
			Uvs Nuur Basin	900880	WH	9 400.34	
		Russian Federation	Kosh-Agachskiy Nature Sanctuary or Partial Reserve	200403	IV	1 486.69	
			Ozero Tore-Khol' Nature Monument	199818	III	73.72	
			Ubsunurskaya Kotlovina State Nature Reserve	67722	Ia	600.80	
			Ukok Resource Reserve	200404	VI	2 550.01	
			Golden Mountains of Altai	168241	WH	16 995.59	
			Uvs Nuur Basin	900882	WH	3 106.91	45 079.04
152		China	Buergenheli Nature Reserve	96125	V	657.82	
		Mongolia	Bulgan River Nature Reserve	11730	III	66.85	724.67
153		China	Wulatelenglenglin-mengguyelv Nature Reserve	315607	V	698.40	
		Mongolia	Small Gobi Strict Protected Area	124309	Ib	17 345.59	18 043.99
154		Mongolia	Khoridal Saridag Strict Protected Area	166790	Ia	1 939.45	
			Khovsgol lake National Conservation Park	93579	II	8 605.46	
		Russian Federation	Badary Nature Sanctuary or Partial Reserve	198868	IV	580.41	
			Irkutnyi Nature Sanctuary or Partial Reserve	203123	IV	422.53	
			Shumakskiy Nature Sanctuary or Partial Reserve	198861	IV	692.58	
			Snezhinskiy Nature Sanctuary or Partial Reserve	198853	IV	2 475.07	
			Tunkinskiy Nature Sanctuary or Partial Reserve	198864	IV	561.80	
			Tunkinsky National Park	68356	II	11 443.41	
			Lake Baikal	124386	WH	82 245.58	106 491.22
155	The Daurian Steppes	Mongolia	Mongol Daguur Strict Protected Area	93538	Ib	930.91	
			Mongol Daguur (Mongolian Dauria)	145817	RS	921.75	
	Dauria International PA (1994)	Russian Federation	Daursky State Nature Reserve	62684	Ia	624.35	
			Torey Lakes	95379	RS	1 786.31	
		China	Dalaihu Nature Reserve	96064	V	3 543.28	7 182.26
156		China	Tiexi Nature Reserve	315740	V	1 083.53	
			Xingkaihu Nature Reserve	95476	V	1 281.00	
		Russian Federation	Khankaisky State Nature Reserve	62691	Ia	360.89	
			Lake Khanka	68150	RS	4 234.35	5 678.78
157		China	Bachadao Nature Reserve	315636	V	68.76	
			Sanjiang Nature Reserve	315728	V	1 244.47	
		Russian Federation	Bolshekhekhtsirsky State Nature Reserve	1715	Ia	487.64	1 800.87
158		China	Zhujiangkouzhonghuabaijitun Nature Reserve	315631	V	465.76	
		Hong Kong	Lantau North Country Park	9924	V	24.24	
			Lantau South Country Park	12404	V	52.73	542.73
159		China	Gulongshanshuiyuanlin Nature Reserve	95872	V	348.39	
		Vietnam	Trung Khanh Nature Reserve	10360	IV	171.55	519.94
160		China	Nongxinshuiyuanlin Nature Reserve	95641	V	118.98	
		Vietnam	Pac Bo HCR Historic/Cultural Site	10329	V	49.65	168.63
161		China	Huanglianshan Nature Reserve	95743	V	708.69	
			Jinpingfenshuiling (Yunnan) Nature Reserve	95742	V	420.27	
			Guanyinshan (Yunnan) Nature Reserve	96139	V	164.10	

NO.	TBPA NAME[A]	COUNTRY[B]	PROTECED AREA NAME[C]	WCMC CODE[D]	IUCN CATEGORY[E]	SIZE (KM²)[F]	SUBTOTAL (KM²)[G]
		Lao PDR	Phou Dene Din National Biodiversity Conservation Area	12182	VI	1 872.13	
		Vietnam	Muong Nhe Nature Reserve	10362	IV	1 820.00	
			Hoang Lien Son Nature Reserve	10357	IV	30.00	5 015.19
162		Vietnam	Sop Cop Nature Reserve	10363	IV	420.96	
		Lao PDR	Nam Et National Biodiversity Conservation Area	61496	VI	2 569.02	
			Phou Loey National Biodiversity Conservation Area	61495	VI	1 521.31	4 511.29
163		Vietnam	Dong Phong Nha Nature Reserve	10345	IV	416.46	
			Pu Mat Nature Reserve	61595	IV	971.05	
			Vu Quang Nature Reserve	10375	IV	576.96	
			Phong Nha-Ke Bang National Park	900883	WH	895.56	
		Lao PDR	Nam Kading National Biodiversity Conservation Area	18896	VI	1 691.90	
			Corridor Nakai-Nam Theun and Phou Hin Poun National Biodiversity Conservation Area	71254	VI	33.23	
			Hin Nam No National Biodiversity Conservation Area	61498	VI	865.59	
			Nakai-Nam Theun National Biodiversity Conservation Area	10130	VI	3 546.02	
			Nam Theun Ext. National Biodiversity Conservation Area	71255	VI	472.56	9 052.87
164		Lao PDR	Phou Xiengthong National Biodiversity Conservation Area	18893	VI	1 137.21	
		Thailand	Kaeng Tana National Park	4674	II	68.83	
			Pha Tam National Park	39518	II	376.82	1 582.86
165		Cambodia	Virachey National Park	68862	II	3 379.84	
		Lao PDR	Dong Ampham National Biodiversity Conservation Area	18872	VI	2 005.47	
		Vietnam	Mom Ray Nature Reserve	12171	IV	488.70	5 874.01
166		Cambodia	Lomphat Wildlife Sanctuary	10121	IV	2 540.24	
			Mondulkiri Protected Forest	313444	IV	4 302.20	
			Phnom Nam Lyr Wildlife Sanctuary	68868	IV	536.24	
			Phnom Prich Wildlife Sanctuary	10120	IV	2 280.20	
		Vietnam	Yok Don National Park	18033	II	1 019.52	10 678.40
167		Cambodia	Preah Vihear Protected Forest	313443	IV	1 908.79	
			Preah Vihear Protected Landscape	12249	V	25.40	
		Thailand	Huai Sa La Wildlife Sanctuary	18467	IV	399.84	
			Phanom Dong Rak Wildlife Sanctuary	1415	IV	391.07	
			Phu Chong-Na Yoi National Park	19672	II	760.79	
			Yod Dom Wildlife Sanctuary	1422	IV	165.48	3 651.37
168	The Lanjak Entimau/ Batang Ai/Batung Kerihun Complex (see Chapter 24)	Indonesia	Betung Kerihun National Park	8673	II	7 905.05	
			Bukit Batutenobang Protection Forest	8678	VI	4 672.62	
		Malaysia	Batang Ai National Park	12250	II	217.44	
			Lanjak-Entimau Wildlife Sanctuary	1300	IV	1 733.39	14 528.50
169	Labi Hills/Gunung Pulu Transboundary Complex	Brunei Darussalam	Labi Hills (Bukit Batu Patam Protection) Forest Reserve	39639	Ia	8.69	
			Labi Hills (Bukit Teraja Protection) Forest Reserve	39641	Ia	72.59	
			Labi Hills (Luagan Lalak Recreation) Forest Reserve	18035	V	3.96	
			Labi Hills (Sungai Ingei Conservation) Forest Reserve	32948	Ia	185.37	
		Malaysia	Gunung Mulu National Park	787	II	530.17	
			Gunung Mulu National Park	220293	WH	535.11	800.79
170	Wasur-Tonda Transboundary Conservation Area (see Chapter 25)	Indonesia	Wasur National Park	29966	II	2 444.75	
		Papua New Guinea	Tonda Wildlife Management Area	4200	VI	5 307.19	
			Tonda Wildlife Management Area	68136	RS	5 137.67	7 751.94
171		China	Yaluzangbudaxiagu Nature Reserve	315616	V	8 982.47	
		India	Dibang Sanctuary	26155	IV	767.51	9 749.98
172		Bhutan	Jigme Singye Wangchuck National Park	5066	II	1 733.46	
			Royal Manas National Park	7996	II	1 024.77	
		India	Buxa Sanctuary	9232	IV	95.63	
			Manas Sanctuary	1818	IV	539.88	
			Manas Wildlife Sanctuary	10745	WH	545.20	3 393.75
173		China	Jiangcun Nature Reserve	95784	V	742.55	
			Quomolangma Nature Rreserve	301953	VI	34 227.39	
			Zhangmukouan Nature Reserve	95785	V	218.04	
			Zhumulangmafeng Nature Reserve	95783	V	18 000.95	
		India	Khangchendzonga National Park	689	II	1 794.26	
		Nepal	Annapurna Conservation Area	10091	VI	7 441.02	
			Kanchanjunga Conservation Area	143001	VI	1 996.93	
			Langtang National Park	803	II	1 635.14	
			Makalu-Barun National Park	26606	II	1 497.61	
			Sagarmatha National Park	804	II	1 112.07	
			Sagarmatha National Park	2007	WH	1 117.65	68 665.95
174		India	Sohagibarwa Sanctuary	12414	IV	425.94	
			Valmiki Sanctuary	4548	IV	401.32	

NO.	TBPA NAME[A]	COUNTRY[B]	PROTECED AREA NAME[C]	WCMC CODE[D]	IUCN CATEGORY[E]	SIZE (KM²)[F]	SUBTOTAL (KM²)[G]
		Nepal	Parsa Wildlife Reserve	10089	IV	477.29	
			Royal Chitwan National Park	805	II	1 181.61	
			Royal Chitwan National Park (Buffer Zone)	303694	VI	764.63	
			Royal Chitwan National Park	10905	WH	1 132.07	3 250.79
175		India	Kachchh Desert Sanctuary	19683	IV	13 616.83	
			Wild Ass Sanctuary	1857	IV	7 183.02	
		Pakistan	Rann of Kutch Wildlife Sanctuary	6684	IV	10 605.39	31 405.24
176		Bangladesh	Sundarbans East Wildlife Sanctuary	4476	IV	210.67	
			Sundarbans South Wildlife Sanctuary	4477	IV	195.87	
			Sundarbans West Wildlife Sanctuary	4478	IV	126.40	
	Sundarbans		Sundarbans Reserved Forest	67808	RS	4 966.12	
			The Sundarbans	145580	WH	1 373.32	
		India	Sajnakhali Sanctuary	4630	IV	2 091.12	
			Sundarbans National Park	14177	WH	1 056.35	8 430.55
177		Azerbaijan	Lachin Nature Sanctuary or Partial Reserve	94018	IV	305.76	
		Armenia	Shikahogh State Reserve		Ia	100.00	405.76
178		China	Changbaishan Nature Reserve	96016	V	2 499.80	
	Turtle Islands	North Korea	Mount Paekdu Biosphere Reserve	17909	BR	1 320.00	
			Mount Paekdu Natural Reserve	17908	IV	1 320.00	5 139.80
179		Malaysia	Pulau Penyu (Turtle Islands) Park	793	II	17.64	
		Phillipines	Turtle Islands Wilderness Sanctuary	198475	IV	2 429.67	2 447.31
180		Bangladesh	Pablakhali Wildlife Sanctuary	9280	IV	236.23	
		India	Dampa Sanctuary	1804	IV	603.07	839.29
181		India	Dudhwa National Park	691	II	717.49	
			Katarniyaghat Sanctuary	1807	IV	397.36	
		Nepal	Royal Bardia National Park	1308	II	910.45	
			Royal Bardia National Park (Buffer Zone)	313264	VI	325.90	
			Royal Suklaphanta Wildlife Reserve	1309	IV	369.95	2 721.15
182		Russian Federation (Kazakhstan)	Volga Delta	68149	RS	9 050.16	9 050.16
183		Iran (Iraq)	Shadegan Marshes and mudflats of Khor-al Amaya and Khor Musa	17157	RS	3 320.13	3 320.13
184		Russian Federation (Kazakhstan)	Tobol-Ishim Forest-steppe	95375	RS	12 756.65	12 756.65
185		Russian Federation (China)	Zeya-Bureya plain	103558	RS	283.48	283.48
186		Russian Federation (China)	Khingano-Arkharinskaya Lowland	103552	RS	4 096.32	4 096.32
187		Nepal (India)	Koshi Tappu	14196	RS	135.54	135.54
188		Iran (Turkmenistan)	Alagol Ulmagol and Ajigol Lakes	17165	RS	14.15	14.15

Total   **3 169 836.50**

On the opposite page, rock formations in Big Bend National Park, Texas, part of one of North America's most important transboundary conservation areas.
© Patricio Robles Gil/Sierra Madre

[A] Official names of transboundary complexes from treaties, Memoranda of Understating, etc. are in italics. Other names are descriptive titles suggested by the authors or appear as chapter titles in this book.

[B] This is the country that manages the individual protected area. In cases where the protected area lies wholly within one country, but there is joint management, responsibility or impact by two or more countries —as frequently is the case for transboundary Ramsar Sites (Wetlands of International Importance)— the country that contains the protected area is listed first, followed by the second or third countries inside parentheses.

[C] This is the official name of the individual protected area as it appears in the UNEP-World Conservation Monitoring Centre (WCMC), World Database on Protected Areas (WDPA).

[D] This is the unique code used by the WDPA to differentiate between protected areas.

[E] IUCN protected area categories are as follows: Ia, Strict Nature Reserve; Ib, Wilderness Area; II, National Park; III, Natural Monument; IV, Habitat/Species Management Area; V, Protected Landscape/Seascape; VI, Managed Resource Protected Area. For more information visit www.iucn.org/themes/wcpa/pubs/pdfs/iucncategories.pdf. Other codes used come from the WDPA. They are: BR, Biosphere Reserve; RS, Wetlands of International Importance (Ramsar Sites); WH, World Heritage Site and, finally, "Unset" when the site is protected at a national level but has not yet been given a category by IUCN.

[F] This is the size of each individual protected area and comes from WDPA data (where it exists) or alternatively from GIS data.

[G] Total size is the total "footprint" of all the protected areas that make up the transboundary complex. When protected areas overlap (as they frequently do for World Heritage Sites, Biosphere Reserves and Ramsar Sites), the size numbers for these overlapping areas are excluded from the totals.

INTRODUCTION

BAILLIE, J.M., S.N. STUART, and C. HILTON-TAYLOR (eds.). 2004. *IUCN Red List of Threatened Species. A Global Species Assessment.* IUCN, Gland, Switzerland and Cambridge, U.K.

BIRDLIFE INTERNATIONAL. 2004. *State of the World's Birds 2004. Indicators for Our Changing World.* Cambridge/ BirdLife International.

CBD. 1992. Convention on Biological Diversity. Rio de Janeiro, Brazil: Secretariat of the Convention on Biological Diversity. http://www.biodiv.org

CHAPE, S., S. BLYTH, L. FISH, P. FOX, and M. SPALDING. 2003. *2003 United Nations List of Protected Areas.* IUCN-The World Conservation Union and UNEP/ World Conservation Monitoring Centre, Gland, Switzerland and Cambridge, U.K.

CONVENTION ON BIOLOGICAL DIVERSITY. June 5, 1992, 31 ILM 818 (1992), *entered into force* Dec. 29, 1993. Malawi Principles, adopted pursuant to decision VII/11 at the Seventh Meeting of the Conference of the Parties to the Convention on Biological Diversity (COP 7) in Nairobi, 2000.

Convention Concerning Indigenous and Tribal Peoples in Independent Countries (ILO No. 169), 72 *ILO Official Bull.* 59, *entered into force* September 5, 1991.

CURRAN, L. M., S. TRIGG, A. McDONALD, D. ASTIANI, Y.M. HARDIONO, P. SIREGAR, I. CANIAGO, and E. KASISCHKE. 2004. Lowland Forest Loss in Protected Areas of Indonesian Borneo. *Science* 303:1000-1003.

Dana Declaration on Mobile Peoples and Conservation. Wadi Dana Nature Reserve, Jordan, April 3-7, 2002. http://www.danadeclaration.org

EKEN, G., L. BENNUN, T. BROOKS, W. DARWALL, L. FISH-POOL, M. FOSTER, D. KNOX, P. LANGHAMMER, P. MATIKU, E. RADFORD, P. SALAMAN, W. SECHREST, M.L. SMITH, S. SPECTOR, and A. TORDOFF. 2004. Key Biodiversity Areas as Site Conservation Targets. *BioScience* 54:1110-1118.

EMSLIE, R. and M. BROOKS (eds.). 1999. African Rhino Status, Survey, and Conservation Action Plan. IUCN/SSC African Rhino Specialist Group. IUCN, Gland, Switzerland and Cambridge, U.K.

EUROPARC. 2003. *Transboundary Parks-Following Nature's Design: A Tool for Improving Transboundary Cooperation in Europe.*

GRIFFIN, J., D. CUMMING, S. METCALFE, M. t'SAS-ROLFES, J. SINGH, E. CHONGUICA, M. ROWEN, and J. OGLETHORPE. 1999. *Study on the Development of Transboundary Natural Resource Management Areas in Southern Africa.* Biodiversity Support Program, Washington, D.C.

ITTO/IUCN. 2003. *Proceedings from an International Workshop on Increasing Effectiveness of Transboundary Conservation Areas in Tropical Forests.* Ubon Ratchathani, Thailand, February 17-21, 2003.

IUCN. 1993. *Parks for Life: Report of the Fourth World Congress on National Parks and Protected Areas.* IUCN, Gland, Switzerland.

IUCN. 1994. *Parks for Life: Action for Protected Areas in Europe.* IUCN, Gland, Switzerland.

IUCN. 1994a. *Guidelines for Protected Area Management Categories.* CNPPA with the assistance of WCMC. IUCN, Gland, Switzerland and Cambridge, U.K.

IUCN/WCPA. 1997. Special Issue on Parks for Peace. *Parks* 7(3):1-56, 6 articles.

IUCN/WCPA. 1997. *Transboundary Protected Areas as a Vehicle for International Co-operation.* Proceedings,

Parks for Peace Conference. Somerset West, South Africa, September 16-18, 1997.

IUCN/WCPA. 1998. International Symposium on Parks for Peace. Draft Proceedings. Bormio, Stelvio National Park, Italy, May 18-21, 1998.

KINNAIRD, M.F., E.W. SANDERSON, T.G. O'BRIEN, H.T. WIBISONO, and G. WOOLMER. 2003. Deforestation Trends in a Tropical Landscape and Implications for Endangered Large Mammals. *Conservation Biology* 17:245-257.

MYERS, N., R.A. MITTERMEIER, C.G. MITTERMEIER, G.A.B. DA FONSECA, and J. KENT. 2000. Biodiversity Hotspots for Conservation Priorities. *Nature* 403: 853-858.

PRESSEY, R.L. 1994. Ad Hoc Reservations. Forward or Backward Steps in Developing Representative Reserve Systems. *Conservation Biology* 8:662-668.

SÁNCHEZ-AZOFEIFA, G.A., G.C. DAILY, A.S.P. PFAFF, and C. BUSCH. 2003. Integrity and Isolation of Costa Rica's National Parks and Biological Reserves: Examining the Dynamics of Land-Cover Change. *Biological Conservation* 109:123-135.

SANDWITH, T.S., C. SHINE, L.S. HAMILTON, and D.A. SHEPPARD. 2001. *Transboundary Protected Areas for Peace and Co-operation.* IUCN, Gland, Switzerland and Cambridge, U.K.

SCOTT, J.M., F.W. DAVIS, R.G. McGHIE, R.G. WRIGHT, C. GROVES, and J. ESTES. 2001. Nature Reserves: Do They Capture the Full Range of America's Biological Diversity? *Ecological Applications* 11:999-1007.

SINCLAIR, A.R.E., S.A.R. MDUMA, and P. ARCESE. 2002. Protected Areas as Biodiversity Benchmarks for Human Impact: Agriculture and the Serengeti Avifauna. *Proceedings of the Royal Society of London* 269:2401-2405, Series B-Biological Sciences.

The World Alliance of Mobile Indigenous Peoples (WAMIP). Proceedings of the Second General Meeting. Kuala Lumpur, Malaysia, February 9-16, 2004.

UNESCO. 2000. *MAB Seville +5 Recommendations for the Establishment and Functioning of Transboundary Biosphere Reserves.* http://www.unesco.org/mab/ mabicc/ 2000/eng/TBREng.htm

UNITED NATIONS. 2000. *Report of the Panel on United Nations Peace Operations (The Brahini Report).* UN document A/55/305, S/2000/809.

VAN SCHAIK, C.P., J. TERBORGH, and B. DUGELBY. 1997. The Silent Crisis: The State of Rainforest Nature Preserves. In R. KRAMER, C.P. VAN SCHAIK, and J. JOHNSON (eds.), *Last Stand: Protected Areas and the Defense of Tropical Biodiversity.* Oxford University Press, Oxford, U.K., pp. 64-89.

WOODROFFE, R. and J.R. GINSBERG. 1998. Edge Effects and Extinction of Populations inside Protected Areas. *Science* 280:2126-2128.

WORLD BANK. 2000a. *Maloti-Drakensberg Transfrontier Conservation and Development Project: Project Appraisal Document.* World Bank, Africa Regional Office, Washington, D.C.

WORLD BANK. 2000b. *Working Paper on Transboundary Reserves: World Bank Implementation of the Ecosystem Approach.* Washington, D.C.

WORLD TOURISM ORGANIZATION. *Tourism Highlights,* 2004 edition. http://www.world-tourism.org

Yaoundé Declaration. Issued in Yaoundé, Cameroon at the Ministerial Conference on Africa Forest Law Enforcement and Governance, October, 2003.

ZBICZ, D.C. 1999a. *Transboundary Co-operation in Conservation: A Global Survey of Factors Influencing Co-operation between Internationally Adjoining Protected Areas.* Ph.D. dissertation, Duke University.

ZBICZ, D.C. 1999b. Transboundary Co-operation between Internationally Adjoining Protected Areas. In D.S. HARMON (ed.), *On the Frontiers of Conservation: Proceedings of the 10th Conference on Research and Resource Management in Parks and on Public Lands.* The George Wright Society, Hancock, U.S., pp. 199-204.

ZBICZ, D.C. 2001. Global List of Internationally Adjoining Protected Areas 2001. In T. SANDWITH, C. SHINE, L. HAMILTON, and D. SHEPPARD (eds.), *Transboundary Protected Areas for Peace and Co-operation.* IUCN, Gland, Switzerland.

ZBICZ, D.C. and M. GREEN. 1997. Status of the World's Transfrontier Protected Areas. In IUCN/WCPA, *Transboundary Protected Areas as a Vehicle for International Co-operation.* Proceedings, Parks for Peace Conference. Somerset West, South Africa, September 16-18, 1997.

THREE EXEMPLARY CASE STUDIES

The Waterton Glacier International Peace Park: The First of Its Kind

BUCHHOLTZ, C.W. 1976. *Man in Glacier.* Glacier Natural History Association, West Glacier, Montana.

DIETTERT, G.A. 1992 *Grinnell's Glacier.* Mountain Press, Missoula, Montana.

LESICA, P. 2002. *A Flora of Glacier National Park, Montana.* Oregon State University Press, Corvallis.

LESICA, P. and B. McCUNE. 1992. Monitoring the Effects of Global Warming Using Peripheral Rare Plants in Wet Alpine Tundra in Glacier National Park, Montana. Glacier National Park, USDI National Park Service, West Glacier, Montana.

LOTHIAN, W.F. 1976. *A History of Canada's National Parks.* Parks Canada, Ottawa.

MARNELL, L. 2004. *Amphibians of Glacier National Park.* http://biology.usgs.gov/s+t/SNT/noframe/ wm149.htm

MITTERMEIER, R.A., C.G. MITTERMEIER, P. ROBLES GIL, J. PILGRIM, G.A.B. DA FONSECA, T. BROOKS and W. KONSTANT (eds.). 2002. *Wilderness: Earth's Last Wild Places.* CEMEX (Monterrey), Conservation International (Washington, D.C.), Agrupación Sierra Madre (Mexico City).

RICKETTS, T.H., E. DINERSTEIN, D.M. OLSON, C.J. LOUCKS, W. EICHBAUM, D. DELLASALLA, K. KAVANAGH, P. HEDAO, P.T. HURLEY, K.M. CARNEY, R. ABELL, and S. WALTERS. 1999. *Terrestrial Ecoregions of North America: A Conservation Assessment.* Island Press, Washington, D.C.

RODNEY, W. 1969. *Kootenai Brown, His Life and Times,* Gray's Publishing, Sydney, British Columbia.

SHEA, D.S. 1995. *Mammals of Glacier National Park.* http://www.nps.gov/glac/resources/ mammalcheck.htm

STANFORD, J.A. 2001. River Ecological Studies of the North Fork of the Flathead River, Montana and British Columbia. Open File Report, Flathead Biological Station, University of Montana, Polson.

SWANSON, L.D. 2003. *Gateway to Glacier: The Emerging*

On the opposite page, sunrise over the Montes Azules Biosphere Reserve in Chiapas, Mexico, an important part of the Maya Forest.
© Patricio Robles Gil/Sierra Madre

Economy of Flathead County. National Parks and Conservation Association, Helena, Montana, and Washington, D.C.

WEAVER, J.L. 2001. *The Transboundary Flathead: A Critical Landscape for Carnivores in the Rocky Mountains*. Working Paper No. 18. Wildlife Conservation Society, Bronx, New York.

The Great Limpopo Transfrontier Park: A Benchmark for International Conservation

BRAACK, L.E.O. 1996. *Globetrotters Guide to the Kruger National Park*. New Holland, Cape Town.

BRAACK, L.E.O. 2004. African Parks under Challenge: Novel Approaches in South Africa May Offer Respite. In M.S. GORDON and S.M. BARTOL (eds.), *Experimental Approaches to Conservation Biology*. University of California Press, Berkeley, pp. 298-322.

BRAACK, L.E.O., H.C. BIGGS, K. ROGERS, C. MARAIS, H. MAGOME, and J. STURGEON. 1997. A Revision of Parts of the Management Plan for the Kruger National Park: Volume 8. Internal unpublished document of South African National Parks, Skukuza, South Africa. http://www. parks-sa.co.za

CARRUTHERS, J. 1995. *The Kruger National Park: A Social and Political History*. University of Natal Press, Pietrmaritzburg, South Africa.

DE VILLIERS, B. 1999. Makuleke Land Claim and the Kruger National Park. Joint Management. A Benchmark for Conservation Areas. *South African Public Law* 1999:309-330.

DU TOIT, J.T., K.H. ROGERS, and H.C. BIGGS. 2003. *The Kruger Experience: Ecology and Management of Savanna Heterogeneity*. Island Press, Washington, D.C.

VENTER, F.J., R.J. SCHOLES, and H.C. ECKHARDT. 2003. The Abiotic Template and Its Associated Vegetation Pattern. In J.T. DU TOIT, K.H. ROGERS and H.C. BIGGS, *The Kruger Experience: Ecology and Management of Savanna Heterogeneity*. Island Press, Washington, D.C., pp. 83-129.

El Carmen-Big Bend: An Emerging Model for Private Public Partnership in Transboundary Conservation

BROCK, J.P. and K. KAUFMAN. 2003. *Butterflies of North America*. Houghton Mifflin Company, Boston.

GARZA DE LEÓN, A. 2003. *Aves de Coahuila. Guía de campo*. Saltillo, Coahuila.

GEHLBACH, F.R. 1993. Mountain Islands and Desert Seas: A Natural History of the U.S.-Mexican Borderlands. Texas A&M University Press, College Station, Texas.

MITTERMEIER, R.A., P. ROBLES GIL, M. HOFFMANN, J. PILGRIM, T. BROOKS, C.G. MITTERMEIER, J. LAMOREAUX, and G.A.B. DA FONSECA (eds.). 2004. *Hotspots Revisited: Earth's Biologically Richest and Most Endangered Terrestrial Ecoregions*. CEMEX (Monterrey), Conservation International (Washington, D.C.), Agrupación Sierra Madre (Mexico City).

National Geographic Field Guide to the Birds of North America. 1987. National Geographic Society, Washington, D.C.

WAUER, R.H. 1992. *A Naturalist's Mexico*. Texas A&M University Press. College Station, Texas.

AMERICA

The Alaska-Yukon-British Columbia Borderlands: The World's Largest Contiguous Protected Area Complex

DANBY, R.K. 2002. Fostering an Ecosystem Perspective through Intergovernmental Cooperation: A Look at Two Alaskan Examples. In S. BONDRUP-NIELSEN, N. MUNRO, G. NELSON, J.H.M. WILLISON, T.B. HERMAN, and P. EAGLES (eds.), *Managing Protected Areas in a Changing World*. SAMPA/PRFO, Wolfville, NS/Waterloo, Ontario, pp. 722-735.

DANBY, R.K., D.S. HIK, D.S. SLOCOMBE, and A. WILLIAMS. 2003. Science and the St. Elias: An Evolving Framework for Sustainability in North America's Highest Mountains. *The Geographical Journal* 169(3):191-204.

DANBY, R.K. and D.S. SLOCOMBE. 2002. Protected Areas and Intergovernmental Cooperation in the St. Elias Region. *Natural Resources J.* 42(2):247-282.

MATZ, G. 1999. World Heritage Wilderness: From the Wrangells to Glacier Bay. *Alaska Geographic* 26 (2):112.

SLOCOMBE, D.S. 1992. The Kluane/Wrangell-St. Elias National Parks, Yukon and Alaska: Seeking Sustainability Through Biosphere Reserves. *Mountain Research and Development* 12(1):87-96.

SLOCOMBE, D.S. and R.K. DANBY. 2004. Complexity, Science and Collaborative Management in Two Very Large Regions: The Australian Alps and the St. Elias. In D. HARMON and G. WORBOYS (eds.), *Managing Mountain Protected Areas: Challenges and Responses for the 21st Century*. Andromeda Editrice, Colledara, Italy, pp. 88-94.

THEBERGE, J.B. (ed.). 1980. *Kluane: Pinnacle of the Yukon*. Doubleday Canada, Toronto.

WRIGHT, R.G. (ed.). 1981. Wrangell-Saint Elias: International Mountain Wilderness. *Alaska Geographic* 8(1):144.

Dry Borders: Linking Nature Reserves across the Sonora-Arizona Border

BRUSCA, R.C., E. KIMREY and W. MOORE (eds.). 2004. *A Seashore Guide to the Northern Gulf of California*. Arizona-Sonora Desert Museum Press, Tucson.

FELGER, R.S. 2000. *Flora of the Gran Desierto and Rio Colorado of Northwestern Mexico*. University of Arizona Press, Tucson.

FELGER, R.S. and B. BROYLES (eds.). 2005. *Dry Borders: Great Natural Areas of the Gran Desierto and Upper Gulf of California*. University of Utah Press, Salt Lake City.

HARTMANN, W.K. 1989. *Desert Heart*. Fisher Books, Tucson.

PHILLIPS, S.J. and P.W. COMUS. 2000. *A Natural History of the Sonoran Desert*. Arizona-Sonora Desert Museum Press, Tucson, and University of California Press, Berkeley.

ROBLES GIL, P., E. EZCURRA, and E. MELLINK (eds.). *The Gulf of California, a World Apart*. Pegaso/Casa Lamm/Agrupación Sierra Madre, Mexico City.

Laguna Madre: A Major Transboundary Wetland on the Texas-Tamaulipas Border

HEDGPETH, J.W. 1947. The Laguna Madre of Texas. *North American Wildlife Conference* 12:364-380.

HEDGPETH, J.W. 1967. Ecological Aspects of the Laguna Madre, a Hypersaline Estuary. In G.H. LAUFF (ed.), *Estuaries*. Publication no. 83. American Association for the Advancement of Science, Washington, D.C., pp. 408-419.

HILDEBRAND, H.H. 1969. Laguna Madre de Tamaulipas: Observations on Its Hydrography and Fisheries. In A. AYALA CASTANARES and F.B. PHLEGER (eds.), *Coastal Lagoons: A Symnposium*. Universidad Nacional Autónoma de México, Mexico City, pp. 679-686.

TUNNELL, J.W. and F.W. JUDD. 2002. *The Laguna Madre of Texas and Tamaulipas*. Texas A&M University Press, College Station, Texas, 346 pp.

The Maya Tropical Forest: Saving a Threatened Tri-National Biological and Cultural Heritage

BREEDLOVE, D. 1973. Phytogeography of Chiapas. In A. GRAHAM (ed.), *Vegetation and Vegetational History*. Amsterdam.

CONSERVATION INTERNATIONAL. 2003. *The Northern Mesoamerica Ecosystem Profile*. Critical Ecosystem Partnership Fund. Conservation International, Washington, D.C.

NATIONS, J.D. 1994. The Ecology of the Zapatista Revolt. *Cultural Survival Quarterly* 18(1):31-33.

NATIONS, J.D. In press. The Maya Tropical Forest: People, Parks, and Ancient Cities. University of Texas Press, Austin.

NATIONS, J.D., R.B. PRIMACK, and D. BRAY. 1998. Introduction: The Maya Forest, Chapter 1. In R.B. PRIMACK, D. BRAY, H.A. GALLETTI, and I. PONCIANO (eds.), *Timber, Tourists, and Temples: Conservation and Development in the Maya Forest of Belize, Guatemala, and Mexico*. Island Press, Washington, D.C.

PARKER, T.A., B.K. HOLST, L.H. EMMONS, and J.R. MEYER. 1993. *A Biological Assessment of the Columbia River Forest Reserve, Toledo District, Belize*. Rapid Assessment Program Working Papers 3. Conservation International, Washington, D.C.

SWANK, W.G. and J.G. TEER. 1989. Status of the Jaguar. *Oryx* 23:14-21.

La Amistad: A Long History of Transboundary Friendship in Central America

ALVARADO, R. 1988 (unpublished). *Resumen de información básica sobre el Parque Internacional La Amistad, Bocas del Toro, Panamá*. Instituto Nacional de Recursos Naturales Renovables, Dirección Regional 1.

DE VRIES, P. *The Butterflies of Costa Rica and Their Natural History*. Volume I: Papilionidae, Pieridae, Nymphalidae (1987), and Volume II: Riodinidae (1997). Princeton University Press, Princeton, New Jersey.

GÓMEZ, L. 1989. *Unidades naturales y uso actual de los ecosistemas, de recursos naturales, beneficios potenciales en la región de Talamanca-Amistad*. Consultancy to OAS. San José, Costa Rica.

GUEVARA, M. 2000. *Perfil de los pueblos indígenas de Costa Rica*. RUTA-Banco Mundial, mayo de 2000.

MIPPE. 1992 (unpublished). *Marco de referencia y características generales del Área Reserva de la Biosfera La Amistad Sector Panamá*. Government of Panama, Panama City.

OAS-CI. 1990. Estrategia para el desarrollo institucional de la Reserva de la Biosfera La Amistad, Costa Rica.

A report to the Government of Costa Rica. MIREN-ME-MIDEPLAN, San José, Costa Rica, 137 pp.

OAS-CI. 1994 (unpublished). *Estrategia para el desarrollo sostenible de la Reserva de la Biosfera La Amistad-Panamá*. A report to the Government of Panama. Panama City, 128 pp.

Vilcabamba-Amboró: Transboundary Collaboration from Andean Peaks to the Amazon Basin

ALONSO, L.E., A. ALONSO, T.S. SCHULENBERG, and F. DALLMEIER (eds.). 2001. Biological and Social Assessments of the Cordillera de Vilcabamba, Peru. Conservation International/Smithsonian Institution, Washington, D.C. RAP Working Papers 12:298.

CONSERVATION INTERNATIONAL. 2004. *Treasures without Borders: Weaving the Vilcabamba-Amboró Conservation Corridor*. Video 26 minutes. Conservation International, Washington, D.C.

GEF/UNDP/UNOPS. 1997. *Amazonia peruana: comunidades indígenas, conocimientos y tierras tituladas. Atlas y base de datos*. UNDP, Lima. 351 pp.

SUÁREZ DE FREITAS, G., C. PONCE, G. LLOSA, and E. MENDOZA. 2000. The Ecological Corridors for the Amazon: The Case of the Peru-Bolivia Conservation Corridor. Conference report of Interactive Session I in the IUCN World Conservation Congress in Amman, Jordan, October 4-11, 2000.

WORLD WILDLIFE FUND. 2004. Terrestrial Ecoregions of the World. http://www.worldwildlife.org/science/ecoregions/terrestrial.cfm

Pantepui: The Roraima and Neblina Regions of Brazil, Venezuela, and Guyana

BOUBLI, J.P. 2002. Lowland Floristic Assessment of Pico da Neblina National Park, Brazil. *Plant Ecology* 160: 149-167

BOUBLI, J.P. In prep. *Biodiversidade de vertebrados do Pantepui*. Final report. Sustainable Development of the Brazilian Biodiversity Program —PROBIO—, Ministry for the Environment, Federal Government of Brazil, The World Bank and the Global Environment Facility.

BREWER-CARIAS, Ch. 1988. *Cerro de la Neblina: resultados de la expedición 1983-1987*. FUDECI, Caracas.

BROWN, N.E. 1901. Report on Two Botanical Collections Made by Messrs. F.V. MCCONNELL and J.J. QUELCH at Mount Roraima in British Guiana. *Transactions of the Linnean Society of London* 6:1-107.

DOYLE, A.C. 1912. *The Lost World*. Hoder & Stoughton, New York.

GENTRY, A. 1986. Exploring the Mountain of the Mist. *Science Year (The World Book Science Annual)*: 125-139.

HUBER, O. 1995. Introduction. In J.A. STEYERMARK, P.E. BERRY, and B.K. HOLST (eds.), *Flora of the Venezuelan Guayana*, Vol. 1. Missouri Botanical Garden, St. Louis. Timber Press, Portland, Oregon.

MAGUIRE, B. 1979. Guayana, Region of the Roraima Sandstone Formation. In K. LARSEN and L.B. HOLM-NIELSEN (eds.), *Tropical Botany*. Academic Press, London, pp. 223-238.

MAYR, E. and W.H. PHELPS, JR. 1967. The Origin of the Bird Fauna of the South Venezuelan Highlands. *Bulletin of the American Museum of Natural History* 136:269-328.

PRANCE, G.T. and H.O.R. SCHUBART. 1978. Notes on the Vegetation of Amazonia I. A preliminary note on the origin of the open white sand campinas of the lower Rio Negro. *Brittonia* 30:60-63.

STEYERMARK, J.A. 1986. Speciation and Endemism in the Flora of the Venezuelan Tepuis. In F. VUILLEUMIR and M. MONASTERIO (eds.), *High Altitude Tropical Biogeography*. Oxford University Press, New York, pp. 317–373.

TATE, G.H.H. 1930. Notes on the Mount Roraima Region. *Geographical Review* (New York) 20:53-68.

The Borderlands of Brazil and the Guianas: The World's Most Intact Tropical Rainforest

HUBER, O. and M.N. FOSTER (eds.). 2003. Conservation Priorities for the Guayana Shield: 2002 Consensus. Conservation International, Washington, D.C., 99 pp.

MITTERMEIER, R.A., S.A. MALONE, M.J. PLOTKIN, F.L.J. BAAL, K. MOHADIN, J. MAC KNIGHT, M.M. WERKHOVEN, and T.H. WERNER. 1990. Conservation Action Plan for Suriname. Conservation International, Suriname Forest Service, WWF-U.S., STINASU, University of Suriname, 45 pp.

Iguaçu-Iguazú: One of the World's Greatest Natural Wonders

BERGALLO, H. DE G. and C.F. DE V. CONDE, 2001. O Park Nacional do Iguaçu e a Estrada do Colono. *Ciência Hoje* 29(174):37-39.

CÂNDIDO-JR., J.F., V.P. MARGARIDO, J.L. PEGORARO, A.R. D'AMICO, W.D. MADEIRA, V.C. CASALE and L. ANDRADE. 2002. *Animais atropelados na rodovia que margeia o Park Nacional do Iguaçu, Paraná, Brazil, e seu aproveitamento para estudos de biologia da conservação*. Anais III Congresso Brazileiro de Unidades de Conservação, Fortaleza, 553 pp.

CHEBEZ, J.C. 1996. *Fauna misionera. Catálogo sistemático y zoogeográfico de los vertebrados de la provincia de Misiones (Argentina)*. Ed. Lola, Bs.As., Argentina, 318 pp.

RODRIGUES, E. 2003. Estrada do Colono: um trilho de burros. *La Insignia* (on line). http://www.lainsignia.org/2003/octubre/ecol_004.htm

SEIBENE, C.A., M. CASTELINO, N.R. REY, J. HERRERA and J. CALO. 1996. *Inventario de las aves del Parque Nacional Iguazú, Misiones, Argentina*. Ed. Lola, Buenos Aires, monografía 9, 70 pp.

STRAUBE, F.C. and A.R. D'AMICO (eds.). 2005. *Relatório final da Expedição Floriano (17 a 23 de março de 2004)*. Relatório. IBAMA-PNI, Foz do Iguaçu.

STRAUBE, F.C. and A. URBEN-FILHO. 2004. Uma revisão crítica sobre o grau de conhecimento da avifauna do Park Nacional do Iguaçu (Paraná, Brazil) e áreas adjacentes. *Atualidades Ornitológicas* 118:6.

STRAUBE, F.C., A. URBEN-FILHO and J.F. CÂNDIDO-JR. 2004. Novas informações sobre a avifauna do Park Nacional do Iguaçu (Paraná). *Atualidades Ornitológicas* 120:10.

EUROPE

The Pyrenees-Mount Perdu: A Shared Gem on the French-Spanish Border

ASSOCIATION MONT PERDU PATRIMOINE MONDIAL (AMPPM). 1995. *Massif Mont Perdu/Tres Serols*. France/Spain. Nomination proposal to the World Heritage Committee. Unpublished report, 100 pp. plus annexes.

BALCELLS R., E. 1992. *Ordesa y Monte Perdido Parque Nacional*. Lunwerg Editores y Ministerio de Agricultura, Pesca y Alimentación, ICONA, Madrid.

DE BELLEFON, P. 2002. *Landscape Description*. MPPM Association. http://www. mppm.org

ESPAÑA-FRANCIA. 1997. Monte Perdido, circos y cañones. Proposition d'Inscription au Patrimoine Mondial de l'UNESCO. February 1997, 21 pp. plus annexes.

MINISTÈRE DE L'ENVIRONNEMENT, FRANCE. 1995. Massif Mont Perdu-Tres Serols. Proposition d'Inscription au Patrimoine Mondial de l'UNESCO. September 1995, 12 pp. plus annexes.

RIVAS-MARTÍNEZ, S. 1969. Las comunidades de las ventiqueros (*Salicetea herbaceae*) del Pirineo Central. *Vegetatio* 17. Madrid.

UNEP-WCMC. 2001. *World Heritage Data Sheet*. http://www.wcmc.org.uk/protected_areas/data/wh/mtperdu.html

VILLAR, L., P. MONTSERRAT, and R. PÉREZ. 1993. *Cartografía vegetal del Parque Nacional de Ordesa y Monte Perdido*. 1:25000. ICONA-CSIC, Huesca.

The European Green Belt: From Vision to Reality

BENNETT, G. 2004. Integrating Biodiversity Conservation and Sustainable Use. Lessons learned from ecological networks. IUCN, Gland, Switzerland and Cambridge, U.K., vi + 51 pp.

EUROPEAN UNION. 2005. http://europa.eu.int/comm/environment/nature/home.htm

GLOBAL TRANSBOUNDARY PROTECTED AREAS NETWORK. 2005. http://www.tbpa.net/docs/pdfs/SEE_Strategy_May%2004_final.pdf

SEPP, K. and A. KAASIK. 2002. *Development of National Ecological Networks in the Baltic Countries in the Framework of the Pan-European Ecological Network*. IUCN Regional Office for Europe, Warsaw.

UNESCO. 2005. *Fertö/Neusiedlersee Cultural Landscape*. http://whc.unesco.org/pg.cfm?CID=31&ID_SITE=772&l=en

AFRICA

West Africa's Upper Guinea Forest Region: Transboundary Conservation in a Conflict Zone

BAKARR, M.I., B.B. BAILEY, D. BYLER, R. HAM, S. OLIVIERI, and M. OMLAND (eds.). 2001. *From the Forest to the Sea: Biodiversity Connections from Guinea to Togo*. Conservation International, Washington, D.C.

DAVIES, A.G. 1987. The Gola Forest Reserves, Sierra Leone: Wildlife Conservation and Forest Management. IUCN, Gland, Switzerland.

KORMOS, R., C. BOESCH, M.I. BAKARR, and T.M. BUTYNSKI (eds.). 2004. *West African Chimpanzees. Status Survey and Conservation Action Plan*. IUCN/SSC Species Specialist Group. IUCN, Gland, Switzerland and Cambridge, U.K.

MARTIN, C. 1991. *The Rainforests of West Africa: Ecology-Threats-Conservation*. Birkhäuser Verlag, Basel, Switzerland.

MERTZ, G. 1986. The Status of the Forest Elephant *Loxodonta Africana cyclotis*, Mastchie, 1900 in the Gola Forest Reserve, Sierra Leone. *Biological Conservation* 36(1):83-94

MITTERMEIER, R.A., N. MYERS, P. ROBLES GIL, and C.G. MITTERMEIER (eds.). 1999. *Hotspots: Earth's Biologically Richest and Most Endangered Terrestrial Ecoregions.* CEMEX (Monterrey), Conservation International (Washington, D.C.), Agrupación Sierra Madre (Mexico City).

MITTERMEIER, R.A., P. ROBLES GIL, M. HOFFMANN, J. PILGRIM, T. BROOKS, C.G. MITTERMEIER, J. LAMOREAUX, and G.A.B. DA FONSECA (eds.). 2004. *Hotspots Revisited: Earth's Biologically Richest and Most Endangered Terrestrial Ecoregions.* CEMEX (Monterrey), Conservation International (Washington, D.C.), Agrupación Sierra Madre (Mexico City).

RICHARDS, P. 1996. *Fighting for the Rain Forest: War, Youth and Resources in Sierra Leone.* James Currey (reprinted with additional material in February 1998), Oxford.

SAYER, J.A., C.S. HARCOURT, and M.N. COLLINS. 1992. *The Conservation Atlas of Tropical Forests: Africa.* IUCN, Gland, Switzerland.

STATTERSFIELD, A.J, M.J. CROSBY, A.J. LONG, and D.C. WEGE. 1998. *Endemic Bird Areas of the World: Priorities for Biodiversity Conservation.* BirdLife International, Cambridge.

The Tri-National de la Sangha: Transboundary Conservation in the Western Congo Forest

BERESFORD, P. and J. CRACRAFT. 1999. *Speciation in African Forest Robins* (Stiphornis)*: Species, Limits, Phylogenetic Relationships, and Molecular Biogeography.* No. 3270. American Museum of Natural History, New York.

BURGESS, N., J. D'AMICO HALES, E. UNDERWOOD, E. DINERSTEIN, D. OLSON, I. ITOUA, J. SCHIPPER, T. RICKETTS, and K. NEWMAN. 2004. *Terrestrial Ecoregions of Africa and Madagascar: A Conservation Assessment.* Island Press, Washington, D.C.

CHRISTY, P. 2002. *Aires protégées de Dzanga-Sangha: République Centrafricaine.* WWF Central Africa Regional Program Office, Libreville, Gabon.

FISHPOOL, L. and M. EVANS (eds.). 2001. *Important Bird Areas in Africa and Associated Islands. Priority Sites for Conservation.* BirdLife Conservation Series No. 11, BirdLife International. Pisces Publications. Newbury and Cambridge, U.K.

IUCN. 2004. *2004 IUCN Red List of Threatened Species.* http://www.redlist.org

KAMDEM-TOHAM, A., J. D'AMICO, D. OLSON, A. BLOM, L. TROWBRIDGE, N. BURGESS, M. THIEME, R. ABELL, R. CARROLL, S. GARTLAN, O. LANGRAND, R. MIKALA MUSSAVU, D. O'HARA, and H. STRAND (eds.). 2003. *Biological Priorities for Conservation in the Guinean-Congolian Forest and Freshwater Region.* WWF Gabon Country Office, Libreville, Gabon.

MITTERMEIER, R.A., C.G. MITTERMEIER, P. ROBLES GIL, J. PILGRIM, G.A.B. DA FONSECA, T. BROOKS, and W. KONSTANT (eds.). 2002. *Wilderness: Earth's Last Wild Places.* CEMEX (Monterrey), Conservation International (Washington, D.C.), Agrupación Sierra Madre (Mexico City).

The Virunga Volcanoes Transboundary Conservation Area: Home of the Mountain Gorilla

BUTYNSKI, T.M. 2001. Africa's Great Apes. In B.B. BECK, T.S. STOINSKI, M. HUTCHINS, T.L. MAPLE, B. NORTON, A. ROWAN, E.F. STEVENS, and A. ARLUKE (eds.), *Great Apes and Humans: The Ethics of Coexistence.* Smithsonian Institution Press, pp. 3-56.

BUTYNSKI, T.M. and J. KALINA. 1993. Three New Mountain National Parks for Uganda. *Oryx* 27:214-224.

BUTYNSKI, T.M. and J. KALINA. 1998. Gorilla Tourism: A Critical Look. In E.J. MILNER-GULLAND and R. MACE (eds.), *Conservation of Biological Resources.* Blackwell Science, Oxford, pp. 280-300.

FISHPOOL, L.D.C. and M.I. EVANS (eds.). 2001. *Important Bird Areas in Africa and Associated Islands: Priority Sites for Conservation.* Pisces Publications, Newbury, U.K.

HOMSY, J. 1999. *Ape Tourism and Human Diseases: How Close Should We Get?* Unpublished report. International Gorilla Conservation Program, Nairobi.

INTERNATIONAL GORILLA CONSERVATION PROGRAMME (IGCP). 1996. *Environmental Sector Profile: Strategic Action Plan for the Great Lakes Region.* Unpublished report. UNEP, Nairobi.

KALPERS, J. 2001. *Volcanoes Under Siege: Impact of a Decade of Armed Conflict in the Virungas.* Unpublished report. Biodiversity Support Program, Washington, D.C.

LANJOUW, A., A. KAYITARE, H. RAINER, E. RUTAGARAMA, M. SIVHA, S. ASUMA, and J. KALPERS. 2001. *Beyond Boundaries: Transboundary Natural Resource Management for Mountain Gorillas in the Virunga-Bwindi Region.* Unpublished report. Biodiversity Support Program, Washington, D.C.

PLUMPTRE, A.J., M. BEHANGANA, T.R.B. DAVENPORT, C. KAHINDO, R. KITYO, E. NDOMBA, P. SSEGAWA, G. EILU, D. NKUUTU, and I. OWIUNJI. 2003. *The Biodiversity of the Albertine Rift.* Unpublished report, Albertine Rift Technical Reports No. 3. Wildlife Conservation Society, New York.

WALLER, D. 1996. *Rwanda: Which way now?* Unpublished report. Oxfam, Oxford.

WOODFORD, M.H., T.M. BUTYNSKI, and W.B. KARESH. 2002. Habituating the Great Apes: The Disease Risks. *Oryx* 3:153-160.

YAKOBO, M. and B. UWIMBABZAI. 2000. *Analysis of the Economic Significance of Gorilla Tourism in Uganda.* Unpublished report. International Gorilla Conservation Programme, Nairobi.

Serengeti-Masai: Land of the Great Migration

BAKER, T., L. NEWTON, M. SWADLING, and J. TREVILLIAN. 1995. *Paradise on Earth: The Natural World Heritage List.* JIDD Publishers, Patonga, Australia.

CAMPBELL, K. and M. BORNER. 1995. Population Trends and Distribution of Serengeti Herbivores: Implications for Management. In A.R.E. SINCLAIR and P. ARCESE (eds.), *Serengeti II: Dynamics, Management and Conservation of an Ecosystem.* University of Chicago Press, Chicago, pp. 117-145.

CHRIST, C. and W.R. KONSTANT. 2002. Serengeti. In R.A. MITTERMEIER, C.G. MITTERMEIER, P. ROBLES GIL, J. PILGRIM, G.A.B. DA FONSECA, W.R. KONSTANT, and T. BROOKS (eds.), *Wilderness: Earth's Last Wild Places.* CEMEX (Monterrey), Conservation International (Washington, D.C.), Agrupación Sierra Madre (Mexico City), pp. 210-219.

FRIEDMANN, H. 1954. Honey-Guide: The Bird that Eats Wax. *National Geographic* 105(4):551-560.

GRZIMEK, B. and M. GRZIMEK. 1961. *Serengeti Shall Not Die.* E.P. Dutton and Co., Inc., New York.

HANKS, J. and S. CHARLTON. 2004. African Plains Game. In R.A. MITTERMEIER, P. ROBLES GIL, C.G. MITTERMEIER, T. BROOKS, M. HOFFMANN, W.R. KONSTANT, G.A.B. DA FONSECA, and R. MAST (eds.), *Wildlife Spectacles.* CEMEX (Monterrey), Conservation International (Washington, D.C.), Agrupación Sierra Madre (Mexico City), pp. 111-117.

IWAGO, M. 1987. *Serengeti: Natural Order on the African Plain.* Chronicle Books, San Francisco.

LAMPREY, R.H. and R.S. REID. 2004. Expansion of Human Settlement in Kenya's Masai Mara: What Future for Pastoralism and Wildlife? *Journal of Biogeography* 31(6):997-1032.

MOSS, C. 1975. *Portraits in the Wild: Behavior Studies of East African Mammals.* Houghton Mifflin Company, Boston.

OLSON, D.M., E. DINERSTEIN, E.D. WIKRAMANYAKE, N.D. BURGESS, G.V.N. POWELL, E.C. UNDERWOOD, J.A. D'AMICO, I. ITOUHA, H.E. STRAND, J.C. MORRSION, C.J. LOUCKS, T.F. ALNUTT, T.H. RICKETTS, Y. KURA, J.F. LAMOREUX, W.W. WETTENGEL, P. HEDAO, and K. KASSEM. 2001. Terrestrial Ecoregions of the World: A New Map of Life on Earth. *Bioscience* 51(11):933-938.

SCHALLER, G. 1973. *Golden Shadows, Flying Hooves.* Alfred A. Knopf, New York.

STATTERSFIELD, A.J., M.J. CROSBY, A.J. LONG, and D.C. WEGE. 1998. *Endemic Bird Areas of the World: Priorities for Biodiversity Conservation.* BirdLife International, Cambridge, U.K.

UNESCO. 2002. *Biosphere Reserves: Special Places for People and Nature.* UNESCO, Paris.

VAN LAWICK-GOODALL, J. 1968. Tool-Using Bird: The Egyptian Vulture. *National Geographic* 133(5):630-641.

ZIMMERMAN, D.A., D.A. TURNER, and D.J. PEARSON. 1996. *Birds of Kenya and Northern Tanzania.* Christopher Helm, London.

|Ai-|Ais-Richtersveld-Sperrgebiet: Transboundary Conservation in an Arid Hotspot

BARNARD, P. (ed.). 1998. *Biological Diversity in Namibia: A Country Study.* Namibian National Biodiversity Task Force, Windhoek, 332 pp.

BARNARD, P., C.J. BROWN, A.M. JARVIS, A. ROBERTSON, and L. VAN ROOYEN. 1998. Extending the Namibian Protected Area Network to Safeguard Hotspots of Endemism and Diversity. *Biodiversity and Conservation* 7(4):531-547.

BARNARD, P. and S. FRAZEE. 2002. The Succulent Karoo Hotspot in Namibia: Securing the Sperrgebiet Wilderness and Its Biological Diversity. Unpublished concept paper for Conservation International's Global Conservation Fund to establish a Sperrgebiet National Park in Namibia. Namibian Ministry of Environment and Tourism (Windhoek), Conservation International-Namibia (Cape Town).

BOHENSKY, E., B. REYERS, A. VAN JAARSVELD, C. FABRICIUS et al. 2004. *Ecosystem Services in the Gariep Basin: A Component of the Southern African Millennium Ecosystem Assessment (SAfMA).* Sun Press, Stellenbosch, South Africa.

BURKE, A. 2002. *Sperrgebiet Conservation Planning Study: Implementation Strategy.* Ministry of Environment and Tourism/Conservation International, Windhoek, Namibia.

BURKE, A. 2004. A Preliminary Account of Patterns of Endemism in Namibia's Sperrgebiet/The Succulent Karoo. *Journal of Biogeography* 31:1613-1622.

COWLING, R.M., P.W. RUNDEL, P.G. DESMET, and K.J. ESLER. 1998. Extraordinarily High Regional-Scale Plant Diversity in Southern African Arid Lands: Subcontinental and Global Comparisons. *Diversity and Distributions* 4:27-36.

DRIVER, A., P.G. DESMET, M. ROUGET, R.M. COWLING, and K. MAZE. 2003. Succulent Karoo Ecosystem Plan: Biodiversity Component Technical Report. Cape Conservation Unit Report No. CCU 1/03, Botanical Society of South Africa.

LOOTS, S. and C. MANNHEIMER. 2003. The Status of *Aloe pillansii* L. Guthrie (Aloaceae) in Namibia. *Bradleya* 21:57-62.

MIDGLEY, G.F. and D. MILLAR. In press. Case Study: Biome and Species Range Shifts in Two Biodiversity Hotspots. In T.J. LOVEJOY and L. HANNAH (eds.), *Climate Change and Biodiversity*, Chapter 17. Yale University Press.

MIDGLEY, J.J., R.M. COWLING, H. HENDRICKS, P.W. RUNDEL, and K.J. ESLER. 1997. Population Ecology of Tree Succulents (*Aloe* and *Pachypodium*) in the Arid Western Cape: Decline of Keystone Species. *Biodiversity and Conservation* 6:869-876.

PALLETT, J. (ed.). 1995. *The Sperrgebiet: Namibia's Least Known Wilderness. An Environmental Profile of the Sperrgebiet or Diamond Area 1 in Southwestern Namibia.* Desert Research Foundation of Namibia and Namibia-DeBeers Corporation, Windhoek, 84 pp.

PIERCE, S.M. and R.M. COWLING. 1999. Succulent Karoo. In R.A. MITTERMEIER, N. MYERS, C.G. MITTERMEIER, and P. ROBLES GIL (eds.), *Hotspots: Earth's Biologically Richest and Most Endangered Terrestrial Ecoregions.* CEMEX (Monterrey), Conservation International (Washington, D.C.), Agrupación Sierra Madre (Mexico City), pp. 228-237.

RUNDEL, P.W., R.M. COWLING, K.J. ESLER, P.J. MUSTART, E. VAN JAARSVELD, and H. BEZUIDENHOUT. 1995. Winter Growth Phenology and Leaf Orientation of *Pachypodium namaquanum* (Apocynaceae) in the Succulent Karoo of the Richtersveld, South Africa. *Oecologia* 101:472-477.

SIMMONS, R.E. 2005 (in press). *Birds to Watch in Namibia: Red, Rare and Endemic Species.* Namibian National Biodiversity Programme/Namibia Nature Foundation, Windhoek.

SIMMONS, R.E., M. GRIFFIN, R.E. GRIFFIN, E. MARAIS, and H. KOLBERG. 1998. Endemism in Namibia: Patterns, Processes and Predictions. *Biodiversity and Conservation* 7(4):513-530.

SPERRGEBIET CONSORTIUM. 2000. *The Sperrgebiet Land Use Plan.* Draft, October 2000. Ministry of Environment and Tourism, Windhoek, 162 pp. + 38 plates.

VAN WYK, A.E. and G.F. SMITH. 2001. *Regions of Floristic Endemism in Southern Africa.* Umdaus Press, Pretoria.

WWF/IUCN. 1994. *Centres of Plant Diversity. A Guide and Strategy for Their Conservation. Volume 1: Europe, Africa, South West Asia and the Middle East.* IUCN Publications Unit, Cambridge, U.K.

Kavango-Zambezi: The Four Corners Transfrontier Conservation Area

CHASE, M. 2004. Ecology, Population Structure and Movements of Elephant Populations in the Okavango-Upper Zambezi Transfrontier Conservation Area. Progress Report. Conservation International, Maun, Botswana.

COWLING, R.M. and C. HILTON-TAYLOR. 1994. Patterns of Plant Diversity and Endemism in Southern Africa: An Overview. In B.J. HUNTLEY (ed.), *Botanical Diversity in Southern Africa.* Strelitzia 1, National Botanical Institute, Cape Town, pp. 31-52.

GRIFFIN, J. 1999. Study on the Development of Transboundary Natural Resource Management Areas in Southern Africa. Main Report. Biodiversity Support Program, Washington, D.C.

HANKS, J. 2003. Transfrontier Conservation Areas (TFCAs) in Southern Africa: Their Role in Conserving Biodiversity, Socioeconomic Development and Promoting a Culture of Peace. *Journal of Sustainable Forestry* 17(1/2):127-148.

ROSS, K. 2003. *Okavango: Jewel of the Kalahari.* Struik, Cape Town.

SANDWITH, T., C. SHINE, L. HAMILTON, and D. SHEPPARD. 2001. *Transboundary Protected Areas for Peace and Co-operation.* Best Practice Protected Area Guideline Series No. 7. IUCN, Gland, Switzerland.

ZBICZ, D.C. 1999. Transboundary Cooperation Between Internationally Adjoining Protected Areas. In D. HARMON (ed.), *On the Frontiers of Conservation.* Proceedings of the Tenth Conference on Research and Resource Management in Parks and Public Lands. The George Wright Society, Hancock, U.S., pp. 199-204.

The Roof of Africa: Transboundary Conservation in the Maloti-Drakensberg Mountains

BIRDLIFE INTERNATIONAL. 2003. *BirdLife's Online World Bird Database: The Site for Bird Conservation.* Version 2.0. BirdLife International, Cambridge, U.K. http://www.birdlife.org

COWLING, R.J. and C. HILTON-TAYLOR. 1994. Patterns of Plant Diversity and Endemism in Southern Africa: An Overview. In B. HUNTLEY, *Botanical Diversity in Southern Africa.* National Botanical Institute, Pretoria.

HILLIARD, O.M. and B.L. BURTT. 1987. The Botany of the Southern Natal Drakensberg. Natal Botanic Gardens and CTP Book Printers, Cape Town.

MITTERMEIER, R.A., P. ROBLES GIL, M. HOFFMANN, J. PILGRIM, T. BROOKS, C.G. MITTERMEIER, J. LAMOREAUX, and G.A.B. DA FONSECA (eds.). 2004. *Hotspots Revisited: Earth's Biologically Richest and Most Endangered Terrestrial Ecoregions.* CEMEX (Monterrey), Conservation International (Washington, D.C.), Agrupación Sierra Madre (Mexico).

POOLEY, E. 2003. Mountain Flowers: A Field Guide to the Flora of the Drakensberg and Lesotho. The Flora Publications Trust, Durban.

SANDWITH, T.S. 1997a. The Drakensberg-Maloti Transfrontier Conservation Area: Experience and Lessons Learned. In IUCN/WCPA (2000), *Parks for Peace: Transboundary Protected Areas as a Vehicle for International Cooperation.* Proceedings of the Parks for Peace International Conference, Somerset-West, South Africa, September 16-18, 1997.

VAN DER LINDE, H., J. OGLETHORPE, T. SANDWITH, D. SNELSON, and Y. TESSEMA (with contributions from A. TIÉGA and T. PRICE). 2001. Beyond Boundaries: Transboundary Natural Resource Management in Sub-Saharan Africa. Biodiversity Support Program, Washington, D.C.

WRIGHT, J.B. 1971. Bushman Raiders of the Drakensberg, 1840-1870: A Study of Their Conflict with Stock-Keeping Peoples in Natal. University of Natal Press, Pietermaritzburg, South Africa.

ASIA/PACIFIC

West Tien Shan: At the Crossroads of Central Asia

IUCN/WCPA. 2003. *Central Asia Transboundary Biodiversity Project: Kyrgiz Republic, Kazakhstan and Uzbekistan.* Case Study in Transboundary Conservation: Promoting Peaceful Cooperation and Development while Protecting Biodiversity. IUCN.

WORLD BANK. 2000. *Transboundary Reserves.* World Bank implementation of the ecosystem approach. World Bank, Washington, D.C.

Manas: Transboundary Conservation on the Assam-Bhutan Border

BLOWER, J.H. 1986. *Nature Conservation in Bhutan: Project Findings and Recommendations.* FO:DP/BHU/83/022. FAO, Rome, 55 pp.

JOHNSINGH, A.J.T. and D. YONTEN. 2004. *Beautiful Buthan.* Frontline, India.

LAHAN, P. 1986. *Report on Ecological Reconnaissance of Manas Wildlife Sanctuary, Namgyal Wangchuk Wildlife Reserve, and Phipsoo Wildlife Reserve and an Outline Master Development Plan for the Reserves.* FO:DP/ BHU/83/022, Field Document No. 9. FAO, Rome, 110 pp.

MALLINSON, J.J.C. 1971. The Pigmy Hog *Sus sulvanicus* (Hodgson) in Northern Assam. *Jour. Bombay Nat. His. Soc.* 68:423-433.

OLIVER, W.L.R. 1984. The Distribution and Status of the Hispid Hare. *J. Jersey Wildl. Preserv. Trust. Dodo* 21:6-23.

SCOTT, D.A. (ed.). 1989. *A Directory of Asian Wetlands.* IUCN, Gland, Switzerland and Cambridge, U.K., 1181 pp.

SINGH, S.K. and D. SINGH. 1994. Changes Between Cover of the Manas Tiger Reserve in between 1989-93. *Cheetal.* 36 (1-2):23-28.

THORSELL, J. and J. HARRISON. 1990. Parks that Promote Peace: A Global Inventory of Transfrontier Nature Reserves. In J. THORSELL (ed.), *Parks on the Borderline: Experience in Transfrontier Conservation.* IUCN, Gland, Switzerland, pp. 3-22.

The Lanjak Entimau/Batang Ai/Betung Kerihun Complex: A Heritage Area in the Heart of Borneo

ITTO, WWF-IP, PHKA, and BETUNG KERIHUN NATIONAL PARK. 2000. *Management Plan Betung Kerihun National Park, West Kalimantan: Executive Summary.* 16 pp.

KAVANAGH, M. 1996. Tale of the Forest Man. In *Duniaku*, WWF-Malaysia, p. 11.

NPWO/WWFM (compiled by M. KAVANAGH). 1983. *Report on an Aerial Survey of Lubok Antu Sub-district by RMAF Alouette Helicopter on Wednesday, 9 March 1983.* National Parks and Wildlife Office, Sarawak Forest Department, Kuching.

NPWO/WWFM (compiled by M. KAVANAGH). 1984. *Report on an Aerial Survey of Parts of the First and Second Divisions, 17 April 1984.* National Parks and Wildlife Office, Sarawak Forest Department, Kuching.

SINGLETON, I., S. WICH, S. HUSSON, S. STEPHENS, S. UTAMI ATMOKO, M. LEIGHTON, N. ROSEN, K. TRAYLOR-HOLZER, R. LACY, and O. BYERS. 2004. *Orangutan Population and Habitat Viability Assessment.* IUCN/SSC Conservation Breeding Specialist Group, Apple Valley.

SUPRIATNA, J. and E.H. WARJONO. 2001. *Panduan Lapangan Primata Indonesia*. Yayasan Obor, Jakarta.

WWF-MALAYSIA. 1998. *The National Parks and Other Wild Places of Malaysia*. New Holland Publishers, London.

Wasur-Tonda: Transboundary Conservation in the New Guinea Wilderness

ALLISON, A. 1994. Biodiversity and Conservation of the Fishes, Amphibians, and Reptiles of Papua New Guinea. In B.M. BEEHLER, (ed.), *Papua New Guinea Conservation Needs Assessment*, Volume 2, Chapter 16. Government of Papua New Guinea, Department of Environment and Conservation (DEC). The Biodiversity Support Program, Boroko, pp. 157-225

BEEHLER, B.M. (ed.). 1994. *Papua New Guinea Conservation Needs Assessment*. Government of Papua New Guinea, Department of Environment and Conservation (DEC). The Biodiversity Support Program, Boroko.

BISHOP, K.D. 2004. *A Review of the Avifauna of the TransFly Ecoregion: The Status, Distribution, Habitats and Conservation of the region's birds*. Unpublished report to the WWF South Pacific Program, Suva, Fiji.

BLEEKER, P. 1983. *Soils of Papua New Guinea*. Australian National University Press, Canberra.

COGGER, H.G. 2000. *Reptiles and Amphibians of Australia*. Sixth Edition. Reed New Holland.

DAVIS, S.D., V.H. HEYWOOD, and A.C. HAMILTON. 1995. *Centres of Plant Diversity: A Guide and Strategy for Their Conservation*. WWF/IUCN.

MACKINNON, J. 1997. *Protected Areas Systems Review of the Indo-Malayan Realm*. Asian Bureau for Conservation/World Conservation Monitoring Center/World Bank publication.

MILLER, S., P. OSBORNE, W. ASIGAU, and A.J. MUNGKAGE. 1994. Environments in Papua New Guinea. In N. SEKHRAN and S. MILLER. 1994. *Papua New Guinea Country Study on Biological Diversity*. Africa Centre for Resources and Environment (ACRE) (Nairobi, Kenya), Department of Environment and Conservation, Conservation Resource Centre, (Waigani, Papua New Guinea).

PAIJMANS, K. 1975. *Explanatory Notes to the Vegetation Map of Papua New Guinea*. Land Research Series No. 35. Commonwealth Scientific and Industrial Research Organization, Melbourne, Australia.

STATTERSFIELD, A, M.J. CROSBY, A.J. LONG, and D.C. WEGE. 1998. *Endemic Bird Areas of the World, Priorities for Biodiversity Conservation*. BirdLife International, Cambridge, U.K.

WURM, S.A. and S. HATTORI (eds.). 1981. *Language Atlas of the Pacific Area. Part 1: New Guinea Area, Oceania, Australia*.

MARINE

The Mesoamerican Reef: A Shared Commitment for the Caribbean Jewel

BEZAURY-CREEL J., R. MACÍAS ORDÓÑEZ, G. GARCÍA BELTRÁN, G. CASTILLO ARENAS, N. PARDO CAICEDO, R. IBARRA NAVARRO, and A. LORETO VIRUEL. 1997. Implementation of the International Coral Reef Initiative (ICRI) in Mexico, Commission for Environmental Cooperation (CEC). In *The International Coral Reef Initiative: The Status of Coral Reefs in Mexico and the United States Gulf of Mexico*. Compact Disk. Amigos de Sian Ka'an, A.C./CINVESTAV/NOAA/CEC/The Nature Conservancy. http://www.nmfs.noaa.gov/prot_res/PR/fpweb/icri/home. htm

DULIN P., J. BEZAURY, M. DOTHEROW-MCFIELD, M. BASTARRECHEA, B. ASPRA DE LUPIAC, and J. ESPINOZA. 2000. *Conservation and Sustainable Use of the Meso-American Barrier Reef System*. Working Paper 1: Threat and Root Cause Analysis. Food and Agriculture Organization. http://www.mbrs.org.bz/dbdocs/en_trca. pdf

WORLD BANK/GEF. 2001. *Mesoamerican Barrier Reef Systems Project* (MBRS-Project Document). http://www.mbrs.org.bz/dbdocs/en_pad. pdf

The Eastern Tropical Pacific Seascape: An Innovative Model for Transboundary Marine Conservation

EDGAR, G.J., S. BANKS, J.M. FARIÑA, M. CALVOPIÑA, and C. MARTÍNEZ. 2004 (in press). Regional Biogeography of Shallow Reef Fish and Macro-Invertebrate Communities in the Galápagos Archipelago. *Journal of Biogeography*.

EDGAR, G.J., J.M. FARIÑA, M. CALVOPIÑA, C. MARTÍNEZ, and S.J. BANKS. 2002. Comunidades submareales rocosas II: peces y macroinvertebrados móviles. In E. DANULAT and G.J. EDGAR (eds.), *Reserva marina de Galápagos, línea base de la biodiversidad*. Charles Darwin Foundation and Galápagos National Park Service, Galápagos, Ecuador, pp. 63-92.

EDGAR, G.J. and L. GARSKE. 2004. *Conservation Outcome Indicators for the Galápagos Marine Reserve*. Report to Conservation International.

FERNÁNDEZ, P., D.T. ANDERSON, P. SIEVERT, and K. HUYVAERT. 2001. Foraging Destinations of Three Low-Latitude Albatross (*Phoebastria*) Species. *Journal of Zoology* 255.

WHITEHEAD, H. 2001. Analysis of Animal Movement Using Opportunistic Individual Identifications: Application to Sperm Whales. *Ecology [Ecology]* 82:1417-1432.

WHITEHEAD, H., J. CHRISTAL, and S. DUFAULT. 1997. Past and Distant Whaling and the Rapid Decline of Sperm Whales off the Galápagos Islands. *Conservation Biology [CONSERV. BIOL.]* 11:1387-1396.

Antarctica: The Last Global Commons

BIRDLIFE INTERNATIONAL. 2000. *Threatened Birds of the World*. Lynx Edicions/BirdLife International, Barcelona, Spain and Cambridge, U.K.

BONNER, W.N. 1985. Birds and Mammals: Antarctic Seals. In W.N. BONNER and D.W.H. WALTON (eds.). *Key Environments: Antarctica*. Pergamon Press, Oxford, pp. 202-222.

CLEMENTS, J.F. 2000. *Birds of the World: A Checklist*. Pica Press, Robertsbridge, East Sussex, U.K.

GILLE, S.T. 2002. Warming of the Southern Ocean since the 1950s. *Science* 295:1275-1277.

LOEB, V., V. SIEGEL, O. HOLM-HANSEN, R. HEWITT, W. FRASERE, W. TRIVELPIECE, and S. TRIVELPIECE. 1997. Effects of Sea-Ice Extent and Krill or Salp Dominance on the Antarctic Food Web. *Nature* 387(6636):897-900.

MITTERMEIER, R.A. and G.S. STONE. 2002. Antarctica. In MITTERMEIER, R.A., C.G. MITTERMEIER, P. ROBLES GIL, J. PILGRIM, G.A.B. DA FONSECA, T. BROOKS, and W. KONSTANT (eds.). 2002. *Wilderness: Earth's Last Wild Places*. CEMEX (Monterrey), Conservation International (Washington, D.C.), Agrupación Sierra Madre (Mexico City), pp. 544-555.

PYNE, S.J. 1986. *The Ice: A Journey to Antarctica*. University of Iowa Press, Iowa City.

STONE, G. 2003. *Ice Island: Expedition to Antarctica's Largest Iceberg*. Bunker Hill Publishing, Charlestown, U.S., 88 pp.

STONEHOUSE, B. 2000. *The Last continent: Discovering Antarctica*. SCF Books, Norfolk, U.K., 278 pp.

APPENDIX. GLOBAL LIST OF INTERNATIONALLY ADJOINING PROTECTED AREAS AND OTHER TRANSBOUNDARY CONSERVATION INITIATIVES

HANKS, J. 2003. Transfrontier Conservation Areas (TFCAs) in Southern Africa: Their Role in Conserving Biodiversity, Socioeconomic Development, and Promoting a Culture of Peace. *Journal of Sustainable Forestry* 17(1/2):127-149.

IUCN. 1994. *Guidelines for Protected Area Management Categories*. CNPPA with the assistance of WCMC. IUCN, Gland, Switzerland and Cambridge, U.K. http://www.iucn.org/themes/wcpa/wcpa/protectedareas.htm

UNEP-WCMC (United Nations Environmental Programme-World Conservation Monitoring Centre). 2005. *World Database of Protected Areas*. http://sea.unep-wcmc.org/wdbpa

ZBICZ, D.C. 2001. Global List of Internationally Adjoining Protected Areas: Revised and Updated, 2001. In T.S. SANDWITH, C. SHINE, L.S. HAMILTON, and D.A. SHEPPARD, *Transboundary Protected Areas for Peace and Co-operation*. IUCN, Gland, Switzerland and Cambridge, U.K.

ZBICZ, D.C. and M. GREEN. 1997. Status of the World's Transfrontier Protected Areas. In IUCN/WCPA, *Transboundary Protected Areas as a Vehicle for International Co-operation*. Proceedings, Parks for Peace Conference. Somerset West, South Africa, September 16-18, 1997.

Rosario Álvarez / The Nature Conservancy-
Programa México
Manuel M. Ponce 322, 2° piso, Guadalupe Inn,
01020 Mexico City, Mexico
ralvarez@tnc.org

Mohamed Bakarr / World Agroforestry Centre
United Nations Avenue, P.O. Box 30677-00100,
Nairobi, Kenya
M.Bakarr@cgiar.org

Phoebe Barnard / Global Invasive Species Programme
SA National Botanical Institute
Private bag X7, Claremont 7735, South Africa
barnardp@sanbi.org

Robert Bensted-Smith / Center for Biodiversity
Conservation, Andes
Conservation International
Av. Coruña N29-44 y Noboa Caamaño, Quito, Ecuador
r.bensted@conservation.org

Charles Besançon / IUCN World Commission on
Protected Areas
C.A.P.E Office, Private Bag X7, Claremont, Cape
Town 7735, South Africa
charlesbesancon@yahoo.com

Juan Bezaury / The Nature Conservancy-Mexico
4245 North Fairfax Drive, Arlington, VA 22203, U.S.A.
jbezaury@aol.com

Jean-Philippe Boubli / Conservation and Research of
Endangered Species
Zoological Society of San Diego
Escondido, CA, U.S.A.
jpboubli@yahoo.com

Michele Bowe / WWF-PNG Madang Office
PMB Madang, Papua New Guinea
mbowe@wwfpacific.org.pg

Leo Braack / Southern African Trans-frontier
Conservation Area, Conservation International
Paardevlei Building, AECI Heartlands Complex
De Beers Avenue, Somerset West 7129, South Africa
l.braack@conservation.org

Bill Broyles / Sonoran Desert National Park Friends
5501 North Maria Drive, Tucson, AZ 85704, U.S.A.
bibroyles@aol.com

Phillip Brylski / Vietnam Office, The World Bank
1818 H Street, NW, Washington, D.C. 20433, U.S.A.
Pbrylski@worldbank.org

Thomas Butynski / Eastern Africa Biodiversity Hotspots
Conservation International c/o IUCN
P.O. Box 68200, City Square 00200, Nairobi, Kenya
t.butynski@conservation.org

Jose Maria Cardoso da Silva / Conservation
International-Brazil
Av. Nazaré 541, sala 310, Ed. José Miguel Bitar
66035-170 Belém, Pará, Brazil
jmc.silva@uol.com.br

Richard W. Carroll / West and Central Africa and
Madagascar Regions, World Wildlife Fund
1250 24th Street, N.W., Washington, D.C. 20037, U.S.A.
richard.carroll@wwfus.org

Marco Vinicio Cerezo / Fundación para el
Ecodesarrollo y la Conservación de Guatemala
(FUNDAECO)
7a Calle "A" 20-53, Zona 11, Colonia Mirador,
01011 Guatemala City, Guatemala
fundaeco@quetzal.net

Costas Christ / Bar Harbor Chamber of Commerce
P.O. Box 158, Bar Harbor, ME 04609, U.S.A.
director@barharborinfo.com

Richard M. Cowling / Terrestrial Ecology Research Unit
Nelson Mandela Metropolitan University
P.O. Box 77000, Port Elizabeth 6031, South Africa
rmc@kingsley.co.za

Gustavo A.B. da Fonseca / Conservation
International
1919 M Street NW, Suite 600, Washington, D.C.
20036, U.S.A.
g.fonseca@conservation.org

Ryan K. Danby / Deptartment of Biological Sciences
University of Alberta
Edmonton, Alberta T6G 2E9, Canada
rdanby@ualberta.ca

Jonás A. Delgadillo / CEMEX El Carmen
Av. Independencia 901-A Ote. Colonia Cementos,
64520 Monterrey, N.L., Mexico
jonasvi69@hotmail.com

Susie Ellis / Indonesia and Philippines Programs
Conservation International
s.ellis@conservation.org

Luis Espinel / Conservation International-Peru
Malecón de la Reserva 281, Miraflores, Lima, Peru
l.espinel@conservation.org

Exequiel Ezcurra / Biodiversity Research Center
of the Californias
San Diego Natural History Museum
1788 El Prado, San Diego, CA 92101, U.S.A.
eezcurra@sdnhm.org

Lisa Famolare / Guianas Regional Program
Conservation International
1919 M Street NW, Suite 600, Washington, D.C.
20036, U.S.A.
l.famolare@conservation.org

Richard S. Felger / Drylands Institute
2509 North Campbell Avenue, Suite 405, Tucson,
AZ 85719, U.S.A.
rfelger@ag.arizona.edu

Eduardo Forno / Conservation International-Bolivia
Calle 13 No. 8008, Calacoto, La Paz, Bolivia
e.forno@conservation.org

Sarah R. Frazee / Southern African Hotspots
Programme
Conservation International
Private Bag X7, Claremont 7735, South Africa
s.frazee@conservation.org

Claude Gascon / Regional Programs Division
Conservation International
1919 M Street NW, Suite 600, Washington, D.C.
20036, U.S.A.
c.gascon@conservation.org

Atul K. Gupta / Department of Population
Management Capture and Rehabilitation
Wildlife Institute of India
Chandrabani, P.O. Box. 18, Dehra Dun 248 001,
Uttaranchal, India
akphayre@yahoo.com / akg@wii.gov.in

David Gutiérrez / Comisión Nacional de Areas
Naturales Protegidas, SEMARNAT
Camino al Ajusco 200, Jardines de la Montaña,
Tlalpan, 14210 Mexico City, Mexico
daguti@conanp.gob.mx

John Hanks
P.O. Box 254, Greyton 7233, South Africa
hanksppt@iafrica.com

Jack Hannah / Columbus Zoo and Aquarium
9990 Riverside Drive, P.O. Box 400, Powell, OH
43065, U.S.A.
Jack.Hannah@columbuszoo.org

Ricardo Hernández / Corredor Selva Maya
Conservation International
Boulevar Comitán 191, Colonia Moctezuma, Tuxtla
Gutiérrez Chiapas, Mexico
rhernandez@conservation.org

Michael Hoffmann / Conservation Synthesis
Department, Center for Applied Biodiversity Science
Conservation International
1919 M Street NW, Suite 600, Washington, D.C.
20036, U.S.A.
m.hoffmann@conservation.org

Otto Huber / CoroLab Humboldt, CIET/IVIC
Apartado 21827, Caracas 1020-A, Venezuela
ohuber@ivic.ve

Noel Jacobs / Mesoamerican Barrier Reef Project
Coastal Resources Multicomplex Building
Princess Margaret Drive, P.O. Box 93, Belize City, Belize
mbrs@btl.net

Mikaail Kavanagh / WWF-Malaysia
49 Jalan SS23/15, Taman SEA, 47400 Petaling Jaya,
Malaysia
MKAVANAGH@wwf.org.my

Agi Kiss / Environmentally and Socially Sustainable
Development, Europe and Central Asia
The World Bank
1818 H Street, NW, Washington, D.C. 20433, U.S.A.
akiss@worldbank.org

William R. Konstant / Conservation and Science
Houston Zoo, Inc.
1513 North MacGregor, Houston, TX 77030, U.S.A.
williamkonstant@yahoo.com

Cyril F. Kormos / The WILD Foundation
P.O. Box 1380, Ojai, CA 93024, U.S.A.
cyril@wild.org

Thomas Lacher / Center for Applied Biodiversity
Science, Conservation International
1919 M Street NW, Suite 600, Washington, D.C.
20036, U.S.A.
t.lacher@conservation.org

OLIVIER LANGRAND / Africa and Madagascar Programs
Conservation International
1919 M Street NW, Suite 600, Washington, D.C.
20036, U.S.A.
o.langrand@conservation.org

HARVEY LOCKE
2 Carlton Street, Suite 601, Toronto, Ontario M5B 1J3,
Canada
hlocke@sympatico.ca

KATHY MACKINNON / Environment Department
World Bank
1818 H Street, Washington, D.C. 20433, U.S.A.
kmackinnon@worldbank.org

CARLOS MANTEROLA / Conservation International-
Mexico and Central America
Av. Primero de Mayo 249, San Pedro de los Pinos,
03800 Mexico City, Mexico
c.manterola@conservation.org

DAN MARTIN / Conservation Funding Division
Critical Ecosystem Partnership Fund
Conservation International
1919 M Street NW, Suite 600, Washington, D.C.
20036, U.S.A.
d.martin@conservation.org

VANCE MARTIN / The WILD Foundation
P.O. Box 1380, Ojai, CA 93024, U.S.A.
vance@wild.org

RODERIC MAST / Conservation International
1919 M Street NW, Suite 600, Washington, D.C.
20036, U.S.A.
r.mast@conservation.org

EDDY MENDOZA / Centro de Sistemas de Información
Conservation International-Peru
Malecón de la Reserva 281-Miraflores, Lima, Peru
e.mendoza@conservation.org

CRISTINA G. MITTERMEIER / International League
of Conservation Photographers
432 Walker Rd., Great Falls, VA 22066, U.S.A.
cgmittermeier@aol.com

RUSSELL A. MITTERMEIER / Conservation International
1919 M Street NW, Suite 600, Washington, D.C.
20036, U.S.A.
r.mittermeier@conservation.org

CHABA MOKUKU / Maloti Drakensberg Transfrontier
Conservation and Development Project
7th Floor, Post Office Building, P.O. Box 7271,
Maseru, 100, Lesotho
cmokuku@maloti.org.ls

JOHN MORRISON / Conservation Science Program
World Wildlife Fund
1250 24th St. NW, Washington, D.C. 20037, U.S.A.
john.morrison@wwfus.org

JAMES D. NATIONS / Center for State of the Parks
National Parks Conservation Association
1300 19th St., N.W., Washington, D.C. 20036, U.S.A.
jnations@npca.org

CARLOS PONCE / Conservation International-Peru
Malecón de la Reserva 281-Miraflores, Lima, Peru
c.ponce@conservation.org

MANUEL RAMÍREZ / Southern Mesoamerican Corridor
Conservation International-Programa Mesoamérica Sur
Codigo Postal 2365-2050, San Pedro, San José,
Costa Rica
manuelru@racsa.co.cr

BONNIE REYNOLDS MCKINNEY / CEMEX El Carmen
Av. Independencia 901-A Ote., Colonia Cementos,
64520 Monterrey, N.L., Mexico
brmckinney@hotmail.com

UWE RIECKEN / Department of Biotope Protection
and Landscape Ecology
Federal Agency for Nature Conservation
Konstantinstrasse 110, D-53179 Bonn, Germany
RieckenU@bfn.de

PATRICIO ROBLES GIL / Agrupación Sierra Madre
Av. Primero de Mayo 249, San Pedro de los Pinos,
03800 Mexico City, Mexico
problesgil@agrupacionsierramadre.com.mx

CARLOS RODRÍGUEZ / Oficina del Corredor
Mesoamerica Norte, Región Guatemala,
El Salvador y Honduras
Fundación Conservación Internacional
Avenida Reforma 12-01, zona 10, Edificio Reforma
Montúfar, Oficina 1105, Nivel 11, Guatemala City
crodriguez@conservation.org

JAIME ROJO / Agrupación Sierra Madre
Av. Primero de Mayo 249, San Pedro de los Pinos,
03800 Mexico City, Mexico
jrojo@agrupacionsierramadre.com.mx

TREVOR SANDWITH / Cape Action for People
and the Environment
World Commission on Protected Areas
Private Bag X7, Claremont 7735, Western Cape,
South Africa
trevor@capeaction.org.za

GEORGE L. SCHILLINGER / Conservation International
2933 Lupin Lane, Pebble Beach, CA 93953, U.S.A.
g.shillinger@conservation.org

JOE SINGH / Conservation International-Guyana
266 Forshaw Street, Queenstown, Georgetown, Guyana
jsingh@conservation.org

RAYMOND SKILES / Big Bend National Park
P.O. Box 129, Big Bend National Park, TX 79834, U.S.A.
raymond_skiles@nps.gov

SCOTT SLOCOMBE / Department of Geography
and Environmental Studies
Wilfrid Laurier University
75 University Avenue West, Waterloo, Ontario
N2L 3C5, Canada
sslocomb@wlu.ca

GREGORY S. STONE / Global Marine Programs
New England Aquarium
Central Wharf, Boston, MA 02110, U.S.A.
gstone@neaq.org

FERNANDO C. STRAUBE / Mülleriana: Sociedade Fritz
Müller de Ciências Naturais
Cx. P. 1644, 80011-970, Curitiba/PR, Brazil
urutau@terra.com.br

JATNA SUPRIATNA / Conservation International-
Indonesia
Jl. Pejaten Barat 16A, Kemang, Jakarta-12550, Indonesia
j.supriatna@conservation.org

ANTONIO TELESCA
4505 Cortland Rd., Chevy Chase, MD 20815, U.S.A.
attelesca@hotmail.com

ANDREW TERRY / IUCN-The World Conservation Union
Regional Office for Europe
Boulevard Louis Schmidt 64, 1400 Brussels, Belgium
andrew.terry@iucn.org

ADAM TOMASEK / World Wildlife Fund
1250 24th St. NW, Washington, D.C. 20037, U.S.A.
adam.tomasek@wwfus.org

JOHN W. TUNNELL / Center for Coastal Studies
Texas A&M University-Corpus Christi
6300 Ocean Drive NRC 3200, Corpus Christi,
TX 78412, U.S.A.
jtunnell@falcon.tamucc.edu

WIM UDENHOUT / Conservation International-
Suriname
Kromme Elleboog Straat No. 20, Paramaribo, Suriname
wudenhout@conservation.org

KARIN ULLRICH / Department of Biotope Protection
and Landscape Ecology
Federal Agency for Nature Conservation
Konstantinstrasse 110, D-53179 Bonn, Germany
UllrichK@bfn.de

ALBERTO URBEN-FILHO / Mülleriana: Sociedade Fritz
Müller de Ciências Naturais
Cx. P. 1644, 80011-970, Curitiba/PR, Brazil
mulleriana@aol.com.br

RICARDO VILA / Vila Editorial
Avenida Clavé 57, 50004 Zaragoza, Spain
ricardo@vilaeditorial.com

DOROTHY C. ZBICZ / International Policy Consultant-
World Wildlife Fund
1701 N. Kent St., Box 1104, Arlington, VA 22209, U.S.A.
dorothy.zbicz@zbicz.net

KEVAN ZUNCKEL / Maloti Drakensberg Transfrontier
and Development Programme
P.O. Box 1362, Howick 3290, South Africa
kevan@maloti.org

The authors would like to thank the following people for their contributions to specific chapters of this book. For his assistance with the Introduction, thanks to Alastair Sarre, Editor and Communications Manager of ITTO. The chapter on West Africa benefitted immensely from analytical work conducted through Conservation International's program in that region, and its author is grateful to all who worked in the Regional Program from 1999-2002, especially Mari Omland, Dirck Byler, and Rebecca Kormos. Thanks also to Jennifer Donovan for her input. For the Lanjak-Entimau/Batang Ai chapter, the authors would like to thank Dr. Melvin Gumal; and for the Ai-Ais-Richtersveld-Sperrgebeit, our thanks to Helen Suich for her edits, as well as to EcoAfrica for the use of their map. Special thanks to Shawn Concannon and Doris Swanson for their partial support of the research that went into this book. Also to Conservation International for commissioning this work and to Jeff Jenness for writing a custom GIS script that proved crucial to conducting the analysis. Our appreciation also to Dorothy Zbicz for working with us on methodological issues and to Mary Cordiner, from UNEP-WCMC, for supplying us with recent data. The authors would additionally like to thank the following individuals and organizations for their advice, support, and insight towards the Eastern Tropical Pacific Seascape chapter: Drs. Robert Bensted Smith, Roberto Roca, Barbara Block, and Sylvia Earle for their input and comments; Conservation International's Global Conservation Fund; UNESCO's World Heritage Program; the Walton Family Foundation; the Betlach Family Foundation for their investment in the Seascape Initiative; Sterling Zumbrunn for his assistance with photography and image acquisition; the Environmental Ministries of Costa Rica, Panama, Colombia, and Ecuador; Stanford, Drexel, and Indiana-Purdue Fort Wayne Universities; the Wider Caribbean Sea Turtle Conservation Network (WIDECAST), and the Leatherback Trust (TLT). Last, but not least, our gratitude to Mark Denil of the GIS Department of the Center for Applied Biodiversity Science (CABS) at Conservation International for his help with the maps, to Inés Castro of the Brazil Program for translation, and to Ella Outlaw and Jill Lucena for overall support throughout this project. Agrupación Sierra Madre in turn would also like to thank the following people and institutions for their help and assistance in various aspects relating to the production of this book: Carlos Castillo, Gerardo Ceballos, Jack Dykinga, El Colegio de la Frontera Sur, Ernesto Enkerlin, Billy and Nelly Finan, David Garza, Alberto Garza Santos, Gobierno del Estado de Tamaulipas, John King, Sandy Lanham, Jesús López Reyes, Mauricio Marroquín, Enrique Martínez y Martínez, Benjamín Morales, Antonieta Morales de Yarrington, Carlos Osuna, Doris Osuna del Villar, Guillermo Osuna, Ofelia Osuna, Sandra Osuna, Raúl Pérez Madero, Humberto Pulido, Billy Pat McKinney, Antonio Rivera, Patricia Rojo, Elvira Rojo and Jesús López, Rodolfo and Patricia de los Santos, Manuel Senderos, Héctor Zamora, and Francisco Zavala.

On p. 1, European beech (Fagus sylvatica) *and fir* (Picea abies) *forests in Ordesa y Monte Perdido National Park, Spain.* © Francisco Márquez; *on p. 2. a storm passes and a rainbow appears near Logan Pass in Montana's Glacier National Park, the American portion of Waterton-Glacier —the world's first Peace Park.* © Willard Clay; *on pp. 4-5. snow-covered mountains reflected on the still waters of the Lemaire Channel on the Antarctic Peninsula.* © Ron Naveen/OSF Limited; *on pp. 6-7, a pair of red-and-green macaws* (Ara chloroptera), *one of roughly a thousand bird species recorded from Madidi National Park in Bolivia, part of the Vilcabamba-Amboró Corridor.* © Joel Sartore/National Geographic Image Collection; *on pp. 8-9, attracted by the mineral-rich soil, forest elephants* (Loxodonta cyclotis) *linger in the misty dawn of Dzanga Bai in the Central African Republic.* © Michael Nichols/National Geographic Image Collection; *on p. 10 and cover, granite cliffs in the Maderas del Carmen Flora and Fauna Protection Area, Coahuila, Mexico.* © Patricio Robles Gil/Sierra Madre; *on pp. 12-13, a Serengeti lion* (Panthera leo) *surveys its domain in one of Africa's most important transboundary conservation areas, the Serengeti-Mara on the Tanzania-Kenya border.* © Anup Shah; *on p. 14, the elusive leopard* (Panthera pardus) *is widespread but more difficult to observe than the gregarious lion.* © Thomas Mangelsen/Images of Nature; *on pp. 16-17, a view of the Tien Shan Mountains on the Kyrgyzstan side.* © Patricio Robles Gil/Sierra Madre; *on p. 18, a young rhinoceros hornbill* (Buceros rhinoceros) *feeds on a strangler fig in the lowland rainforest of Borneo.* © Tim Laman/National Geographic Image Collection; *on pp. 20-21, a male moose* (Alces alces) *in Kluane National Park, Canada.* © Patricio Robles Gil/Sierra Madre; *on p. 22, the stark landscape of the Rio Bravo at Boquillas Canyon, on the border between Big Bend National Park in Texas and Maderas del Carmen Flora and Fauna Protection Area in Mexico's state of Coahuila.* © Patricio Robles Gil/Sierra Madre; *on pp. 370-371, rocky mountain bighorn sheep* (Ovis canadensis) *in Glacier National Park, Montana, U.S.* © Patricio Robles Gil/Sierra Madre; *on p. 372, sand verbena or alfombrilla* (Abronia villosa) *blooming in El Pinacate and Gran Desierto de Altar Biosphere Reserve, in Sonora, Mexico, with the Tinajas Altas Mountains of Arizona in the background.* © Jack Dykinga

PRODUCTION
Agrupación Sierra Madre, S.C.
Redacta, S.A. de C.V.

GENERAL COORDINATION
Ana Ezcurra

EDITORIAL COORDINATION
Oswaldo Barrera   Antonio Bolívar

GRAPHIC DESIGN
Juan Carlos Burgoa

PHOTOGRAPHS COMPILATION
Roxana Vega

PRODUCTION COORDINATION
Eugenia Pallares   Elena León

EDITORIAL REVISION
Guillermina Fehér

MAPS
Álvaro Couttolenc

TYPESETTING
Socorro Gutiérrez